Pious Nietzsche

T0340670

INDIANA SERIES IN THE PHILOSOPHY OF RELIGION

Merold Westphal, *general editor*

Pious Nietzsche

Decadence and Dionysian Faith

BRUCE ELLIS BENSON

Indiana University Press

Bloomington and Indianapolis

This book is a publication of

Indiana University Press
601 North Morton Street
Bloomington, IN 47404–3797 USA

http://iupress.indiana.edu

Telephone orders   800-842-6796
Fax orders   812-855-7931
Orders by e-mail   iuporder@indiana.edu

The paper used in this publication meets the minimum requirements of American National Standard for Information Sciences—Permanence of Paper for Printed Library Materials, ANSI Z39.48–1984.

Manufactured in the United States of America

Library of Congress Cataloging-in-Publication Data

Benson, Bruce Ellis, date
    Pious Nietzsche : decadence and Dionysian faith / Bruce Ellis Benson.
      p. cm.   — (Indiana series in the philosophy of religion)
    Includes bibliographical references and index.
    ISBN-13: 978-0-253-34964-4 (cloth : alk. paper)
    ISBN-13: 978-0-253-21874-2 (pbk. : alk. paper) 1. Nietzsche, Friedrich
Wilhelm, 1844–1900. 2. Religion. I. Title.
    B3318.R4B46   2008
    193—dc22

                                      2007021396

1 2 3 4 5   13 12 11 10 09 08

CONTENTS

PREFACE: READING NIETZSCHE

> *If you should come round to writing about me . . . be sensible enough—as nobody has been till now—to characterize me, to "describe"—but not to "evaluate." This gives a pleasant neutrality: it seems to me that in this way one can put aside one's own passionate emphasis, and that it offers all the more to the more subtle minds. I have never been characterized, either as a psychologist, or as a writer (including poet), or as the inventor of a new kind of pessimism (a Dionysian pessimism, born of strength, which takes pleasure in seizing the problem of existence by the horns), or as an Immoralist (the highest form, till now, of "intellectual rectitude," which is permitted to treat morality as an illusion, having itself become instinct and inevitability).[1]*

So Nietzsche writes—near the end of his productive life—providing his own guidelines for interpreting him. It is clear that he desperately *wants* to be interpreted in certain ways—as psychologist, writer, poet, inventor of Dionysian pessimism, and immoralist. But, more than that, he wants to be interpreted by someone who has set "one's own passionate emphasis" aside. Presumably, then, the ideal Nietzsche interpreter is a cool, detached observer, one who only describes and thus keeps herself out of the picture. Indeed, this idea of proper interpretation fits well with Nietzsche's own worries about how he has been received so far: "This is, in the end, my ordinary experience and, if you will, the *originality* of my experience. Whoever thought he had understood something of me, had made himself something out of me after his own image—not uncommonly an antithesis to me; for example, an 'idealist'—and whoever had understood nothing of me, denied that I need be considered at all" (*EH* "Books" 1; *KSA* 6:300). Tracy B. Strong quotes the first part of this passage and then goes on to say: "I take this warning seriously."[2]

Certainly it is a warning. But does not Nietzsche provide us with one of the most difficult cases of interpretation? Can we even speak of a "right" interpretation of Nietzsche, on the basis of what Nietzsche *himself* says? Should our quest be one of *finding/explicating* the "real" Nietzsche or should that quest be something else?

The Quest for the Historical Nietzsche

For at least the past half-century[3]—beginning with Walter Kaufmann's Herculean efforts to rescue Nietzsche from various sorts of strange interpretations and uses—there has been a remarkable attempt to get clear as to what Nietzsche really *did* say, as well as what those sayings could possibly *mean*.[4] That such an effort was needed stems from myriad aspects: the intentional and unintentional lack of clarity in Nietzsche's texts, the "holding hostage" of Nietzsche's writings by his cunning but philosophically challenged sister, Elisabeth Förster-Nietzsche, the use of Nietzsche for Nazi propaganda, and the ways in which Nietzsche's thought challenged (and continues to challenge) not just the conclusions of most philosophers but the very philosophical enterprise and its basic logical premises.[5] No better example could be given of this sort of project than the title of the text *What Nietzsche* Really *Said,* an illuminating popular book by two highly respected Nietzsche scholars.[6] The efforts of Nietzsche scholars over the past fifty years have yielded exemplary Nietzschean scholarship that has clarified much of what can be clarified. Today we are far from the situation of needing to "rescue" Nietzsche.

Or are we? Even today the interpreter of Nietzsche is faced with at least four significant complications, ones that concern not just our position vis-à-vis Nietzsche but also Nietzsche's own views. First, Emmanuel Levinas has made many of us aware of the conceptual violence that is seemingly endemic to the very hermeneutical enterprise.[7] I take Levinas's concern seriously. To encounter Nietzsche is to encounter an "other" that (to speak with Hans-Georg Gadamer) "breaks into my ego-centeredness and gives me something to understand."[8] Yet it may be safe to say that *any* interpretation of Nietzsche—simply because it's an interpretation—ends up doing at least some sort of conceptual violence to Nietzsche's thought. Although Gadamer at one point insists that, in reading a text, the interpreter "disappears—and the text speaks,"[9] such is never the case. The text may indeed speak, but the interpreter never *disappears*—for the interpreter is the very possibility condition for the text to speak at all. No texts come to us "uninterpreted."

A second complication is Nietzsche's own so-called perspectivism and his criticism of the "true world." Here the problem is not merely one of sifting through the extant texts that seem at times contradictory or incoherent with the goal of discovering the real Nietzsche. Even if there were something analogous to the "Jesus Seminar" (a "Nietzsche Seminar" perhaps) to give a final pronouncement (deciding, say, once and for all that Nietzsche really *was* a Polish noble [*EH* "Wise" 3; *KSA* 6:628] and identifying which fragments of the *Nachlass* truly represent his "final" thinking), such a pronouncement would be at odds with Nietzsche's own thought. If Nietzsche is right in denying the existence of the "true world" (*TI* IV; *KSA* 6:80–81), then claims to "perspectives" of what we might call the "true Nietzsche" become problematic. Certainly any pretension to having the ultimate perspective on Nietzsche—whether defined as Platonic *eidos* or Kantian *noumenon*—would be self-defeating, since such a claim would be profoundly un-Nietzschean. But the problem cuts more deeply than that. For Nietzsche's stated view actually undercuts itself. If there are only "perspectives" and no "true" Nietzsche, then Nietzsche neither has any privileged perspective on "himself" nor can he continue to speak in such terms. There are only interpretations of interpretations, traces of traces. Despite that, most interpretations of Nietzsche at least *imply* that they are giving us a perspective of the "true Nietzsche," and the usual implication is that this particular perspective is somehow closer to the "true Nietzsche." Moreover, Nietzsche himself seems to be seeking after what we might call "the highest possible perspective." In other words, Nietzsche is not simply a perspectival relativist who judges all perspectives of equal validity. Even for Nietzsche, then, some perspectives are better than others. Better? In what *way* better? There are at least two ways of answering that question. On the one hand, some perspectives are better in the sense that they *promote life*. Living by certain perspectives, for Nietzsche, simply brings about a better quality of life. On the other hand, some perspectives are more "true." This leads us to a third aspect of Nietzsche interpretation.

That Nietzsche interpreters find it so difficult to leave behind the quest for the historical Nietzsche demonstrates that we clearly have *not* left the correspondence theory of truth behind (something that Nietzsche's account would seem to suggest we do). For the notion of the "true Nietzsche" still functions (to use a term of Edmund Husserl's) as a kind of idea *"in the Kantian sense,"*[10] a regulative ideal toward which to strive. And it's hard to imagine any text of Nietzschean scholarship *without* that goal (even if a more minimal sort). When we say that certain interpretations of Nietzsche are more "true," we do not mean that in some kind of heavy-duty Platonic sense of that term, but at least they are more true in that they better reflect the human condition (or, in the case of Nietzsche, better reflect what Nietzsche thought). So Nietzsche may wish to give up "the true world"—what Maudemarie Clark refers to as a "metaphysical correspondence theory"; he holds on to (again to quote Clark) a "minimal" correspondence theory.[11]

There is one last complication, and it is twofold. On the one hand, while Nietzsche displays a concern for hermeneutical violence, in his advice on how he is to be interpreted he adds: "It is not necessary at all—not even desirable—that you should argue in my favor; on the contrary, a dose of curiosity, as in the presence of a foreign plant, with an ironic resistance, would seem to me an incomparably more intelligent attitude" (*SL* 305; *KSB* 8:375–76). Isn't the "invitation" to "ironic resistance" already a green light for interpreting Nietzsche in a way that goes beyond pure description? It is strange that this passage completes the earlier quote from Nietzsche's letter to Fuchs, for the two parts truly seem to be at odds with one another. On the other hand, if we take Nietzsche as an example of an interpreter, when does Nietzsche *ever* read anyone except with his "own passionate emphasis" not merely present but also *first and foremost* in his interpretation? One can hardly imagine an interpreter who is further from the stance of neutral observer than Nietzsche. So why should we read Nietzsche in a way that he does not read others? Is this because Nietzsche thinks he deserves a certain privilege? It is hard to imagine any reason to support such a privilege. Perhaps one might instead respond that a cool objectivity could reveal some things in Nietzsche that might otherwise be overlooked. Probably so. However, one can easily turn this argument around: for *without* that passionate emphasis, we will undoubtedly *miss* other things. Our concern—the concern that we bring to the text—is important in helping us *understand* the text, in a way that cold "objectivity" or "neutrality" may miss.

More important, Nietzsche's very writing style is such that it encourages the interpreter *not* to disappear but to become part of the text. The result is that a "proper" reading of Nietzsche requires the interpreter to insert herself into the text, blurring the lines not only of interpretation (versus, say, appropriation) but even of the notion of authorship itself.[12] To interpret Nietzsche *requires* that one do *more* than give a literally "faithful" interpretation. But this leaves interpreters with a dual sort of role. While my own view is that such a role is present in the interpretation of *any* text, it is particularly prominent in Nietzsche. In order to do *justice* to Nietzsche's texts, one is forced to follow at least something like the quest for the historical Nietzsche (however problematic that may be in light of Nietzsche's own views). For one must attend to what Nietzsche *said* and could possibly have *meant* (even if one officially renounces the rule of authorial intent). But one must likewise go beyond that quest. On the whole, given Nietzsche's *own* readings of texts designed to get out of them what *he* wants, he can hardly condemn his readers for doing the same. Indeed, were one *not* to do so, one would be an *unfaithful* reader of Nietzsche.[13] Anything less—it seems to me—would be an injustice to his thought, even though this leaves the Nietzsche interpreter in a double bind.

Nietzsche frequently does "violence" to those he interprets. One might even argue that some of Nietzsche's most interesting and valuable interpretations are clearly violent in nature. Moreover, there is good reason to think that Nietzsche knew what he was doing, as opposed to committing hermeneutical violence unawares. Yet perhaps Nietzsche's call for simultaneous "description" and "ironic resistance" is not so alien as it might seem. Jacques Derrida reminds us there are two sides of the hermeneutical spectrum (not to mention an infinity of shades in between). On the one hand, one can provide a kind of "doubling commentary" of a text that uses "the instruments of traditional criticism." Such commentaries, insists Derrida, serve as a kind of "indispensable guardrail" to protect the text, and he provides us with fine examples of such scrupulous readings. Needless to say, all attempts at "doubling" commentaries are merely that—*attempts*. For, as much as one tries, one cannot get rid of oneself. But, even if one could get rid of oneself, such commentaries have "only *protected*" and "never *opened*" a text.[14] When Geoffrey Bennington describes Derrida's interpretation as being (likewise) "immodesty itself, forcing these same old texts to say something quite different from what they had always seemed to say," we have a picture of this kind of *opening,* in which texts are read not *merely* with faithful interpretation as the goal.[15]

Or, applying this to Nietzsche, we have a picture of what Nietzsche himself does, not merely with texts but with concepts, previous thinkers, and even the basic conception of philosophy itself. Nietzsche appropriates to suit his purposes. Speaking of his essay "Schopenhauer as Educator," Nietzsche says that "it is admittedly not 'Schopenhauer as Educator' that speaks here, but his opposite, 'Nietzsche as Educator.'" He likewise admits that the essay is really about "my innermost history, my *becoming*" (*EH* "Books" UM 3; *KSA* 6:320). And this pattern recurs frequently in Nietzsche's discussions of philosophers or poets. He speaks of them in order to speak of himself. He adapts their characteristics to describe either what he is or what he wishes to be.

Derrida's "doubling commentary" is certainly a beginning, but it is not an end in itself. To understand Nietzsche is not simply to read his texts, but to juxtapose them with his life. Yet even that is not enough: interpretation is possible only in juxtaposing *oneself* with his texts. With that caveat in mind, I fully admit that what follows is an "interpretation" of Nietzsche that goes beyond what he strictly says—and that is my intention. For instance, my account of Nietzsche's view of decadence and his turn to a musical *askêsis* is best described as "extrapolated" from Nietzsche's texts in an interpretive move that goes beyond any strict "doubling commentary." As far as I can tell, Nietzsche never speaks of either decadence or his way of resisting decadence in *musical* terms.[16] Indeed, he rather speaks of decadence in terms of disarray of instincts. However, my interpretation of decadence as "de-cadence" (falling out of rhythm with life) certainly fits with Nietzsche's own description of decadence and also his way of resisting it. In other words, what I attempt to do in my interpretation of Nietzsche is connect certain elements that he himself did not quite connect, and so go beyond his own interpretation of himself. Although I think this "makes sense" of certain aspects of Nietzsche's thought in a helpful way, I fully admit that my interpretation is much more than a "strict description" of what Nietzsche says and likely thought. But, again, strict descriptions or doubling commentaries of Nietzsche's thought seem all too un-Nietzschean. If there is anything that Nietzsche authorizes us to do, it is to go beyond mere description.

Reviving the *Ad Hominem*

That Nietzsche often stoops to what seem—at least to philosophers, who pride themselves to be above such tactics—below-the-belt punches should not keep us from taking them seriously.[17] Indeed, the very aversion to *ad hominem* itself needs to be addressed. For, if Nietzsche is right about philosophy being in service of life and not the other way around, then his use of *ad hominem* may not merely be justified but actually warranted.[18] Of course, Nietzsche at one point seems to want to draw a strict line between himself and his works. He claims: "I am one thing, my writings are another matter" (*EH* "Books" 1; *KSA* 6:298). But does that attempt to provide a clean break work? It certainly doesn't fit with Nietzsche's own arguments. The metaphysical truism that Nietzsche's life and his writings are ontologically different turns out to be less true than it seems. For the entity we call "Nietzsche" is composed of both life and writings, and it seems impossible to separate—and certainly not possible to *interpret*—one without the other. Moreover, *other things* that Nietzsche says clearly contradict that statement. About the same time that he was writing *Ecce Homo,* Nietzsche writes to Peter Gast: "I never write a sentence now in which the whole of me is not present" (*SL* 334; *KSB* 8:528).[19] Much earlier, though, Nietzsche had written: "I have gradually come to realize what every great philosophy so far has been: a confession of faith on the part of its author, and a type of involuntary and unself-conscious memoir" (*BGE* 6; *KSA* 5:19). So Nietzsche himself sees a very strong connection between one's self and one's writings. And with that realization comes the freedom to criticize the thought of others by criticizing *them.*

Nietzsche's accusation that Socrates was ugly and characterized by a "*rickety nastiness*" and his description of George Eliot as one of the "little moral females" who belongs to the class Nietzsche terms "the English dimwits" are two of the more memorable of his numerous *ad hominem* arguments (*TI* II:3–4 and IX:5; *KSA* 6:68–69, 113–14). A typical way that Nietzsche interpreters deal with these arguments is to suggest that Nietzsche wants to grab our attention, and is willing to employ any strategy necessary. No doubt, that is *also* the case. That these charges stand out so vividly in the minds of both commentators and casual readers provides ample evidence of Nietzsche's success in that regard. Yet I think there is a much more important reason why Nietzsche employs such tactics: he actually takes them to be *arguments.*

In the case of Socrates, Nietzsche's charge is that ugliness "was among the Greeks virtually a refutation" (*TI* II:3; *KSA* 6:68), for it indicates who one *is.* When Nietzsche speaks here of the "Greeks," he means the "more" ancient Greeks, the ones prior to Plato and Aristotle. As he puts it: "With Socrates, Greek taste takes a turn in favor of dialectic" (*TI* II:5; *KSA* 6:69). So what counted earlier as a "refutation" [*Widerlegung*]—a charge that someone or something was untrue or wrong—ceased to have argumentative force. The assumption was that one's personality and even one's looks are connected to the views one holds. While the connection between one's looks and one's views seems to us implausible at best, the connection between character or personality and one's views has far more plausibility. Note that Nietzsche also charges Socrates with being "nasty," and Nietzsche thinks that nastiness is closely connected to the ways in which Socrates' moral views are exhibited in his personal life. Whether Nietzsche is right, of course, is open to question. But this characterization sounds considerably more like an *argument* (or at least the basic premise of an argument) against Socrates. In the charge against George Eliot, the assumption of a connection is even more pronounced. By calling her a moral dimwit, Nietzsche in effect comments on Eliot's *motive*—a classic *ad hominem* move. Like other English "moralists," Eliot seeks to hold on to Christian morality even while jettisoning its metaphysical base. For Nietzsche, she's a dimwit because he thinks she ought to have known better—what we would colloquially call "putting two and two together." Here was someone who had translated Ludwig Feuerbach's *The Essence of Christianity*—in which Feuerbach argues that "God" is merely an anthropomorphic projection—and David Strauss's *Life of Jesus*—in which the "historical Jesus" is replaced by the "ideal Christ"—and still didn't understand that (to quote Nietzsche) "if you give up Christian faith, you pull the *right* to Christian morality out from under your feet" (*TI* IX:5; *KSA* 6:113). Instead of having both the insight and the courage to go beyond Christian morality (at least on Nietzsche's read), Eliot merely gives us a sentimentalized version of Christian morality that has no metaphysical basis. Such is basically Nietzsche's charge against Eliot. So, having started with *ad hominem,* he goes on to provide what sounds more like a standard argument. Nietzsche likewise supplies an argument against Socrates to complement the *ad hominem* (though admittedly Nietzsche's use of *ad hominem* is not always followed by argument).

Is Nietzsche really alone in his use of *ad hominem*? Despite all the claims of philosophers to the contrary, it seems to me that such attacks have *always* been part and parcel of the philosophical enterprise. Perhaps the difference between Nietzsche and "respectable" philosophers is more a matter of degree and *subtlety*. One of the oldest examples of ancient *ad hominem* is the Platonic dismissal of the sophists for (among other things) charging fees—hardly an argument against their "positions." More recently, one can cite the attack on Derrida as "making a career out of what we regard as translating into the academic sphere tricks and gimmicks similar to those of the Dadaists or of the concrete poets" by Barry Smith and the other writers of the now infamous letter to *The Times* of London when Cambridge University planned to award him an honorary doctorate.[20] Whether one judges this letter to make a valid point or to support Plato in his war against the sophists is—for our purposes here—of no account. My only reason for citing them is to demonstrate that *ad hominem* arguments have always been included in the philosophical quiver. One only need attend a philosophy conference to make that clear.

But there is a much more important issue at stake. Does *ad hominem* rightly have a place in the argumentative arsenal? Or, to switch from war metaphors, does the consideration of another's philosophical position actually *warrant* taking the person—and her motives, character, and lifestyle —into account? I think it does. Indeed, if one takes the recent moves of virtue ethics and virtue epistemology seriously, then one has no other choice but to allow arguments regarding motives and character to have their place. If the point of ethics is not theory but the shaping of character and thus one's practice, then attacking—or praising—someone's character (or person) should be connected to (even if not simply a replacement for) attacking or praising someone's theory.

An *ad hominem* argument can be deemed a fallacy—or misuse of argument—only if we decide that theory and practice are separable. To connect them is already to provide legitimation for *ad hominem.* That hardly means that just *any* attack on another's character or motives—let alone *personal appearance*—is thereby legitimated.[21] Moreover, deciding *exactly* what sort of status they should be accorded is open to question. Yet such aspects cannot merely be dismissed.

Given this recognition, I think it fully appropriate to judge Nietzsche's philosophical positions—at least to some extent—on precisely the basis of his own life. In other words, having recognized the albeit limited legitimate use of *ad hominem,* it's perfectly acceptable to direct it back at Nietzsche. The question of whether Nietzsche lived the life he either directly or indirectly commends is, I think, although not of *equal* importance with the validity of those instructions, certainly of *significant* importance. Or, perhaps we ought to say that those instructions are not simply detachable from that life, precisely because those instructions are partially *defined* by that life. To recognize that, of course, is merely to recognize something that is almost as old as philosophy itself, though it has taken the recent work of Pierre Hadot and others (such as Martha Nussbaum) to remind us that—at least early on—philosophy was not merely a theoretical enterprise but a "way of life."[22] Nietzsche has clearly been an important force in returning us to this way of thinking, so it seems right to consider both *what he says* and *how he lives.*

And it is from this perspective—with the *ad hominem* ever in mind—that this book is written.

ACKNOWLEDGMENTS

Like so many projects, this book began to take shape long before it was written. Teaching Nietzsche in senior seminars at Wheaton College provided the catalyst for working through his texts.

Much of the initial planning for this project took place while I was a visiting scholar at the New School for Social Research, which provided a lively philosophical environment. For that, I am grateful to Richard J. Bernstein and J. M. Bernstein. I am indebted to Wheaton College for providing release time through an Aldeen Grant and to my dean, Jill Peláez Baumgaertner.

Merold Westphal has been a source of encouragement and sage advice throughout the project. I am grateful to my colleagues for their helpful responses to particular chapters presented in our departmental colloquium. Thanks to Thomas Brobjer, who kindly read an early draft of part of the text, and to Sharon Baker for proofreading an early version of the manuscript. Daniel Conway, one of the readers for Indiana University Press, provided extensive comments on the manuscript that have proven invaluable and strengthened the manuscript in ways too numerous to count. Dee Mortensen has been a fine editorial guide on this and other projects. Thanks also to my copy editor, David Anderson.

An early version of certain parts of this text appeared as "The Prayers and Tears of Friedrich Nietzsche" in *The Phenomenology of Prayer,* ed. Bruce Ellis Benson and Norman Wirzba (New York: Fordham University Press, 2005). Thanks to Fordham University Press for permission to republish that material here.

Finally, thanks go to James F. DiFrisco for indexing and helping proofread the text.

ABBREVIATIONS

Numbers following the English translations of Nietzsche's texts refer to sections, rather than pages (except where noted). Numbers following the German texts (*KSA, KSB,* and *KGW*) refer either to page numbers (in the case of published texts and letters) or else to the numbering of Nietzsche's notebooks (in the case of unpublished texts). Although I have usually followed the translations listed below, I have modified the translations in some cases.

Since it has become standard practice to indicate how one treats the *Nachlass* (i.e., the unpublished writings from his notebooks), let me say that I consider the published writings to have a considerably higher status than those that Nietzsche left unpublished. However, given that the notebooks often shed helpful interpretative light upon the published works, I refer to them when I deem it appropriate and when they appear to be in line with published material.

GERMAN EDITIONS

KGW	Werke. Kritische Gesamtausgabe
KSA	Sämtliche Werke, Kritische Studienausgabe in 15 Bänden
KSB	Sämtliche Briefe, Kritische Studienausgabe in 8 Bänden

ENGLISH TRANSLATIONS

AC	The Anti-Christ(ian)
BGE	Beyond Good and Evil: Prelude to a Philosophy of the Future
BT	The Birth of Tragedy and Other Writings
CW	The Case of Wagner
D	Daybreak: Thoughts on the Prejudices of Morality
DD	Dithyrambs of Dionysus
EH	Ecce Homo
GM	On the Genealogy of Morality
GS	The Gay Science
HC	Homer's Contest
HH	Human, All Too Human: A Book for Free Spirits
NCW	Nietzsche contra Wagner

OM   "On Moods"

OMW "On Music and Words"

PPP   *The Pre-Platonic Philosophers*

PT   *Philosophy and Truth: Selections from Nietzsche's Notebooks of the Early 1870's* (numbers refer to pages in the text)

SL   *Selected Letters of Friedrich Nietzsche*

TI   *Twilight of the Idols*

UM   *Untimely Meditations*

WP   *The Will to Power*

Z   *Thus Spoke Zarathustra*

Pious Nietzsche

INTRODUCTION
Improvising Pietism

> *Christianity is essentially a matter of the heart. . . . The main
> teachings of Christianity only relate the fundamental truths of
> the heart. . . . To become blessed through faith means nothing
> other than the old truth, that only the heart, not knowledge can
> make one happy.*[1]

> *The "kingdom of heaven" is a state of the heart—not something
> that is to come "above the earth" or "after death." . . . it is an
> experience of the heart; it is everywhere, it is nowhere.*[2]

> *When one had lost the proper tension and harmony of the Soul,
> one had to dance to the beat of the singer—that was the prescrip-
> tion of this healing art.*[3]

The deeply religious nature of Nietzsche's thought and his attempts
to overcome his early religiosity in order to move to a *new* religiosity are the focus of this text. I contend that Nietzsche not only
begins as a Pietist but also ends as one. Though the content of Nietzsche's
"new" Dionysian Pietism is different from the Pietism of his childhood,
the form remains virtually unchanged. *Both* versions of Pietism are for
Nietzsche matters "of the heart."

To reach this new Dionysian Pietism, Nietzsche must break with
the Christian Pietism of his youth. Nietzsche comes to recognize that
not only his early Pietism but also his philosophical and artistic attach-
ments are "decadent." To move beyond his decadence—or, better put,
to "resist" it—Nietzsche employs the strategy of *askêsis*. As it turns out,
Nietzsche's *askêsis* is twofold. On the one hand, he claims that he must
"take sides against everything sick in me" (*CW* P; *KSA* 6:12). This is
what we might call Nietzsche's "no-saying *askêsis*," which consists of his
warfare against all that is "sick" in him. Practically, this takes the form
of Nietzsche resisting the decadent influences to whom he feels so close:

Socrates, Wagner, and Paul. On the other hand, Nietzsche realizes he needs an *askêsis* that teaches him to say "Yes and Amen." I argue that, in order to reach that stage, Nietzsche needs a "musical" *askêsis*. But why exactly is *music* so important to Nietzsche's *askêsis*? It is, of course, well known that music was an overwhelmingly important aspect of Nietzsche's life. Rüdiger Safranski's biography of Nietzsche opens with these words: "Nietzsche experienced music as authentic reality and colossal power. Music penetrated the core of his being, and it meant everything to him."[4] As strong as this statement is, it in no way overestimates for Nietzsche the centrality of music to life. Georges Liébert notes in his book *Nietzsche and Music:* "Nietzsche's repeated avowal is often cited: 'Without music, life would be an error,' but almost as though it were a quip. Rarely is the decisive importance music, in fact, had for the economy of his thought recognized."[5] As right as he is in recognizing the centrality of music for Nietzsche's life and thought, Liébert is clearly wrong is claiming that Nietzsche's relationship to music has gone unexamined; rather, it has been the subject of numerous studies.[6]

However, my focus on Nietzsche and music is unique in that I argue that music is crucial to reaching his Dionysian Pietism. As Nietzsche himself puts it: "When one had lost the proper tension and harmony of the Soul, one had to *dance* to the beat of the singer—that was the prescription of this healing art" (*GS* 84; *KSA* 3:441). For Nietzsche, music restores the proper harmony of the soul, a harmony that is directly proportional to being in harmony with life itself. Music allows for the possibility of the "ecstasy of the Dionysiac state, in which the usual barriers and limits of existence are destroyed" (*BT* 7; *KSA* 1:56). Nietzsche was often lost in this sense of rapture while improvising at the piano. It is not just that musical improvisation was at the top of his list of things in life that provide pleasure (*KSA* 8:23 [57]); rather, musical improvisation—in both the literal and the more metaphorical sense (a sense that will become clearer later on)—is at the heart of Nietzsche's project. A significant component of my argument is that it is this very ecstatic rapture—in which one transcends oneself—that helps Nietzsche "improvise" upon *himself.* Nietzsche's improvisation both upon himself and upon Pietism go hand in hand: the one facilitates the other.

Equally important, though, is my reading of decadence in terms of "falling out of rhythm with life." As mentioned in the preface, although Nietzsche never explicitly speaks of decadence in terms of "de-cadence" (falling out of rhythm), that way of thinking about decadence actually fits quite well with what Nietzsche says about decadence. Given that *mousikê*—which, for the ancient Greeks, includes not only rhythm, tones, dance, and words but also the development of oneself—is central to Nietzsche's life and thought, then reading decadence in this distinctly *musical* way seems particularly appropriate.[7] Although my account is different in certain respects from that of George H. Leiner, he also thinks that music is central to Nietzsche's self-overcoming, claiming that "there must be a rhythm, a rhyme, a meter to the lives of those who would overcome themselves."[8]

In short, then, my thesis is as follows: Nietzsche wishes to move from orthodox Christian Pietism to a Dionysian Pietism in which the content is somewhat different but the form remains virtually unchanged. For Nietzsche, Pietism is not so much a mode of belief but a way of being that fully embraces life, vicissitudes and all. To reach that place of complete acceptance, Nietzsche practices both a "yes-saying" and "no-saying" *askêsis* designed, on the one hand, to affirm life and, on the other hand, to overcome everything within him that fails to affirm life. That affirmative *askêsis*—most clearly worked out in *Thus Spoke Zarathustra*—is one that is best understood *musically,* which is why central passages in *Zarathustra* involve both singing and dancing. Music is key precisely because it makes possible the kind of ecstatic transcendence so crucial to affirming life and improvising upon Nietzsche's very self. Finding a new rhythm is the only way in which Nietzsche can replace the rhythm of decadence. On my account, Nietzsche's decadence is not merely connected to his Dionysian Pietism; it is *synonymous* with his failure to live out that Pietism.

The remainder of this introduction articulates the basic contours of that thesis. The remainder of the book, in turn, develops those contours.

Nietzsche's Shifting Pietism

That Nietzsche was—and continually remained—a deeply *religious* thinker is certainly a contentious claim. It goes almost without saying that—since Nietzsche was a critic of Christianity, an atheist, and a nihilist —his credentials as "secular thinker" are impeccable. Indeed, many would see Nietzsche as having either ushered in the current secular age, or at least having set the stage for its entry. One need only peruse the Nietzsche scholarship that has proliferated in the past few decades to see that it is overwhelmingly secular in nature and that Nietzsche has largely been appropriated for decidedly secular purposes.[9] On such a reading, Nietzsche is the quintessentially postmodern, posttheistic philosopher for whom the true world has finally become a fiction.

Thus, it is not surprising that the editors of a recent collection of papers regarding Nietzsche's relation to religion write: "Many readers of Nietzsche will, no doubt, be uneasy about the tendency of a number of papers in this collection to complicate considerably and to render ambiguous Nietzsche's relation to the 'divine.' They will be even more nervous when, as in some cases, a 'religious' sensibility is said to underpin and pervade Nietzsche's thought."[10] Yet Nietzsche is considerably closer to religion than many commentators have either realized or admitted. Tyler Roberts is right in saying that "the place of religion in Nietzsche's writing begs to be examined."[11] Rereading Nietzsche as *homo religiosus* is precisely what Roberts does. More recently, Alistair Kee, the writers in two recent anthologies—*Nietzsche and the Divine* and *Nietzsche and the Gods*—Giles Fraser, and Julian Young, have joined him in that project.[12] To be sure, there are precedents for such readings. For instance, in *Nietzsche and Christianity,* Karl Jaspers points out: "A study of Nietzsche will surprise those who know only this hostility [toward Christianity]. They will find lines which seem wholly at odds with the anti-Christian portions of his work. 'After all,' he could say of Christianity, 'it is the best example of the ideal life I have really come to know; I have pursued it from my childhood on, and I do not think my heart has ever dealt meanly with it.'"[13] Here Jaspers quotes from Nietzsche's letter of 21 July 1881 to Peter Gast.[14] Moreover, Jaspers (rightly) goes on to note that Nietzsche says remarkably positive things about the Bible and about Christians who take their faith seriously. One might argue, of course, that the Nietzsche of 1888 that produces *The Anti-Christ(ian)* has completely moved from that position. But a close inspection of *The Anti-Christ(ian)* would not necessarily lead to that conclusion, as I will later argue. Indeed, Young concludes his study of Nietzsche's thinking about religion by saying that not only is Nietzsche "not anti-religious" but also that he is *"above all a religious thinker."*[15] The result is that Nietzsche's "atheism" is hardly straightforward, as dismaying as that may be to many of both Nietzsche's dismissive denouncers and fawning disciples. Indeed, if my account is correct, then Nietzsche is simply *not* an atheist (and, for that matter, also not a nihilist). Instead, he remains a kind of theist throughout his life, even though he moves from one god to another.

So what accounts for this apparent disjunction—that Nietzsche is largely interpreted as being against Christianity (not to mention the fact that he actually *is* against Christianity) and these positive comments? Fraser's answer to "why it is that Nietzsche manages to come across simultaneously as both atheistic and pious" is that "Nietzsche is obsessed with the question of human salvation." As he goes on to explain, "Nietzsche's work is primarily soteriology: experiments to design a form of redemption that would work for a post-theistic age."[16] Yet, while Fraser correctly sets that concern within Nietzsche's Lutheran Pietistic upbringing, he wrongly takes the question "How are we saved?" to be the central question of Lutheran Pietism. In contrast, I argue that Nietzsche—far from seeking a new soteriology—is seeking to overcome the perceived notion that we *need* some sort of salvation. Not only does he wish to be free from the God of Christianity, he also wishes to be free from the very idea of redemption. Speaking of Wagner, Nietzsche uses the phrase "redemption *from* the redeemer" [*Erlösung dem Erlöser*] (*CW* Postscript; *KSA* 6:42). The problem with Wagner (or at least *one* particularly important problem) for Nietzsche was that Wagner still sought a kind of salvation. In fact, Wagner's project is salvific from the ground up. It is that very project that Nietzsche wishes to give up. Whether he succeeds, of course, is another matter. As we will see, it is only in *that* sense that Nietzsche can be said to be concerned about salvation (though we will also note that, at times, Nietzsche at least *seems* to lapse into precisely what he wishes to escape). In any case, while I agree with Thomas Brobjer's claim that "most of Nietzsche's philosophy can be seen as a critique of Christianity and as an attempt to construct an alternative to Christian views and values,"[17] I think that Nietzsche never escapes the logic of Christianity—in a number of ways.

On my reading, then, Nietzsche remains essentially a Pietist to the end of his life. No doubt, he becomes a rather unorthodox Pietist, for his goal is to create a new—and significantly different—Pietism. But both the Pietism he tries to leave behind and the one that he hopes to create have to do with the *heart*, not with salvation. And so they—despite all appearances and Nietzsche's seeming hostility toward everything Christian—bear a remarkable family resemblance. In 1862 Nietzsche writes to his young friends Gustav Krug and Wilhelm Pinder: "Christianity is essentially a matter of the heart. . . . To become blessed through faith means nothing other than the old truth, that only the heart, not knowledge can make one happy" (*KSB* 1:202). And, as late as 1888, he writes something that sounds remarkably similar: "The 'kingdom of heaven' is a state of the heart—not something that is to come 'above the earth' or 'after death.' . . . it is an experience of the heart" (*AC* 34; *KSA* 6:207). Having the right kind of heart is what concerns Nietzsche, and his move from one kind of Pietism to another is really about a *"change* of heart." Nietzsche wants to be the kind of person who can truly say: "So be it. Yes and Amen." But that "change of heart" requires finding a new rhythm to life. More accurately, it requires getting back into life's true rhythm, which means that Nietzsche needs to move from a decadent rhythm to one that is truly life *affirming.* As we will discover, that project is considerably more complicated than it might at first seem.

Resisting Decadence—Or, Getting Back into Rhythm

"Nothing has preoccupied me more profoundly than the problem of *décadence*—I had reasons" (*CW* P; *KSA* 6:11).[18] Such is the unexpectedly strong statement that Nietzsche writes in the last year of his sanity. After all, throughout his life, Nietzsche had been deeply concerned with a seemingly wide variety of questions and problems. He is much better known for such themes as the will to power, nihilism, the death of God, and the overman. And, yet, here Nietzsche singles out decadence as his primary concern. That statement is all the more surprising in that he begins using the term in his published writings only in 1888, his last year of sanity. Yet the term is not only to be found but also plays a major role in each of his texts written that year—*The Case of Wagner, Twilight of the Idols, The Anti-Christ(ian),* and *Ecce Homo.*[19] Each, in its own way, can be read as a treatise on decadence, and each provides a different angle on what Nietzsche takes to be ultimately the same phenomenon.

Yet what exactly is "decadence," and how does it relate to Nietzsche's improvised Pietism? In its most literal sense, "decadence" simply means "to fall down."[20] Metaphorically, it denotes decline or decay from a previous state of vitality. But one can also interpret decadence *musically,* as a "de-cadence" in the sense of a loss of rhythm. On that read, decadence is the loss of life's rhythm in which we are out of step both with our true selves and with the earth. Earlier, we noted that—*pace* Fraser—Nietzsche hopes to escape from the logic of soteriology—to be saved from the perceived need for salvation. By its very logic, having a soteriology assumes one needs to be "saved"—that something needs to be made right. Nietzsche wants to move to a position in which he is able to *affirm* all that is, not wish that it be somehow "redeemed."

One can argue that the term "decadence" in effect supplants and sublates *Entartung* [degeneration], *ressentiment,* and *Nihilismus*—all of which are reactive in nature.[21] As such, decadence has a reactive logic. Further, all of the characteristics against which Nietzsche had so vehemently railed—such as slave morality, weakness, pity, and "otherwordliness"—are symptoms of decadence. So it becomes a general term that sums up everything Nietzsche considers to be "bad" (including the notion of "evil"). Moreover, the logic of decadence is diametrically opposed to the logic of Nietzsche's improvised Pietism. If Nietzsche's Pietism can be summed up as "Yes and Amen," then decadence is an ultimate "No" to life. In effect, decadence is the will to something else, the will to change the world, the will that opposes life—the will to *salvation.* One is decadent precisely when one fights against life. Conversely, one overcomes decadence by getting back into step with life.

Decadence can manifest itself in various ways. Philosophically, decadence can be exemplified by the attempt to combat suffering and chaos by way of dialectic and system (Socrates). Artistically, it manifests itself by overly exciting the nerves and promoting "metaphysical solace" and "redemption" (Wagner). Religiously, one finds it in theodicy, the denial of the body, and—of course—soteriology (Paul). But all of these manifestations come down to the same thing—a devaluation of life, both practically and theoretically. On the one hand, Nietzsche says "to choose instinctively what is harmful to *oneself,* to be *enticed* by 'disinterested' motives, is virtually the formula for *décadence.*" So one acts decadently by choosing against one's own interests and thus choosing against life. Theoretically, one's decadence is manifested by considering life to be of no value: "Instead of naively saying, '*I'm* not worth anything anymore,' the lie of morality says in the mouth of the *décadent:* 'Nothing is worth anything—*life* isn't worth anything'" (*TI* IX:35; *KSA* 6:133).

Although Nietzsche singles out such figures as Socrates, Wagner, and Paul as particularly exemplifying decadence, the problem is far more widespread. Nietzsche sees decadence as *the* illness of his time, one that infects all of western culture. And that infection is not simply accidental.

For the entire course of western history—particularly as manifested in morality, religion, and philosophy—has inexorably led to the current state of decline. Western history *is* the history of decadence. So the only way to overcome decadence is to radically alter the course of that history—or to find some way to escape it altogether. To say that Nietzsche faces a tall order is the greatest of understatements.

However, Nietzsche also has a much more personal interest in the phenomenon of decadence. To be sure, he writes as a physician to culture in general, but his prescription is also for himself. And, while Nietzsche questions whether that prescription will work, he sees himself as having at least one major advantage over Socrates or Wagner. The problem with decadence is that it is usually accompanied by blindness to it or—even worse—the ability to see but a denial of what one sees. Such blindness or lying to oneself is even a chief characteristic of decadence. Given that, it is no wonder that decadence is so difficult to battle. But Nietzsche thinks that he is both able to see and honest enough to admit his decadence. As he says, "I am, no less than Wagner, a child of this time; that is, a decadent" (*CW* P; *KSA* 6:11). Elsewhere, he goes so far as to claim: "I am, in questions of *décadence,* the highest authority on earth."[22] That "authority" clearly comes from both personal experience and much rumination on the subject.

Nietzsche's *Askêsis*

According to Nietzsche, his ability to recognize his own decadence, coupled with what he terms "the philosopher in me," enables him to "resist" it. After admitting his complicity, he goes on to say, "but I comprehended this, I resisted it." Yet what sort of resistance is this? How is Nietzsche to overcome something so deeply ingrained not merely in culture but also in himself? Nietzsche says, "for such a task I required a special self-discipline." And he goes on to describe this discipline as "self-overcoming" and "self-denial" (*CW* P; *KSA* 6:12). Yet this ascetic formula comes as something of a surprise from someone who has so soundly excoriated those who engage in at least certain ascetic practices. Section three of *On the Genealogy of Morality*—titled "What Do Ascetic Ideals Mean"—could be read as a complete repudiation of ascetic ideals. Yet Nietzsche's attack in the *Genealogy* is not necessarily against ascetic ideals per se but rather against "the ascetic ideal" of a particular sort.[23] Whereas asceticism (at least as it has been practiced) is *sometimes* a denial and devaluation of life (and, therefore, inherently decadent), the adoption of an ascetic ideal could well be in the service of life. Such is what Nietzsche proposes.

In effect, Nietzsche gives us a particular sort of *askêsis* (i.e., the practice of spiritual exercises), designed as an "opposing ideal" (*GM* III:23; *KSA* 5:395) to the ascetic ideals of both religion and philosophy. Its purpose is to get one back into rhythm. Appropriately enough, then, Nietzsche gives us what I have already described as a "twofold" *askêsis,* a "no-saying" that requires waging war against his "sickness" and a "yes-saying" that takes a musical form. We first get a glimpse of this "yes-saying" *askêsis* in the music-practicing Socrates of *The Birth of Tragedy.* There Nietzsche recalls Socrates' claim on his deathbed that he has often been called to "practice music."[24] After referring to this passage, Nietzsche then asks: "Perhaps art may even be a necessary correlative and supplement of science" (*BT* 14; *KSA* 1:96). While there are only the beginnings of Nietzsche's musical *askêsis* in *The Birth of Tragedy* (1871–72), the problem he identifies is clear. Socrates has failed to listen to the muse (who has spoken over and over again), and the result is that he has fundamentally misunderstood his role not only as philosopher but also as human being. But what does it mean to "practice music"? We find a further piece of Nietzsche's musical *askêsis* in *The Gay Science* (1882), where he criticizes the "true" philosopher who "didn't listen to life insofar as life is music; he *denied* the music of life" (*GS* 372; *KSA* 3:623–24). Precisely in fearing the senses and thus embodiment (the very things with which philosophical analysis, with its emphasis on mind, is nearly incapable of dealing), philosophers have negated their true selves and thus life itself.

In contrast, Nietzsche wants to *affirm* this "music of life." To affirm the music of life—to practice music—is to cultivate one's creative vitality (which Nietzsche often calls the "will to power"). This rather broad conception of "practicing music" may seem strange to us (since we today define "music" in a relatively narrow sense), but it would have been perfectly sensible to Nietzsche, who would have had the ancient Greek sense of *mousikê* in mind. Practicing music for the ancient Greeks was much more than "playing" or "listening" to music. Indeed, as we will see, it also included any art that developed oneself or cultivated one's soul. For Nietzsche, cultivating the soul means that we attune our instincts back to the earth, rather than attempt to squelch them or orient them toward a world beyond. Nietzsche makes it clear that his "yes-saying" *askêsis* is "solved" in *Thus Spoke Zarathustra* and that the "no-saying" part is worked out in later texts.[25] One of Nietzsche's central metaphors for the attunement of "yes-saying" in *Zarathustra* is *dance*. As we shall see, learning to follow the rhythm of life and let *Life* lead can be accomplished only by dancing.

It is this musical *askêsis*—which involves both specific positive practices and a kind self-denial—that is central for Nietzsche to move from traditional Pietism to his improvised Pietism. To replace Christian faith with Dionysian faith (which he terms "the highest of all possible faiths," *TI* IX:49; *KSA* 6:152), Nietzsche needs a new sort of rhythm—the rhythm of new sorts of dances, prayers, songs, and even creeds. Although Michel Haar is speaking of the doctrine of the eternal return, what he says about how it is able to "take hold" is likewise true for Nietzsche's Dionysian faith: it can take hold only "in the same way a religion does."[26] For what Nietzsche offers us in the end is something much less like a "philosophy" and much more like a "faith" or a Pietism of the earth.

Learning to "practice" that Dionysian Pietism—to truly have a "change of heart"—is the challenge that Nietzsche faces. Whether he succeeds is the central question of this study.

PART 1

From Christian Pietism to Dionysian Pietism

ONE

The Prayers and Tears of Young Fritz

I have firmly resolved within me to dedicate myself forever to His service. May the dear Lord give me strength and power to carry out my intention. . . . Yes, dear Lord, let Thy face shine upon us forever! Amen![1]

When I have looked into my Zarathustra, I walk up and down in my room, unable to master an unbearable fit of sobbing.[2]

From Nietzsche's first work to his last, one finds the intonation of prayer and the stain of tears. The child who weeps over the deaths of father and brother becomes the man who sobs peering into the abyss of the tragic or encountering a horse being abused. The child who instinctively knew how to pray becomes the adult who struggles to find a new way to pray, one that follows new and cultivated instincts.[3]

That transition from one sort of prayer to another is neither easy nor simply instinctual for Nietzsche. Both Augustine's *Confessions* and Nietzsche's *Ecce Homo* can justly be called "books of tears," as Derrida maintains. Yet to what degree is *Ecce Homo* truly characterized as "Dionysian counter-confessions," as Derrida also claims?[4] Does Nietzsche *reach* the Dionysian? Or does he merely tearfully long for it? As we have noted, the extent to which Nietzsche fully reaches the Pietistic Dionysian—in which Nietzsche is truly *Dionysian at heart*—is open to question. And Nietzsche's own claims—and strategies—would lead one to think that he is ever on his way but never wholly there. Indeed, *Ecce Homo* provides significant evidence that Nietzsche has failed to become truly Dionysian in heart.

One might be tempted to characterize Nietzsche's "confessions" in *Ecce Homo* as the inverse of Augustine's—not the tortured move *to* faith but the tortured move *away* from faith. But my argument is that Nietzsche moves—or attempts to move—from one faith to *another. Ecce Homo* is thus a "confession" in both senses of that term: simultaneously a recognition of things "done and left undone" and a statement of belief that is characterized by both a measure of belief and an aspiration to further belief. As such, it follows the very formula of faith as given by the man who brings to Jesus a son seized by a spirit in the gospel of Mark. The father says to Jesus: "if you are able to do anything, have pity on us and help us" (Mk. 9:22). To which Jesus (indignantly) replies: "If you are able!—All things can be done for the one who believes" (Mk. 9:23). It is in that context that the father provides a perfect description of faith: "I believe; help my unbelief" (Mk. 9:24). Such is Nietzsche's Dionysian belief: he believes, but he likewise needs help to believe fully. Where exactly this "help" comes from is something to which we turn to later. As we will see, Nietzsche's mature faith still seems "all too Christian" rather than "purely Dionysian," so that *Ecce Homo* bears a surprising connection to *Aus meinem Leben*. As it turns out, Nietzsche's childhood faith proves decisive for his later philosophy. What I hope to show is not merely the deeply religious quality of Nietzsche's thought but also the role that prayer plays in shaping that thought.

There are two aspects to my analysis. First, I argue that Nietzsche remains a person of faith and prayer, though he attempts to shift both the logic and the content of that faith and prayer. Of course, I am using the terms "faith" and "prayer" in a broad rather than narrow sense. Nietzsche's "Dionysian faith" is not a "faith" in the sense of "belief in the Christian God." Yet it *is* a belief in some sort of god, the definition of which shifts over time. Further, whereas Nietzsche's early prayers are addressed to someone, it is not clear to whom (or *what*) some of his later "prayers" are addressed. Second, I argue that Nietzsche retains not only the basic logic that emerges in his early prayers but much of its content (which proves to have both positive and negative implications).

To see how Nietzsche arrives at *Ecce Homo,* we need to follow the path that leads from *Aus meinem Leben*. In so doing, we shall see the evolution of Nietzsche's God and thus the evolution of his relation to that God. We shall also see just how "faithful" Nietzsche turns out to be. In this chapter our focus is primarily on the prayers of the young Fritz and the shifting conception of God already found in Nietzsche's early years. In later chapters we will consider how those prayers are continually transformed, while remaining constant in certain respects throughout Nietzsche's life.

From the God of Pietism to the *Unbekannter*

What was the faith of the young Fritz, known for his "ability to recite Scriptural passages and religious songs with great pathos" and hence called the "little pastor"?[5] That Nietzsche came from a long line of Lutheran pastors going back to the beginning of the seventeenth century is well known. His father was a pastor, as were both of his grandfathers. Nietzsche was deeply influenced by Luther (and Lutheranism), as is clear from both his life and texts, even if he in the end spurns Luther. Yet what was the character of the Lutheranism that Nietzsche experienced? One need look no farther than his household environment for some important clues. The young Fritz was personally familiar with the examples of faith as practiced by his mother and aunt Rosalie, who lived with the Nietzsche family. At least in his early years, the effect of the mother on young Nietzsche clearly outweighs that of the aunt. Although both had a faith deeply influenced by German Pietism, the outworking of that faith was significantly different in mother and aunt. Whereas Nietzsche's mother had a "practical faith" that was entirely lacking in "theological reflection and sophistication," the faith of his aunt was more "rationalistic" in nature.[6] Although Luther is best known for his emphasis on salvation by grace (i.e., his soteriology), the Lutheranism that Nietzsche inherits is deeply mediated by German Pietism. While it is true that Nietzsche's father was strongly influenced by a particular strand of revivalism in which conversion plays a central role (and such an aspect is certainly a part of German Pietism), Nietzsche's mother "preferred an emotional, sincere quiet piety to a dogmatic Christianity based on prescriptions. She was deeply influenced by the pietist beliefs in her parental home."[7] Nietzsche seems to be far more influenced by this emotional piety than by the emphasis on salvation.[8] Thus, when Nietzsche says in *Ecce Homo* that he has never been concerned with "redemption," *that claim* is probably correct (*EH* "Clever" 1; *KSA* 6:278)—in the sense that Nietzsche rejects the Christian conception of redemption. In contrast, Nietzsche's piety emphasizes the role of having a right relationship with God and thus having a right *heart*. For the young Fritz, Christian praxis was considerably more important than Christian doctrine. From that Pietistic perspective, Christianity is primarily a way of *being*, one characterized primarily by childlike trust in God rather than doctrinal correctness. As such, it was truly a *faith*, instead of being a set of rational propositions. It is a relationship of utter dependence. Practically, that relationship was evidenced in Nietzsche's life by fervent prayer, Bible study, and attending services. That Nietzsche read Scripture extensively is amply demonstrated by his writings.

We get a vivid picture of young Fritz's faith in the following prayer, which closes *Aus meinem Leben* (1858):

> I have firmly resolved within me to dedicate myself forever to His service. May the dear Lord give me strength and power to carry out my intention and protect me on life's way. Like a child I trust in His grace: He will preserve us all, that no misfortune may befall us. But His holy will be done! All He gives I will joyfully accept: happiness and unhappiness, poverty and wealth, and boldly look even death in the face, which shall one day unite us all in eternal joy and bliss. Yes, dear Lord, let Thy face shine upon us forever! Amen! (*KGW* I/1, 4 [77])[9]

Although the depth of religious zeal in this prayer may seem strange when juxtaposed to Nietzsche's later writings, it should not surprise us. None of the elements of this prayer are unusual. They are all typical of the German Pietism of Nietzsche's upbringing. Further, given Nietzsche's later vehemence against Christianity, one would expect that level of criticism to be matched by a previous level of devotion.[10]

Note how all of the Pietistic aspects of Nietzsche's early faith come out in this prayer. What we find, first, is an outpouring of the heart, one that is clearly more interested in Christian practice than any set of beliefs. Second, there is the sense of a very close relationship to God. It is that sense of personal relationship that is crucial to German Pietism. Third, it is a prayer of bold resolution: there is no room for inconstancy here. Nietzsche sounds absolutely unshakable in his trust in God, a trust built upon the relationship. Fourth, that resolve is—nonetheless—tempered by an admission of inability. Only by way of the strength of another (God) can that resolution be carried out. Fifth, with an openly proclaimed and even celebrated childlike trust, Nietzsche is convinced that God will provide. Sixth, even if God brings what seems like misfortune, Nietzsche still affirms it as God's will. Whatever happens, Nietzsche is content to "joyfully accept" it, to say "yes and amen" to all that comes. Seventh, although God is not specifically identified here, Nietzsche clearly has no questions regarding who he is, nor any doubt about his relation to God.

What makes this fervent devotion and trust all the more remarkable is the ways in which these various elements are put into question in a poem written only a few years later (1862), "Entflohn die holden Träume" ("Fled are the Lovely Dreams").[11] It, too, is an outpouring of the heart. But *this* heart is disillusioned, uncertain, and full of tears. What exactly has fled becomes clear when Nietzsche says:

> I do not know what I love
> I have neither peace nor rest.
> I do not know what I believe
> Or why I'm still living. For what?

The poem ends with three incomplete stanzas. One senses Nietzsche struggling for words, unable even to follow the basic form of the poem:

> Man is not a worthy image
> Of God
>
> From day to day more distorted
> . . . . [the line is simply left blank]
> According to my rudimentary character
> I form God.
>
> I awoke from heavy dreams
> Through a dull ringing.[12]

Nietzsche no longer affirms his close relationship to God, his earlier promise to serve God, his unwavering childlike trust that God is good, his willingness to accept whatever God gives, and his certainty of who God is. These have become part of a "lovely dream" from which he has—quite sadly—awakened. Having realized that God—*as earlier configured*—does not exist, Nietzsche is now uncertain what to put in its place. One should read Nietzsche's claim "Der Mensch is nicht der Gottheit / Würdiges Ebenbild" [Man is not a worthy image / Of God] in light of the claim "Nach meinem Urcharakter / Gestalt ich mir auch Gott" [I form God / According to my rudimentary character].[13] Nietzsche's picture of God has changed because he himself has changed, and thus he sees God differently. But this new picture of God is one that he is reluctant to accept. It is all too human—too Feuerbachian—and so "unworthy."

Surprisingly, Nietzsche's statement that "I do not know what I love" bears a strange but I think telling resemblance to Augustine's question "Quid ergo amo, cum Deum amo?"—What do I love when I love my God? Although Augustine is sure he loves the God of the Bible—whoever and whatever that may be—in a way analogous to Nietzsche, Augustine is struggling to articulate who this God is.[14] In the same way that Jacques Derrida cannot get rid of this question, and so finds himself still asking it, so Nietzsche cannot get rid of this question. It is a continual struggle for Nietzsche, as we will see. Nietzsche like Derrida "quite rightly pass[es] for an atheist" (to quote Derrida's own self-description).[15]

Yet it takes Nietzsche quite some time to come to the place where he recognizes who his "replacement god" is. That Nietzsche was struggling with how to conceive of god is evident from two slightly later poems. The first, "Du hast gerufen—Herr ich komme" ["You Have Called—Lord, I Come"], was also written in 1862 and seems—at first glance—to revert to Nietzsche's earlier conception of God:

> You are so gentle,
> Faithful and sincere,
> Genuinely earnest,
> Dear savior image for sinners!

It is hard to imagine a more "Pietistic" image of God. And it is to *this* God that Nietzsche says:

> You have called
> Lord, I rush
> With circumspection
> To the steps of your throne.
> Glowing with love,
> Your gaze shines into
> My heart so dearly,
> So painfully: Lord, I come.[16]

Still, it would be too simple to assume that Nietzsche has here simply reverted to Pietism. For his prayer is clearly tempered by hesitation, fear, and growing uncertainty. Nietzsche presents us with a Pietistic conception of God and promises to heed His call. But then he says "Herr: ich eile / Und weile" [Lord, I rush / With circumspection]. It is the religious double gesture: he hurries, but he also holds back [*weile*]. Nietzsche seems to be unsure *even in the midst of* rushing back to God. Why is he so reluctant? While he first says he feels "a shudder" [*ein Grauen*] "from the sin" [*Vor der Sünde*], he expands on this by describing it as the abyss of night [*Nachtgründe*]. Is Nietzsche's problem simply remorse for sin? It is hard to think of *sin* as the abyss for him at this point. Much more likely is that his "sin" is that of having peered into the abyss—the nothingness—of unbelief. Moreover, note that God's gaze [*Blick*] shines into Nietzsche's heart. This idea of God gazing into the human heart is certainly a basic Christian idea, but it is particularly strong in German Pietism. That gaze is something that, at this point, Nietzsche merely acknowledges. But, later, it will become an intolerable burden, and a reason for God's death. Yet here the question is whether Nietzsche can really return to his earlier conception of God. Given both the earlier poem and the ambivalence expressed in this one, he seems to be well aware that this attempt may (and likely will) fail. So the prayer seems like a move of desperation, a desperation that will characterize all of Nietzsche's further attempts to deal with God, Christianity, and religion in general.

In the Introduction, we noted that Nietzsche writes (in 1862) the following to his childhood friends: "Christianity is essentially a matter of the heart. . . . The main teachings of Christianity only relate the fundamental truths of the heart. . . . To become blessed through faith means nothing other than the old truth, that only the heart, not knowledge can make one happy."[17] Here it sounds as if Nietzsche still holds to classic German Pietism. But that would be too quick and easy a conclusion to draw. For Nietzsche prefaces these remarks by saying that we "recognize that we are only responsible to ourselves, that a reproach over a failed direction in life only relates to us, not to any higher power." So, instead, we have a Pietism that is already reconceived under the influence of Feuerbach. As such, it provides the model for Nietzsche's continually improvised Pietism that continues throughout his life.

By 1864, although Nietzsche has not completely given up on God's existence, he certainly sounds as if he has finally given up on his Pietistic conception of God. The second poem, "Dem unbekannten Gott" (To the Unknown God), was written at the time of his graduation from Pforta at age nineteen:

> . . . I lift up my hands to you in loneliness—
> you, to whom I flee,
> to whom in the deepest depths of my heart
> I have solemnly consecrated altars
> so that your voice
> might summon me again.
>
> On them glows, deeply inscribed,
> the word: To the unknown god
> I am his. . . .
>
> I want to know you, Unknown One,
> you who have reached deep into my soul,
> into my life like the gust of a storm,
> you incomprehensible yet related one!
> I want to know you, even serve you.[18]

Nietzsche desperately wants to know this *Unbekannter* [Unknown One].
Moreover, this is not the first time he has cried out to this *Unbekannter*.
He says: "Noch einmal" [once more]. His "consecration" of altars suggests an ongoing willingness to know God, for the inscription on them is
"tief eingeschrieben" [deeply inscribed]. Further, Nietzsche says, "Sein
bin ich" [I am his] and (once again) expresses his desire to serve God:
"Ich will dich kennen, selbst dir dienen" [I want to know you, even
serve you]. But he is no longer sure who this "God" is. It is, to be sure,
the God who "tief in meine Seele greifender" [has reached deep into
my soul]. But Nietzsche now identifies this God as the *Unbekannter,* the
Unfaßbarer [Incomprehensible One]—in short, the "Other" whose identity has not been revealed and cannot be known. So he has not exactly left
god behind, even if he has left a particular *sort* of god behind. Yet, that
Nietzsche wants both to identify and to *serve* this *Unbekannter* is telling.
For the rest of his writings are obsessed with these questions—who or
what is god and what does it mean to *serve* this god?

From the *Unbekannter* to Dionysus and Life

At the time of his confirmation (1861), Nietzsche's faith was particularly strong. Paul Deussen, who was confirmed with Nietzsche, writes of
that time in their lives: "How well I still remember the holy, otherworldly

feeling, which filled us during the weeks before and after confirmation. We would have been completely ready, at once, to depart in order to be with Christ, and all our thinking, feeling, and striving were filled with a heavenly joy."[19] It is in this year that Nietzsche writes "Du hast gerufen— Herr ich komme." However, we have seen that Nietzsche's faith gradually erodes over time, with increasing questions regarding not simply God's existence but also who or what this god is.

What, though, are the factors that lead to Nietzsche's crisis of Christian faith? In *On The Genealogy of Morality* (1887), Nietzsche claims that his skepticism "first appeared so early in my life, so spontaneously, so irrepressibly, so much in contradiction to my environment, age, models, origins, that I almost have the right to call it my *a priori*" (*GM* P 3; *KSA* 5:249). To some extent, we can read this quotation as the later Nietzsche's attempt to "reread" his earlier life in order to see it differently and thus "create" another Nietzsche (or, to use Nietzsche's later way of speaking, wearing a mask). In contrast, I find it simply implausible to interpret the thirteen-year-old who prays fervently in *Aus meinem Leben* as wearing a "mask." Of course, it should be pointed out that this wearing of masks *too* is part of Nietzsche's attempt at a different sort of "prayer."

Yet it is true that skepticism does appear relatively earlier in Nietzsche's life. Although commentators are agreed on neither the precise factors nor the precise point at which Nietzsche can no longer be classified as a believer, there are clearly a number of indications of a loss of faith. H.-J. Schmidt's argument that Nietzsche had already lost his faith as a young boy because of his father's death seems strongly at odds with the prayers and poems that we've considered. To follow Schmidt's interpretation, we would have to see these prayers and poems as completely disingenuous.[20] Further, the death of Nietzsche's father, if anything, seems only to have strengthened his faith and resolve to become a pastor.

However, having ruled the death of Nietzsche's father out as a factor, we can point to a number of factors that clearly influenced Nietzsche's apostasy. Reading Feuerbach in 1861 was no doubt an important influence. In *The Essence of Christianity,* Feuerbach argues that the concept of God is merely the product of wish projection, and thus God is essentially anthropomorphic. Then, in April 1862 Nietzsche writes an essay titled "Fate and History" (*KGW* I/2, 13 [6]). There he indicates that historical criticism of Scripture—then gaining currency in Germany—leaves Christian doctrines with little credibility.[21] The year 1865 proves to be a particularly important one in the loss of Nietzsche's Christian faith. Although he had signed up the previous year to study both theology and philology, in 1865 he drops theology.[22] That same year he also reads David Strauss's *The Life of Jesus,* Daniel Schenkel's *The Profile of Jesus,* and Schopenhauer. On Easter Sunday of that year, he refuses communion, which shocks both family and friends. The following year Nietzsche uses Schopenhauer to criticize Christianity in a letter to his friend Carl von Gersdorff (letter of April 7, 1866; *SL* 10–13; *KSB* 2:119–23). Reading Schopenhauer helps Nietzsche develop his critique of Christianity. For Schopenhauer, religion is a surrogate for those unfortunates who find themselves incapable of philosophizing. Schopenhauer also thought of Christianity's tenets as myths rather than demonstrable truths, and this fit well with Nietzsche's idea that Christianity's principal doctrines had been discredited by historical criticism. That same year Nietzsche writes to his sister: "If you prefer peace of mind and happiness, then believe. If you would like to be a disciple of truth, do research."[23] It is not just the dichotomy of faith/research that Nietzsche sets up here; it is likewise the dichotomy of happiness/truth. For, at this point in Nietzsche's life, they become at odds with one another. It will take many years before Nietzsche can embrace a view in which happiness and truth are not mutually exclusive. In any case, in 1870 Nietzsche identifies himself as being part of the category of those "who have completely forgotten Christianity" (letter to Erwin Rohde, April 30, 1870; *KSB* 3:120).[24] Probably not coincidentally, beginning in 1870, Nietzsche rooms with Franz Overbeck, who was to prove influential in shaping Nietzsche's reading list with books that were generally hostile to Christianity—or at least orthodox Christianity.

But then who—or what—takes over the role of "God" for Nietzsche? And to whom—or what—does Nietzsche now "pray"? It is not as if Nietzsche now leaves the "god question" behind; rather, it remains with him throughout his life. Lou Salomé, who knew Nietzsche well, points out that Nietzsche remains obsessed with God throughout his life:

> Only when we enter Nietzsche's last phase of philosophy will it become completely clear to what extent the religious drive always dominated his being and his knowledge. His various philosophies are for him just so many surrogates for God, which were intended to help him compensate for a mystical God-ideal outside of himself. His last years, then, are a confession that he was not able to do without this ideal. And precisely because of that, time and again we come upon

his impassioned battle against religion, belief in God, and the need for salvation because he came precariously close to them.[25]

Yet it is not just that Nietzsche's "philosophies" function as "surrogates for God." Nietzsche actually gives us at least two "gods" who are surrogates for the God to whom the young Fritz once prayed: Dionysus and Life. Both are variations on the *Unbekannter,* and Nietzsche eventually comes to use them almost interchangeably. Moreover, Nietzsche later comes to contrast what he terms "Dionysius" and the "Crucified" as two different *religious types.* Whereas the follower of the Crucified (the Christian) denies life, the follower of Dionysus affirms life (*WP* 1052; *KSA* 13:14 [89]).

Just how far Nietzsche gets in his attempt to become (to use his phrase) a "godless anti-metaphysician" (*GS* 344; *KSA* 3:577) is open to question. Martin Heidegger has famously questioned whether Nietzsche is truly an "anti-metaphysician," accusing him of elevating "'will to power,' 'becoming,' 'life,' and 'Being' in the broadest sense" to metaphysical principles.[26] But my assertion here—and throughout this book—is that Nietzsche is not truly *godless.* For Nietzsche, "Life" is the *Unbekannter* who replaces God. So Nietzsche moves from one God to another. Of course, even *this* move of replacing God with Life proves difficult for Nietzsche. So one can level at least three charges against Nietzsche: (1) he has not completely left metaphysics (and thus transcendence) behind, (2) his move from the God of Christianity to the *Unbekannter* known as "Life" means that he has not truly left religion behind, and (3) his attempt to replace "God" with "Life" is itself only partially successful. We shall take up these charges in later chapters. Although they are different charges, if Nietzsche is guilty of any one of them (and I think he is guilty of all three), then he is not truly "godless."[27] And, as we shall see, Nietzsche still "prays."

As any careful reader can see from what I have noted so far, I clearly think that Nietzsche's thought develops significantly over time. And, yet, there is a complication with that view, one probably best mentioned at the outset. One basic question can be asked regarding the Nietzschean corpus: put bluntly, is that corpus better viewed as a literary whole or a series of disjointed texts? As will be increasingly clear, my view tends toward the former over the latter, even with notable exceptions. Without doubt, there are important twists and turns in the development of Nietzsche's thought. For instance, the preface that Nietzsche later adds in 1886 to *The Birth of Tragedy* significantly distances him from certain beliefs he had championed in that early work. But Nietzsche has hardly left the entire book behind, and his preface makes it equally clear that those earlier concerns continue to motivate him. As much as he criticizes himself for being (in his words) a "Deifier of Art" (*BT* P 7; *KSA* 1:21), it is quite significant that this very section of the preface concludes with a long citation from *Thus Spoke Zarathustra* in which Zarathustra is depicted as a dancer and dancing as being clearly "key" to living life aright. So, while Nietzsche changes his mind over the course of his writing career—adopting new ideas, reworking old ideas, or simply abandoning certain ideas that had served him well early on but prove less useful in later texts—on the whole, I see Nietzsche's concerns and even ideas remarkably continuous over time. My interpretation, then, takes into account *both* that continuity *and* the ways in which Nietzsche's thought changes in later texts.

That continuity amid difference is particularly evident in the development of Nietzsche's continuing piety. To see how that piety develops, we need to examine his explicit break with the God of Christianity. As we will see, that story proves to be far more complicated than it is often made out to be.

TWO

The Euthanasia of Christianity

> *At the deathbed of Christianity.—Really active people are now inwardly without Christianity, and the more moderate and reflective people of the intellectual middle class now possess only an adapted, that is to say marvelously simplified Christianity. . . . [I]n short, resignation and modest demands elevated to godhead—that is the best and most vital thing that still remains of Christianity. But one should notice that Christianity has thus crossed over into a gentle moralism: it is not so much "God, freedom and immortality" that have remained, as benevolence and decency of disposition . . . it is the euthanasia of Christianity.[1]*

H ow does a God die? We must count the ways. In the above quotation, Nietzsche's answer is that it is a "happy death" in which God slowly morphs from a genuine metaphysical entity into "a gentle *moralism*." This is the way a God dies, "not with a bang but a whimper."[2] The change is so subtle that most people don't even notice. They still say "Christianity," but they no longer mean "God, freedom and immortality." They still say "God," but they mean "resignation and modest demands." But they don't necessarily *know* that this is what they mean. The old language remains, but it is now eviscerated of its old meaning. Of course, language often morphs in precisely this way.

Yet Nietzsche's account of the *Gottdämmerung*—the twilight of God— is more complex than either the account he provides here or the accounts provided by many who read him. That should come as no surprise, given that Zarathustra says "when gods die, they always die several kinds of death" (*Z* IV "Retired from Service"; *KSA* 4:324). In what follows, we will trace those various deaths and consider their relations to one another.

Murder by Truth

It takes Nietzsche some years after abandoning the Christian faith before he begins to criticize it. From roughly the mid-1860s to the mid-1870s, Nietzsche makes relatively few negative comments about Christianity, either in publication or in personal correspondence. In *Ecce Homo,* he notes that *The Birth of Tragedy* was characterized by a "profound, hostile *silence* about Christianity" (*EH* "Books" BT 1; *KSA* 6:310—my italics). The full-frontal attack against Christianity—with which most readers of Nietzsche are familiar—comes out only in his late philosophy. In contrast, his early "criticism" usually takes the form of observation and description of the state of Christianity in nineteenth-century Germany.

Nietzsche nowhere provides a sustained argument against belief in God or Christianity. The reason for that lack of argument is simple: Nietzsche thinks it is no longer necessary to refute God's existence. Instead, one need merely explain how belief in God—and other religious entities—came into being, and thus explain it away:

> In former times, one sought to prove that there is no God—today one indicates how the belief that there is a God could *arise* and how this belief acquired its weight and importance: a counter-proof that there is no God thereby becomes superfluous.—When in former times one had refuted the "proofs of the existence of God" put forward, there always remained the doubt whether better proofs might not be adduced than those just refuted: in those days atheists did not know how to make a clean sweep. (*D* 95; *KSA* 3:86–87)

Although Nietzsche does not use such terminology here, "genealogy" effectively replaces refutation. By showing the distinctly *human* origins of belief in God, one shows that such belief is no longer plausible. So it is no longer incumbent upon those who do not believe to prove their point or refute arguments on behalf of God's existence; instead, believers are now put on the defensive to prove *theirs.* Or, as Nietzsche puts it: "When on a Sunday morning we hear the bells ringing we ask ourselves: is it possible! this is going on because of a Jew crucified 2000 years ago who said he was the son of God. The proof of such an assertion is lacking.—In the context of our age the Christian religion is certainly a piece of antiquity intruding out of distant ages past (*HH* I:113; *KSA* 2:116–17)." Of course, Nietzsche could make this move only given the direction in which German intellectual life was heading. In a previous age, the burden of proof would have been on *his* side. Yet, given the remarkable changes that had come about in Christian theology *itself,* Nietzsche thinks that Christianity has effectively undermined its own truth claims. The result is that it is no longer intellectually respectable to believe in God or Christianity: "Given the current state of knowledge, one can no longer have any association with [Christianity] without incurably dirtying one's intellectual conscience" (*HH* I:109; *KSA* 2:108–9).

Nietzsche's comments about the end of Christianity in *Human, All Too Human* are remarkably dispassionate. As such, they sound like a clinical diagnosis. In contrast, that (in)famous passage in *The Gay Science* in which the death of God is announced is anything but dispassionate. There Nietzsche describes the madman [*der tolle Mensch*] as entering the marketplace crying: "I'm looking for God! I'm looking for God." Yet the madman goes on to provide the answer to his own question: "I'll tell you! *We have killed him*—you and I! We are all his murderers. But how did we do this? How were we able to drink up the sea? Who gave us the sponge to wipe away the entire horizon?" (*GS* 125; *KSA* 3:480–81). Here it is clear that the death of God necessarily involves the death of the true world (i.e., the entire horizon). But it is likewise clear that wiping away that horizon is something that could never happen overnight; it could take place only over a long period of time, and with a great number of conspirators.

It is interesting to compare this famous passage with one (from the same text) that is considerably less cited: "*How to understand our cheerfulness.*—The greatest recent event—that 'God is dead'; that the belief in the Christian God has become unbelievable—is already starting to cast its first shadow over Europe. To those few at least whose eyes—or the *suspicion* in whose eyes is strong and subtle enough for this spectacle—some sun seems to have set" (*GS* 343; *KSA* 3:573). Although Nietzsche here refers to the death of God as an "event" (indeed, "the greatest" of recent events), it seems far more accurate to describe it as a lingering "twilight" [*Dämmerung*]. So the *Gottdämmerung* [twilight of God] is much like the *Götzen-Dämmerung,* the title of one of Nietzsche's last books and a word play on the last opera (*Götterdämmerung*) in Richard Wagner's *Ring* cycle. It is not merely that it takes time for the "shadow" to cast itself over Europe (and even longer to spread over the rest of the world) but also that it takes time for God to die. While Nietzsche seems to act as if God's death is now "over and done," the dying is more like that of a patient whose feeding tube has been removed—slow, agonizing, and without certainty when the final breath will be taken. Of course, the death of God is not constituted by some actual mortal "event." Nietzsche here clearly equates "God is dead" with the fact that "the belief in the

Christian God has become unbelievable." But loss of faith usually (even if not always) takes place over a long period of time. Rarely does it take place in a moment. Those who "suddenly" find themselves without belief (in a religion, an ideology, a political party, or something else) can often point to a series of "moments of disbelief" in which belief is slowly eroded. Such, it would seem, is precisely what happens to Nietzsche. As we have seen, the poems and prayers of his teens display an eroding belief.

Yet, given that the madman says *"we have killed him,"* there is clearly a conspiracy. It would be too much to detail Nietzsche's complicit predecessors in the death of God here. One could point to Immanuel Kant's rationalistic reconfiguration of Christianity in *Religion within the Boundaries of Mere Reason* (1794). Or cite David Strauss's *Life of Jesus* (1835), in which he argued for mythical interpretations of Jesus' life and miracles and then, in *The Old Faith and the New* (1872), proclaims the "new" faith to be simply Christian moral teachings. Or mention Ludwig von Feuerbach's *The Essence of Christianity* (1841), in which the concept of God is reduced to a composite of human characteristics.[3] But there was a whole host of German philosophers, theologians, and biblical exegetes who were putting both Christian theology and the biblical writings under close and critical scrutiny.

Nietzsche is not the first to announce the death of God. That distinction probably goes to Max Stirner (the pen name of Johann Caspar Schmidt), who published *The Ego and His Own* in 1844. Even though there is no evidence to demonstrate that Nietzsche read Stirner—or even was significantly influenced by him—there are some interesting parallels between Stirner's thought and that of Nietzsche.[4] One need merely compare Stirner's motto "Realize yourself!" with Nietzsche's "Become Who You Are," taken from Pindar.[5] More than that, Stirner anticipates Nietzsche's rejection of metaphysics, his criticism of Christianity's denunciation and suppression of human instincts, the call for strong individuals, the freedom to decide one's own moral values, and the critique of the ascetic priest (which Stirner terms the "cleric"). Most important, it was Stirner who writes "man has killed God in order to become now—'*sole* God on high.'"[6]

So there is a precedent for the madman's pronouncement. Indeed, many of the madman's hearers are not at all surprised by the news. They respond with laughter. "Has he been lost?" they ask. "Did he lose his way like a child?" While some of those in the crowd might well have read Stirner, more likely they were people who attended church and made pretensions to belief—all the while believing in something like Strauss's "new faith." After all, attending church was a social behavior still expected of any respectable person in nineteenth-century Germany.

Unlike his hearers, the madman is considerably perturbed by this dramatic event:

> How can we console ourselves, the murderers of all murderers? The holiest and the mightiest thing the world has ever possessed has bled to death under our knives: who will wipe this blood from us? With what water could we clean ourselves? What festivals of atonement, what holy games will we have to invent for ourselves? Is the magnitude of this deed not too great for us? Do we have to become gods merely to appear worthy of it? There was never a greater deed—and whoever is born after us will on account of this deed belong to a higher history than all history up to now! (GS 125; KSA 3:481)

That Nietzsche thinks something remarkable—even unprecedented—has taken place is clear. It is important to note that section 343 of *The Gay Science,* in which Nietzsche speaks of God's death with "cheerfulness," is part of book five, which he added to *The Gay Science* five years after initial publication of the first four books. In marked contrast, in the famous section 125 there is no cheerfulness at all—only a sense of weight, a guilty feeling of having done something "unclean," and a deep sorrow. Is it the madman who sings *"requiem aeternam deo"*? Or is it Nietzsche? Is this Nietzsche speaking from deep in his heart about the gravity of what he (not to mention others) has done? It seems hard to read this passage without catching a sense of sadness—and more than a whiff of regret. But does section 343 mean that Nietzsche has moved through the stages of grief and arrived at cheerfulness? Or is this an attempt by Nietzsche to convince *himself*? Speaking this way can be read as part of Nietzsche's strategy for reshaping himself and reconfiguring his piety. To interpret the death of God in a cheerful way is to put Nietzsche's celebrated ability to switch perspectives to work.[7]

In any case, the reason for the death of God in *The Gay Science* seems relatively straightforward: belief in God is no longer possible due to such nineteenth-century factors as the dominance of the historical-critical method of reading Scripture, the rise of modern science (and thus the rise of incredulity toward anything miraculous), the growing sense that

Scripture is merely a human product, and the idea that God is the creation of wish projection. Oddly enough, Nietzsche contends that the *death* of God is actually the result of the *belief* in God—taken to its logical conclusion: "One can see *what* it was that actually triumphed over the Christian god: Christian morality itself, the concept of truthfulness that was taken ever more rigorously; the father confessor's refinement of the Christian conscience, translated and sublimated into a scientific conscience, into intellectual cleanliness at any price" (*GS* 357; *KSA* 3:600). So Christianity's drive toward truth—its relentless honesty—proves its own undoing. The "price" of belief in God is that belief in God can no longer be accepted. Nietzsche interprets the drive toward historical-critical readings of Scriptural texts as motivated by a love of truth and even a sense of moral responsibility. It is the sheer rigor of Christian values that undermines both God, and even themselves. To be totally committed to truth is to be truthful enough to be able to admit that there is no "Truth" (at least in the Platonic sense of the term) and that there is no "Morality." Whereas Plato had originally lied in constructing the Forms,[8] Christianity ultimately destroys itself because of its very logic. But, in so doing, it stays true to itself.

Murder by Jealousy, Death by Pity

Having considered the account of the death of God in *The Gay Science*, it is highly illuminating to juxtapose that account with what we find in *Thus Spoke Zarathustra*. There we discover a couple of curious but important variations. First, we get a motivation for God's death that is strangely lacking in *The Gay Science*. Second, we get a different account of the death of God, one that at least seems strangely at odds with the account we've considered above.

While Zarathustra is speaking to his disciples ("friends," to use his term)—and he freely admits that "God is a conjecture"—he goes on to speak very frankly: "But let me reveal my heart to you entirely, my friends: *if* there were gods, how could I endure not to be a god! *Hence* there are no gods. Though I drew this conclusion, now it draws me" (*Z* II "Blessed Isles"; *KSA* 4:109–10). This is a strikingly *different* reason for rejecting God, and one that is hardly intellectually defensible. In fact, its logic is childish in the worst possible way: "I don't get to be God, so no one gets to be God." No wonder that Zarathustra realizes he is revealing something from deep in his heart. For here the motivation for the death of God turns out to be purely emotional and selfish.

This psychological account for the death of God is further strengthened by what the "ugliest man" says. Zarathustra encounters the ugliest man and recognizes him as *"the murderer of God"* (*Z* IV "Ugliest Man"; *KSA* 4:328). He accuses him of having taken revenge upon God, and the ugliest man admits that this is exactly what he has done. Speaking of God, the ugliest man says:

> He *had to* die: he saw with eyes that saw everything; he saw man's depths and ultimate grounds, all his concealed disgrace and ugliness. His pity knew no shame: he crawled into my dirtiest nooks. This most curious, overobtrusive, overpitying one had to die. He always saw me: on such a witness I wanted to have revenge or not live myself. The god who saw everything, *even man*—this god had to die! Man cannot bear it that such a witness should live. (*Z* IV "Ugliest Man"; *KSA* 4:331)

Because of what Nietzsche elsewhere says about Socrates being ugly (*TI* II:3: *KSA* 6:68), some commentators identify Socrates with the ugliest man.[9] Yet the God that has to die here sounds much very like the Pietistic God of Christianity (both in the sense of knowing all and in being so pitying in nature), so Socrates seems an inappropriate assassin. The logic here is essentially the same as the previous reason given by Zarathustra. It is the logic of *ressentiment,* a resentful, vengeful logic. The principal difference between Zarathustra's version and that of the ugliest man is that the latter is so obsessed and angry. It is largely that obsession that makes the ugliest man so truly ugly: he has become *racked* with revenge, and it has taken a physical toll upon his facial features. Yet there is another reason for his ugliness. As Zarathustra leaves the ugliest man, he remarks: "None have I found yet who despised himself more deeply." On the one hand, Zarathustra goes on to say, "I love the great despisers" and even asks, "was *he* perhaps the higher man whose cry I heard?" (*Z* IV "Ugliest Man"; *KSA* 4:332). To despise oneself is a part of the overcoming that Zarathustra seeks. On the other hand, the reason why this man is so ugly is that he is riddled with shame. He has so internalized the morality of the God—who is now dead—that he still feels the burden of that shame and so despises himself.

So far, we have examined only deaths by murder. The first is a murder by way of the truth; the second is a murder by way of revenge. Yet Nietzsche also speaks of death by way of pity.[10] In the section just preceding "The Ugliest Man," Zarathustra encounters a "retired" pope. Zarathustra asks him: "You know *how* he died? Is it true what they say, that pity strangled him, that he saw how *man* hung on the cross and that he could not bear it, that love of man became his hell, and in the end his death?" (*Z* IV "Retired From Service"; *KSA* 4: 323).[11] The old pope doesn't answer, but his lack of an answer seems to be affirmation of Zarathustra's supposition. The reason why pity would cause one to die is that *Mitleid* (or, as Nietzsche puts it, *das Mitleiden*) is simply the compounding of suffering. "Pity (*Mitleid*), insofar as it really causes suffering (*Leiden*)—and this is here our only point of view—is a weakness, like every losing of oneself through a *harmful* affect. It *increases* the amount of suffering in the world" (*D* 134; *KSA* 3:127–28). So God dies from taking on all of the suffering of the world—it becomes simply overwhelming. But, of course, God *could* have chosen not to do so. In that respect, one could interpret this "death by pity" as a suicide.

Thus, Nietzsche's genealogy of the deaths of God turns out to be rather complicated. God dies in more than one way and for more than one reason. Moreover, Nietzsche leaves us with these various perspectives, not choosing any one over the others. Such is a quintessentially Nietzschean thing to do. Yet it leaves the reader with a question: are these accounts all *equally* plausible, or is one more plausible than the others? In other words, while Nietzsche's loss of faith seems to have been more due to a sense of Christianity's implausibility, does the psychological account have anything to do with him personally? The question is, at bottom, whether Nietzsche's own reasons for rejecting the metaphysics of Christianity are simply intellectual or whether the psychological account plays a role too. While such a question is ultimately impossible to answer, the psychological account certainly fits with the kind of individualism to which Nietzsche aspires.

Consider what Nietzsche writes in the section *"Excelsior"* [literally, higher] of *The Gay Science*: "You will never pray again, never adore again, never again rest in endless trust; you refuse to let yourself stop to unharness your thoughts before any ultimate wisdom, goodness, or power" (*GS* 285; *KSA* 3:527). What would make it easier to refuse to pray or adore or trust than to *remove* anything or anyone to whom one might pray or show adoration or trust? Of course, Nietzsche realizes just how overwhelming such a task is for humankind, for he goes on to say, "Man of renunciation, all of this you wish to renounce? Who will give you the strength to do so? No one yet has had the strength!" (*GS* 285; *KSA* 3:528). Whether

Nietzsche has the strength will be the focus of the following chapter. There I will argue that—in the end—Nietzsche *does not* have the power to renounce all adoration and truth, for he ends up transferring that adoration and trust from God to Life.

Who Dies?

But who dies? On my reading, there are three deaths for Nietzsche.[12] The first is of what Pascal had called "the God of the philosophers." Nietzsche terms this "the last, thinnest, emptiest" being, the *ens realissimum* (*TI* III: 4; *KSA* 6:76). Nietzsche, of course, doesn't really argue against this concept, in the same way that he never really argues against Plato's Forms. On Nietzsche's view, this concept of "God" had been spun out of thin air (by what Nietzsche calls "sickly web-spinners"). Nietzsche is certainly right on that score. As Jean-Luc Marion points out, "That which dies does not have any right to claim, even when it is alive, to be 'God.'"[13] On this point, Marion and Nietzsche are agreed: what dies is no less than an idol. One can be grateful to Nietzsche for using his subtle hammer to detect such an idol.

Yet the death of the *ens realissimum* turns out to be effectively the death of metaphysics and the end of the True World. For Nietzsche, it is also—by logical extension—the death of ethics and aesthetics. For, if there is no Truth, there is no Goodness nor Beauty either. No one has described this death more effectively than Heidegger: "The pronouncement 'God is dead' means: The suprasensory world is without effective power. It bestows no life. Metaphysics, i.e., for Nietzsche Western philosophy understood as Platonism, is at an end. Nietzsche understands his own philosophy as the countermovement to metaphysics, and that means for him a movement in opposition to Platonism."[14] The countermovement that Heidegger describes is simply the shifting of gravity from Platonic "otherworldliness" to "this worldliness." In other words, Nietzsche thinks he is simply "undoing" Platonism. For Platonism effectively "places life's center of gravity not in life but in the 'beyond'—*in nothingness*—one deprives life of its center of gravity altogether." Once Nietzsche's shift back is complete, "now becomes the 'sense' of life" (rather than some *other* time or place) (*AC* 43; *KSA* 6:217).

There are two significant caveats that we have to add to this account of the death of God as the death of metaphysics. The first is that Heidegger thinks that Nietzsche has not quite left metaphysics behind, which we briefly noted in the previous chapter. As he puts it: "Nietzsche holds this overturning of metaphysics to be the overcoming of metaphysics. But every overturning of this kind remains only a self-deluding entanglement in the Same that has become unknowable."[15] To be sure, Nietzsche no longer wishes to ascribe power to the suprasensory world. Yet Heidegger argues that Nietzsche is still engaged in the metaphysical project, for two reasons. First, the very logic of overcoming metaphysics leaves one entangled in the metaphysical web. For one cannot simply give up metaphysics by walking away from it. Instead, one in effect exchanges one metaphysical position for another. Heidegger claims that the same logic is to be found in irrationalism. Because the parallel between "overcoming" metaphysics and rationalism is so striking, it is worth quoting Heidegger's comments in full: "Irrationalism is a way out of rationalism that does not lead us out into the open but only gets us stuck *still* farther in rationalism, because it promotes the opinion that rationalism is overcome by merely saying no to it, whereas in fact it now just plays its games more dangerously, because it plays them covertly and in a manner less vulnerable to interference."[16] Certainly Heidegger thinks that this is what happens to Nietzsche: he tries to escape from metaphysics but ends up being "stuck" within its grasp. Yet the worst part is that one *thinks* one has successfully escaped. Second, and illustrative of the first, Heidegger's charge is that Nietzsche reduces everything to the "will to power" (since, to quote Heidegger, "the pronouncement 'God is dead' can be thought adequately only from out of the essence of the will to power").[17] That is, God's death is the result of a human will to power. Since Heidegger reads the will to power as the overarching metaphysical principle in Nietzsche's thought (in which Nietzsche becomes a kind of monist), Nietzsche still remains entangled in the metaphysical project.

But there are at least two problems with Heidegger's charges. On the one hand, various commentators have argued that Heidegger—being particularly influenced by the posthumously published volume *The Will to Power*—makes the will to power far too central to Nietzsche's thought (or at least far more central than Nietzsche ever intended it, to whatever extent we can determine Nietzsche's "intentions").[18] On the other hand, there is an open question regarding the status of "will to power" itself: "Even if there exists a doctrine, one that can be unpacked 'analytically' as a psychological principle, is it to be grasped ontologically, as discarded notes from the *Nachlass* [his literary estate] seem to suggest?"[19] As should be clear, since these questions are intertwined, their answers are likewise intertwined. But the issue here is not *merely* the status of the *Nachlass*. The question of whether the "will to power" is meant as a metaphysical principle can *not* be determined simply by whether one does or does not accept the *Nachlass* as authoritative. For the *Nachlass* in no way makes it clear that the will to power either is or is not a metaphysical principle (despite the fact that Magnus and Higgins think it is somehow suggested). I, for one, am unable to find any passage in the *Nachlass* that makes any such reading "obvious." On the contrary, given everything that Nietzsche says, it would seem that the will to power is *not* a metaphysical but what we might call a *physical* principle. To shift the center of gravity back to this world and to make life central is to leave metaphysics behind, which means we are left with only the physical world.

Despite all that, Heidegger's point is one that cannot simply be ignored, though it must be recast. For the problem is not really whether Nietzsche *sees* himself as overcoming metaphysics (which seems clear enough) but whether he *can*. That is, are there still vestiges of metaphysics in his thought? Or, to put this question much more pointedly and broadly, can metaphysics *ever* be left behind—merely by claiming to "overcome" it? Here I have in mind the problem Kant raises in the first preface to the *Critique of Pure Reason*: while science can in no way adjudicate between competing metaphysical claims, one is still left with the fact that one cannot help but make such claims. As Kant puts it, the problem is that "these so-called **indifferentists**, to the extent that they think anything at all, always unavoidably fall back into metaphysical assertions, which they professed so much to despise."[20] So the question then becomes: just what counts as a "metaphysical assertion"? The answer from a Kantian point of view would be: any ultimate principle that cannot be given a scientific basis (but is instead the basis for science). Given *that* definition, then Nietzsche's "will to power" (or various kinds of forces that are found throughout his writings) *must be* metaphysical in nature. The only other possibility would be just to start talking differently. That, at least, is Richard Rorty's solution (and he thinks he's simply borrowing the strategy from Nietzsche). He writes: "We simply refuse to talk in a certain way, the Platonic way. The views we hope to persuade people to accept cannot be stated in Platonic terminology."[21] It is true that Nietzsche speaks of learning "to think differently" and ultimately "to feel differently"

(*D* 103; *KSA* 3:92)—a topic we'll take up in the next chapter. Moreover, Nietzsche thinks that such notions as God can be replaced only by what he terms "other metaphysical plausibilities (at bottom likewise untruths)" (*HH* I:109; *KSA* 2:108).

At this point, though, we must leave behind the realm of Nietzsche scholarship (i.e., "what did Nietzsche really mean?"). It is perfectly clear that Nietzsche wants to overcome metaphysics. What is less clear is whether Nietzsche (or Rorty) can do so simply by proclaiming to do so. And there is no way to adjudicate this dispute. One simply *believes* one way or the other. It is ultimately a matter of "faith." On the one hand, even someone as "postmodern" as Derrida insists that "it was a Greek who said, 'If one has to philosophize, one has to philosophize; if one does not have to philosophize, one still has to philosophize (to say it and think it). One always has to philosophize.'" By which Derrida means that one cannot escape from metaphysics. On the other hand, Levinas responds: "*Not to philosophize would not be 'to philosophize still,' nor succumb to opinions.*"[22] But—at best—it can be only Levinas the *theologian* who makes that claim, not Levinas the *philosopher*. One cannot escape philosophy—and thereby metaphysics—by making a philosophical argument against it. So it is perfectly appropriate that Nietzsche ultimately comes to call his own belief system a faith that is "the highest of all possible faiths," one that he baptizes "with the name of *Dionysus*" (*TI* IX:49; *KSA* 6:152).

Earlier I noted that there is a second caveat regarding the death of God. Assuming (for the sake of argument) that gods can die and that one can truly escape from metaphysics, then where are we now? Unlike the more complicated twelve-step program of Alcoholics Anonymous, "How the 'True World' Finally Became a Fiction" is a mere six-step program. However, to get to the sixth step, there must be no more talk of either the true or the apparent world. Again, the comparison with Rorty is warranted, for Rorty wants to arrive at the place where we do not talk about "relativism," since that talk supposes an oppositional term (say, "absolutism"). Whatever one thinks about either Nietzsche's or Rorty's project, it is clear that we are not even close to having done away with the True World. It still functions in most philosophical discussions, even in antirealist ones such as Rorty's. So there may be a time when God is dead and the True World has passed away, but we are far from that at this point. Which is to say that the *Gottdämmerung* continues to linger.

Even though the death of God is for Nietzsche primarily metaphysical in nature, there are clearly two other deaths involved. There is the death of what we might term "the God of Abraham, Isaac, and Jacob," who self-identifies with the elusive formula "I AM WHO I AM" (Ex. 3:14), and "the Christ of faith." Later, in chapter 7, we'll note that Nietzsche has remarkable respect for the God of the Old Testament. Here we could also take up the "deaths" of the historical figure of Jesus and the "Christ of faith," but we'll instead consider those deaths in chapters 7 and 8.

Of course, once God is dead, the question is: what kind of "piety" does Nietzsche put in place of Christian piety? That is the subject of the following chapter.

THREE
The Piety of Zarathustra

That God became man only shows that man should not seek his blessedness in eternity, but instead ground his heaven on earth.[1]

T hat quotation comes from the same letter in which Nietzsche proclaims to his young friends that Christianity is "essentially a matter of the heart." Already by 1862, then, Nietzsche had come to think in terms of a purely earthly piety. Admittedly, Nietzsche's conception of Christian Pietism is less than orthodox. Yet my point in this chapter is to show how remarkably true Nietzsche remains to the structure of Pietism. As we will see, it is likewise the case that Nietzsche remains relatively well disposed toward Christian Pietism, even if his own Pietism takes a different direction.

Nietzsche and Christian Pietism

While Nietzsche was living with Franz Overbeck, the latter wrote an essay titled "On the Christian Spirit of Our Contemporary Theology" (1873). Although most forms of Protestant theologies come in for criticism, Overbeck affirms Pietism as "a form of Christianity that attempts as much as possible to assimilate original Christianity to contemporary Christianity."[2] Overbeck diagnoses the problem of modern theology as being too concerned with theory and not enough with practice—and so Pietism is the answer to contemporary theology's problems. That Nietzsche and Overbeck were good friends and spoke frequently on theological matters leads Martin Pernet to conclude that this judgment likely characterized Nietzsche's own, which seems a plausible conclusion. That plausibility is considerably strengthened when we consider what Nietzsche has to say in *The Anti-Christ(ian)* regarding the true spirit of Christianity (and how it has been distorted by the church):

> I go back, I tell the *genuine* history of Christianity. . . . It is false to the point of nonsense to find the mark of the Christian in a "faith," for

> instance, in the faith in redemption through Christ: only Christian *practice*, a life such as he *lived* who died on the cross, is Christian. Such a life is still possible today, for certain people even necessary: genuine, original Christianity will be possible at all times. Not a faith, but a doing; above all, a *not* doing of many things, another state of *being*. (*AC* 39; *KSA* 6:211)

Such was the essence of true Christian faith for Nietzsche, this *practice* that is a state of *being*. It is telling that Nietzsche singles out "faith in redemption through Christ" as a quintessential example of what he considers a Christian teaching that is "false to the point of nonsense." For Nietzsche, Christianity simply isn't about redemption. When he says "there was only *one* Christian, and he died on the cross," he means that subsequent church teachings were "'*ill* tidings,' a *dysangel*" (*AC* 39; *KSA* 6:211)—and redemption is a key component of that false gospel. Of course, even though Nietzsche no longer follows Christian Pietism, he continues to think that it is still a possible way to live. Moreover, Nietzsche goes out of his way not to disturb the faith of those like his mother who lived a true faith of piety, even though he scathingly attacks those who hold to a more rationalistic version of Christianity.[3] Although Nietzsche's sister Elisabeth may not always be the most trustworthy reporter of facts relating to her brother, she seems to be correct when she writes "my brother had the greatest possible respect for sincere, honest Christianity."[4]

As it turns out, his most scathing attack on Christianity—the "Decree against Christianity," a document so vehement that even Nietzsche's editors and friends were reluctant to include it as the culmination to *The Anti-Christ(ian)*—is a particularly good example. For there Nietzsche makes it clear whom he is truly against: "Be more severe toward Protestants than toward Catholics and more severe toward liberal Protestants than toward those of strict belief. The criminality of being a Christian increases in so far as the Christian approaches science."[5] Relatively speaking, Nietzsche lets those who truly believe off rather lightly. Of course, he thinks that the truly religious person "is an exception" in any religion (*GS* 128; *KSA* 3:484). In contrast, he thinks that those who take a "scientific" approach toward Christianity are the ones to be most strongly criticized. There are at least two reasons for that severity. First, Nietzsche sees those who have a scientific view of Christianity as not being true believers. They may have retained some of the trappings of Christianity (usually its morality), but they have left its metaphysics behind. And, in so doing, they are not really believers but hypocrites. Second, Nietzsche would see people like David Strauss or George Eliot as either disingenuous or simply stupid (or both). Nietzsche's essay "David Strauss, the Confessor and the Writer" is a merciless tirade against Strauss's *The Old Faith and the New*. Repeatedly labeling Strauss a "philistine," Nietzsche mocks Strauss's "new faith" as having nothing to do with Christianity. Strauss wants the same thing as does Nietzsche—that "heaven" be "a Heaven on earth" (*UM* I:4: *KSA* 1:178). Yet, whereas Nietzsche propounds such a theory as decidedly non-Christian, Strauss tries to make himself out as still following in the Christian tradition. We already noted the criticism of George Eliot (Marian Evans) and other "English dimwits" (to use Nietzsche's phrase). In Eliot's case, she fails to understand that the destruction of Christian metaphysics inevitably results in the destruction of Christian morality. Eliot, like Strauss, wants to jettison the former but retain the latter. Yet this move means that she ends up being "a moral fanatic in the most frightening way." That is, she clings all the more strongly to Christian morality but counts as a "fanatic" in that she has absolutely no justification for doing so.[6] Nietzsche goes on to insist that such a project is simply contradictory:

> If you give up Christian faith, you pull the *right* to Christian morality out from under your feet. This morality is simply *not* self-evident: one has to bring this point home again and again, despite the English dimwits. Christianity is a system, a view of things conceived as a connected *whole*. If you break off a major concept from it, faith in God, you break up the whole as well: there are no necessities left to hold onto anymore. Christianity presupposes that human beings do not know, *cannot* know, what is good and evil for them: they believe in God, who is the only one who knows it. Christian morality is a commandment; its origin is transcendent; it is beyond all criticism, all right to criticism; it is only true if God is truth—it stands and falls with faith in God. (*TI* IX:5; *KSA* 6:113–14)

Yet the true believer, one who believes both the metaphysical and ethical parts of Christianity, comes out looking far more respectable than the rationalistic or "scientific" Christian. He writes: "Who could possibly feel an aversion for pious people strong in their faith? To the contrary, do we not regard them with a silent respect and take pleasure in them, with a profound regret that these excellent people do not feel as we do?" (*D* 56; *KSA* 3:57). While Nietzsche certainly thinks pious believers are *wrong*, he doesn't single them out for attack. Of course, one might be tempted to argue that—given Nietzsche's rules for warfare, in which he only engages in an "*honest* duel" against an equal opponent—he sees devout Christians as unworthy or unequal opponents (*EH* "Wise" 7; *KSA* 6:274). Yet he nowhere says this. In fact, in the passage quoted above, he speaks of treating true believers with "respect," given that they are "excellent people." He does indeed single out the Apostle Paul for a scathing attack, but that attack is not against Paul's *belief* but what Nietzsche perceives as his *distortion* of the gospel for personal reasons. Interestingly enough, Nietzsche claims "the most serious Christians have always been well disposed toward me." Given the positive ways in which later Christian theologians such as Karl Barth, Dietrich Bonhoeffer, and Eberhard Jungel appropriate (and affirm) aspects of Nietzsche's thought, that claim is not without at least some merit. Further, Nietzsche claims that in waging war against Christianity, he is not "blaming individuals" (*EH* "Wise" 7; *KSA* 6: 275).

Of course, while Nietzsche thinks that such criticism is necessary, that criticism is only a means to his personal goal to arrive at a wholly natural sort of piety.

Learning to *Think and Feel Differently*

Given that belief in God is simply untenable for Nietzsche and many of his generation, he sees a need to *think differently*. After all, it is one thing to recognize that belief in God and belief in Christianity are no longer tenable; it is another thing for that lack of belief to sink in and change one at the core of one's being. It is this deep change that Nietzsche seeks throughout the rest of his life, though the extent of his success in this self-experimentation is open to question—increasingly so in the works of 1888. In any case, he is clear as to what needs to happen: "We have to *learn to think differently*—in order at last, perhaps very late on, to attain even more: *to feel differently*" (*D* 103; *KSA* 3:92). One way of making this happen—or perhaps *the only way of making this happen*—would be to create what Nietzsche calls "other metaphysical plausibilities":

> How one would like to exchange the false assertions of the priests
> that there is a God who desires that we do good, is the guardian and
> witness of every action, every moment, every thought, who loves

us and in every misfortune wants only what is best for us—how one would like to exchange these for truths that would be as salutary, pacifying and beneficial as those errors are! Yet such truths do not exist; the most philosophy can do is to set against them other metaphysical plausibilities (at bottom likewise untruths). (*HH* I:109; *KSA* 2:108)

This passage is particularly revealing in that it lays out Nietzsche's strategy. While Nietzsche disbelieves Christian truths, he sees no need for a "refutation" (as we noted in the previous chapter). Instead, his positive strategy is that one best counters metaphysical untruths with what he sees as equally untrue metaphysical claims. Of course, at the time Nietzsche wrote out this "prescription" for a life change (1878), he is not at all clear as to which counter-metaphysical claims he will put in their place. Only in later works—particularly *Thus Spoke Zarathustra*—does he begin to assemble his arsenal of metaphysical counterclaims.

In *Daybreak: Thoughts on the Prejudices of Morality* (1880–81), Nietzsche pursues a strategy of genealogy that causes us to think differently. In order to rethink morality, Nietzsche needs to show that our moral beliefs are actually prejudices for which we have no real support. He claims, for instance, that *we* are the ones who have created the notion of sin (*D* 81; *KSA* 3:78) and that Christianity creates a way to "save" people from this invented type of deed (*D* 59; *KSA* 3:59–60). Seen from this perspective, morality and the need for salvation look very different: if there really isn't any sin, then there is no need for salvation. On Nietzsche's read, Christianity has invented "nothing but imaginary *causes* ('God,' 'soul,' 'ego,' 'spirit,' 'free will')" and "nothing but imaginary *effects* ('sin,' 'redemption,' 'grace,' 'punishment,' 'forgiveness of sins')," making Christianity both the illness and the cure (*AC* 15; *KSA* 6:181). Eliminating Christianity, then, eliminates the whole mess. We will turn to Nietzsche's read of Paul in chapter 7, but it is worth pointing out here that Nietzsche credits Paul with "inventing" Christianity by reinterpreting Christ's death (*D* 68; *KSA* 3: 64–68). So there is an important sense in which Nietzsche—at least from his point of view—is "undoing" what Paul had done.

Nietzsche thinks there *is* another way to think and feel: we just need to make that move. For instance: "The passions become evil and malicious if they are regarded as evil and malicious" (*D* 76; *KSA* 3:73). Nietzsche's message is clear: if thinking has made the passions seem evil to us, then thinking can just as well make them into something positive. Or, as Nietzsche puts it elsewhere, we cultivate "a new habit, a new instinct, a second nature, so that our first nature withers away" (*UM* II:3; *KSA* 1:270). It is this same kind of "thinking differently" that Nietzsche applies to Pietism.

In the previous chapter, we considered Zarathustra's conversation with the retired pope. What comes at the end of that section is somewhat surprising, for the pope senses a kind of kinship with Zarathustra. Just as Zarathustra is about to leave, the pope says: "O Zarathustra, with such disbelief you are more pious [*frömmer*] than you believe. Some god in you must have converted you to your godlessness. Is it not your piety itself that no longer lets you believe in a god? . . . although you want to be the most godless, I scent a secret, sacred, pleasant scent of long blessings" (*Z* IV "Retired from Service"; *KSA* 4:325). It is interesting that it takes a truly pious person to recognize piety in someone else. Although Zarathustra no longer believes in God, he still retains his piety. Indeed, he responds to the pope by saying: "I love all who are pious." So Zarathustra has not left his piety behind. Along the lines of the logic that we sketched in the previous chapter, the pope even suggests that it is Zarathustra's piety that causes him to be godless. Yet *is* there a god "in Nietzsche" that leads him to think as he does? And who might that god be?

Refiguring Pietism

That the pope has a better read on Zarathustra than Zarathustra has on himself will become amply clear. Assuming that Zarathustra is one of the masks Nietzsche wears—not exactly Nietzsche per se but *a* Nietzsche or a perspective on Nietzsche—then Zarathustra provides us with a good idea of Nietzsche's own *Versuch* [attempt] to leave the God of his youth behind and become a truly free spirit.[7] Here we will trace the steps that Zarathustra/Nietzsche takes to refigure Pietism.

From the opening lines of *Thus Spoke Zarathustra,* it is clear that Zarathustra has not left the form of religion behind—even if he is *attempting* to leave its content behind. For Zarathustra begins with a prayer to the sun. That alone would be remarkable, but the content is even more telling. Zarathustra addresses the sun as the "great star" and even says "we waited for you every morning, took your overflow from you, and blessed you for it" (*Z* I "Prologue" 1; *KSA* 4:11). What is striking about this prayer is that, only a year before, Nietzsche had written the following (as we noted in chapter 2): "You will never pray again, never adore again, never again rest in endless trust; you refuse to let yourself stop to unharness your thoughts before any ultimate wisdom, goodness, or power" (*GS* 285; *KSA* 3:527). That Zarathustra prays a *prayer* is evident from its opening, Zarathustra's declaration of dependence upon the sun, and the admission of having "blessed" the sun for its gifts. And this opening prayer is actually mirrored by another prayer that originally closed *Thus Spoke Zarathustra*—subtitled "The Song of Yes and Amen."[8] So the theme of prayer runs throughout the text.

Yet, in some ways, the presence of prayer should not be so surprising. For, although the prayers of dependence that Nietzsche condemns may be something he wishes to leave behind, Higgins rightly notes that prayers *can* be "a means to revitalize one's spirit."[9] Nietzsche criticizes prayers designed as distractions so that believers never stop to think about what they are really doing. But he does admit that some believers *do* have "thoughts and elevations of their own." Even such believers "have their tired hours, when a string of venerable words and sounds and mechanical piety do them good" (*GS* 128; *KSA* 3:484). Thus, for example, the Anglican Book of Common Prayer is not merely a repository of deep religious insight and piety; it is also a useful tool for precisely those moments when one does not feel very pious or inspired.

Prayer, then, can have an important function in shaping one's character. But it is not alone in this respect. Right after praying to the sun, Zarathustra encounters a saint who says to him: "I make songs and sing them; and when I make songs, I laugh, cry, and hum: thus I praise God. With singing, weeping, laughing, and humming I praise the God who is my God" (*Z* I "Prologue" 2; *KSA* 4:13). Although Zarathustra has nothing to say to the saint, the saint's formula of "singing, weeping, laughing, and humming" will soon become his own, in praise to the god who is *his* god.

Zarathustra is painfully aware that leaving the God who has died behind requires a change of heart as well as the invention—as we noted earlier—of a new set of "metaphysical plausibilities." As soon as Zarathustra leaves the saint, he enters the next town and declares: "Behold, I teach you the overman. The overman is the meaning of the earth. Let your will say: the overman *shall be* the meaning of the earth! I beseech you, my brothers, *remain faithful to the earth,* and do not believe those who speak to you of otherworldly hopes! . . . Despisers of life are they" (*Z* I "Prologue" 3; *KSA* 4:15). The overman [*Übermensch*] is the first of Zarathustra's new metaphysical plausibilities (not metaphysical *realities* but stand-ins for such realities), and it is expressly designed to replace otherworldly hopes. It is still a kind of hope, to be sure, for Zarathustra can only hold out the hope of the coming of this greatly underspecified new being. Moreover, Zarathustra also goes on to redefine the notion of "sin": whereas once it had been something against God, now it is something against the world. Of course, this new notion of sin would have fit with Nietzsche's *Christian* Pietism, too, even though he seems not to recognize this.

However, Zarathustra finds that simply stating these new metaphysical plausibilities hardly invokes faith in them. His speech is greeted with a mixture of silence and laughter. But Zarathustra notes that "one must still have chaos in oneself to be able to give birth to a dancing star" (*Z* I "Prologue" 5; *KSA* 4:19). Although his listeners still have that chaos, when he goes on to speak of the "last men," they actually want to *become* last men, which means that they have no desire to take risks but are content to live in utter mediocrity. They are unwilling to embrace that chaos and instead seek comfort in Christian morality. However, none of this should come as a surprise to Zarathustra. For *coming to believe* in metaphysical plausibilities requires a complete change in which one learns to think and feel differently. Thus, the Prologue leads to "The Three Metamorphoses," the essential changes that must take within oneself in order to become a different person. One begins as a camel, the bearer of burdens. No doubt, these burdens are those of sin and guilt (the "thou shalts" and "shalt nots"), but they also include the burden of giving up metaphysical comfort. The camel is replaced by a lion, which puts "I will" in place of "Thou Shalt." The lion symbolizes the ability to destroy the old metaphysical plausibilities and to create a space—a new freedom—in which new values can be created. However, the lion is unable to create new values, only to destroy the old. Only the child who replaces the lion can create new values, since the child is "innocence and forgetting, a new beginning, a game, a self-propelled wheel, a first movement, a sacred 'Yes.' For the game of creation, my brothers, a sacred 'Yes' is needed" (*Z* I "Three Metamorphoses"; *KSA* 4:31).

The reason why the child is needed for the creation of new values is that only the child is innocent in the sense of having no memory of the past. To give a "sacred Yes" to new values, one must be utterly unaware of the old ones (in the same way that the True World has become a fiction). Yet this raises a fundamental question, not just for Zarathustra but for Nietzsche as well. If becoming a child is essential to beginning again, then does (or *can*) Nietzsche accomplish that goal? Here it is merely a doctrine laid out by Nietzsche. But, in only few short years, it becomes a question that one *must* ask regarding Nietzsche himself. In *Ecce Homo*, Nietzsche portrays himself as somehow reaching this stage. Yet his claim seems disingenuous at best, for Nietzsche—unlike the child—seems filled with *ressentiment*. But we will return to this problem in the last chapter.

In stark contrast to Nietzsche, Zarathustra ends book one with a penetratingly honest evaluation of himself. After an at times nauseating collection of sermons, Zarathustra has the honesty to question his own proclamation. He goes so far as to say that he may have actually deceived his disciples and advises them: "Now I bid you lose me and find your-selves; and only when you have all denied me will I return to you" (*Z* I "Gift-Giving Virtue" 3; *KSA* 4:101). Zarathustra has certainly not reached the stage of being a child, but he also makes no pretensions to having done so.

While Nietzsche wants to think and feel differently, the goal of "starting over" is far easier prescribed than accomplished. This practi-cal inability to *be* different is particularly evident in the section "On the Tarantulas" in which Zarathustra characterizes them as "secretly venge-ful." Their formula for "justice" is "that the world be filled with the storms of our revenge." Yet Zarathustra goes on to admit that he has been bitten by them, and that they "make my soul, too, whirl with revenge" (*Z* II "Tarantulas"; *KSA* 4:128, 131). The problem is that he has not yet learned to practice what he preaches. Zarathustra is particularly forced to confront his inadequacies in "The Stillest Hour." There he is told "with-out voice": "You must yet become as a child and without shame. The pride of youth is still upon you; you have become late; but whoever would become as a child must overcome his youth too." To this, Zarathustra replies (quite honestly): "I do not want to." Not surprisingly, the voice-less voice then responds: "O Zarathustra, your fruit is ripe but you are not ripe for your fruit." At this, Zarathustra "wept loudly" (*Z* II "Stillest Hour"; *KSA* 3:189–90). For he admits that he is at best a lion, but still cannot become a child. And, as we will see, this inability to believe and live out his own doctrines—of not yet being "ripe"—recurs not merely in *Zarathustra* but in Nietzsche's later works as well.

Another one of Nietzsche's new "metaphysical plausibilities" is the doctrine of the eternal return. While there are myriad ways of interpreting this doctrine (and a Nietzschean cottage industry to go along with it),[10] one thing is clear: to affirm the eternal return is to affirm whatever has happened, does happen, and will happen. Nietzsche first introduces this doctrine in a section titled *"The Heaviest Weight"*: "What if some day or night a demon were to steal into your loneliest loneliness and say to you: 'This life as you now live it and have lived it you will have to live once again and innumerable times again.' . . . [H]ow well disposed would you have become to yourself and to life *to long for nothing more fervently* than for this ultimate eternal confirmation and seal?" (*GS* 341; *KSA* 3:570). On one perspective, such a doctrine is the heaviest of weights. For, if what happens will happen over and over again, there is no possibility of "changing" the course of events. Yet Nietzsche puts this forth in precisely the opposite spirit of "futility": to *embrace* this idea that life is a continual repetition is to embrace *whatever* happens. One's attitude is one not merely passively "accepting" whatever happens, then, but rather of very actively longing for whatever happens.

Although there is a significant difference between the eternal return and *amor fati* (simply because loving one's fate need not involve any sense of recurrence), they go together well, and seem to be connected in Nietzsche's mind: "My formula for greatness in a human being is *amor fati:* that one wants nothing to be different, not forward, not backward, not in all eternity. Not merely bear what is necessary, still less conceal it—all idealism is mendaciousness in the face of what is necessary—but *love* it" (*EH* "Clever" 10; *KSA* 6:297). Nietzsche calls the embracing of *amor fati* "redemption": "To redeem those who lived in the past and to transform every 'It was' into an 'I wanted it thus!'—that alone do I call redemption!" (*Z* II "Redemption"; *KSA* 4:179). To make it clear that this is the only form of "redemption" that Nietzsche accepts, he virtually repeats this formula in the third section of *Zarathustra*. Speaking of his disciples, he says:

> I taught them all *my* creating and striving, to create and carry together into One what in man is fragment and riddle and dreadful accident; as creator, guesser of riddles, and redeemer of accidents, I taught them to work on the future and to redeem with their creation all that *has been*. To redeem what is past in man and to re-create all "it was" until the will says, "Thus I willed it! Thus I shall will it"—this I called redemption and this alone I taught them to call redemption. (*Z* III "Old and New Tablets" 3; *KSA* 4:248–49)

Even though Nietzsche uses the term "redemption" in both this passage and the one before, it is crucial to note that he is using it in the exact *opposite* sense of its usual meaning. His use of the phrase "that alone do I call redemption" clearly calls attention to the fact that he employs the term in a very different way. For the underlying assumption of "redemption" as normally defined is that something is *wrong* and needs to be *fixed*. For Christianity, the assumption is that sin is wrong, and so we need to be "redeemed" from sin. Alternatively, for Karl Marx, the assumption is that capitalism is wrong, and so we need communism to "redeem" us. On Nietzsche's account, "the spirit of revenge" is the source of the usual conception of redemption. One wants to punish someone or something and, in so doing, right what is perceived as wrong.[11]

Conversely, redemption for Nietzsche means not thinking there is something wrong in the first place: if we can call it "redemption," then it is in effect a redemption *from* redemption. The logic of *amor fati,* then, is the antithesis of the logic of redemption. On the one hand, making this change from the usual concept of redemption to *amor fati* would seem to be a truly gargantuan task. For it requires both a thinking and feeling differently that would seem difficult to accomplish. On the other hand, *amor fati* is remarkably close to the sentiments of the Pietistic prayer of the young Fritz: "All He gives I will joyfully accept: happiness and unhappiness, poverty and wealth, and boldly look even death in the face" (*KGW* I/1, 4 [77]).[12] It would be hard to think of a better expression of *amor fati* than this prayer. Yet now Nietzsche's trust is not in God but in Life.

In chapter 8, we will turn to Nietzsche's dances and the ways in which they both negate the spirit of gravity and affirm Life. But here we should note that "The Yes and Amen Song" (the subtitle of "The Seven Seals") has the repeated refrain "For I love you, O Eternity."[13] Here eternity is effectively equivalent to Life. Thus, to love the "eternal return" is to love Life. Of course, given the fact that Life accuses Zarathustra of not being faithful to her, this song seems less to represent "Zarathustra the faithful" but more a Zarathustra who *longs* for faithfulness, who sings a song of affirmation of faith but still lacks faith.[14] Like many hymns, this hymn is clearly a prayer—addressed to Life. But what kind of prayer is this? One would suppose that is *not* the prayer of which Nietzsche speaks in "Excelsior," in which there is adoration and trust and sharing one's thoughts with an "ultimate wisdom, goodness, or power" (*GS* 285; *KSA*

3:527). In contrast, Nietzsche calls for "faith in oneself" (*GS* 284; *KSA* 3:527).

Yet, as noted earlier, even Nietzsche questions whether this project of renunciation of reliance on another is truly possible, for he asks: "Who will give you the strength to do so? No one has yet had the strength?" (*GS* 285; *KSA* 3:528). Does Zarathustra/Nietzsche really give up such prayer? I think he does not, in at least two ways. On the one hand, his dance with Life ends by his saying that now "Life was dearer to me than all my Wisdom had ever been" (*Z* III "Other Dancing Song" 2; *KSA* 4:285). So we have transference of adoration—and trust—to Life. Further, other important elements of Nietzsche's prayer of 1858 can be found in these songs. First, there is an outpouring of the heart in "The Yes and Amen Song" that sounds remarkably like Pietistic devotion. Although Nietzsche remains inconstant, he at least *wants* to be faithful to Life. Second, even though Nietzsche *wants* to give up prayer, the question "who will give you the strength to do so?" implies that Nietzsche realizes that he may not be strong enough to give up prayer and reliance on his own. But then *on whom or what is Nietzsche relying*? It would seem to be Life herself, even if that reliance is shot through with unbelief. Third, what Nietzsche had earlier said to the God of Christianity ("I have firmly resolved within me to dedicate myself for ever to His service") and then to the *Unbekannter* ("I want to know you, even serve you") he now pledges to life.[15] To say "I love you, O Eternity" is in effect a pledge of service to life. Finally, Nietzsche's earlier affirmation of God's will—"His holy will be done! All He gives I will joyfully accept"—now becomes the prayer of "Yes and Amen." The doctrine of eternal return—of *amor fati*—is functionally the equivalent of "All He gives I will joyfully accept." So, while Nietzsche is no longer a Christian Pietist, he retains the basic framework of Pietism. In the final chapter, we will turn to whether Nietzsche is fully able to embrace his Dionysian Pietism.

Does Nietzsche actually get beyond a dependence upon "ultimate" wisdom or power? In speaking to Life, he says that now she is more valued "than all my wisdom ever was" (*Z* III "Other Dancing Song" 2; *KSA* 4:285). But, even if Nietzsche *does* leaves wisdom behind (and it's not at all sure that he does), Life certainly seems to be Nietzsche's ultimate "power." So Nietzsche himself does precisely what he warns against. And, yet, Nietzsche later admits that he is a decadent. That very decadence has much to do with his relation to Life, as we will see in the next chapter.

PART 2

Profiles in Decadence

FOUR

Nietzsche's Decadence

A long, all too long, series of years signifies recovery for me; unfortunately it also signifies relapse, decay, the periodicity of a kind of decadence. Need I say after all this that in questions of décadence I am experienced?[1]

Apart from the fact that I am a décadent, I am also the opposite. My proof for this, among other things, that I have always instinctively chosen the right means against wretched states; while the décadent typically chooses means that are disadvantageous for him. . . . I took myself in hand, I made myself healthy again.[2]

O nly a page apart, we have two highly contrasting accounts of Nietzsche's own decadence. The first account gives us a picture of a Nietzsche who is not dealing particularly well with his decadence: there are signs of hope, points of progress, and then relapse. It is an account in which *periodicity* is the operative term. Like a cancer, decadence flourishes for a season and then goes into remission. In contrast, the second account is like the removal of an inflamed appendix: a quick surgical cut and all is well.

So which is it? Strange that Nietzsche would give us these two varying accounts in rapid succession. Or is even that strange juxtaposition—which sounds like the dance between depression and mania—*itself* another manifestation of decadence? That one could see the situation so clearly, so desperately—and then suddenly retreat into the pyrrhic victory of mania. We will need to keep these two descriptions of Nietzsche's decadence in mind as we consider just how successful he is in "resisting" decadence.[3] Of course, given the decadent penchant for self-deception, it may be hard to know how seriously to take Nietzsche's account of himself.

The Reactive Logic of Decadence

Although Nietzsche uses the term *décadence* in one of his notebooks from late 1876/early 1877 (*KSA* 8:23 [140]), it is clearly his reading Paul Bourget's essay on Charles Baudelaire (titled "Théorie de la décadence") that inspires him to make decadence the central theme of his late work.[4] Kaufmann is partly right when he says that reading Bourget "does not introduce an entirely new turn into Nietzsche's thought; it merely strengthens a previously present motif."[5] To be sure, Nietzsche has been concerned with *Verfall* and *Niedergang* [decline], *Entartung* [degeneration], and *Nihilismus* [nihilism]. Yet Nietzsche's newly found interest in decadence does considerably more than merely strengthen "a previously present motif." Nietzsche now comes to see decadence as both inescapable and a hallmark not only of the modern age but also of western history in general. But, then, how does decadence relate to decline, degeneration, and nihilism? Are the latter three subspecies of the former?

Michael Silk claims that decadence is not the same as *Verfall* and *Niedergang*.[6] Yet the distinction he draws between them is questionable. Silk points to one of Nietzsche's own statements regarding decadence: "Decadence itself is nothing *to be fought:* it is absolutely necessary and belongs to every age and every people. What should be fought vigorously is the creeping contagion of the healthy parts of the organism" (*WP* 41; *KSA* 13:15 [31]).[7] To this citation he adds the following: "All priests and moralists have . . . *wanted* to bring humanity back. . . . It's no use: one *must* go forwards, that is to say *further, step by step, into déca-dence* (this is *my* definition of modern progress)" (*TI* IX:43; *KSA* 6:144).[8] With these texts in mind, Silk draws the conclusion that "decadence, on Nietzsche's usage, often has a limiting, rather than a wholly negative value."[9] On Silk's account, then, the difference between "decline" (*Verfall* and *Niedergang*) and "decadence" would seem to be that the former is always negative, whereas the latter is partially positive. However, in making this distinction, it seems that Silk mistakes Nietzsche's statement of *strategy* for dealing with decadence as a statement of approval. When Nietzsche claims that one should not fight against decadence but instead go further into it, he is merely stating what he takes to be the only possible strategy regarding decadence (not that decadence is sometimes "positive"). That he labels this strategy his "definition of modern 'progress'" is sheer irony. Nietzsche had long abandoned any notion of modern progress (which is why progress is in quotation marks for Nietzsche), so his point here is simply that the most "progress" one can make is by recognizing decadence's absolute inevitability and avoiding the hopeless strategy of fighting against it.[10] A very paltry sort of progress, to say the least.

As it turns out, Nietzsche is often imprecise in his use of the term *décadence*. While decadence for Nietzsche may not be *exactly* the same as *Entartung, Niedergang, Verfall, Nihilismus,* and *romantische Pessimismus,* they are strongly connected—which means that anything like a complete distinction between them is simply impossible.[11] For instance, the first three of these terms are virtually synonymous with one another. *Entartung* can be translated as "degeneration" (which is how Kaufmann translates it in *Z* I "Gift-Giving Virtue" 1; *KSA* 4:98). Certainly degeneration is an expression of decadence. For Nietzsche, one degenerates (or is *already* degenerate) when one no longer instinctively chooses what is best for one and instead chooses "unselfishly." *Niedergang* and *Verfall* are clearly similar to *Entartung:* one "declines" precisely when one "degenerates" (in the sense of degeneration given above).[12] And Nietzsche's definition of decadence likewise sounds very much like *Nihilismus:* "Instead of naively saying, '*I'm* not worth anything anymore,' the lie of morality says in the mouth of the *décadent:* 'Nothing is worth anything—*life* isn't worth anything'" (*TI* IX:35; *KSA* 6:133). It is hard to imagine a stronger definition of *Nihilismus* than that "*life* isn't worth anything." If nihilism is the idea that there are no values, then a blanket pronouncement against life *itself* seems about as a nihilistic statement as one can make. While *romantische Pessimismus* is the idea that life can be "redeemed" only by way of art (a belief that Nietzsche admits to having held earlier in life—see his self-criticism in *BT* P 7; *KSA* 1:21)—this idea too is based on the belief that life is essentially worthless (and thus needs to be "saved").

With that in mind, I think it is safe to say "the problem of *décadence* has burdened [Nietzsche] throughout his philosophical career—indeed, throughout his life."[13] Moreover, it can be read as a central term for Nietzsche—at least in his late philosophy—meaning that *Entartung, Niedergang, Verfall, Nihilismus,* and *romantische Pessimismus* can be subsumed under it. Yet what exactly *is* decadence? Nietzsche does give us a helpful clue for making one sort of distinction between decline and decadence when he says the following. "Basic insight regarding the nature of decadence: *its supposed causes are its consequences.* This changes the whole perspective of *moral problems*" (*WP* 41; *KSA* 13:15 [31]). Once one gets clear as to which is the cause and which the results, one truly understands the nature of decadence. Nietzsche claims that "to choose instinctively what is harmful to *oneself*, to be *enticed* by 'disinterested' motives, is virtually the formula for *décadence*" (*TI* X:35; *KSA* 6:133). Selfless motives are already more a symptom than the cause. At root, decadence is simply being against life. And, since instincts (which are, for Nietzsche, inherently concerned with the *self*) are the expression of life, being against them is equivalent to being against life. This is why the decadent's condemnation is against life itself. Moreover, once one despises life, one's own instincts *develop into* instincts that reject life. Although Nietzsche is speaking of the decadence of politicians in the following passage, what he says is true of all decadents: "*they instinctively prefer* what dissolves them, what makes the end come faster" (*TI* IX:39; *KSA* 6:141). In contrast, the "well-turned-out person . . . has a taste only for what is good for him" (*EH* "Wise" 2; *KSA* 6:267). In other words, the instincts of the decadence are dangerous: as a decadent, one seeks that which is unhealthy. But some decadents—such as Nietzsche—are able to turn their illness to their own advantage: "To sense that what is harmful is harmful, to be *able* to forbid oneself something harmful, is a sign of youth and vitality. The exhausted are *attracted* by what is harmful: the vegetarian by vegetables. Sickness itself can be a stimulant to life: only one has to be healthy enough for this stimulant" (*CW* 5; *KSA* 6:22).

The difference between decline and decadence becomes clearer in a later passage: "Life itself is to my mind the instinct for growth, for durability, for an accumulation of forces, for *power:* where the will to power is lacking there is decline" (*AC* 6; *KSA* 6:172). So decline (whether *Verfall* or *Niedergang*) is very much connected to decadence, but it is a *symptom* rather than the disease itself. In contrast, the term *Entartung,* which Nietzsche first uses (in published writings) in *Thus Spoke Zarathustra,* is closer to decadence.[14] In fact, Nietzsche virtually equates the two in *Twilight of the Idols.* In speaking of the modern conception of individual freedom, Nietzsche says that it is "a symptom of *décadence:* our modern concept of 'freedom' is another proof of the degeneration [*Entartung*] of the instincts" (*TI* X:41; *KSA* 6:143). So freedom is the symptom, while *décadence/Entartung* is the root cause.

Talk of decadence was all the rage in fin de siècle Europe, so Nietzsche was hardly alone in commenting on the phenomenon.[15] Nietzsche follows Bourget's analysis of decadence as a kind of over-civilization, in which the basic drives and instincts are (we might say) "civilized away." Although decadence is defined as being against life, it is manifested by a lack both of energy and of a central, organizing drive to control that energy.[16] So it is not enough simply to *have* that energy; for Nietzsche, it must also be brought under control by a dominant instinct so that one functions as a coherent whole. The importance of such integrity is clear from what Nietzsche says about literary decadence, which—*mutatis mutandis*—applies to decadence in general: "Life no longer dwells in the whole. The word becomes sovereign and leaps out of the sentence, the sentence reaches out and obscures the meaning of the page, the page gains life at the expense of the whole—the whole is no longer a whole. But this is the simile of every style of *decadence*" (*CW* 7; *KSA* 6:27). Nietzsche goes on to say that decadence reveals itself in the "disgregation of the will," a kind of "anarchy" in which the instincts are no longer controlled.

What is perhaps most frightening about decadence is how it manifests itself. If Nietzsche is right, decadence in effect operates with a kind of centripetal force that constantly sweeps one back into its center. No matter how much one attempts to overcome decadence, one can never really escape its overwhelming pull. Even the self-aware attempt to overcome decadence still ends up being one more manifestation—and perhaps even the most *virulent* manifestation—of decadence. Not surprisingly, then, Nietzsche himself claims only to have "resisted" decadence (*CW* P; *KSA* 6:12). Any claim of overcoming would itself be a decadent claim.

Yet what is the structure of decadence? Simply put, it is a viciously reactive logic. Decadence is always a reaction to a prior action, rather than a pure acting. But, more than that, the reaction of decadence is usually characterized by revenge or *ressentiment*: it is the reaction of the weak who realize their weakness, and resent the strong. Summing up Nietzsche's view as well as any, Max Scheler describes *ressentiment* as follows:

> Thirst for revenge is the most important source of *ressentiment*. ... The desire for revenge—in contrast with all active and aggressive impulses, be they friendly or hostile—is also such a reactive impulse. It is always preceded by an attack or an injury. ... Revenge is distinguished by two essential characteristics. First of all, the immediate reactive impulse, with the accompanying emotions of anger and rage, is temporarily or at least momentarily checked and restrained, and

the response is consequently postponed to a later time and to a more suitable occasion. . . . Furthermore, it is the essence of revenge that it always contains the *consciousness* of "tit for tat," so that it is never a mere emotional reaction.[17]

Without the contrast to the strong, the weak would not perceive their weakness and so not be resentful. Moreover, precisely because they are weak, they are unable to act immediately and obviously. So their anger is internalized and can be acted upon only in a clever, unobtrusive way. Thus, the reaction is vicious in the sense of being malicious and spiteful. Yet it is also vicious in the sense of being self-perpetuating. The more one reacts, the more vicious the reaction. The result is a vicious circle that ends up being a downward spiral. Both *ressentiment* and decadence have the character of begetting more *ressentiment* and decadence. That spiral can end only in complete and utter decay, with only death cutting it short. The problem that Nietzsche faces, of course, is how one can possibly extricate oneself from this spiral. Or, put both more and less strongly, how can one even "resist" without that resistance turning into simply another manifestation of decadence or *ressentiment*?

In terms of practical manifestations, decadence works itself out in all of western culture. Nietzsche provides us with a list of symptoms that is as dizzyingly encyclopedic as a cure-list for snake oil: "vice—the addiction to vice; sickness—sickliness; crime—criminality; celibacy— sterility; hystericism—weakness of the will; alcoholism; pessimism; anarchism" (*WP* 42; *KSA* 13:14 [73]).[18] In another one of his notes, he writes: "Philosophy as *décadence*. Morality as *décadence*. Religion as *décadence*. Art as *décadence*. Politics as *décadence*" (*KSA* 13:15 [101]). So many manifestations of decadence!

So what is Nietzsche's "cure"?

Nietzsche as Personal Physician

Throughout his career, Nietzsche saw himself as a physician to culture. As early as 1873, he writes the outline for text that he tentatively titles "The Philosopher as Cultural Physician" (*PT* 69–76; *KSA* 7:23 [7]–[45], 28 [2]), which eventually becomes "Philosophy in the Tragic Age of the Greeks." In that early sketch, he characterizes "the *value* of philosophy" as useful to "cleanse muddled and superstitious ideas." But he notes that the cultural physician "is most useful when there is *a lot to be destroyed,* in times of chaos or degeneration" (*PT* 72; *KSA* 7:28 [2]). Clearly, Nietzsche himself is in the midst of such a time.

For those who are truly decadent, the best cure might simply be *death*. In *The Birth of Tragedy,* Nietzsche had invoked the wisdom of Silenus (the companion of Dionysus): "The very best thing is utterly beyond your reach: not to have been born, not to *be,* to be *nothing*. However, the second best thing for you is: to die soon" (*BT* 3; *KSA* 1:35). Much later, in *Twilight of the Idols,* he invokes it again, this time as the only sure "cure" for decadence: "Finally, a recommendation for those gentlemen the pessimists and other *décadents*. It is not up to us to prevent ourselves from being born, but we can make up for this mistake—for sometimes it is a mistake. When one *does away* with oneself, one does the most honorable thing there is: it almost earns one the right to live" (*TI* IX:36; *KSA* 6:135). It is hard to know exactly what to make of this piece of advice. Ironically, it is within a section titled *"Morality for Doctors."* Given Nietzsche's propensity for irony, it is hard not to see him as playing off one of the supposed tenets of the Hippocratic Oath—"First, do no harm."[19] Nietzsche suggests that—in such drastic cases of decadence—death makes the most sense. So he appears to be giving a piece of advice that applies particularly to the worst of the decadents. True, the only thing that really cures decadence is death. And perhaps Nietzsche really *is* suggesting suicide for the truly sickly. Yet some—like Nietzsche—have the strength to "resist" decadence. Their "death" is one of *self*-overcoming by way of *askêsis,* something we will consider in more detail in chapter 9.

In the preface (of 1886) to *The Gay Science,* when Nietzsche is already well aware of his decadent predicament, he writes: "I am still waiting for a philosophical *physician* . . . someone who has set himself the task of pursuing the problem of the total health of a people, time, race or of humanity" (*GS* P 2; *KSA* 3:349). Yet, by 1888, Nietzsche realizes that finding a cure for the culture is hopeless, since it is far too mired in decadence. The only hope (and a slim one at best) is that perhaps a few strong individuals—like Nietzsche, of course—will be able to muster enough strength within them to resist the pandemic decadence of modernity.

One way of describing decadence is as a lack of organization of the instincts. In one sense, this jostling of the instincts is just part of life. Since there is "no will" per se (as in the sense of some unified force), it is natural that there are constantly shifting "treaty drafts of will" in which given instincts "are constantly increasing or losing their power" (*WP* 715; *KSA* 13:11 [73]). What Nietzsche terms the "will to power" is better described as a concatenation of wills or forces or instincts that are continually shifting in their hierarchy. At any given point, there can be a kind of "contract" that spells out the hierarchy of forces, although it is always subject to revision. Yet when that healthy jostling turns into bitter combat—or all-out anarchy—then health quickly turns into illness. Nietzsche describes this condition as "very unhealthy, inner ruin, disintegration, betraying and increasing and inner conflict and anarchism—unless one passion at last becomes master" (*WP* 778; *KSA* 13:14 [157]). One cannot help but think here of a Hobbesian state of nature, in which, instead of there being a war of "every man, against every man," there is a war of every instinct against every instinct.[20] As long as the instincts are in such disarray, there can be no sense of health.

Interestingly enough, this war is actually the result of "perspectivism," in that each of the instincts has a different perspective that it wishes to make the ruling perspective: "Before knowledge is possible, each of these impulses must first have presented its one-sided view of the thing or event; then comes the fight between these one-sided views, and occasionally out of it a mean, an appeasement, a concession to all three sides, a kind of justice and contract" (*GS* 333; *KSA* 3:558–59). Elsewhere, he notes "it is our needs that interpret the world"; these needs in effect determine what we are "For and Against" (*WP* 481; *KSA* 12:7 [60]). Nietzsche recognizes that there are always multiple perspectives—and that it is perfectly consistent to move from one to the other. Yet, ultimately, we must decide which perspective we wish to accept as the "ruling" perspective. In this sense, Nietzsche is not quite a "perspective relativist": that is, while there are different perspectives that have different levels of "validity," he clearly seeks to find the "highest" perspective. Presumably, this perspective would be not merely "higher" in the sense of taking into account other perspectives but also higher in the sense of more conducive to the flourishing of life. But exactly what perspective this might be is a question to which we turn in the final chapter.

The most important thing that the physician can do is to provide a kind of cohesion of the forces—whether within a community or an individual.[21] What marks the "real philosophers of Greece" ("those before Socrates") is that they "bring themselves into a system" (*WP* 437; *KSA* 13:14 [100]). For Nietzsche, one is healthy when the various "powers" (forces, instincts) of the individual are unified so that one of them proves dominant. When one instinct can bring the others into control by becoming a dominating passion, the organism experiences a kind of "health." Nietzsche points out that "since only the ultimate reconciliation scenes and final accounts of this long process rise to consciousness, we suppose that *intelligere* must be conciliatory . . . essentially opposed to the instincts." But the reality of the matter is just the opposite: "in fact *it is only a certain behaviour of the drives towards one another*" (*GS* 333; *KSA* 3:559). In effect, the setting up of one drive as the "dominant" drive leads to kind of "contract" among the drives.

"*True philosophers are commanders and legislators:* they say, 'That is how it *should be*'" (*BGE* 211; *KSA* 5:145). This, at least, is what Nietzsche aims for. But *clever* philosophers are those who know *which* drive to make dominant. We will note in the following chapter that Socrates chooses dialectic, a form of reason. While reason is also an instinct for Nietzsche, it is one of the less developed of the instincts. Indeed, he makes a crucial distinction between two types of reason. "Little reason" for Nietzsche is conscious reason, that known by the mind. In contrast, "great reason" is the unconscious reason known by way of the body (*Z* I "Despisers of the Body"; *KSA* 4:39).[22] Simply put, the great reason known by the body is simply more primordial epistemologically for Nietzsche. As he puts it: "The problem of consciousness . . . first confronts us when we begin to realize how much we can do without it" (*GS* 354; *KSA* 3:590). Zarathustra likewise claims "there is more reason in your body than in your best wisdom" (*Z* I "Despisers of the Body"; *KSA* 4:40). Here the difference is between the reason of the body and the reason of consciousness. Yet, in one important sense, there is no difference between them in that they are both aspects of the body. Nietzsche maintains: "body I am entirely, and nothing else; and soul is only a word for something about the body" (*Z* I "Despisers of the Body"; *KSA* 4:39). So speaking of "reason" is simply speaking of a particular *aspect* of the body.

Clever philosophers/physicians, then, understand that we are simply constituted by a body with its multiple drives or instincts that must be unified. Here it is important to be precise. Nietzsche thinks that "to *have* to fight the instincts—that is the formula for *décadence*" (*TI* II:11; *KSA* 6:73).[23] So one does not resist decadence by fighting *against* the instincts. That would lead only to further decay and decline. Instead, one *organizes* the instincts in such a way that *one* instinct predominates. That may require putting the other instincts "in their place" (so to speak), but it does not means doing battle with them. Nietzsche is very clearly against the kind of "self-control" demanded by certain "moralists" that consists of being "armed against [oneself]" (*GS* 305; *KSA* 3:543). Such a posture can at best preserve an organism, but not help it to *grow*. Instead, growth requires precisely what Nietzsche recognizes we are afraid to admit is at work all the time: "exploitation":

> Life itself is *essentially* a process of appropriating, injuring, overpowering the alien and the weaker, oppressing, being harsh, imposing your own form, incorporating, and at least, the very least, exploiting. . . . "Exploitation" does not belong to a corrupted or imperfect, primitive society: it belongs to the *essence* of being alive as a fundamental organic function; it is the result of genuine will to power, which is just the will of life. (*BGE* 259; *KSA* 5:207–8)

As much as we are reluctant to recognize life as exploitation and appropriation, Nietzsche insists that such is the brute reality of existence. Not to admit this is simply to be dishonest, to lie to oneself. And, of course, Nietzsche is to a great extent simply right. Probably the best example is nutrition: even the kindest, gentlest vegetarian lives only because other things must be sacrificed (i.e., eaten). The cultural physician, then, will admit that the way we become healthy is by allowing ourselves to be ourselves. Which means letting the instincts be expressed.

Of course, since Nietzsche recognizes that the instincts have already been highly compromised, just letting them thrive would not be enough. Instead, one must "take oneself in hand" by way of *askêsis*. In chapter 9 we will carefully examine Nietzsche's own musical *askêsis*. Here, though, we must consider the very project of asceticism. For some would claim that Nietzsche *rejects* "asceticism," making this the last thing to which he would turn.

Rethinking Asceticism

One could certainly read the opening question to the third treatise of *On The Genealogy of Morality*—"What do ascetic ideals mean?"—as an open question. In fact, whether Nietzsche intended that treatise as an "answer" is itself open to question. Yet interpreters have not infrequently assumed that Nietzsche is against both asceticism and the ascetic ideal—

and often equate the two. Clark, for instance, interprets Nietzsche's phrase "the ascetic ideal" as denoting a particular ideal characterized by a dualist belief in the "True World" and an accompanying self-deception.[24] With that read in mind, when Nietzsche says "the ascetic ideal expresses a will" and goes on to ask "*where* is the opposing will in which an *opposing ideal* expresses itself?*" Clark takes Nietzsche's comment in *Ecce Homo* that "a *counter-ideal* was lacking—*until Zarathustra*" to mean that Zarathustra provides us with a counter-ideal to the ascetic ideal—namely, the doctrine of eternal recurrence.[25] With that doctrine, then, Nietzsche is read as turning his back on asceticism.

However, it is neither clear that Nietzsche is simply "against" asceticism nor clear that his "counter-ideal" must necessarily be "nonascetic" in nature. True, Nietzsche is somewhat ambivalent about ascetic ideals. On the one hand, they have been used to the detriment of life. On the other hand, they have been crucial to the development of human beings. It is not just that the rise of the priestly class finally made human beings "*interesting*" and gave their souls "*depth*" (*GM* I:6; *KSA* 5:266); it is also that "*the ascetic ideal springs from the protective and healing instincts of a degenerating life* that seeks with every means to hold its ground and is fighting for its existence." As Nietzsche goes on to say, even though its proponents do not realize it, "the ascetic ideal is an artifice for the *preservation* of life" (*GM* III:13; *KSA* 5:366). So the ascetic ideal has been a way of promoting life, even if not necessarily the most efficient or honest way.

One thing *is* clear: we have ascetic ideals because "the basic fact of the human will" is "its *horror vacui: it needs a goal*—and it would rather will *nothingness* than *not* will" (*GM* III:1; *KSA* 5:339). The human will's greatest fear is not a "bad" ascetic goal but *none at all*. Ascetic ideals provide us with a goal, even if that goal is one of self-deprivation. Moreover, that goal is always one that promotes life. Admittedly, some ascetic ideals do a better job of this than others, but all of them promote life in some sense or another, as we noted above. This is why Nietzsche cannot be read as simply against asceticism: to be against asceticism would mean being against life. Although it may seem that the ascetic represents "life *against* life," Nietzsche labels any such view as "simply nonsense." Any ascetic "attack" on life, then, "can only be *apparent*" (*GM* III:13; *KSA* 5:365).

Of course, Nietzsche does admit in *Ecce Homo* that the ascetic ideal (which he quite specifically defines as "the priests' ideal") is "the *harmful* ideal *par excellence*, a will to the end, an ideal of decadence" (*EH* "Books"

GM; *KSA* 6:353). Although Nietzsche undoubtedly wants to leave *that* ideal behind, we cannot thereby conclude that he would want to leave *all* ascetic ideals behind. Actually, there are at least two reasons why Nietzsche *cannot* do so. First, if he really hopes to move from the burden-bearing camel to the value-destroying lion and finally to the child that is "innocence and forgetting," "a sacred 'Yes,'" then Nietzsche must do battle *with himself* (*Z* I "Three Metamorphoses"; *KSA* 4:29–31). He fully admits that he must "take sides against everything sick in me." And that would seem impossible to do so apart from *some version* of ascetic practice. Nietzsche asks rhetorically: "what sacrifice wouldn't be fitting? what 'self-overcoming'? what 'self-denial' to resist decadence?" (*CW* P; *KSA* 6:12). Moreover, as an "immoralist," Nietzsche makes it clear that there is a "no-saying" that is an integral *part* of "yes-saying: "Fundamentally, my term *immoralist* involves two negations. For one, I negate a type of man that has so far been considered supreme: the good, the benevolent, the beneficent. And then I negate a type of morality that has become prevalent and predominant as morality itself—the morality of decadence or, more concretely, *Christian* morality. . . . [N]egating *and destroying* are condition of saying Yes" (*EH* "Destiny" 4; *KSA* 6:367–68). Nietzsche's need for saying "No" stems from the fact that his status as "immoralist" (i.e., as beyond the categories of good and evil) is in no way already "accomplished." That Nietzsche is speaking in the *present tense* in *Ecce Homo* makes this fact even more pronounced. So Nietzsche needs to "take sides" against that which is sick in *him* by saying No.

Second, even though the ascetic ideal both *attacks* and *preserves* life (making it a true *pharmakon*), "attacking" is actually what Nietzsche thinks *constitutes* life. In *Thus Spoke Zarathustra*, Nietzsche defines "spirit" as "life that itself cuts into life," which is why the "happiness of the spirit" is precisely its self-sacrifice (Z II "Famous Wise Men"; *KSA* 4:134). Moreover, Life herself confides to Zarathustra a secret: "I am *that which must always overcome itself.* . . . Whatever I create and however much I love it—soon I must oppose it and my love; thus my will wills it" (*Z* II "Self-Overcoming"; *KSA* 4:148). That Nietzsche continues to think of life this way is evident from his preface to the second edition of *The Gay Science,* in which he says, "Life—to us, that means constantly transforming all that we are into light and flame, and also all that wounds us; we simply *can do* no other. . . . Only great pain is the liberator of the spirit" (*GS* Preface 3; *KSA* 3:349–50).[26] Similarly, in *Twilight of the Idols,*

Nietzsche speaks of a *"spirit* that has become free" from "the contempt-ible sort of well-being dreamt of by grocers, Christians, cows, women, Englishmen, and other democrats. The free human being is a *warrior"* (*TI* IX:38; *KSA* 6:139–40). So it is hard to see how Nietzsche either *could* escape from asceticism or *would* wish to do so.

The question, then, is not whether Nietzsche is against asceticism but rather what *sort* of asceticism he opposes. I take it that Nietzsche's asceticism should have at least three qualities. First, it must be honest: "All my reverence to the ascetic ideal," Nietzsche writes, *"as long as it is honest!"* (*GM* III:26; *KSA* 5:407). As he goes on to say, an "honest" asceti-cism is one that actually "believes in itself and does not present us with a façade of clownery." But I take it there is likely another sense in which Nietzsche means that it is "honest," the sense of not making extravagant claims (such as "justifying" suffering) and so not being self-deceptive. We could say that Nietzsche's "sacrifice" here is giving up notions of metaphysical comfort such as the "True World" and "Morality." Second, Nietzsche wants an asceticism that promotes life. True, he admits that the otherworldly asceticism of the ascetic priests ends up promoting life too. But the asceticism of the ascetic priests merely *preserves* life rather than *increases* power. Clearly, Nietzsche's asceticism should do the latter. Third, Nietzsche particularly needs an asceticism that is effective against his own decadence. He speaks of a "Selbstdisciplin von Nöten," which could be translated either as a "special self-discipline" (as Kaufmann has it) or more literally as an *"emergency* self-discipline." Given the lateness of the hour and Nietzsche's acute sense of his own peril, the latter seems to be more what he has in mind.

With these desiderata for a truly Nietzschean ascetic practice in mind, perhaps we might use the notion of *askêsis* as a way of avoiding the nega-tive connotations of "asceticism." Hadot has recently reminded us of the prominent place that *askêsis* played in ancient philosophy. *Askêsis*—the practice of spiritual exercises—is designed so that we *"let* ourselves be changed, in our point of view, attitudes, and convictions. This means that we must dialogue with ourselves, and hence we must do battle with ourselves."[27] The parallel here between *askêsis* and Nietzsche's account of life as that which "cuts into life" and transforms itself by self-overcoming is striking. Hadot points out that *askêsis* is designed to bring about "a conversion which turns our entire life upside down, changing the life of the person who goes through it."[28] It is probably not coincidental that the Christian conception of "conversion" [*metanoia*] denotes precisely the same thing—a 180-degree change of direction. Of course, Nietzsche's *askêsis* is designed to turn the decadent Nietzsche in quite the opposite direction.

Practically, though, what does *askêsis* involve? Although most of the many Stoic treatises on spiritual exercises have been lost, Philo of Alexandria provides us with two lists of exercises. One includes the following: research, investigation, reading, listening, attention, self-mastery, and indifference to indifferent things.[29] The first three of those items are relatively straightforward. Nietzsche was certainly engaged in research, investigation, and reading. While the Stoics, for example, wouldn't have had in mind anything like an investigation into the genealogy of morality, genealogy proves an important spiritual exercise for Nietzsche. I will turn to "listening" in chapter 9, but here we need to expand on the exercise of attention [*prosoche*]. For the Stoics, *prosoche* meant being constantly aware of all one says and does. The goal is to choose consciously rather than act instinctively. Although it might seem that Nietzsche would favor acting "by instinct,"[30] he too would need to pay close attention to his actions. After all, Nietzsche realizes that he is a decadent and his instincts have been corrupted. Moreover, he is hardly in favor of *simply* following the instincts, given his goal of self-overcoming and thus the continual transformation of instincts. He says his "supreme guideline" is: "one must not 'let oneself go,' not even when one is by oneself" (*TI* IX:47; *KSA* 6:149). So Nietzsche realizes that at least some sort of "self-denial"—however broadly or narrowly construed—is essential.

Yet how does *askêsis* differ from asceticism? Consider Hadot's way of distinguishing them: *askêsis* designates "inner activities of the thought and of the will," while asceticism is (and here Hadot borrows a definition from Karl Heussi) "complete abstinence or restriction in the use of food, drink, sleep, dress, and property, and especially continence in sexual matters."[31] There are at least two problems with Hadot's distinction. First, it relies on (and perpetuates) the very sort of bifurcation of mind and body that seems so foreign to early practitioners of spiritual exercises—not to mention Nietzsche.[32] *Askêsis* has to do with techniques of the self (to use Michel Foucault's phrase) that are as much bodily as intellectual. It is hard to imagine either "self-mastery" (from Philo of Alexandria's first list) or "therapies of the passions" (from his second list) as *merely* "inner activities of the thought and of the will." Not surprisingly, then, Foucault cites "dietary regimens" as one example of *askêsis*.[33] Foucault actually provides a more accurate distinction between asceticism and *askêsis* when he says: "Asceticism as the renunciation of pleasure has bad connotations. But the askesis is something else: it's the work that one performs on oneself in order to transform oneself or make the self appear that happily one never attains." For Foucault, then, what distinguishes asceticism is its "renunciation of pleasure."[34] In contrast, *askêsis* is about transforming the self. So the distinction between the *askêsis* and asceticism should not be based on a dichotomy of mind and body.[35] Second, Hadot uses a definition for asceticism (and why he picks this *particular* definition is unclear) that seems unnecessarily extreme. While it is true that we tend to think of the ascetic as someone who takes extreme measures, it is just as possible to define asceticism in a much more moderate way. It is telling, for instance, that the fourth-century desert "mother" Amma Syncletica claims the mark of true Christian fasting—as opposed to its pagan counterpart—is precisely its moderation. Of course, as Eastern Orthodox theologian Kallistos Ware goes on to point out, "'moderation,' however, is a vague term."[36] Still, *that* moderation is taken as the distinguishing characteristic of proper fasting shows that extremity in ascetic matters is hardly the rule, and perhaps rather the exception. To some extent, this point also somewhat blunts Nietzsche's criticism of the ascetic ideal in general, for he at least gives the impression throughout *The Genealogy of Morality* that asceticism has usually been extreme in nature. In contrast, the reality would seem to be much more complicated.

Yet a more important question is whether asceticism is simply world-denying or whether it actually affirms *this* world and our bodily existence. Ware claims that Christian asceticism (at least as he construes it) denies this world precisely in order to affirm it.[37] Would Nietzsche agree with this statement? At first glance, it would seem that Nietzsche thinks of Christians as classic "deniers" of this-worldly values in favor of otherworldly values. And such an interpretation of Nietzsche seems perfectly valid. Yet the question is whether that interpretation is either complex or subtle enough to capture Nietzsche's true assessment of Christians and their values. Nietzsche's charge is not *simply* that Christians eschew worldly values to attain otherworldly values. Rather, he thinks that desires for otherworldly values end up being covert expressions of desire for reward in this world *too*. Certainly the ascetic priests—for example—have a highly elaborate system that produces both this-worldly and otherworldly values.[38]

Although I take it that this latter case is fully exemplary of the kind of *dishonest* asceticism which Nietzsche is so strongly against, it seems quite possible to imagine an *askêsis* that is both inherently "this-worldly" (in the sense of *valuing* this world) and not self-deceptive. Not only is Hellenistic philosophy filled with examples of this-worldly *askêsis,* but one could also argue that there are religious versions that are not necessarily otherworldly.[39] In any case, we can just as easily speak of an *askêsis* in the service of life, one that affirms life and recognizes that certain ways of living are better. Precisely that sort of *askêsis* is what Nietzsche seeks.

In chapter 9, we will consider Nietzsche's "affirmative" *askêsis.* Here—and in the next three chapters—we are concerned with the "no-saying" that must precede the "yes-saying." For, in order to get to the place of affirmation, Nietzsche must first wage war.

Nietzsche's Guerrilla Warfare

> I am warlike by nature. Attacking is one of my instincts. Being *able* to be an enemy, *being* an enemy—perhaps that presupposes a strong nature; in any case, it belongs to every strong nature. It needs objects of resistance: hence it *looks for* what it resists. . . . The strength of those who attack can be measured in a way by the opposition they require: every growth is indicated by the search for a mighty opponent . . . [O]pponents that are our *equals.* (*EH* "Wise" 7; *KSA* 6:274)

The "warlike" Nietzsche sees himself as *needing* "objects of resistance." As he says, attacking for him is instinctual. He *needs* to fight against those decadents to whom he finds himself coming ever so close. For that fighting is *itself* a way of resisting decadence, a part of his therapy. Of course, those objects themselves must be *equally* strong, or else they could not provide sufficient resistance and would prove poor sparring partners. In other words, Nietzsche wants and needs truly *worthy* opponents—ones who are *equal* in strength. "We do not want to be spared by our best enemies," writes Nietzsche. Remarkably, he even feels a kind of kinship with those who are his "best enemies," for he writes: "My brothers in war, I love you thoroughly; I am and I was of your kind. And I am also your best enemy" (*Z* I "War and Warriors"; *KSA* 4:58).

So we are left with a not-so-strange dialectic of love and hate, in which the two turn out to be sides of one coin. That dynamic would explain quite a lot about Nietzsche's battles, and about his feelings for his opponents. It is not a question of either loving or hating one's enemies: Nietzsche admits to both. And that should not come as a surprise, since worthy enemies can easily arouse both sorts of feelings in us. Worthy opponents usually evoke admiration, and that can turn into a form of love. Yet one feeling they do not evoke is despising. As Nietzsche says, "you may only have enemies whom you can hate, not enemies you despise" (*Z* I "War and Warriors"; *KSA* 4:59). Properly speaking, enemies only worth despising are no enemies at all. Nietzsche speaks of a kind of "equality before the enemy: the first presupposition of an *honest* duel." In contrast, "where one feels contempt, one *cannot* wage war" (*EH* "Wise" 7; *KSA* 6:274). One can only despise.

In the year in which Nietzsche does intensive battle with Socrates, Wagner, and Paul, he writes: "This time, as an old artilleryman, I bring out my heaviest artillery: I fear that I will shoot the history of mankind into two halves. . . . [*The Anti-Christ(ian)*] is already a hundredfold declaration of war, with a distant thunder in the mountains; in the foreground, much 'merriment,' of the sort of merriment related to me" (letter to Franz Overbeck, October 18, 1888; *KSB* 8:453). Nietzsche is well aware that he is fighting the battle of his life. It is his last productive year—1888—and he wages warfare with no holds barred. If *The Anti-Christ(ian)* is "a hundredfold declaration of war," *Twilight of the Idols* and *The Case of Wagner* are hardly much less explosive and vituperative. Of course, Nietzshe's "warfare" is less like a "normal" war than a series of calculated raids. The longest section of *Twilight of the Idols* is titled "Streifzüge eines Unzeitgemässen," which can be translated as "raids of an untimely man." *Streifzüge* are the kinds of raids typical of guerrilla warfare or commando missions. Rather than a straight-out war, Nietzsche's attacks are more on the order of harassment and sabotage. They are likewise "aggressive," "radical," and "unconventional." And they are certainly also "untimely," as the reception history of Nietzsche's late works makes clear.[40]

Yet, for Nietzsche, these raids are absolutely necessary—for personal reasons. It is in the context of dwelling on his *own* "periods of decadence" and tendencies toward *ressentiment* that Nietzsche speaks of the need for war (*EH* "Wise" 6; *KSA* 6:273). By the time of writing *Ecce Homo* (October–December 1888), Nietzsche had come to understand much about himself. His 1886 prefaces to earlier works show that he had made great strides in self-understanding, and now recognized significant errors in his earlier thought.[41] In his "Attempt at a Self-Criticism" appended to *The Birth of Tragedy,* he scathing writes (to himself): "But, Sir, if *your* book is not Romanticism, what on earth is it?" and goes on to refer to himself as "Mr. Pessimist and Deifier of Art" (*BT* P 7; *KSA* 1:21). He fully admits to his own complicity in the project of seeking "metaphysical comfort," in this case through art. So waging war on the positions that he has left behind—and perhaps to which he is still attracted—is part of his therapy, or the military counterpart to his musical *askêsis.*

In the midst of war, Nietzsche pauses to reflect on his own rules of engagement, of which he provides us with four. His first rule is "I only attack causes that are victorious; I may even wait until they become victorious" (*EH* "Wise" 7; *KSA* 6:274).[42] Given that rule, Nietzsche is certainly free to fight Platonism and Christianity, for they have been wildly successful. Of course, one might wonder about the German Christendom of Nietzsche's time: wasn't the madman's proclamation of the death of God precisely about the loss of Christianity's influence on culture—that it was no longer victorious? Nietzsche would likely respond that, even having lost considerable ground, Christianity still remained a largely "victorious cause." And, even today, Platonism has proved its continuing viability, albeit with significant modifications along the way.

Second, Nietzsche claims: "I only attack causes against which I would not find allies, so that I stand alone." Here Nietzsche's assertion is somewhat less convincing, for he certainly was not alone in attacking Christianity. However, one could argue that his critique of it was simply unparalleled in both its force and sheer honesty. Even Max Stirner did not have the intestinal fortitude to bring about a full-frontal attack on Christianity of the likes of *The Anti-Christ(ian).* While others were in effect whittling away at Christian narrative and doctrine bit by bit, Nietzsche was taking on the entire thing—including its morality, to which so many (like the English dimwits) still clung.

Nietzsche's third rule is: "I never attack persons; I merely avail myself of the person as a strong magnifying glass that allows one to make visible a general but creeping and elusive calamity." Realizing that any reader might raise Nietzsche's savage assault of David Strauss as an example of attacking a person, Nietzsche immediately goes on to defend his attack against Strauss as precisely an attack rather on "the 'cultured' people of Germany," who had so easily bought into Strauss's critique. On the one hand, this claim might not be completely believable. Nietzsche's critique of

Strauss in "David Strauss, the Confessor and Writer" is an attack not just upon Strauss's views but also his writing style and grammar.[43] Moreover, Strauss is repeatedly denounced as a "philistine." On the other hand, Nietzsche really does think that Strauss is simply an example of the philistine culture of the Germany of his day. So, as nasty and seemingly personal as Nietzsche's attack may be, it is much more an indictment of German culture in general than an attack on Strauss (who just happens—pity for Strauss—to be a convenient example). Much later, for example, Nietzsche will exclaim: "How much tiresome heaviness, lameness, humidity, dressing-gown stupor—how much *beer* there is in the German intellect! . . . I was talking about the German spirit: about how it's getting coarser, how it's getting shallower" (*TI* VIII:2–3; *KSA* 6:104–5). Not surprisingly, in this passage he once again brings up Strauss—as an example of the "degeneration" [*Entartung*] of German culture as a whole.

As for Wagner, Nietzsche contends that, in attacking Wagner, he was really criticizing "the falseness, the half-couth instincts of our 'culture' which mistakes the subtle for the rich, and the late for the great." One can certainly read the attack on Wagner as an attack on all that was artistically degenerate in German culture. Yet, when Nietzsche introduces his fourth rule of warfare—"I only attack when every personal quarrel is excluded"—it becomes harder to be convinced that Nietzsche is truly following his own rules. Can one really read *The Case of Wagner* without reading it as being not even slightly motivated by a personal quarrel? Nietzsche may be "over" Wagner, but there is still an open wound.

Yet why does Nietzsche pick battles with Socrates, Wagner, and Paul? It would seem to be because Nietzsche finds himself so close to them.

Too Close for Comfort

"Simply to acknowledge the fact: *Socrates* is so close to me that I am almost continually fighting with him" (*PT* 127; *KSA* 8:6 [3]). Don't we get a clear formula here? Nietzsche admits that he fights with those who are closest to him. True, he mentions only Socrates, but the reason given for fighting is *proximity*. It would seem reasonable to suppose that proximity —at least for Nietzsche—breeds quarrels.[44] Admittedly, there are different ways in which one can be "close" to someone else. In Nietzsche's relationship to Socrates, Wagner, and Paul, that closeness takes various forms (as will become clear).[45] Moreover, one can also extrapolate from this statement that, the closer Nietzsche feels himself to an opponent, the more "continual" the engagement. Yet can we draw a further inference from what Nietzsche says? Is it not likely that Nietzsche is inclined to fight all the more *viciously* against that to which he feels himself attracted? Certainly that was the judgment of Salomé, who (as we noted earlier) explains Nietzsche's "impassioned battle against religion, belief in God, and the need for salvation *because he came precariously close to them.*"[46] On her read, it is in his last writings that Nietzsche's connection to religious concepts—and a desperate need for some figure to replace the God of Christianity—becomes particularly apparent. And it is, of course, in these last writings that Nietzsche brings out the firepower against three particular figures: Socrates, Wagner, and the apostle Paul.

That Nietzsche felt the need to fight those who were "close" to him also seems clear from his engagements with Wagner and Paul. Curt Paul Janz notes that *The Case of Wagner* is really a "frightful self-portrait," in which Nietzsche "discovers in Wagner everything that he sees as a danger, as a dangerous possibility in himself."[47] It does not take a very close reading of *The Case of Wagner* to see that Janz is correct. Certainly the most obvious way in which Nietzsche is close to Wagner is that the chief charge against Wagner—namely, his decadence—is one that Nietzsche explicitly turns back upon himself. Moreover, Nietzsche is all too well aware how deeply under Wagner's influence he had come, and how difficult it is for him to shake it off. When in July 1882 he hears the piano reduction of *Parsifal,* he immediately recognizes stylistic similarities between it and his own piano composition "Der Tod der Könige" [The Death of Kings]. He subsequently writes to Gast with alarm: "I confess: with true shock, I am once again made aware of *how* closely I have been *related* to Wagner" (letter of July 25, 1882; *KSB* 6:231).[48] As it turns out, he has for years been "working through" the influence of Wagner upon him. Oddly enough, Nietzsche is not simply interested in ridding himself of Wagner's influence; instead, he wants to "incorporate" all that he has learned from Wagner to help him learn to *resist* Wagner. In other words, any strategy of simply "overcoming" Wagner is bound to fail. For instance, as much as Nietzsche disdains *Parsifal,* he openly admits "I admire this work; I wish I had written it" (*CW* Postscript; *KSA* 6:43).[49] So Nietzsche realizes that he has been thoroughly "Wagnerized." The question, then, is how one responds to *that*. His answer is that he needs to use Wagner's help—what he has learned from Wagner—to resist Wagner. Of course, any sort of break with Wagner could never be "complete" in such a case.

The case of the apostle Paul is much more complicated. For, even though Nietzsche writes nearly as viciously about him as he does about Socrates and Wagner, there is no obvious textual evidence to which one can point to confirm Nietzsche's sense of being close to Paul. Jörg Salaquarda notes—with considerable skepticism—that some have claimed a kind of kinship between the two.[50] For example, Ernst Bertram claims to see what he takes to be an important similarly between Nietzsche and Paul.[51] On Nietzsche's view, it was Paul who reinterpreted the crucifixion in terms of salvation for sin. Thus, in overturning Paul's "perversion" of Jesus' gospel, Nietzsche would be like Paul—a kind of modern Paul or even an "anti-Paul." Whether Nietzsche recognized this, of course, is open to question, for Nietzsche himself never makes any such explicit comparison. Yet it is hard to imagine that Nietzsche *wouldn't* have seen the irony of criticizing Paul for doing precisely what Nietzsche is doing, not just because of Nietzsche's acute appreciation of irony but also his deeply self-conscious awareness of exactly what he is doing. He openly proclaims himself to be a "revaluator" of all values, and that would make him very much like Paul.

Another commentator who thinks there is a deep connection between Nietzsche and Paul is Carl Bernoulli. In discussing Calvin and Nietzsche, Bernoulli claims that "when [Nietzsche] takes someone especially severely to task" there is "a secret kinship always behind it."[52] From what we have seen with Socrates and Wagner, that claim would seem to have some warrant. Where Bernoulli's connection becomes much more speculative is when he makes a comparison between Nietzsche's dramatic experience in Sils-Maria (in which Nietzsche supposedly moves from No to Yes in the sense that he has a vision of the idea of eternal recurrence) and that of Paul on the road to Damascus.[53] It is clear that Nietzsche *did* have some such experience in Sils-Maria, for he writes of it in several places. In *Ecce Homo,* he speaks of a day in August 1881 when he "was walking through the woods along the lake of Silvaplana; at a powerful pyramidal rock not far from Surlei I stopped. It was then that this idea [of eternal recurrence] came to me. If I reckon back a few months from this day, I find as an omen a sudden and profoundly decisive change in my taste, especially in music" (*EH* "Books" Z 1; *KSA* 6:335).

In his journal, he speaks of having a vision near what has since come to be known as the "Zarathustra Stone" (i.e., the Surlej boulder), and he describes himself as being "6,000 feet above the sea and much higher than all human things" (*KSA* 9:11 [141]). The seriousness of this vision is clear from what he writes to Gast (August 14, 1881):

> On my horizon, thoughts have arisen the likes of which I have never seen before. . . . Oh, friend, from time to time the thought goes through my head that I am actually living a highly dangerous life, since I am one of those machines that could explode! The intensities of my feelings make me shudder and laugh—a couple of times I couldn't leave the room for the ridiculous reason that my eyes were inflamed—because of what? I had in each case wept too much the day before, and they were not tears of sentimentality but tears of joy; I sang and said nonsensical things, filled with a new vision that puts me ahead of everyone else. (*KSB* 6:112)

Could it be Paul to whom one would have to go back to find a similar sense of vision? Bernoulli seems at least to think so, though there is clearly a lack of textual evidence for that view. Bernoulli connects this vision with what Nietzsche says of Paul:

> Paul conceived the idea, and Calvin appropriated the idea, that countless numbers have from all eternity been condemned to damnation and that this lovely universal plan was thus instituted so that the glory of God might be revealed in it; Heaven and Hell and humanity are thus supposed to exist so as to—gratify the vanity of God! What a cruel and insatiable vanity must have flickered in the soul of him who first conceived or first appropriated such a thing!—Paul thus remained Saul after all—*the persecutor of God*. (*HH* II:85; *KSA* 2:591)

On Bernoulli's read, Paul (or Saul) is like Nietzsche—a fellow "*persecutor of God*." No doubt there is at least some justification for that connection. Whether Nietzsche would have noted it is again open to question. So the connection is indeed speculative, though it is not simply without justification. In any case, it would seem that both Paul and Nietzsche underwent a powerful experience that changed their lives.

Actually, it is Salomé's observation that seems particularly apt in regard to Paul. For Nietzsche does—as we will later see—seem to come dangerously close to Christianity. And, since Nietzsche labels Paul "*the *first Christian,*" it would not be surprising that Nietzsche would feel both a kinship and a deep antipathy (*D* 68; *KSA* 3:64).

Perhaps we might sum up the severity of Nietzsche's critique of Socrates, Wagner, and Paul with the following quotation from Edmund Husserl/Goethe. Whereas early in his career Husserl had accepted the view of psychologism, the *Logical Investigations* marks a stark repudiation of that view. At the end of the foreword to the first edition, Husserl quotes Goethe as saying: "There is nothing to which one is more severe than the errors that one has just abandoned."[54] Yet here we might perhaps add that one is likely to be *even more severe* against those views one wishes to abandon but can't quite find the strength to do so.

In the following three chapters, we turn to philosophical, artistic, and religious forms of decadence. As we will see, Nietzsche holds up the individuals Socrates, Wagner, and Paul as representatives of larger movements. Thus, although Nietzsche should be read as quite explicitly criticizing Socrates and Platonism, the criticism he levels against Socrates should likewise be read as a criticism against philosophy itself. Similarly, Nietzsche's attacks on Wagner and Paul represent attacks on the movements that they represent. In Wagner's case, it is a kind of art; in Paul's case, it is a certain kind of Christianity.

While Nietzsche is often read as being much "harder" on religion as a decadent phenomenon, an examination of his critique of Socrates and Wagner shows that he is equally savage in his attack on philosophy and art. Assuming I am right in the claim that there are various manifestations of decadence and that Nietzsche gives them more or less equal criticism, then interpreting Nietzsche on decadence presents us with an important choice. Either it is the case that philosophy, religion, *and* art may be inherently decadent and thus should be abandoned. Or else there are possible versions of each that could—at least in principle—avoid or (more accurately) minimize decadence. I will be arguing for the latter of these two theses—which means there could be a form of *religion* that is not necessarily decadent. This I take to be Nietzsche's view: that there is a form of religion available not just to him but to anyone who escapes the charge of decadence. Later in life, Nietzsche forms his "own" religion that is designed precisely to go beyond decadence.

Whether Nietzsche is successful in this venture is certainly open to question. But, in any case, the possibility of abandoning religion and/ or philosophy in favor of art or "aesthetics"—and thereby necessarily overcoming decadence—is simply *not* an option that Nietzsche's later philosophy leaves open, despite interpretations to the contrary. As should be clear, I expressly wish to argue against interpreters such as Nehemas or Rorty, who claim that Nietzsche suggests we abandon philosophy in favor of art or literature. Of course, that claim is usually nuanced by defining philosophy as "systematic" or "analytic" in nature. But, on my read, what makes philosophy decadent is similar to what makes religion or art decadent. Thus, escaping from one to the other solves *nothing*.

FIVE

Socrates' Fate

> *In my own case this disrespectful thought, that the great sages are declining types, first occurred to me precisely in regard to an instance where learned and unlearned prejudice most strongly opposes it: I recognized Socrates and Plato as symptoms of decay, as instruments of the Greek dissolution, as pseudo-Greek, as anti-Greek. . . . [T]hese wisest ones, were somehow in physiological agreement, so that they took the same negative stance toward life—and had to take it.*[1]

Who would have guessed? Socrates, the murderer of tragedy—or so Nietzsche thinks (*BT* 12; *KSA* 1:87)—turns out to be tragic himself. Not a hero exactly, but a tragic figure. As a decadent, Socrates *had* to turn to the *pharmakon* of dialectic, and he couldn't help but drag Athens along with him. Although Socrates chooses a decadent way of dealing with decadence, Nietzsche thinks that he really had no choice.

The Valuation Game

Where does decadence first manifest itself in Athenian society and what is its primary manifestation? Note how Nietzsche begins the section "The Problem of Socrates": "The wisest sages of all times have reached the same judgment about life: *it's worthless*" (*TI* II:1; *KSA* 6:67). Such is hardly Nietzsche's judgment; instead, he thinks that it is the judgment of philosophers in general. But the problem here is only secondarily the conclusion that Socrates and the other "wisest sages" reach. That conclusion is itself a symptom rather than the "essence" of decadence. Although Nietzsche is hardly clear as to the precise moment of the beginning of decadence, perhaps we can pinpoint it to the beginning of what we could term the "valuation game."[2] Decadence begins the moment we begin to ask whether life has value or how it can be justified. Nietzsche says that "value judgments about life, for or against, can in the final analysis never be true; they have value only as symptoms" of decadence (*TI* II:2; *KSA* 6:68). But, if those are symptoms, then "catching the disease" (as opposed to having it manifest itself) is the point at which one starts to *feel the need of justification*. It is precisely at this moment that one moves from what Nietzsche calls "*ascending*" life to declining life. As long as "happiness is the same as instinct"—as long as one feels no need to justify one's choices or justify one's life—then one is still ascending (*TI* II:11; *KSA* 6:73). For Nietzsche, every age can be classified as an age of "ascent" or one of "descent": "Either it has the virtues of *ascending* life: then it will resist from the profoundest depths the virtues of declining life. Or the age itself represents declining life: then it also requires the virtues of decline, then it hates everything that justifies itself solely out of abundance, out of the overflowing riches of strength" (*CW* Epilogue; *KSA* 6:50).

But what is this valuation game that is a mark of such a drastic change in living? Fundamentally, it concerns the value of life itself, and is only secondarily about particular value judgments. How exactly does this work in practice? Nietzsche believes that we are forced to do something that is inherently harmful to life—put a "price tag" on it: "Man has gradually become a fantastic animal that must fulfill one condition of existence more than any other animal: man *must* from time to time believe he knows *why* he exists; his race cannot thrive without a periodic trust in life—without faith in the *reason in life*!" (*GS* 1; *KSA* 3:372). Yet, even though Nietzsche thinks that we have become animals who demand an answer to the question "what is the meaning of life?" he clearly thinks that all such justifications are impossible and criticizes all who make such statements (whom he goes on to term "*the teachers of the purpose of existence*"). But it is *how* they promote existence that troubles Nietzsche:

> "Life is worth living," each of them shouts, "there is something to life, there is something behind life, beneath it, beware!" This drive, which rules the highest as well as the basest of human beings—the drive for the preservation of the species—erupts from time to time as reason and passion of the mind; it is then surrounded by a resplendent retinue of reasons and tries with all its might to make us forget that fundamentally it is drive, instinct, stupidity, lack of reasons. Life *ought* to be loved, *because*—! Man *ought* to advance himself and his neighbour *because*—! What names all these Oughts and Becauses have been given and may yet be given in the future! (*GS* 1; *KSA* 3:371)

What these teachers of "the meaning of life" want to do is *justify* life by way of their "oughts" and "becauses." Nietzsche has no problem with the basic drive that causes us instinctively to preserve the species. In fact, the problem comes when we forget that this drive—this drive toward life—is *itself* without any ground or purpose. In other words, life simply *is*. Nietzsche notes: "Whether I regard human beings with a good or with an evil eye, I always find them engaged in a single task, each and every one of them: to do what benefits the preservation of the human race" (*GS* 1; *KSA* 3:369). So we all do this instinctively. But some forget—or else are unable to face the fact that—the drive of self-preservation is itself ungrounded, and simply cannot be grounded on anything. Thus, they suggest that there is something "behind" or "beneath" life. Inevitably, these claims take the form of: "life is valuable because . . ." And one has to fill in the blank with *something*.

Even though we have become animals who expect a *why*—and even though Nietzsche writes "if you have your *why* for your life, you can get by with almost any *how*" (*TI* I:12; *KSA* 6:60–61)—Nietzsche clearly is trying to get beyond this stage of human development. He wants to be able to say "life is good" without adding any "because." But can he really get to that stage—and how? Nietzsche gives us a clue in *The Gay Science*, when he writes "*in the long run* each of these great teachers of a purpose was vanquished by laughter, reason and nature: the brief tragedy always changed and returned into the eternal comedy of existence" (*GS* 1; *KSA* 3:372). Laughter is the only "cure" to what Nietzsche elsewhere calls "the spirit of gravity" (*Z* III "Spirit of Gravity"; *KSA* 4:241–45). This is why Nietzsche proposes a *"fröhliche Wissenschaft"*—a light-hearted kind of science that refuses to give answers where there are none and doesn't worry about that inability to give answers—to the point of not even thinking it *is* an inability. When Nietzsche praises the Greeks for being "superficial—*out of profundity*" (*GS* P 4; *KSA* 3:352), he is speaking of those truly ancient philosophers—before Socrates and Plato—who not only gave superficial answers because they realized that such was all they had but also were *content* with such answers.

While Nietzsche has no problem with value judgments per se, he takes issue with any value judgments that stem from the need to put a value on life. Nietzsche claims *"the value of life cannot be assessed"* (*TI* II:2; *KSA* 6:68). Even more important, he thinks that life's value *should not* be assessed. Yet what exactly makes such a judgment impossible?

And, further, why would Nietzsche see such a judgment as inherently wrong?

Regarding the first question, Nietzsche sees it as simply impossible for us to put any kind of value on life. Since we are *living* beings, we are "parties to the dispute" (*TI* II:2; *KSA* 6:68). Part of the problem here is that the justification of life is simply unable to make any claims of "objectivity." To speak in Kantian language, such a judgment cannot be "scientific," for we are unable to find anything like a view "from the outside."[3] Given that Nietzsche has long given up the notion of scientific objectivity in favor of perspectivism, his reasoning here seems inconsistent. Why would *Nietzsche* require that we be able to step back from life in this sense? However, the difficulty goes deeper than that. As living beings, how can we come up with any other answer than "life is meaningful"? We may, of course, decide that life is *theoretically* meaningless. But, in the end, could we really be convinced? As living beings, to say that life is meaningless is to say that we are meaningless. Yet that claim seems impossible to take seriously without severe problems of self-referentiality, for it is a meaningless claim.[4]

There is another way, though, in which the game or project of valuing life is simply misguided. Nietzsche believes that life simply *is* valuable. Nietzsche in no way puts forth an argument for that claim. Rather it is something that he simply takes on faith or else sees as self-evident.[5] Thus, any kinds of claims that attempt to *provide* a meaning or justification for life simply miss the fundamental character of life. We could put this problem in a slightly different way. Since there is nothing greater than life for Nietzsche, there is simply no way to value it. For any kind of value claim would require an appeal to something else that is above life. The project, then, would be similar to that of a religious believer attempting to "justify" or "value" God (which is why some religious believers take the project of theodicy—the "justification" of God's existence in the face of evil—to be heretical). Since God is the very definition of what is good (at least on most theistic accounts, and certainly all Christian accounts), one would inevitably end in circularity. In neither case could any meaningful justification be given.

Yet the valuation game is not merely misguided. It is also fundamentally pernicious, since it goes against life. In order to make any judgment regarding life, one would inevitably have to set oneself *above* it. In Socrates' case, the attempt is to set reason above life by giving a rational justification for why life is of value. The religious move is a similar "setting above," but by way of placing God (and, more important, a very particular *sort* of God) above life. Thus, on a Christian account, life is good precisely because it proceeds from God. But both moves (secular or religious) require that one simultaneously *devalue* life, for life is either less important than oneself or God. Or such is how Nietzsche sees it: one undermines life in either case.

As an antidote to this devaluation of life, Nietzsche gives us his Dionysian faith in life. Although we will look at this later in more detail, it is important to realize that Nietzsche *does* think he has an alternative to valuing life.[6] Even though he realizes that human beings up until now have had to have a "why," he wants to move beyond that. Instead, Nietzsche aspires to "a glad and trusting fatalism in the midst of the universe, with a *faith* that only the particular is to be rejected, that as a whole, everything redeems and affirms itself" (*TI* IX:49; *KSA* 6:152). If everything "redeems and affirms itself," then no *further* justification is needed. Whether Nietzsche ever reaches this place, of course, is another question.

The *Pharmakon* of Dialectic

Socrates' own version of the valuation game works out as follows. Clever fellow that he is, Socrates rightly realizes that Athenian life is in decline. In Nietzsche's version of "the good old days," nobility is the state of life *without* a valuation game. One gives no justification for life because one feels no need to do so. And one gives no justification for one's actions. There is no need for correction, redemption, or improvement —precisely because one operates with the assurance that whatever one does is right. One acts with authority "so that one does not 'give reasons' but commands." Given such a situation, "the dialectician is a sort of clown" whose perceived need to justify himself is precisely the signal that his action is unjustified (*TI* II:5; *KSA* 6:70). In contrast, nobility simply sees itself as right to such an extent that it is not even self-conscious about that rightness. It is a pure assurance of oneself in which there is no moment of self-assurance. Consider what Nietzsche says about the nobles of ancient Greece: "'We who are truthful'—that is what the nobility of ancient Greece called themselves. . . . The noble type of person feels that *he* determines value, he does not need anyone's approval, he judges that 'what is harmful to me is harmful in itself,' he knows that he is the one who gives honor to things in the first place, he *creates values*. He honors everything he sees in himself: this sort of morality is self-glorifying" (*BGE* 260; *KSA* 5:209). Somewhat surprisingly, Nietzsche terms this attitude a "faith" that one has in oneself: "It is not works, it is *faith* that is decisive here, faith that establishes rank order (this old, religious formula now acquires a new and deeper meaning): some fundamental certainty that a noble soul has about itself, something that cannot be looked for, cannot be found, and perhaps cannot be lost either.—*The noble soul has reverence for itself*" (*BGE* 287; *KSA* 5:233).

And, yet, somehow it is lost. Or is forgotten. Or else a new generation comes along that no longer has that complete self-assurance. In any case, though, once one begins to question oneself and then feels a need to justify one's existence and one's actions, one is on the road to decline. Not surprisingly, given the political misfortunes of Athens, the noble warrior in Socrates' day was no longer able to have that undisturbed sense of being right and justified. Socrates was a decadent, but so was all of Athens. So one can hardly *blame* Socrates. Yet, as fate would have it, the good doctor Socrates just happens to show up at precisely the right time with a *pharmakon,* a remedy that turns out to be (in the literal sense of that term) both medicine and poison. Following Plato, Derrida notes that, while a *pharmakon* might "worsen the ill," it can likewise ameliorate.[7] The extent to which the Socratic *pharmakon* is more cure than poison—or poison than cure—remains to be seen.

As is to be expected in a mass epidemic, Socrates is himself ill, and— just like the other wise sages—a little "shaky" (*TI* II:1; *KSA* 6:67). But he has a medicine that, as long as the patient continues to take it, should stave off the effects of decadence. Socrates' medicine is a new sort of *agôn* [contest]. Whereas the noble warrior was defined by *arête* [excellence] in physical warfare, Socrates substitutes an *arête* of mental warfare.[8] Although Socrates had distinguished himself as a warrior in battle, Nietzsche overlooks this and accuses Socrates of coming from the "rabble" (*TI* II:3; *KSA* 6:68).[9] But Nietzsche *is* right that the Socratic dialectic represents a change in how one "proves" oneself. Yet Nietzsche thinks this change is effected only due to desperation, like most medicine. As he puts it, "dialectic is chosen only as a last resort" (*TI* II:6; *KSA* 6:70). Unlike physical battle—in which "winning" is more clearly defined—Nietzsche points out that reasoning is really not that convincing. Moreover, it can easily breed mistrust, since either one's listener or even oneself may not be entirely convinced.

Yet Nietzsche takes his critique of Socrates far beyond the criticism of his use of dialectic. *Twilight of the Idols* contains a number of *ad hominem* attacks, but none is so memorable as that against Socrates (which we noted in the Preface). Already in *The Pre-Platonic Philosophers,* Nietzsche had characterized Socrates as "ugly" with a "flat nose, thick lips, bulging eyes," and "prone to violent outbursts" (*PPP* 144; *KGW* II/4, 353). Here Nietzsche is mainly recounting some of the nastier things that had been said by Socrates' contemporaries. Yet, in *Twilight of the Idols,* these "facts" are transformed into an argument:

> Ugliness, which in itself is an objection, was among the Greeks virtually a refutation. Was Socrates Greek in the first place? Ugliness is often enough the expression of interbreeding, of a development *thwarted* by interbreeding. In other cases it appears as a development in *decline*. Forensic anthropologists tell us that the typical criminal is ugly: *monstrum in fronte, monstrum in animo* [monster in the face, monster in the soul]. But the criminal is a *décadent*. . . . A visitor who knew about faces, when he passed through Athens, said to Socrates' face that he *was* a *monstrum*—that he contained all bad vices and cravings within him. And Socrates simply answered: "You know me, sir!" (*TI* II:3; *KSA* 6:68–69)[10]

Leaving aside Nietzsche's questionable views on eugenics, let us consider his equally questionable views on ugliness and its relation to one's true self. Nietzsche's view that ugliness is connected to criminality was a widely accepted view by criminologists, psychologists, and novelists in his time.[11] Moreover, his claim that, for the Greeks, ugliness was almost a "refutation" is not quite as far-fetched at it might at first seem. Jacob Burckhardt well describes the Greek conception of beauty when he writes: "Not only were the Greeks most strongly affected by beauty, but they universally and frankly expressed their conviction of its value, in sharp contrast to the moderns, who do their best to see it from the ethical viewpoint as a very fragile gift. . . . The first wish made for sons who are to rule is that their appearance should match their destiny; the essential is that physique should have its own claim to high rank."[12] So Nietzsche has good reason to claim that the Greeks saw a strong connection between one's outer appearance and one's inner self. Certainly this was true of the ancient Greeks (i.e., those who preceded Socrates and Plato). An *aesthetic* justification was for them legitimate. Presumably, then, both beauty and ugliness could be taken as signs of one's inner nobility—or lack thereof. Interestingly enough, in Socrates this relation is more or less inverted. Whereas for the ancient Greeks beauty was an indication of goodness, what Nietzsche calls "*aesthetic Socratism*" produces the formula "'In order to be beautiful, everything must be reasonable'" (*BT* 12; *KSA* 1:85). So Socrates' hyper-rational nature makes him—in a sense—"beautiful." Thus, Nietzsche's *ad hominem* is a mixture of ancient Greek belief and the criminology and eugenics of his day. Does it work as an *argument*? Probably not for most of us today. Yet, given both ancient Greek theory and nineteenth-century criminology, one cannot simply write Nietzsche off as being simply "unfair." He at least had both precedent and (then) current theory on his side.[13]

But how does the *pharmakon* of dialectic work? For Nietzsche, reason *too* is an instinct, albeit one that is severely *underdeveloped* in relation to the others and therefore not primary. However, Socrates takes reason to be the *supreme* instinct—and lords it over the others. In the midst of Athenian decadence, "Socrates believed that he was obliged to correct existence, starting from this single point" (*BT* 13; *KSA* 1:89). Here a brief account of Socrates' view of the soul is in order. Among Socrates' most memorable metaphors is that of the charioteer driving a pair of winged steeds. In the *Phaedrus,* Socrates describes the soul as composed of three parts: reason (the charioteer), spirit (the steed that is "noble and good"), and appetites (the steed of "opposite character").[14] Whereas the former steed responds relatively easily to the pull of the reins of reason, the latter can only be brought under control by great exertion. But Plato's goal here is clear: the unity of these three elements can only be achieved with reason in charge, a state which enables the soul to ascend "beyond the heavens" where she can "contemplate" truth and be "nourished."[15] The result is an ordered soul, one that exhibits the same sort of well-regulated harmony we find in the works of fine craftsmen.[16]

Nietzsche, too, is interested in achieving the harmony of the soul. Indeed, that ordering is just as important to Nietzsche as it is to Socrates.[17] So it is the *kind* of ordering that Socrates proposes that Nietzsche rejects, as well as the way in which it is *imposed.* Nietzsche's criticism of Socratic decadence can be taken as a propaedeutic to restoring life's proper rhythm. No doubt, Socrates gives us a kind of rhythm, but it is a cadence achieved by both the dominance of reason and a heavy dose of "otherworldliness." Nietzsche objects to both of these, and sees them as going hand in hand. Socrates assumes that there is a fundamental deficiency of the soul precisely because it tends to be ordered by that which is *not* rational. On Nietzsche's account, the assumption of the need for correction of the soul—as if its natural state was somehow deficient—is already a manifestation of decadence, and that decadence is simply expanded and developed by the correction. Moreover, the formula for overcoming decadence that we find in Socrates ends up being remarkably similar to that of Christianity, which is one of the chief reasons why Nietzsche sees Christianity as simply a continuation of Platonism. Later, we shall consider what Nietzsche takes to be a "right" ordering of the soul. But, first, we need to see how Socrates in effect "disorders" the soul and thus is decadent.

Whereas the noble warrior was quite happy in following his appetites or instincts, Socrates assumes that the appetites and instincts are precisely the problem. Yet, once they come under suspicion and are deemed "base," one has to look to something else for guidance. That something else for Socrates is reason. Even though Socrates is following one of his instincts—reason—he does so in a way that both disorders the "true" order of life (at least as Nietzsche sees it) and accords reason a stature that it does not deserve. On Nietzsche's read, Socrates recommends taking control of oneself—or, perhaps more accurately, fighting against oneself—by way of the *agôn* of dialectic. In contrast to the idea that happiness is to be found simply in following one's appetites or instincts, Socrates presents an alternative formula—which Nietzsche labels "the most bizarre equation that there is"—"reason = virtue = happiness" (*TI* II:4; *KSA* 6:69). Happiness is now to be found in curbing the appetites and instincts, in doing what does *not* come naturally. Whereas "the drives want to play the tyrant" (and Nietzsche is perfectly happy with that), Socrates feels the need "to invent a stronger *counter-tyrant*" (*TI* II:9; *KSA* 6:71). But, since the appetites and instincts are what express life—or even *are* life for us—then their suppression is the suppression of life. It is hard for Nietzsche to imagine a more obvious case of decadence. "To *have* to fight the instincts—that is the formula for *décadence*" (*TI* II:11; *KSA* 6:73). Thus, although purporting to cure his patients, Socrates' *pharmakon* turns out to be a poison that makes them even sicker.

But what are these instincts [*Instinkte*] and drives [*Triebe*]? And how do they control our lives? Often Nietzsche uses these terms interchangeably to denote whatever is *not* rational, and thus not conscious. In fact, Nietzsche uses a bewildering array of terms that he seems—more or less—to equate with the instincts and drives: will, life, power, strength, energy, and force. To return to Socrates' charioteer metaphor, the instincts and drives are the horses that power the chariot. Thus, instincts and drives are what give our lives their vitality and direct us in certain ways. But it is important to see that, for instance, the term "instinct," as we normally predicate it of animals, is not exactly the same as what Nietzsche means by *Instinkt*. For human instincts and drives are never purely "natural" and thus "unformed" by culture.[18] In early essays Nietzsche speaks of various drives, such as the drives to knowledge [later, the will to truth], art, myth, and science. So the drives or instincts are not simply natural, nor are they entirely disconnected from reason. The problem with Socrates' dialectic is twofold. First, it puts in place a very particular *sort* of reason, one that is fundamentally otherworldly. In fact, the further removed from physical reality reason is, the more it is truly "rational." But Nietzsche, of course, would dispute this, arguing that rationality is connected only to *this* world. Any claims of rationality being connected to some other world are—simply put—*irrational*. Second, Socrates' conception of rationality is such that it should *rule*. Nietzsche is not against science or reason per se, but his idea of a "reformed" Socrates would be one who recognized that "art may even be a necessary correlative and supplement of science" (*BT* 14; *KSA* 1:96).

Just like Socrates, Nietzsche sees the need to organize the instincts. His goal is certainly not that of letting them run wild, nor is it the return to some state of nature. Since instincts are always organized by cultural forces, the question is rather one of *which* cultural forces are allowed to mold the instincts and *how* those instincts are molded. In the case of the noble warrior, the instincts were properly "civilized," and it is this *sort* of civilization to which Nietzsche wants to return. Yet Nietzsche realizes that turning back the clock is impossible, as well as undesirable. So who might he have in mind as an example? Nietzsche *does* speak of Napoleon in glowing terms, calling him a "master" and one of the "great human beings" (*TI* IX:44; *KSA* 6:145). Still, he lacks what Nietzsche terms *"noblesse* of character" (*WP* 1026; *KSA* 10:7 [27]). Goethe, on the other hand, provides a much better example for Nietzsche: "Goethe conceived of a human being who was strong, highly cultivated, skilled in everything bodily, with self-control and self-respect—a human being who is allowed to dare to accept the entire scope and wealth of naturalness, who is strong enough for this freedom; a tolerant human being, not out of weakness but out of strength" (*TI* IX:49; *KSA* 6:151). It is the simultaneous control of that which is body and that which is "spiritual" that so impresses Nietzsche. Goethe is "a spirit who has *become free*" precisely by having "disciplined himself into wholeness." The result is that "he *created* himself" (*TI* IX:49; *KSA* 6:151–52). Such is the goal that Nietzsche has for himself.[19]

The "Egyptianized" World

Decadence turns out to have a much less personal and far more global sort of manifestation. Nietzsche does not see dialectic as merely fighting one's own personal appetites and instincts but also as fighting all that is worldly—whatever is physical and thus subject to change. Since this world for Nietzsche is synonymous with life, then to go against it is to go against life itself. Having dealt with the way in which Socrates combats the appetites and instincts (in effect, the body), Nietzsche turns to the way reason has been used to do battle with the physical world as a whole. Here we find a parallel to the strategy used in the *agôn* against the body. The physical is demeaned by the postulation of something that is non-physical. That nonphysical something is what Nietzsche calls the "true world." Whereas the "apparent world" (again to use his language) is the world that is immediately obvious by way of the senses, the true world can be known only by reason. The ultimate purpose of this true world is to provide an escape from the apparent world, and this is merely a symptom of decadence: "Dividing the world into a 'true' and 'apparent' world . . . is merely a move inspired by *décadence*—a symptom of *declining* life" (*TI* III:6; *KSA* 6:79).

Perhaps the most important section in *Twilight of the Idols* is that entitled "How the 'True World' Finally Became a Fiction," in which Nietzsche gives us a tantalizingly brief outline of the demise of the true world. But here we might ask: how ever did the true world become a fact in the first place? Unlike Nietzsche's account of the true world's demise, in which there are six relatively sharply delineated steps, Nietzsche gives us at best a kind of genealogy of the "creation" of the true world in which there are number of factors. The simplest of these, of course, is that "the 'true world' is just *added to* [the apparent world] *by a lie*" (*TI* III:2; *KSA* 6:75). Philosophers—and he really means Socrates and Plato—have postulated the true world out of thin air. Although Nietzsche doesn't give us a clear sense of motivation in *Twilight of the Idols* (other than it is inspired by decadence), we find one in a much earlier essay. There Nietzsche gives an account of what he refers to as the "fable" of knowledge: "Once upon a time, in some out of the way corner of that universe which is dispersed into numberless twinkling solar systems, there was a star upon which clever beasts invented knowledge. That was the most arrogant and mendacious minute of 'world history,' but nevertheless, it was only a minute" (*PT* 79; *KSA* 1:874).

Since knowledge and the true world are equated by Plato, it would hardly be unreasonable to say that the true world comes about on Nietzsche's view by way of the same haughtiness. And there is something about this move—the very audacity of it—that should impress Nietzsche, who himself exhibits and seems to condone brazenness. After all, Plato gives us no real support for postulating the Forms. He simply does so, in a purely dogmatic fashion. And, indeed, Nietzsche says, "we should not be ungrateful towards dogmatism" (*BGE* P; *KSA* 5:12). But, of course, Nietzsche immediately goes on to say that Plato's dogmatism stands as "the worst, most prolonged, and most dangerous of all errors to this day." It is an audacity that has had seriously deleterious effects.

The result is a "true world" in which all the life has been sucked out. On Nietzsche's account, philosophical reason (as inherited from the Greeks) despises change and privileges stasis. The result is that everything important turns out to be whatever has no history. Nietzsche accuses philosophers of being "idiosyncratic" in "their hatred for the very notion of becoming." Why this is strange is that—if anything seems obvious—it is that things change. Instead of facing what their senses so clearly tell them, they exclaim "there has to be an illusion, a deception at work that prevents us from perceiving what *is*." Rather than accept this aspect of worldly existence, philosophers construct a world in which *nothing* changes. Thus, Nietzsche accuses philosophy of "Egyptianism," in which philosophers "kill and stuff whatever they worship" (*TI* III:1; *KSA* 6:74). For Nietzsche, this otherworldliness is a slander against *this* world—and thus against life itself. As such, it is simply another manifestation of decadence.

Yet Socrates requires this Egyptianism to combat his instincts. One might be tempted to accuse Socrates of being hyper-rational (what Nietzsche terms *"absurdly rational"*), but his move toward dialectic and Egyptianism has a very *practical* motive. As a decadent, he latches onto dialectic as a way of combating his decadence. Unfortunately, instead of relying on the body's intelligence ("big reason"), Socrates turns to the least developed of our human ways of knowing—consciousness. He is forced to "make a tyrant out of *reason.*" Nietzsche is quite clear that this was Socrates' fate: "neither Socrates nor his 'sick patients' were rational by choice—it was *de rigueur,* it was their last resort" (*TI* II:10; *KSA* 6:72).

Even though Socrates has no other alternative, Nietzsche sees the legacy of "Socratism" as immensely negative. In effect, Socrates has created an alternative world as a way of escaping the real world. Everything that Socrates says turns out to be a negation of the way the world really is. Take, for example, the formula "reason = virtue = happiness." For anyone who has been deeply influenced by the ethics of Plato and Aristotle, it might be difficult—at least at first glance—to see what is wrong with it. If one acts according to reason, then one will be virtuous and thereby be happy. Yet Nietzsche reads this as a complete inversion of not only the so-called apparent world but also the *truly* ancient Greek way of thinking. As Nietzsche puts it: "'Virtue is knowledge; sin is only committed out of ignorance; the virtuous man is a happy man'; in these basic three forms of optimism lies the death of tragedy. For the virtuous hero must now be a dialectician" (*BT* 14; *KSA* 1:94). In effect, Socrates creates a world in which everything is reasonable, a cosmos that is truly ordered by reason.

It is not merely the fact that, in the "real" world, virtue does not necessarily lead to happiness. Rather, it is the very notion that everything can be made "reasonable." Socrates expects both that one *can* give a rationale for everything and that one *should* give one. Whenever he encounters those who act only from instinct, he finds them deficient. Or, as Nietzsche puts it: "'Only by instinct': the phrase goes to the heart and centre of the Socratic tendency. With these words Socratism condemns existing art and existing ethics in equal measure; wherever it directs its probing gaze, it sees a lack of insight and the power of delusion, and it concludes from this lack that what exists is inwardly wrong and objectionable" (*BT* 13; *KSA* 1:89). Such a view represents both the death of tragedy and the death of the ancient Greek way of thinking. In contrast to Socrates, the early Greeks viewed life as inherently tragic. Not only is existence full of suffering, but there is no explanation for it. In an important sense, the early Greeks were *not* philosophical: that is, they did not live with an acute sense of the contingency of their existence, wondering *why* suffering takes place and asking deep philosophical questions about it. Rather, they simply accepted its existence—and its inexplicability—as a matter of fact.[20] "Tragedy" was thus their way of thinking about the world (without providing an ultimate *explanation*).

But "tragic reasoning" is not really "reasoning" at all (at least from Socrates' perspective), for it begins—and ends—with the assumption that things *don't* make sense. As Nietzsche puts it, the universe "is neither perfect, nor beautiful, nor noble, nor does it want to become any of these things; in no way does it strive to imitate man!" (*GS* 109; *KSA* 3:468). It is —viewed from our perspective—simply irrational and tragic. And this is why Aristotle's account of tragedy is so decidedly "anti-tragic." For Aristotle requires that (at least for what he terms the "perfect plot") that tragedy befall the character because of "some great fault on his part,"[21] as opposed to happening out of mysterious and inexplicable fate. Tragedy, on Aristotle's account, needs to make sense. All of this fits with Socrates' optimistic and rational view of the world: everything must be explained, and that includes suffering. As Nietzsche puts it: "What actually arouses indignation against suffering is not suffering in itself, but rather the senselessness of suffering" (*GM* II:7; *KSA* 5:304). In response, Socrates gives us the formula "reason = virtue = happiness." So now suffering has some explanation: if one suffers, one must have done something to deserve it. Conversely, if one is virtuous, then one will be happy. Suffering, then, is brought under control of "the optimistic dialectic" which "destroys the essence of tragedy" by bringing it "under the lash of its syllogisms" (*BT* 14; *KSA* 1:95). And all of this is in complete opposition to the truly ancient Greek view of suffering and the tragic.

For Nietzsche, returning to such a tragic view of the world represents a *positive* step forward (in contrast to which Socrates represents a step backward). Since Socrates is an optimist (though Nietzsche thinks he dies as a pessimist, as I note below), one might assume that the Greeks were pessimists. Yet Nietzsche insists that "precisely their tragedies prove that the Greeks were *not* pessimists" (*EH* "Books" BT 1; *KSA* 6:309). They acknowledged that suffering is an inevitable part of life and yet still kept living. For them, life itself is its own justification.

Nietzsche *contra* Socrates

Given that Socrates is forced to take his path of hyper-rationality, one might just say that Nietzsche is simply "describing" Socrates and his situation. In fact, one might interpret Nietzsche's "attack" on Socrates as following his third rule of warfare, namely, that of only attacking persons in order to bring to light a greater cultural phenomenon. Such would certainly be true in the case of Socrates, for all of Athens was decadent. Moreover, Nietzsche's attack on Socrates also follows his rule of attacking only victorious causes. And we might add that even Nietzsche admits that his attack on Platonism (and thus Socrates) is a bit of a caricature.[22]

But it is hard to read Nietzsche's critique of Socrates as simply detached and neutral, all the more so given Nietzsche's admission of continually fighting with Socrates.[23] In that sense, Nietzsche's claim to attack only when "every personal quarrel is excluded" may not apply in this case. Moreover, Nietzsche was ill disposed toward Socrates from virtually the beginning of his career. It begins with *The Birth of Tragedy* and ends with *Twilight of the Idols,* in which Nietzsche speculates that Socrates eventually came to realize what he'd done. Socrates saw that he hadn't cured anyone, least of all himself. Thus, he drank the hemlock willingly. Quite fittingly, the doctor who had dispensed poison now got his own medicine. "Socrates *wanted* to die: not Athens, but *he* gave himself the poison cup, he forced Athens to give him the poison cup . . . 'Socrates is no doctor,' he said to himself softly, 'death is the only doctor here'" (*TI* II:12; *KSA* 6:73). On Nietzsche's reading, when Socrates says "Crito, we ought to offer a cock to Asclepius," Socrates is admitting that death is the only cure for decadence.[24] But it is also the only cure for life. In a slightly different version of Socrates' death scene, Nietzsche brings a further charge against Socrates—that he was ultimately against life itself: "Whether it was death or the poison or piety or malice—something loosened his tongue and he said: 'O Crito, I owe Asclepius a rooster.' This ridiculous and terrible 'last word' means for those who have ears: 'O Crito, *life is a disease.* . . . Socrates, Socrates *suffered from life*! And then he still avenged himself—with this veiled, gruesome, pious, and blasphemous saying" (*GS* 340; *KSA* 3:569–70). In dying—and Nietzsche certainly interprets Socrates' death as a suicide—Socrates blasphemes against the god who has become Nietzsche's god: Life.[25] Moreover, Nietzsche at least asks the question of whether Socrates turns out to be a corruptor of youth after all. In *Beyond Good and Evil,* the charge is in connection to Platonic dogmatism (*BGE* P; *KSA* 5:12); yet the charge could just as easily be put in terms of leading the youth of Athens down a decadent path that ends with them adopting his own aversion to life.

In any case, Nietzsche thinks that Socrates gives us "the virtual *philosopher's pose in itself*": "world-negating, hostile to life, not believing in the senses, de-sensualized" (*GM* III:10; *KSA* 5:360). But this raises the crucial question: can Nietzsche really escape from Socrates? As we have already noted, Nietzsche's relationship to Socrates is best characterized as a love-hate relation. Nietzsche is right: he is so close to Socrates. But that only heightens the question. Nehemas puts the point perfectly: "Escaping Socrates might prove for him as impossible as escaping himself."[26] And, of course, Nietzsche needs to do *both* in order to "escape" from decadence.

How might Nietzsche accomplish such a feat? We get at least a partial answer in section two of "What I Owe to the Ancients"—where it becomes clear that Nietzsche doesn't think he "owes" much to Socrates or Plato. Indeed, Plato is a mixer of "all the stylistic forms together, and thus he is one of the *first décadents* in style," "boring," and "overmoralized." In contrast, though, Nietzsche's *"cure* for all Platonism has always been *Thucydides,"* whom Nietzsche sees as closely related by his "unconditional will to fabricate nothing and to see reason in *reality—not* in 'reason,' and still less in morality." For Nietzsche, Thucydides is "the great summation, the final appearance of that strong, strict, hard factuality that was a matter of instinct for the older Hellenes":

> What marks the difference between Thucydides and Plato?
>
> *Courage* in the face of reality is, in the final analysis, the point of difference between natures such as Thucydides and Plato. Plato is the coward in the face of reality—*consequently* he flees into the ideal; Thucydides has control over *himself*—consequently he also has control over things. (*TI* X:2; *KSA* 6:155–56)

Note the formula here: it is lack of *courage* that drives Plato into the realm of the ideal. Since Thucydides is unafraid of reality—even in all its brute force—he both has control over himself *and* over things.[27] He says "Yes" to life. Socrates and Plato, on the other hand, are driven to postulate the realm of the Forms and practice dialectic in order to function. They do not actually deal with reality, but instead attempt to escape from it. Hence, while they *think* they are dealing with "reality," they are instead merely dealing with the Egyptianized world that they've created. Elsewhere, Nietzsche writes: "To the rabble, wisdom seems like a kind of escape, a device or trick for pulling yourself out of the game when things get rough" (*BGE* 205; *KSA* 5:133). The plebian Socrates uses reason as his escape. In contrast, Nietzsche exalts the sophists, for "they deliver what they promise" (*PPP* 148; *KGW* II/4, 358)—a practical way of dealing with *this* world.

Nietzsche thinks that precisely this strategy is what makes Socrates (and, by extension, Plato) even *more* decadent:

> It is a self-deception on the part of philosophers and moralists to think that they can escape from *décadence* merely by making war against it. Escape is beyond their strength: for what they choose as a means, as salvation, is itself just another expression of *déca-dence*—they *alter* its expression, they don't do away with it itself. Socrates was a misunderstanding, *the whole morality of improvement, Christian morality included, was a misunderstanding. (TI* II:11; *KSA* 6:72–73)

Clearly the alternative must be that of following Thucydides—to face reality without fleeing into the ideal.

Yet, like Thucydides, does Nietzsche truly face reality? Or does he—in his own way—find solace in *another* kind of ideal? Before answering that question, we need to consider two other figures of decadence in order to see both how decadence can manifest itself in various ways and why Nietzsche is tempted by both artistic and religious decadence.

SIX

Wagner's Redemption

> *The problem of redemption is certainly a venerable problem.*
> *There is nothing about which Wagner has thought more deeply*
> *than redemption: his opera is the opera of redemption. Somebody*
> *or other always wants to be redeemed in his work: sometimes a*
> *little male, sometimes a little female [bald ein Männlein, bald ein*
> *Fräulein]—this is his problem.*[1]

That Wagner was obsessed with the problem of redemption—even before he encountered the philosophy of Arthur Schopenhauer—is no doubt true. All of his operas are, in one way or another, stories of redemption. It is this redemption—and, more important, the very *longing* for redemption—that Nietzsche wishes to leave behind. Ultimately, his goal is redemption *from* redemption: that is, redemption from the thought that somehow the world *can* and *should* be redeemed. Although Nietzsche speaks of his own "redemption," it is clear that he uses the term both ironically and in a sense that is exactly opposite the notion of redemption in Christianity, Schopenhauer, and Wagner. Precisely because of this, Nietzsche speaks of Wagner's need for redemption as *"his* problem."

Yet to understand why Nietzsche wants to reject the notion of redemption, we must first turn to Schopenhauer. As we will see, the *Leitmotif* of redemption continually sounds in Schopenhauer, and it echoes repeatedly in the music of Wagner. Redemption proves to be the key to understanding both Schopenhauer's philosophy and Wagner's theory of opera's therapeutic effect upon us.

The Pessimism of Schopenhauer

Just how deeply did Schopenhauer influence both Nietzsche and Wagner? And, in the case of Nietzsche, to what degree does that influence diminish over time? How we answer these questions greatly affects how we view the late Nietzsche. Clearly, Nietzsche sees himself moving away from

Schopenhauer in a radical way—and he tries at every turn to emphasize their differences and thus to intensify the chasm between them. However, their connection is never truly severed, and Schopenhauer remains a kind of lens through which Nietzsche continues to view the world.

That Schopenhauer was a pessimist is not only the most widely known aspect of his thought but also its logical conclusion. If one sees the world as Schopenhauer does, then pessimism naturally follows. Yet, as we will see, there are different *sorts* of pessimism, and Schopenhauer represents what Nietzsche would later come to think of as a "gloomy" pessimism. Schopenhauer's pessimism has to do with his peculiar brand of Kantianism. Although Schopenhauer takes over Kant's notion of the "noumenal" (that is, "thing-in-itself," as opposed to the object as perceived), he claims it can be *known*. To this reworked Kantianism, Schopenhauer adds two insights gleaned from his study of the *Upanishads*.[2] First, in accord with the Hindu doctrine of *maya,* Schopenhauer thinks that the world as we know it is ultimately an illusion—a play of representations [*Vorstellungen*]. Second, having accepted the Sanskrit saying "Tat tvam asi" [This art thou], Schopenhauer believes that behind the world of illusion lies what he terms "will," the basic force behind all life. Although we experience the world in terms of plurality—by way of what Schopenhauer calls the *"principium individuationis"*—metaphysical reality is actually "One." Even though we think we are individuals, at bottom we are fundamentally united to each other—and also to the will.

Schopenhauer's pessimism stems from his view of the will, which is neither rational nor good. Rejecting any kind of pantheism, in which the world turns out to be God, Schopenhauer instead embraces an almost demonic sense of the will. So this will—which we could also call "nature"—is an impersonal, inexplicable, blind, destructive (and yet also constructive) force. Although it is the force behind everything, it itself cannot be understood. Schopenhauer insists that the will cannot be viewed in terms of causality (since that is a feature of human consciousness, rather than a feature of the will). So no "explanation" can be given for why things are the way they are. The result is a view of human life that is about as grim as can be imagined: "But let us merely look at it; this world of constantly needy creatures who continue for a time merely by devouring one another, pass their existence in anxiety and want, and often endure terrible afflictions until they fall at last into the arms of death."[3]

Here one is reminded of the wisdom of Silenus: better not to have been born or, having been born, best to die soon. And, indeed, Schopenhauer *does* think that it would be better not to have been born. That would be one kind of salvation, but one that is not open to those who already exist. However bleak this outlook may seem, Schopenhauer sees it as simply an honest recognition of the way life *is:* "Everything in life proclaims that earthly happiness is destined to be frustrated, or recognized as an illusion. The grounds for this lie deep in the nature of things."[4] So Schopenhauer's pessimism is simply a kind of "realism" which he takes to be brutally honest. He is absolutely adamant against those who optimistically argue that this is "the best of all possible worlds." In response, and with ironic reference to Leibniz, he contends: "The world is as bad as it can possibly be, if it is to exist at all. *Q.E.D.*"[5] Even though this view turns out to be less than convincing (if for no other reason than it would seem that one could *always* imagine some feature of the world being worse than it is), it is indeed Schopenhauer's view.

Here one might ask how is it possible to know so much about the will, a seemingly inscrutable force. Schopenhauer's answer is that we have a direct *experience* of the will by way of our bodies: "My body is the only object of which I know not merely the one side, that of the representation, but also the other, that is called *will*."[6] In an important sense, then, we are actually part of the will and thus part of the thing-in-itself: "The *will* is what is real and essential in man, whereas the *intellect* is only the secondary, the conditioned, and the produced."[7]

As to pessimism, Schopenhauer realizes that there are different sorts of pessimism, and that some sorts call for redemption:

> I cannot, as is generally done, put the *fundamental difference* of all religions in the question whether monotheistic, polytheistic, pantheistic, or atheistic, but only in the question whether they are optimistic or pessimistic, in other words, whether they present the existence of this world as justified by itself, and consequently praise and commend it, or consider it as something which can be conceived only as the consequence of our guilt, and thus really ought not to be, in that they recognize that pain and death cannot lie in the eternal, original, and immutable order of things, that which in every respect ought to be. The power by virtue of which Christianity was able to overcome first Judaism, and then the paganism of Greece and Rome, is to be found solely in its pessimism, in the confession that our condition is

> both exceedingly sorrowful and sinful, whereas Judaism and pagan-
> ism were optimistic. That truth, profoundly and painfully felt by
> everyone, took effect, and entailed the need for redemption.[8]

Everything here turns on the phrase "whether they present the existence of this world as justified by itself." From what we have seen, it is hard to read Schopenhauer as holding the view that the world is "justified by itself." If anything, the world is *not* justified—and it certainly is not inherently "good." Thus, it is not surprising to find that, despite his criticism of religions for their pessimism, Schopenhauer himself turns out to be a pessimist. Moreover, he also calls for some sort of "salvation"—even though, in the final analysis, it fails to truly save.

Schopenhauer's "road to salvation" (to use his phrase) turns out to be metaphysical in nature. And its two basic components have much to do with both Nietzsche and Wagner. While that road begins with the recognition that "there is only one inborn error, and that is the notion that we exist in order to be happy,"[9] it continues on—paradoxically enough—with "seeing through the *principium individuationis*" and resulting in "the entire surrender of the will-to-live." That will is replaced by love, and Schopenhauer asserts that "all love (ἀγάπη, *caritas*) is compassion."[10] Despite the fact that the will is fundamentally egoistical—and so are we—salvation comes when we are guided by *Mitleid*. Given the centrality of compassion to his ethics, it is not surprising that Schopenhauer openly says that "my ethical teaching agrees with the Christian [ethics] completely and in its highest tendencies."[11]

Becoming compassionate turns out to have everything to do with understanding oneself as one truly is:

> If that veil of Maya, the *principium individuationis,* is lifted from the
> eyes of man to such an extent that he no longer makes the egoistical
> distinction between himself and the person of others, but takes as
> much interest in the sufferings of other individuals as in his own,
> and thus is not only benevolent and charitable in the highest degree,
> but even ready to sacrifice his own individuality whenever several
> others can be saved thereby, then it follows automatically that such a
> man, recognizing in all beings his own true and innermost self, must
> also regard the endless suffering of all that lives as his own, and thus
> take upon himself the pain of the whole world.[12]

Here we have a transcendence of sorts, in which one sees things in the truest possible way. Schopenhauer characterizes this transformation as a "transition from virtue to *asceticism.*"[13] Yet, as he goes on to point out, this asceticism is "here for the first time expressed in abstract terms and free from everything mythical, as *denial of the will-to-live.*"[14] Here the eastern influence on Schopenhauer is particularly evident, for he thinks that the demands of the body can be silenced only by ignoring them: "True salvation, deliverance from life and suffering, cannot even be imagined without complete denial of life."[15] Again, one is reminded of the wisdom of Silenus, for Schopenhauer is in effect giving a "salvation" that literally leads to death. But here Schopenhauer is not talking about suicide, which he takes to be "a phenomenon of the will's strong affirmation."[16] Instead, he is talking about a carefully considered decision—one based on *knowledge*—that is the only true way of salvation. As chilling an outlook on life as this is, Schopenhauer thinks that at least it avoids the error of optimism, which is "not only a false but also pernicious doctrine, for it presents life as a desirable state and man's happiness as its aim and object."[17] Once the veil of *maya* is lifted, optimism becomes simply untenable, and death is seen as the truly desirable state.

There is actually one other way in which a kind of salvation takes place—but it is only a temporary salvation. It is through art. Schopenhauer theorizes that there is a particular kind of awareness or consciousness that is aesthetic in nature. Normally, consciousness is aware of particulars in the world. Yet art directs our attention away from particulars to the abstract. Schopenhauer is clearly following a Kantian conception of appropriate artistic contemplation as being disinterested and allowing the art object "just to be." In other words, we relate to the object being contemplated in a very different way:

> We relinquish the ordinary way of considering things, and cease to follow under the guidance of the forms of the principle of sufficient reason merely their relations to one another, whose final goal is always the relation to our own will. Thus we no longer consider the where, the when, the why, and the whither in things, but simply and solely the *what*. Further, we do not let abstract thought, the concepts of reason, take possession of our consciousness, but, instead of all this, devote the whole power of our mind to perception, sink ourselves completely therein, and let our whole consciousness be filled by the calm contemplation of the natural object actually present. . . . We *lose* ourselves entirely in this object, to use a pregnant expression; in other words, we forget our individuality, our will, and continue to exist only as pure subject.[18]

Our usual way of perceiving things is by submitting everything to the categories of the mind for inspection. We want to make sense of what we perceive, which is what the will drives us to do. But, in contemplating art, we are actually able to "lose" ourselves and be taken over by the object itself. We become one with the object contemplated. This requires that we relate to the object without "personal participation," which is to say that we remain detached from ourselves:[19] "At the moment when, torn from the will, we have given ourselves up to pure, will-less knowing, we have stepped into another world, so to speak, where everything that moves our will, and thus violently agitates us, no longer exists. . . . Happiness and unhappiness have vanished; we are no longer the individual; that is forgotten; we are only pure subject of knowledge."[20] While this sort of salvation is short-lived—and Schopenhauer goes on to remind us that, once it is over, "we are again abandoned to all our woe"—it does provide a kind of momentary release from the will and from the anxiety and suffering that are for Schopenhauer the hallmarks of human existence. So it is truly a kind of salvation, albeit temporary. All of this is particularly true in experiencing the sublime, in which we both have pleasurable sensations yet also sensations of "our own nothingness."[21]

Of all the poetic arts, Schopenhauer ranks tragedy as supreme. What tragedy teaches us is "the terrible side of life." We come to see "the unspeakable pain, the wretchedness and misery of mankind, the scornful mastery of chance." But it also has a kind of salvific effect, for "the *motives* that were previously so powerful now lose their force."[22] The veil of *maya* is lifted, and we realize that our motives are simply those of the will—rather than our "own." Schopenhauer is careful to distinguish "true" tragedies from Christian ones, since the latter cannot do any more than depict heroism in the face of tragedy brought on by the hero's own sinfulness. In contrast, "the true sense of the tragedy is the deeper insight that what the hero atones for is not his particular sins, but original sin, in other words, the guilt of existence itself."[23] What tragedy teaches us is both the realty of the human condition and that renunciation of willing is ultimately the only way of dealing with that condition.

Even though tragedy is the highest of the poetic arts, Schopenhauer takes the view—one very common among German Romantics—that music is the highest art of all. Here he has in mind *absolute Musik,* or music without words. Precisely because such music is fully abstract, Schopenhauer thinks it is capable of revealing the highest truth—which means that it is likewise above words in terms of sheer power of expression. Music reveals the "thing in itself," which of course for Schopenhauer is the will. Music expresses the will in a way that is utterly unmediated by ideas or conceptions. So music is *pure* expression. Even though what music expresses is unpleasant, music itself "remains pleasant even in its most painful chords . . . even in the most sorrowful melodies."[24] Again, music is like tragedy in that it reveals the truth regarding the will, and that revelation has its own salvific power.

With even this cursory overview of Schopenhauer in mind, it should become amply clear just how much Schopenhauer influences both Nietzsche and Wagner. For his need for redemption becomes theirs, and even their way of obtaining salvation owes a debt to him.

The Price We Are Paying for Schopenhauer

Wagner had already discovered Schopenhauer by 1854, and Nietzsche discovered him eleven years later. Both were swept off their feet. Though Nietzsche would later claim that *Schopenhauer as Educator* was really about himself,[25] the text certainly reads as an enthusiastic encomium to Schopenhauer. Nietzsche chanced upon *The World as Will and Representation* [Die Welt als Wille und Vorstellung] in a secondhand bookshop and was immediately enthralled. He describes his reading of it as follows: "Here every line shouted renunciation, negation, resignation, here I saw a mirror in which I caught sight of the world, life, and one's own mind in frightful grandeur" (*KGW* I/4, 60 [1]).[26] What is most remarkable about Nietzsche's discovery of Schopenhauer is that—for a brief time—he adopted an extreme asceticism and self-criticism. For two weeks, he allowed himself only four hours of sleep per night and spent his days lamenting his shortcomings. Writing to a friend, he lists "my Schopenhauer" as one of his three forms of recreation, the others being "Schumann's music" and "solitary walks." Interestingly enough, in that same letter Nietzsche goes on to indicate what kind of Christianity he is willing to accept:

> If Christianity means "Belief in an historical event or in an historical person," then I'll have nothing to do with Christianity. But if it means simply the need for redemption, then I can value it highly, and do not even object to its attempt to discipline philosophers, who are too few in comparison with the mass of those needing redemption though made of the same stuff—yes, even if all those who practice

> philosophy were to be followers of Schopenhauer! (*SL* 12–13; *KSB* 2:121–22)

We will return to Nietzsche's rejection of the historical claims of Christianity, but here it important to note Nietzsche's sympathy for "redemption." Having read Schopenhauer—and taken him seriously—Nietzsche thinks there is the need for redemption of some sort, even if not the Christian sort. It is this need for redemption that motivates *The Birth of Tragedy* (and it is likewise this need for redemption that he later repudiates).

As to Wagner, Nietzsche first discovers him through his friend Gustav Krug, who became an arch-proponent for the Wagnerian cause.[27] Initially, Nietzsche did not share Krug's enthusiasm, preferring more traditional music. But he eventually came under the piper's spell, particularly after hearing the overture to *Die Meistersinger*. One important link between Nietzsche and Wagner was their admiration of Schopenhauer. Nietzsche writes: "In Wagner, as in Schopenhauer, I like the ethical air, the Faustian odor, Cross, Death, Grave, and so on" (letter to Erwin Rohde, October 8, 1868; *SL* 33; *KSA* 2:322). Shortly thereafter, Nietzsche recounts a conversation between them: "I had a longish conversation with [Wagner] about Schopenhauer; you will understand how much I enjoyed hearing him speak of Schopenhauer with indescribable warmth, what he owed him, how he is the only philosopher who has understood the essence of music" (letter to Erwin Rohde, November 9, 1868; *SL* 39; *KSB* 2:340–41). Even more enthusiastically, Nietzsche exclaims: "For me, all that is best and most beautiful is associated with the names Schopenhauer and Wagner" (letter to Carl von Gersdorff, March 11, 1870; *SL* 65; *KSB* 3:105).

It is the combination of Schopenhauer with Wagner that produces the backdrop for *The Birth of Tragedy*. As Nietzsche puts it, "I have made an alliance with Wagner. You cannot imagine how close we are now and how our plans coincide" (letter to Erwin Rohde, January [28], 1872; *SL* 92; *KSB* 3:279). And that feeling was mutual: Wagner writes to Nietzsche saying, "strictly speaking, you are the only real gain that life has brought me, and second only to my wife in that respect."[28] Although Nietzsche clearly brews his own magical elixir in *The Birth of Tragedy*, it is remarkable how much of Schopenhauer's philosophy Nietzsche appropriates. First, Nietzsche takes over Schopenhauer's basic metaphysical framework—the will, the *principium individuationis*, the idea that life is essentially suffering. Second, Nietzsche likewise believes that tragedy teaches us the true nature of life and that music is somehow salvific. But Nietzsche also begins the text—the full title of which is *The Birth of Tragedy out of the Spirit of Music*—with a "Foreword to Richard Wagner." So Wagner is a key element too.

Essentially, the "plot" of the text is that the ancient sense of Greek tragedy has been lost—through becoming "less tragic" in the hands of Euripides and Socrates—and needs to be regained.[29] Nietzsche celebrates the god Dionysus, whose wild festivals served to bring about "the tearing-apart of the *principium individuationis*" (*BT* 2; *KSA* 1:33). Yet he likewise recognizes the existence of the Apollonian principle, that which gives the wild, unbridled Dionysian principle order and clarity and serves as the *principium individuationis*. While Nietzsche recognizes the need for both the Apollonian and Dionysian in art, the overpowering of the Dionysian by the Apollonian has meant that the ancient Greeks eventually lost contact with the truth of their existence—viz., that life is truly tragic. In place of tragedy is put the optimism of Socrates' dialectic.

In an important sense, Nietzsche is trying to break from the pessimism of Schopenhauer, though this escape proves problematic (as most escapes do). On the one hand, he wants to recognize just as grim a human reality as does Schopenhauer. He is in no way willing to attenuate the description of the bleakness of the human condition. On the other hand, he seeks through tragedy what he terms "metaphysical solace." This is "the solace that in the ground of things, and despite all changing appearances, life is indestructibly mighty and pleasurable" (*BT* 7; *KSA* 1:56). As Nietzsche says more than once in the text (and in his later preface), the principal message of *The Birth of Tragedy* is that "only as an aesthetic phenomenon do existence and the world appear justified; which means that tragic myth in particular must convince us that even the ugly and disharmonious is an artistic game which the Will, in the eternal fullness of its delight, plays with itself" (*BT* 24; *KSA* 1:152). So, in Nietzsche's view, the world is *not* justified by itself; rather it needs a kind of "redemption" of the world by way of art. Nietzsche makes it clear that it is Richard Wagner who is to carry on this Dionysian "task." With reference to Wagner's own comments on the role of music, Nietzsche says that civilization is "absorbed, elevated, and taken up [*aufgehoben*] by music, just as lamplight is superceded by the light of day" (*BT* 7; *KSA* 1:55–56).

Yet one of the crucial questions concerning *The Birth of Tragedy* concerns the extent to which it reflects Schopenhauer's pessimism. And this question turns out to be far more problematic than one might expect. Kaufmann argues that "Nietzsche discovers in Greek art a bulwark against Schopenhauer's pessimism. . . . One can face the terrors of history and nature with unbroken courage and say Yes to life." Yet Young is clearly right in contending—*pace* Kaufmann—that Nietzsche's "solution" is truly "a flight from, a 'denial' of human life."[30] What complicates this is not merely the meaning of the term "pessimism" (again, considerably less obvious than it might seem), but also what Nietzsche later says in his preface to the text that he adds in 1886, what he says in *Ecce Homo,* and his various comments from the *Nachlass.* What emerges is a complicated assessment of the text. Yet we must follow these complications, for they are instructive as to the extent Nietzsche remains indebted to Schopenhauer—and, indirectly, to Wagner.

If we turn to *Ecce Homo*—in which Nietzsche is trying to create a picture of himself that is often more what he *hopes to be* than truly is—we discover him saying "the Greeks got over their pessimism. . . . Precisely their tragedies prove that the Greeks were *not* pessimists: Schopenhauer went wrong at this point, as he went wrong everywhere" (*EH* "Books" BT 1; *KSA* 6:309). Yet this idea that Schopenhauer got all sorts of things wrong already appears in a note from 1880 or 1881: "When I lauded Schopenhauer as my educator, I had forgotten that for a long time not one of his dogmas had resisted my misgivings; but it troubled me little how often I had underlined his sentences with 'imperfectly proven,' or 'undemonstrable,' or 'over-stated'" (*KSA* 9:10 [B31]). Given that Nietzsche never published this note, it cannot be read with the same intent (i.e., establishing a break with Schopenhauer, except perhaps in Nietzsche's own mind). Moreover, it is not insignificant that Nietzsche says that he has had these misgivings for a "long time."

Using Young's own criterion for pessimism, it is not at all clear that the Greeks were pessimists (i.e., that they used art as an escape). But it *is* clear that Nietzsche was, at least at the time of *The Birth of Tragedy.* While one might point to the statement that "the cadaverous perfume sticks to only a few formulas" in the text (*EH* "Books" BT 1; *KSA* 6:310), what Nietzsche says in the preface is absolutely damning. With dripping sarcasm, Nietzsche addresses *himself:*

> But, Sir, if *your* book is not Romanticism, what on earth is it? . . . Just listen, Mr Pessimist and Deifier of Art. . . . Is not your pessimist's book itself a piece of anti-Graecism and Romanticism [?] . . . No, three times no, you young Romantics; it should *not* be necessary! But it is very probable that it will *end* like this, that *you* will end like this, namely "comforted" . . . "metaphysically comforted" . . . as Romantics end, namely as *Christians*. (*BT* P 7; *KSA* 1:21–22)

Nietzsche clearly recognizes himself as being a pessimist at the time of *The Birth of Tragedy*. Moreover, he further characterizes the text as representing the "true Romantic's confession of 1830 beneath the mask of pessimism of 1850, behind which one can hear the opening bars of the usual Romantic finale" (ibid.). The term "Romantic" for him is just another name for being a pessimist, as is Christianity. For Romantics and Christians seek "comfort," as mediated by stories of salvation. Nietzsche connects "*Romantic pessimism*" with "Schopenhauer's philosophy of the will or Wagner's music" (*GS* 370; *KSA* 3:622). It is from *this* sort of pessimism that Nietzsche wishes to escape.

However, Nietzsche goes on to insist that there is a *different* kind of pessimism, which he identifies as "*Dionysian* pessimism." It is this pessimism that Nietzsche wants to affirm—one that fully recognizes that life is full of suffering and is inexplicable, and yet affirms life with the highest possible affirmation. In a note from 1887, Nietzsche indicates that already in 1876 he realized that he had "*compromised*" by going along with both Schopenhauer and Wagner. Even then he recognized that his move away from Schopenhauer was "toward a *justification of life*, even at its most terrible, ambiguous, and mendacious; for this I had the formula '*Dionysian'*" (*WP* 1005; *KSA* 12:9 [42]). Although Young thinks that "what is common to both Schopenhauer and Nietzsche is romanticism, 'romantic pessimism'" (presumably, which would require some kind of "comfort"), it strikes me that there is a significant difference between Schopenhauer and Nietzsche.[31] Theoretically, there is clearly a difference, for one kind of pessimism looks for solace and the other does not. Although Nietzsche puts the following in the form of a question, it is clear that the answer is "no": "Is pessimism *necessarily* a sign of decline, decay, malformation, of tired and debilitated instincts?" (*BT* P 1; *KSA* 1:12). This sort of pessimism is in effect another name for decadence. But Nietzsche goes on to ask: "Is there a pessimism of *strength*?" Clearly, he thinks there is. Yet, more important, Nietzsche is clearly trying to *live* the life of the Dionysian pessimist, rather than the Romantic pessimist. So, when Nietzsche talks about a *"justification of life,"* he does *not* have in mind a kind of justification by way of appeal to *something else,* the kind of "justification" of life we considered in the previous chapter, in which one must appeal to an "in order to" or a "because" to justify life. Rather, it is a justification of life in which *life is its own justification.*

Of course, putting this forth as a philosophical doctrine is relatively easy. *Living* it is another matter. Whether Nietzsche succeeds in his quest to live out this doctrine (for it is indeed a doctrine, one central to his Dionysian faith) is a question to which we shall return in the last chapter.

The Redemption of Parsifal

Already in *Richard Wagner in Bayreuth* there is an implied criticism. Nietzsche criticizes other composers—though not Wagner—for pandering to the public. However, given Wagner's almost insatiable need for adulation (which he was indeed receiving), Nietzsche's comments can be read as a warning, if not already a mild critique. But it was with *Human, All Too Human* that the serious attack begins. Nietzsche notes the irony of his having sent copies of the text to Wagner, only to receive from Wagner a copy of *Parsifal* inscribed "for his dear friend, Friedrich Nietzsche, Richard Wagner, Church Councilor" (*EH* "Books" HH 5; *KSA* 6:327). Nietzsche likens the crossing of the books to the crossing of two swords.

What exactly had Nietzsche said that was so damning? In a section that Nietzsche titles "Wagner as a Danger" in *Nietzsche contra Wagner,* Nietzsche accuses Wagner of leading the listener to swimming. In contrast, "in older music, what one had to do in the dainty, or solemn, or fiery back and forth, quicker and slower, was something quite different, namely, to *dance*" (*NCW* "Wagner as a Danger" 1; *KSA* 6:422). In effect, Nietzsche charges Wagner with having lost all sense of proportion in his music and thus producing "non-music." Or, as he goes on to say, with Wagner we have "*chaos* instead of rhythm." Given the importance of rhythm—literal *and* metaphorical—in Nietzsche, one could hardly imagine a stronger criticism. For Wagner is out of step with music and that means being out of step with life. Although Nietzsche is not using the term "decadence" at this point (1878) with much frequency, the charge here is really one of decadence. But it is in the preface to that work (also from 1886) in which Nietzsche is truly blunt: "At that time [Nietzsche later identifies this as the summer of 1876] it was indeed high time *to say farewell*. . . . Richard Wagner, seemingly the all-conquering, actually a decaying, despairing romantic, suddenly sank down helpless and shattered before the Christian cross" (*HH* II P 3; *KSA* 2:372). In line with his usage of the term in 1888, it is not surprising that Nietzsche replaces "romantic" with "decadent" when quoting the passage above in *Nietzsche contra Wagner.* Nor is it surprising that, in *The Gay Science,* Nietzsche talks about Wagner in terms he typically uses to describe decadents: "Here is a musician who, more than any other musician, is master at finding the tones from the realm of suffering, dejected, tormented souls. . . . he knows how the soul wearily drags itself along when it can no longer leap and fly, nor even walk" (*GS* 87; *KSA* 3:445).

Looking back at the time of *The Gay Science* (1882), Nietzsche realizes that he had made a terrible mistake. Although he took "Wagner's music as the expression of the Dionysian power of the soul" (*NCW* "We Antipodes"; *KSA* 6:425),[32] he now realizes that he had misunderstood both Schopenhauer and Wagner because he had read *himself* into them. It is at this point that Nietzsche makes a crucial distinction, one that he should have made as far back as *The Birth of Tragedy:*

> Every art, every philosophy, may be considered a remedy and aid [*Heil- und Hülfsmittel*] in the service of either growing or declining life: it always presupposes suffering and sufferers. But there are two kinds of sufferers: first, those who suffer from the *overfullness* of life and want a Dionysian art as well as a tragic insight and outlook on life—and then those who suffer from the *impoverishment* of life and demand of art and philosophy, calm, stillness, smooth seas, or, on the other hand, frenzy, convulsion, and anesthesia. Revenge against life itself—the most voluptuous kind of frenzy for those so impoverished! (ibid.)

The Nietzsche of *The Birth of Tragedy* is some sort of mixture of these two types of "sufferers," and probably more like the second than the first. Although Nietzsche uses the term "Dionysian" throughout his corpus, its meaning changes over time in subtle but important ways. Whereas the Dionysian in *The Birth of Tragedy* is still connected to "metaphysical comfort" (which would be more or less in the second category listed above), the later Dionysian has a *truly* tragic "outlook on life" and does not seek revenge on life either through calm or convulsion. It is only with the prefaces of 1886—a truly pivotal year for Nietzsche—that he comes to realize his own earlier self-deception. But it is also only later that Nietzsche comes to realize that some "remedies" turn out to be harmful. Certainly the "remedy" Nietzsche initially proposes—metaphysical solace—is the choice of those who suffer from impoverishment of life.

Up until 1888, we have only scattered criticisms of Wagner. But suddenly everything changes. One can hardly chalk that change up to Nietzsche's having a new revelation regarding Wagner, for most of the charges of *The Case of Wagner* have been anticipated, even if not necessarily spelled out in full. More likely, the newly found ferocity has everything to do with Nietzsche's own development.[33] If there is anything remarkable that takes place in 1888, it is that Nietzsche realizes that, in order to truly combat the decadence within him, he must turn his decadence to good use. Decadence affords him a certain perspective—that is, the perspective of one who is ill—and understanding his own illness enables him to pass beyond decadence. Or at least that is Nietzsche's hope. Having seen that he is decadent and that his decadence is partially caused by Wagner, an important aspect of Nietzsche's *askêsis* for resisting decadence is waging war with Wagner. And wage war he does—with the aid of Bizet. Later on we shall turn to how Bizet provides Nietzsche with a positive model for music, but here it is helpful to contrast Bizet with Wagner to see where Wagner goes wrong.

If Wagner is the composer of decadence—the Romantic pessimist—then Bizet is the composer of Dionysian pessimism. Rather than "Senta-Sentimentality,"[34] Bizet gives us "love as *fatum,* as fatality, cynical, innocent, cruel." All of this is best summed up by Don José's cry: "*Yes. I have killed her, I—my adored Carmen*" (*CW* 2; *KSA* 6:15). There is no "redemption" in Bizet; instead, there is simply the statement of brute fact. Don José kills Carmen, and the opera ends tragically. Yet, despite the brutality of the message of fate, the music is *cheerful:* "Another sensuality, another sensibility speaks here, another cheerfulness. This music is cheerful, but not in a French or German way. . . . fate hangs over it; its happiness is brief, sudden, without pardon. I envy Bizet for having had the courage for this sensibility which had hitherto had no language in the cultivated music of Europe" (*CW* 2; *KSA* 6:15). So Bizet is able to come to terms with suffering, death, and loss—with cheerfulness. There is no attempt to "redeem" that loss by giving us a "happy ending." Yet there is a kind of cheer in the midst of suffering. It is this kind of "cheerful pessimism" that is so far away from the gloomy pessimism of Schopenhauer, and it is this kind of art that Nietzsche had called for in his preface to *The Gay Science:* "If we convalescents still need art, it is *another kind* of art—a mocking, light, fleeting, divinely untroubled, divinely artificial art that, like a bright flame, blazes into an unclouded sky! Above all: an art for artists, only for artists! In addition we will know better what is first and foremost needed *for that:* cheerfulness—any cheerfulness, my friends!" (*GS* P 4; *KSA* 3:351). Of course, there is a sense in which *Carmen* "redeems." Nietzsche says "this work, too, redeems; Wagner is not the only 'redeemer.'" Yet it is important to note *how* its "redemption" takes place: "With this work one takes leave of the *damp* north, of all the steam of the Wagnerian ideal. Even the plot spells redemption from that" (*CW* 2; *KSA* 6:16). So Bizet gives us the redemption from the *need* for redemption.

Wagner, in contrast, cannot merely put forth the human condition and *celebrate* it; he has to *fix* it by way of redemption. Nietzsche makes it clear that this pattern of redemption is to be found in *Der fliegende Holländer, Tannhäuser, Die Meistersinger,* and *Der Ring.* Moreover, he maintains that these are all *Christian* operas, in one way or another. So, for example, *Tannhäuser* "represents the Christian concept, 'you ought to and must *believe*'" (*CW* 3; *KSA* 6:17). But it is *Parsifal* that most spectacularly represents Wagner's capitulation not just to redemption but, more specifically, to Christian redemption. Of course, the "Christianity" of *Parsifal* has long been disputed, beginning already at the time of its premiere. What is remarkable is that Wagner comes in for criticism from all sides. On the one hand, many have interpreted *Parsifal* as not really Christian at all. Writing not long after its premiere, Houston Stewart Chamberlain claimed: "It is superfluous . . . to state that *Parsifal* is not the glorification of religious dogma. There is no more Christianity in *Parsifal* than there is paganism in the *Ring* or *Tristan.*"[35] More recently, Carl Dahlhaus has put that view as follows: "Wagner's faith was philosophical, not religious, a metaphysic of compassion and renunciation, deriving its essential elements from Schopenhauer's *World as Will and Idea* and—via Schopenhauer—from Buddhism. Wagner found these elements also present in Christianity, and to that extent he was a Christian."[36] Dahlhaus's is probably the reigning view today. But, on the other hand, there have long been listeners—like Nietzsche—who saw the work as profoundly Christian in nature. Not surprisingly, such interpreters have criticized Wagner for his strange appropriation of Christian rites and symbols. So, for example, the blood from the holy Grail changes into wine, a kind of Eucharist in reverse. Likewise, the main character Parsifal—in some ways a Christ figure—needs *himself* to be redeemed, clearly a departure from Christian orthodoxy.

What complicates any account of *Parsifal* is that, to some extent, *all* of the above views capture certain aspects of it, without exhausting its complexity. So Chamberlain is right that *Parsifal* does not really champion religious dogma, any more than other operas champion paganism. And yet one must admit that, to the extent that many of Wagner's other operas are deeply influenced by pagan myths, so *Parsifal* is deeply influenced by Christianity. But it is hardly an orthodox Christianity.[37] Dahlhaus charges anyone who criticizes Wagner for being "an unscrupulous theatromane who dissipated Christianity's myths and symbols" as simply being a "fundamentalist." Indeed, he simply points out that, by the nineteenth century, the dominant view of Christianity was a "myth that was once believed as literal truth."[38] Interestingly enough, some contemporaries of Wagner found *Parsifal* problematic precisely for being too *old-fashioned* with its "Christianity abounding in miracles" and his harkening back to a time that "many centuries separate from our age of historic and philologic research."[39] Certainly Wagner felt free to use whatever symbols and rites of Christianity that suited his purposes. After all, this is exactly what he had earlier said that art was supposed to do in *Religion and Art:*

> One might say that where Religion becomes artificial, it is reserved for Art to save the spirit of religion by recognizing the figurative value of the mythic symbols which the former would have us believe in their literal sense, and revealing their deep and hidden truth through an ideal presentation. Whilst the priest stakes everything on the religious allegories being accepted as matters of fact, the artist has no concern at all with such a thing, since he freely and openly gives out his work as his own invention.[40]

Given the ways in which Christian doctrines were being treated in late-nineteenth-century Germany (i.e., they had become "artificial"), it is hardly surprising that Wagner felt himself at liberty to appropriate Christian rites and symbols for his own purposes.

But Wagner was doing more than appropriation. For his appropriation has the effect of reversing the logic of Christianity. Cosima Wagner writes that Wagner interpreted the changing of blood in such a way that it "permits us to turn our gaze refreshed back to earth, whereas the conversion of wine into blood draws us away from the earth."[41] She makes this point even more sharply in a letter: "*Parsifal* has nothing in common with any Church, nor indeed with any dogma, for here the blood turns into bread and wine, whereas it is the other way around in the Eucharist. *Parsifal* picks up where the Gospels leave off."[42] Or, as Slavoj Žižek puts it:

> [Wagner] interprets Christ's death and the Good Friday miracle as a pagan myth of seasonal death and rebirth. This gesture is profoundly anti-Christian: by breaking with the pagan notion of cosmic Justice and Balance, Christianity also breaks with the pagan notion of the circular death and rebirth of the Divinity—Christ's death is *not* the same as the seasonal death of the pagan god; rather, it designates a *rupture* with the circular movement of death and rebirth.[43]

Of course, just how "Christian" *Parsifal* truly is remains an open question. Perhaps Cosima Wagner is right that *Parsifal* is all about *reversing* the logic of Christianity. However, that interpretation is hardly the only one possible, nor even the reigning interpretation. Whether Wagner *really* became a Christian in some sense is open to question, though he does speak to Nietzsche of "the joy he felt in receiving Christian communion" and, as noted, he identifies himself as "church councilor" [*Kirchenrath*] in his inscription to the copy of *Parsifal* he sent to Nietzsche.[44] Nietzsche's sister's gloss on what happens to Wagner is particularly interesting:

> My brother's amazement may, therefore, be imagined when Wagner began to speak of his religious feelings and experiences in a tone of the deepest repentance, and to confess a leaning towards the Christian dogmas. For example, he spoke of the delight he took in the celebration of the Holy Communion. . . . [My brother] considered it quite impossible that Wagner, the avowed atheist, should suddenly have become a naive and pious believer. He could only regard Wagner's alleged sudden change of heart, as having been prompted by a desire to stand well with the Christian rulers of Germany and thus further the material success of the Bayreuth undertaking. My brother was confirmed in this belief by a remark Wagner made when referring to the unsatisfactory attendance at the first Festival; almost angrily, he

exclaimed: "The Germans do not wish to hear anything about gods and goddesses at present, they are only interested in something of a religious character."[45]

Quite apart from the question of the reliability of the source for these comments, the comments themselves pose a significant complication. On the one hand, it seems as if Wagner truly has a "change of heart" toward Christianity, given what he says about taking communion and his avowal of (or at least a "leaning towards") Christian dogmas. That would seem to indicate that Wagner had undergone some sort of change in his relation to Christianity. On the other hand, Nietzsche interprets Wagner's move as not truly sincere—as a kind of "selling out" to what "sold" well at Bayreuth. So which is it? While it could be one *or* the other, it would seem that the more likely interpretation is that it is some combination of both. But, at the end of the day, for Nietzsche it would not much matter which interpretation was correct. For Wagner had effectively "sold out" on either read. Thus, he sums up *Parsifal* as follows: "*Rome's faith without words*" (*BGE* 256; *KSA* 5:204).

In any case, the Wagner that he once loved was gone. Nietzsche writes: "I only loved the Wagner that I knew, that is, an upright atheist and immoralist, who had invented the character Siegfried, a very free man" (*KSA* 11:34 [205]). In its place was a Wagner who had fallen before the cross. But, of course, it is the theme of redemption—intertwined with compassion—that truly galls Nietzsche. Whether that redemption and compassion goes under the name "Christian" or "pagan" really makes no difference to Nietzsche. In taking up these themes, Wagner is in one sense a follower of Schopenhauer, and that is already enough for Nietzsche's charges against him. Yet the problem is more serious: Wagner trades Schopenhauer's pessimism for a Socratic optimism in which true redemption takes place and all is well. Nietzsche sees this as simply metaphysical comfort.

Just a précis of *Parsifal* makes it clear why Nietzsche exclaims: "Incredible! Wagner had become pious" (*EH* "Books" HH 5; *KSA* 6:327).[46] Act 1 opens with the wounded Amfortas (who has been pierced by the sword that pierced Jesus' side) living at Monsalvat [Mount of Salvation] with the knights of the Holy Grail, from which is poured blood that becomes wine. For his cure, Amfortas awaits "the one appointed to me: 'enlightened through compassion [*Mitleid*],'" "the innocent fool" [*reine Tor*]. Parsifal [from "*fal parsi*," innocent fool] arrives on the scene and proves his innocence by killing a swan without remorse. Gurnemanz—who represents the "good man"—tries to explain the gravity of Parsifal's deed, but Parsifal fails to understand. Nor does he understand when he shares in the *Liebesmahl*, at which the youths sing:

> As once His blood flowed
> with countless pains
> for the sinful world—
> now with joyful heart
> let my blood be shed
> for the great Redeemer.
> His body, that He gave to purge our sin,
> lives in us through His death.

Act 1 closes with Gurnemanz sending Parsifal on his way.

Up until act 2, Parsifal knows neither his name nor lineage. He is truly innocent, due to his mother's having protected him from the story of his father (Lohengrin). Under the command of the evil Klingsor, Kundry attempts to seduce Parsifal. But her kiss only serves to fill him with compassion for Amfortas's suffering. Klingsor hurls the famous spear (that pierced Christ's side) at Parsifal, but he grabs it and with it makes the sign of the cross. Finally, in act 3, Parsifal returns to Monsalvat, having gone through "the path of suffering." He baptizes Kundry, in a move that both continues the Buddhist metamorphoses that she undergoes throughout the opera and now—strangely—turns her into a Christian. After healing Amfortas with the spear, the chorus sings, "Höchsten Heiles Wunder! Erlösung dem Erlöser!" [Highest holy wonder! Redemption of the Redeemer!].

Although Nietzsche would have recognized this concoction as a strange mixture of Schopenhauer, Buddhism, and Christianity, its primary emphasis on *Mitleid* and *Erlösung* marks it as Christian for him. The twist at the end—redemption *of* the redeemer—can be read as strange if Parsifal is taken as an ersatz Christ figure.[47] But, if one interprets Parsifal as a human being in need of redemption, then the twist makes sense: Parsifal is at once redeemed and becomes the possibility condition for the redemption of Amfortas.[48] In any case, upon receiving a copy of the score, Nietzsche complains that it partakes of the "spirit of the Counter-Reformation" and "is all too Christian, time-bound, limited;

sheer fantastic psychology; no flesh and much too much blood (especially too much blood at the Holy Communion)" (letter to Reinhart von Seydlitz, January 4, 1878; *SL* 166; *KSB* 5:300). For Nietzsche, whether Wagner had actually become a Christian or merely appropriated its rites and symbols made no difference whatsoever. Even if Wagner's versions of *Mitleid* and *Erlösung* are only partially Christian, he has still "knelt at the cross." And he ends with Socratic optimism!

What truly irritates Nietzsche is how successful Wagner is in his seduction.[49] Although there is no doubt some envy in the midst of that worry, Nietzsche thinks that Wagner has inflicted his decadence upon all of his disciples. Wagner has fostered "an ever growing indifference against all severe, noble, conscientious training in the service of art." But Nietzsche extends this critique even further:

> Thus Wagner is a seducer on a large scale. There is nothing weary, nothing decrepit, nothing fatal and hostile to life in matters of the spirit that his art does not secretly safeguard; it is the blackest obscurantism that he conceals in the ideal's shrouds of light. He flatters every nihilistic (Buddhistic) instinct and disguises it in music; he flatters everything Christian, every religious expression of decadence. Open your ears: everything that ever grew on the soil of *impoverished* life, all of the counterfeiting of transcendence and beyond, has found its most sublime advocate in Wagner's art.

So Nietzsche concludes: "One pays heavily for being one of Wagner's disciples" (*CW* Postscript; *KSA* 6:42–43).

That Nietzsche has a similar love-hate relation to Wagner as he does to Socrates is even clearer in this case. On the one hand, we have the withering critique of *The Case of Wagner* and *Nietzsche contra Wagner*. Although he writes "it is not merely pure malice when I praise Bizet in this essay at the expense of Wagner" (*CW* P; *KSA* 6:11), one can only conclude from that admission that it is at least *partly* out of malice.[50] On the other hand, Nietzsche admits: "In the art of seduction, *Parsifal* will always retain its rank—as *the stroke of genius* in seduction.—I admire this work; I wish I had written it myself" (*CW* 2nd Postscript; *KSA* 6:43).[51] Moreover, he realizes his own "closeness" to Wagner: "Perhaps nobody was more dangerously attached to—grown together with—Wagnerizing; nobody tried harder to resist; nobody was happier to be rid of it" (*CW* P; *KSA* 6:11).[52]

But, at the end of the day, the question remains: from what does all of this warring against Wagner arise? That question is significant because of a contrast that Nietzsche himself draws: "The desire for *destruction*, for change and for becoming can be the expression of an overflowing energy pregnant with the future (my term for this is, as is known, 'Dionysian'); but it can also be the hatred of the ill-constituted, deprived, and under-priviledged one who destroys and *must* destroy because what exists, indeed all existence, all being, outrages and provokes him" (*GS* 370; *KSA* 3:621–22).

As we have noted, Nietzsche feels a need to break with Wagner as part of resisting his own decadence. That would be Nietzsche's "Dionysian break." Yet does his break with Wagner have anything to do with Romantic pessimism? In other words, is there none of this Romantic pessimism that can be found in Nietzsche himself? It seems hard to think that Nietzsche does not take part in this pessimism. Indeed, his admission that he is like-wise a decadent is in effect a recognition of his complicity. But, then, isn't what he has said of Wagner *at least partially* true of *him*? So we can read *Nietzsche contra Wagner* as *Nietzsche contra Nietzsche*. Clearly, Nietzsche's anti-Wagner stance must be taken with a great degree of nuance. For Nietzsche clearly shares much with Wagner, even at the end. Nietzsche's move to distance himself from Wagner is surely motivated by his realiza-tion that they are so much alike. Just as his opposition to Socrates owes so much to their "closeness," so Nietzsche is far too close for his own comfort to Wagner. Moreover, Nietzsche gives us the same "formula" for getting over Wagnerian decadence as he did for Socratic decadence: "There is no way out, one must first become a Wagnerian" (*CW* P; *KSA* 6:12). The only question then is: since we know that Nietzsche becomes a Wagnerian, just how far does Nietzsche truly move *beyond* Wagner? It would seem that he remains much closer to Wagner than he would like to admit.

Yet Wagner turns out to be merely one of three principal figures of decadence. Having seen how close Nietzsche comes to Socrates and Wagner—so close that he must continually do battle with them—the further question to be asked is: how close does Nietzsche come to Paul?

SEVEN

Paul's Revenge

In Paul was embodied the opposite type to that of the "bringer of glad tidings": the genius in hatred, in the vision of hatred, in the inexorable logic of hatred! How much this dysangelist sacrificed to hatred! Above all, the Redeemer: he nailed him to his own cross. The life, the example, the doctrine, the death, the meaning and the right of the entire evangel—nothing remained once this hate-inspired counterfeiter realized what alone he could use. . . . he invented his own history of earliest Christianity.[1]

I f Nietzsche is right, then what we know as "Christianity" is ultimately an invention of Paul's. Ignoring the "glad tidings" preached by Jesus, he invented his own tidings—ones deeply rooted in his hatred, his lust for power, and (most important) his desire for revenge. Ultimately, Paul wants to take revenge upon not only the Jewish law but life itself by retelling the story of Jesus to suit his own purposes. Yet, if Nietzsche's read of Paul is correct, then Nietzsche turns out to be a "second Paul," whose kinship to Paul is actually constituted by their commonality. Of the three figures of decadence—Socrates, Wagner, and Paul—it is Paul who turns out to be the most important for Nietzsche. As Jacob Taubes puts it: "Who has determined the values of the Occident, in Nietzsche's own sense, more deeply than Paul? So he must be the most important man. Because what did Nietzsche want? The transvaluation of values. Well, so there we have someone who pulled it off! And on this point, Nietzsche is very envious too."[2]

Indeed, Nietzsche thinks that the course of history would have been quite different if only Paul had lost: "Epicurus would have won; every respectable spirit in the Roman Empire was an Epicurean. Then Paul appeared" (*AC* 58; *KSA* 6:246–47). One can't really argue on the basis of a counterfactual, of course, so Nietzsche can offer this only as speculation. While it is a reasonable enough speculation, one could also speculate that Stoicism would have won. In any case, the fact is that Paul won—and the course of history in the west was forever changed. But just how did Paul manage to pull that off?

The Genealogy of Christianity

We have already noted that Nietzsche's use of genealogy as a form of argument goes back to some of his earliest writings. Already in "On Truth and Lies in a Nonmoral Sense," Nietzsche uses genealogy to discredit the notion of truth, his argument being that "truth" is invented out of hubris. In chapter 2 we noted that Nietzsche thinks Christianity can be refuted simply by explaining "how the belief that there is a God could *arise* and how this belief acquired its weight and importance" (*D* 95; *KSA* 3:86). Nietzsche labels this "historical refutation," an argument based simply on exposing something's origins. But Foucault notes that Nietzsche uses the term *Ursprung* [origin] in two senses, and this has significant implications for the nature of genealogy.[3] On the one hand, it is used synonymously and interchangeably with other German terms for orgin: *Entstehung, Herkunft, Abkunft,* and *Geburt.* On the other hand, as early as *Human, All Too Human,* Nietzsche contrasts the "miraculous source" [*Wunder-Ursprung*] of metaphysics with "historical philosophy," in which one considers the complex origins of thought (*HH* I:1; *KSA* 2:23). As Nietzsche puts it: "Everything has become: there are *no eternal facts,* just as there are no absolute truths. Consequently what is needed from now on is *historical philosophizing,* and with it the virtue of modesty" (*HH* I:2; *KSA* 2:25).

In *On The Genealogy of Morality,* Nietzsche announces his project of considering the *"origins* [*Herkunft*] of our moral prejudices" (*GM* P 2; *KSA* 5:248). Nietzsche notes that he had first become interested in such a project upon reading Paul Rée's *The Origin of Moral Sensations.*[4] Yet it was not because he agrees with Rée's analyzes that he undertakes such a project, but rather because he finds Rée's analyses problematic in that they constitute a search for a pure *Ursprung* of morality. What Rée fails to understand is that morality has a complicated history with no one point of origin.[5] As Foucault points out, whereas the source for an *Ursprung* is for "the exact essence of things, their purest possibilities, and their carefully protected identities," the search for *Herkunft* stems from the recognition that things "have no essence, or that their essence was fabricated in a piecemeal fashion from alien forms."[6] But, of course, if our concepts and beliefs do not fall "ready-made" from the sky, then it is *also* the case that alternative genealogies are possible. Here we will consider Nietzsche's own genealogy regarding the origins of Christianity—viz., as constructed by Paul—but later we will turn to examine just how plausible those origins are. For one can always counter a genealogy with another genealogy.

Although Nietzsche's early and most important account of Paul's "invention of Christianity" occurs in *Daybreak,* those comments themselves need to be prefaced with a late note from the *Nachlass* that explains the "psychology" behind Paul:

> Toward a psychology of *Paul.*—The given fact is the death of Jesus. This has to be explained—That an explanation may be true or false has never entered the minds of such people as these: one day a sublime possibility comes into their heads: "this death *could* mean such and such"—and at once it *does* mean such and such! A hypothesis is proved true by the sublime impetus it imparts to its originator— "The proof of power": i.e., an idea is proved true by its effect—("by their fruits" as the Bible naively says); what inspires must be true. (*WP* 171; *KSA* 13:14 [57])

Nietzsche is making a twofold claim. On the one hand, he is claiming that Paul and his ilk were too simpleminded to realize that simply because a given interpretation can make an event "sublime" doesn't mean that it is true. Paul is able to "reinterpret" Christ's death and make the resurrection into a truth claim merely by making the claim. On the other hand, the "truth value" of that claim turns out to be justified precisely by its effects: over the past two millennia, the truth "Christ's death provides forgiveness for sins" has proven to be inspiring to millions, which in effect validates it. What is particularly important about this move (what Alain Badiou calls a "truth procedure")[7] is that it is precisely the move that Nietzsche himself wants to make, as we'll consider in more depth at the end of the chapter. Of course, as we'll also see, this account of Paul—that he is really not bright enough to know what he's doing—fails to square with Nietzsche's accounts of Paul in which he is attempting to abolish the law or pushing for power or taking revenge on life. All of these accounts make Paul out not to be a simpleton but a mastermind. And Nietzsche simply can't have it both ways.

But first to the story of Paul as narrated in *Daybreak,* in which Paul's move is motivated by his inability to fulfill the law. One can't help but read Nietzsche's story of Paul without being immediately reminded of Erik Erikson's *Young Man Luther*. For Erikson, we can best understand Martin Luther when we realize how obsessed he is with his sinfulness, his inability to live up to the morality laid down in the Bible, and the coming day of judgment. Luther himself writes: "From childhood on, I knew I had to turn pale and be terror-stricken when I heard the name of Christ; for I was taught only to perceive him as a strict and wrathful judge."[8] On Erikson's reading, Luther's discovery of Paul's notion of "justification by faith" in Romans 5 is as much a product of his biography as it is a theological advancement in Luther's understanding of Scripture. Although Erikson makes a number of references to Nietzsche, surprisingly he never makes the connection between Paul and Luther as being equally obsessed with their sinfulness. Yet Nietzsche does. He observes: "Luther may have felt a similar thing [to what Paul felt] when he wanted in the monastery to become the perfect man of the spiritual ideal" (*D* 68; *KSA* 3:66).[9] It is this very *personal* problem—this inability to live up to the ideal of the law—that drives Paul to reinterpret the crucifixion so as to take revenge upon the law. Or at least that is *one* of Nietzsche's accounts of Paul.

If we turn back to the early Christian context, it is not hard to understand why Nietzsche might interpret Paul as he does. First, things appeared not to have gone according to plan. Jesus was supposed to set up his kingdom on earth—which is what the disciples expected. Instead, he dies the ignoble death of crucifixion. How, then, can one "redeem" this story? Paul immediately sees this as his way to escape from the law, at least on Nietzsche's account. Nietzsche reads Paul as "the fanatical defender and chaperone of this God and his law," who "was constantly combating and on the watch for transgressors and doubters, harsh and malicious towards them and with the extremest inclination for punishment" (*D* 68; *KSA* 3:65). But then Paul comes to realize something startling about himself: the great defender of the law "*could* not fulfill the law": "Many things lay on his conscience—he hints at enmity, murder, sorcery, idolatry, uncleanliness, drunkenness and pleasure in debauch—and however much he tried to relieve this conscience, and even more his lust for domination, through the extremest fanaticism in revering and defending the law, there were moments when he said to himself: 'It is all vain! The torture of the unfulfilled law cannot be overcome'" (*D* 68; *KSA* 3:66).[10]

Nietzsche is certainly right that Paul is well aware of his inabilities to live up to the law. In Romans 7 Paul writes: "For I do not do the good I want, but the evil I do not want is what I do" (Rom. 7:19). He then goes on to exclaim, "Wretched man that I am! Who will rescue me from this body of death?" (Rom. 7:24). Moreover, Paul accuses the *law* of helping create the desire for sin: "If it had not been for the law, I would not have known sin. I would not have known what it is to covet if the law had not said 'You shall not covet.' But sin, seizing an opportunity in the commandment, produced in me all kinds of covetousness" (Rom. 7:7). So Paul is clearly frustrated with the law—with his inability to fulfill it and its very logic that contributes to one's stumbling.

It is this "perverse" logic to which Žižek calls our attention, a logic that Žižek argues long precedes Paul. It begins in the Garden of Eden, when God says: "You may freely eat of every tree of the garden; but of the tree of the knowledge of good and evil you shall not eat, for in that day that you eat of it you shall die" (Gen. 2:16–17). What *else* were they expected to do than go after the forbidden object? As Žižek puts it: "If it is prohibited to eat from the Tree of Knowledge in Paradise, why did God put it there in the first place? Is it not that this was a part of His perverse strategy first to seduce Adam and Eve into the fall, in order to save them? That is to say: should one not apply Paul's insight into how the prohibitive law creates sin to this very first prohibition also?"[11] While it seems far too much to say that God's strategy is to "seduce Adam and Eve into the fall, in order to save them," Žižek's point that the law has almost a kind of perversity to it seems hard to escape. The logic of forbidding is that of creating a temptation, which means that the law creates a kind of logic from which would seem impossible to escape. The more one tries to *keep* from doing a particular act, the more one acutely *wants* to do that act.

Yet Paul opens Romans 8 with a way around the law: "There is therefore now no condemnation for those who are in Christ Jesus. For the law of the Spirit of life in Christ Jesus has set you free from the law of sin and death" (Rom. 8:1–2). On Nietzsche's read, what happens on the road to Damascus is not that Paul has a vision of Jesus but that he has a vision of how to overcome the law:

> What essentially happened then is rather this: his *mind* suddenly became clear: "it is *unreasonable*," he says to himself, "to persecute precisely this Christ! For here is the way out, here is perfect revenge, here and nowhere else do I have and hold the *destroyer of the law*!" . . . Hitherto that shameful *death* had counted with him as the principal argument against the "Messiahdom" of which the followers of the

new teaching spoke: but what if it were *necessary* for the *abolition* of
the law!—The tremendous consequences of this notion, this solution
of the riddle, whirl before his eyes, all at once he is the happiest of
men. (*D* 68; *KSA* 3:66–67)

By way of the death of Jesus, Paul is able to take his revenge against
the law, which he has come to hate so much. Paul is able to make this move
because, in effect, he is the first theologian of Christianity.[12] Nietzsche
actually calls him the "first Christian." As the first Christian, he has an
almost blank palimpsest with which to work: "Consider with what degree
of freedom Paul treats, indeed almost juggles with, the problem of the
person of Jesus: someone who died, who was seen again after his death,
who was delivered over to death by the Jews—A mere 'motif': *he* then
wrote the music to it—A zero in the beginning" (*WP* 177; *KSA* 13:15
[108]). Nietzsche is clear that the God of Christianity is a sheer invention
of Paul's. In fact, he claims that *"deus, qualem Paulus creavit, dei negatio"*
[God, as Paul created him, is the negation of God] (*AC* 47; *KSA* 6:225).

Yet Nietzsche thinks that Paul has another—though closely related—
motive. Speaking of Paul's "extravagant lust for power" (*D* 68; *KSA* 3:66),
Nietzsche thinks that Paul wants the power of the ascetic priest. Although
Nietzsche does not develop that argument in *Daybreak,* it becomes clear
in *The Anti-Christ(ian):* "In Paul the priest wanted power once again—he
could use only concepts, doctrines, symbols with which one tyrannizes
masses and forms herds. What was the one thing that Mohammed later
borrowed from Christianity? Paul's invention, his means to priestly tyr-
anny, to herd formation: the faith in immortality—*that is, the doctrine of
the 'judgment'"* (*AC* 42; *KSA* 6:216–17).

Elsewhere Nietzsche claims that Paul brews up a concoction for the
"religiously excited masses" by way of "a sacrifice, a bloody phantasma-
goria which will stand up in competition with the images of the mystery
cults: God on the cross, blood-drinking, the *unio mystica* with the 'sacrifice'" (*WP* 167; *KSA* 13:11 [282]). Of course, as we saw in the previous
chapter, this is *exactly* the sort of thing that would appeal to Nietzsche.
Writing about Schopenhauer and Wagner, he says: "I like the ethical
air, the Faustian odor, Cross, Death, Grave, and so on" (letter to Erwin
Rohde, October 8, 1868; *SL* 33; *KSA* 2:322). But, according to Nietzsche,
tyrannizing the masses was not quite enough. Paul's lust for power was
so great that he effectively wanted to take God's place: "The 'God' whom

Paul invented, a god who 'ruins the wisdom of the world'[13] (in particular, philology and medicine, the two great adversaries to superstition), is in truth merely Paul's own resolute *determination* to do this: to give the name of 'God' to one's own will" (*AC* 47; *KSA* 6:225–26).

The world, of course, is that which has power. Paul, powerless Jew that he is in the midst of the mighty Roman Empire, can exert power only by *overturning* the wisdom of the world. Moreover, Paul's move is against *both* Roman and Jewish power: he claims that "the word of the cross" [*ho logos gar ho tou staurou*] confounds both the Jews who "demand signs" and the Greeks who "desire wisdom" (I Cor. 18:22).[14] Paul's logic is simple: what was once called foolishness is now called wisdom. He writes: "God's foolishness is wiser than human wisdom, and God's weakness is stronger than human strength" (I Cor. 1:25).

Here we have a prime example of what Nietzsche terms the "slave revolt." Although it is often thought that Nietzsche restricts this to morality, the revolt is more encompassing than that. For it has to do with power and with self-understanding.[15] Thus, Paul's move of putting down "worldly" wisdom by way of what he claims is heavenly wisdom is surely part and parcel of that revolt. We noted in chapter 5 that noble morality simply affirms itself, with the concept of "bad" being a negation of that which is valued. In place of the noble conception of good is put the slave's conception of "good" and "evil," which are *moral* conceptions. According to Nietzsche, "the slave revolt in morality begins when *ressentiment* itself becomes creative and gives birth to values" (*GM* I:10; *KSA* 5:270). At root, then, this move to assert power is actually connected to and *stems from* the desire for revenge. However, that revenge can only take place at the cost of eviscerating life itself. On Nietzsche's read, such is what Christianity has done ever since its inception by Paul.

Castrating Life

> The Church fights passion by cutting it out, in every sense; its practice, its "therapy" is *castration*. It never asks, "How does one spiritualize, beautify, deify a desire?"—its discipline has always emphasized eradication (eradication of sensuality, pride, the ambition to rule, coveteousness, vengefulness).—But ripping out the passions by the root means ripping out life by the root; the practice of the Church is *an enemy to life*. (*TI* V:1; *KSA* 6:83)

Instead of attempting to mold and shape the passions to prevent their "stupidity" (as Nietzsche puts it), Christianity simply responds with a stupidity of its own.[16] But that stupidity ends up going against life itself. The result is that Christianity is fundamentally a "No to everything on earth that represents the ascending tendency of life" (*AC* 24; *KSA* 6:192). Nietzsche thinks that denial of life is so fundamental to Christianity that it is the very motto on its escutcheon (*AC* 7; *KSA* 6:173). In practice, this means that Christianity (1) does battle against the instincts, (2) engages in—and is uniquely characterized by—pity [*Mitleid*] and love, and (3) preaches a message of redemption from suffering and sin.

In the sense that Christianity takes the passions to be bad, it is in effect a religious form of Platonism. Of course, since morality is inherently against nature (according to Nietzsche), any moral system is inherently against the instincts. Yet Christianity does this in a way that turns God into a vicious enemy. "By saying, 'God looks into the heart,'[17] it says no to the lowest and highest desires of life, and takes God to be *life's enemy*" (*TI* V:4; *KSA* 6:85). Thus, the Christian God ends up being "the deity of decadence," since God promotes precisely the decadent turning against life (*AC* 17; *KSA* 183). Christianity is not merely the religion of the weak, in the sense that it is a refuge for the weak (something to which one turns when one realizes one's weakness). It is also the religion that *makes one weak*, in that it encourages all that is decadent.

Yet Nietzsche is *not* simply against religion per se. He actually says things that are quite complimentary about Judaism, at least in its early form. Interestingly enough, Nietzsche thinks that "the Jews are the antithesis of all decadents" (*AC* 24; *KSA* 6:192), and he has high respect for the Old Testament. While he says "I have no love for the 'New Testament,'" he goes on to proclaim: "I take my hat off to the Old Testament! In it I find great human beings, a heroic landscape, and something most rare on earth, the incomparable naïveté of the *strong heart*" (*GM* III:22; *KSA* 5:393). Whereas New Testament characters are weak, the Old Testament is chock full of strong, courageous characters who attain greatness against tremendous odds. Israel Eldad notes that Nietzsche's description of the history of Israel is "almost Dionysian" in character:[18] "Its Yahweh was the expression of a consciousness of power, of joy in oneself, of hope for oneself: through him victory and welfare were expected; through him nature was trusted to give what the people need" (*AC* 25; *KSA* 6:193). So Judaism had built into it a deep "self-affirmation."

Yet Nietzsche draws a sharp contrast between the early and later portions of the Old Testament. Whereas the early part is healthy and affirmative in nature, the later part turns sickly. One needs only consider the political fortunes of the Jews throughout the Old Testament. From the noble Abraham springs a new nation, Israel. While that nation suffers the ignominy of being slaves in Egypt, it triumphantly escapes and finds rest in the promised land. Yet, after many good years of rule by kings such as David and Solomon, the nation is divided and conquered. As Nietzsche puts it, "Yahweh the god of 'justice'" was "no longer one with Israel." The result is an entirely new relation to God in which the priests were now in control:

> The concept of God becomes a tool in the hands of priestly agitators, who now interpret all happiness as a reward, all unhappiness as punishment for disobeying God, as "sin": the most mendacious device of interpretation, the alleged "moral world order," with which the natural concepts of cause and effect are turned upside down once and for all. . . . A god who *demands*—in place of a god who helps, who devises means, who is at bottom the word for every happy inspiration of courage and self-confidence. (*AC* 25; *KSA* 6:194)

It is when the ascetic priests take over the conception of God and use it for their own purposes that Nietzsche sees this God as no more worthy of being called "God." Properly speaking, if Nietzsche is right regarding God's becoming merely a "tool" of the priests, then he is likewise right that such a God has lost all sense of divinity. Rather it becomes an idol. But here Nietzsche fails to make a crucial distinction between the creation of an idol on the part of the ascetic priests and the existence of Yahweh. For Yahweh is not the creation of the ascetic priests but the institutor of the priesthood. Of course, Nietzsche would hardly recognize that point. In any case, by the time Paul arrives on the scene, the priestly class is already in place.

The rise of the priestly class is very closely connected to the slave revolt, which takes place when noble values are inverted into vices and the nobles' vices into virtues. Although it might at first seem that Christianity simply *is* that slave revolt, Nietzsche sees Christianity as continuing the revolt already begun by the Jews—even if deepening and carrying it to its ultimate conclusions.[19] Whereas morality was once "the expression of the conditions for the life and growth of a people," it now becomes "abstract" and "the antithesis of life" (*AC* 25; *KSA* 6:194). However, Nietzsche makes clear in *On The Genealogy of Morality* that a number of factors are needed for the slave revolt to take place. First, "slave morality needs an opposite and external world" (*GM* I:10; *KSA* 5:271), "the true world." The reason for the external world is that the slave needs something to *oppose* to this world by which to denounce this world as evil. Only if there is *another* world that represents the *true* and the *good* can *this* world be devalued:

> The concept of "God" invented as a counterconcept of life—every-
> thing harmful, poisonous, slanderous, the whole hostility unto death
> against life synthesized in this concept in a gruesome unity! The con-
> cept of the "beyond," the "true world" invented in order to devalu-
> ate the only world there is—in order to retain no goal, no reason, no
> task for our earthly reality! The concept of the "soul," the "spirit,"
> finally even "*immortal* soul," invented in order to despise the body,
> to make it sick, "holy"; to oppose with a ghastly levity everything
> that deserves to be taken seriously in life. (*EH* "Destiny" 8; *KSA*
> 6:373–74)

Second, for there to be a revolt, the slave must become *cleverer* [*klüger*] than the noble. That development takes place precisely because the slave is forced to be silent, to remember, and to wait (*GM* I:10; *KSA* 5:272–73). Third, the slave needs a strong sense of agency, in which there is both the idea of a "doer" behind the deed as well as "free choice" (*GM* I:13; *KSA* 5:279–80). Although Nietzsche thinks there are neither "doers" nor free choice, the notion of agency is crucial to the possibility of holding the nobles culpable for their wrong. Fourth, there needs to be an acute sense of suffering, along with the expectation that suffering somehow should *make sense* As Nietzsche points out, "what actually arouses indignation against suffering is not suffering itself, but rather the senselessness of suffering" (*GM* II:7; *KSA* 5:304). Thus, one must find a meaning behind suffering in order for it to be bearable.

Finally, Nietzsche asks: "how then did that other 'gloomy thing,' the consciousness of guilt, the entire 'bad conscience' come into the world?" For Nietzsche, the answer is by way of the notions of creditor and debtor, along with the idea that "every injury has its *equivalent* in something and can really be paid off, even if only through the *pain* of the agent" (*GM* II:4; *KSA* 5:297–98). Although it might seem that *punishment* is what creates the sense of guilt, punishment actually serves to blunt the force of guilt. Rather, it is being able to construe certain kinds of actions *as* reprehensible that enables the creation of a sense of guilt. Strangely enough, though, before the nobles can be accounted guilty, the slaves must first identify *themselves* as guilty. Thus, bad conscience first emerges in the slaves. How, exactly, does this happen? Nietzsche observes that "all instincts that do not discharge themselves outwardly *turn themselves inwards*—this is what I call the *internalizing* of man: thus first grows in man that which he later calls his 'soul.'" Not being in a position to exercise their instincts (or at least not fully or honestly), the slaves' instincts are internalized. Thus, the "hostility, cruelty, pleasure in persecution, in assault, in change, in destruction" that the slaves feel ends up turning "against the possessors of such instincts." Nietzsche concludes: "*that* is the origin of 'bad conscience'" (*GM* II:16; *KSA* 5:322–23). And it is also the origin of *ressentiment*.

As an outstanding example of success in inversion of values, Nietzsche cites the Jews, that "priestly people." In opposition to the ancient Greek idea that "good = noble = powerful = beautiful = happy = beloved of God," they put in place the idea that "the miserable alone are the good; the poor, powerless, lowly alone are the good" (*GM* I:7; *KSA* 5:267). Yet, remarkably, out of this intense hate and desire for revenge grows "something just as incomparable, a *new love,* the deepest and most sublime of all kinds of love." Judaism produces "the embodied Gospel of Love, this 'Redeemer' bringing blessedness and victory to the poor, the sick, the sinners. . . . Has not Israel reached the final goal of its sublime desire for revenge precisely via the detour of this 'Redeemer'" (*GM* I:8; *KSA* 5:268–69). It is at this point that Paul enters the picture. Paul takes the Jewish inversion of values and makes it into something distinctly Christian. But how? First, although Judaism had a notion both of God and that of another world, Paul makes the promise of heaven the ultimate goal of following Christ. In effect, Christianity is far more "otherworldly" than Judaism ever was.[20] Second, by turning Christ's death into the payment for sins, Paul provides a way of escaping the logic of guilt and atonement. Although it wasn't until Anselm that the satisfaction theory of the atonement was worked out in full, it is clearly implied in Paul when he says that "we have been justified by [Christ's] blood" (Rom. 5:9). Third, even though Paul does not provide a justification for all suffering, he claims that "all things work together for good for those who love God" (Rom.

8:28). So, somehow, suffering is "redeemed."[21] And the central message of Christianity is that Christians can be redeemed and rewarded with eternal life—so suffering is redeemed in more than one sense. Suffering both brings about "good," and those who suffer will be "rewarded."

But all of that is precisely what the *Christian* thinks. In contrast, Nietzsche has a completely different interpretation. If we want to understand the priest and his effect upon the believer, Nietzsche thinks we need look no further than the Bible itself:

> The beginning of the Bible contains the *whole* psychology of the priest. . . . "man must be made unhappy"—this was the logic of the priest in every age. It will now be clear what was introduced into the world for the first time, in accordance with this logic: "*sin*." The concept of guilt and punishment, the whole "moral world order," was invented *against* science, *against* the emancipation of man from the priest. Man *shall not* look outside, he shall look into himself. . . . And he shall suffer in such a way that he has need of the priest at all times. Away with physicians! *A Savior is needed.* (*AC* 49; *KSA* 6:228)

In *On The Genealogy of Morality,* Nietzsche seems to waver between claiming that the priest is a kind of noble versus being part of the slave class.[22] In Paul's case, although he claims to have exemplary credentials as an exemplary Jew,[23] he comes from what Nietzsche would consider to be a slave nation. Moreover, Nietzsche seems to have no end of epithets for Paul, calling him (among other things) a "carpet-weaver" [*Teppichwirker*] (*GM* I:16; *KSA* 5:287) and "a very tormented, very pitiable, very unpleasant man who also found himself unpleasant" (*D* 68; *KSA* 3:65).[24] Yet Paul finds a way to elevate himself, as all priests do. What is most striking, though, about Nietzsche's account of Paul is that Paul *single-handedly* elevates himself to the role of priest. Whereas the normal route for a priest is either to be born into a priestly family or else elevated to this position by a body possessing such a power, Paul actually invents *his own* priesthood—all in the elaborate guise of *dissolving* the priesthood.

Earlier we noted that Nietzsche reads Paul's move of destroying the law as a power play. In order to exercise priestly power, Nietzsche says that the "*priestly* type" has "a life interest in making mankind sick" (*AC* 24; *KSA* 6:193). For Nietzsche, the role of priest is to exercise "*dominion over ones who suffer.*" As such, he serves as "savior, shepherd, and advocate of the sick herd." Of course, it is important to note that the priest is "sick himself" and so "related to the sick." Further, since both sheep and shepherd are filled with *ressentiment,* the priest has a dangerous force with which he must reckon: "That most dangerous blasting and explosive material, *ressentiment,* is constantly mounting and mounting." So the priest "*changes the direction of ressentiment*": he directs it back at the sufferer. The priest tells the sufferer: "*you alone are to blame for yourself!*" In order to become indispensable to the patient, the physician "first needs to wound." After that, he "stills the pain that the wound causes," but he also "*poisons the wound at the same time.*" Such is the logic of the priest that Nietzsche lays out.[25]

In addition to making the slaves sick by way of keeping them guilty, the priest also uses the *pharmakon* of pity. In the previous chapter, we noted that Nietzsche attacks Wagner for succumbing to *Mitleid* in *Parsifal.* But one of Nietzsche's chief criticisms against Christianity is that it is "the religion of pity [*Mitleiden*]" (*AC* 7; *KSA* 6:172). For Nietzsche, pity is enervating, and thus goes against life. As he puts it, "Schopenhauer was consistent enough: pity negates life and renders it *more deserving of negation.*" Nietzsche goes on to lay out the logic of pity as follows:

> Pity stands opposed to the tonic emotions which heighten our vitality: it has a depressing effect. We are deprived of strength when we feel pity. That loss of strength which suffering as such inflicts on life is still further increased and multiplied by pity. Pity makes suffering contagious. Under certain circumstances, it engenders a total loss of life and vitality out of all proportion to the magnitude of the cause. (*AC* 7; *KSA* 6:172–73)

Not surprisingly, Nietzsche thinks that pity is "the *practice* of nihilism." Pity is the will to nothingness. Yet, not only does pity sap one's strength, it also "multiplies misery" (*AC* 7; *KSA* 6:173). Instead of one person suffering, now there are two. As Nietzsche asks (rhetorically): "what in the world has caused more suffering than the folly of the pitying?" (*Z* II "Pitying"; *KSA* 4:115). Yet there is a further problem with pity: for Nietzsche, it is ultimately a disguised form of superiority: "To offer pity is as good as to offer contempt" (*D* 135; *KSA* 3:128). Precisely in the act of pitying, one places oneself above the one being pitied. Thus, pity turns out to be a form of revenge, a way of retaliating against the other.[26]

With the advent of Christianity, then, the spiraling logic of decadence reaches a new depth. It becomes subterranean. To which Nietzsche responds: "Bad air! Bad air!" (*GM* I:14; *KSA* 5:282). Of course, we already noted that Nietzsche claims Socrates himself came from the "lowest folk" [*niedersten Volk*] (*TI* II:3; *KSA* 6:68). So the implication at least is that Socrates had already managed to drag down his followers (and Nietzsche extends the charge of leveling down to Socrates' philosophical successors). If ascending life is characterized by an unshakable self-assurance regarding the rightness of one's instincts and the flourishing of those instincts, then Christianity clearly puts that self-assurance into even further question and clamps down on the instincts even more tightly. Understandably, Nietzsche claims that what is called "the kingdom of God" is actually "an underworld kingdom, a hospital, a *souterrain* kingdom, a ghetto kingdom" (*AC* 17; *KSA* 6:184). Nietzsche claims that Christianity, rather than give us a view of life "from a height" (an explicit reference to the Sermon on the Mount), instead views everything from the lowest possible point (*TI* V:1; *KSA* 6:82).

But, having seen that Socrates' dialectic goes against life, how is Christianity any different, let alone worse? They are different in at least two respects. First, although Socrates' *pharmakon* ultimately has the effect of poisoning its patients, the dialectic is two-sided. True, the systemic opposition to the instincts that are the source of life ultimately wears one down. So the dialectic's long-term effect is enfeebling. Yet dialectic is *also* an expression of the vitality and power that characterize life. So its effect is not simply destructive. While Socrates gives up the *agôn* of the noble warrior, he exchanges it for the *agôn* of dialectic. Since Nietzsche thinks "one has relinquished *great* life when one relinquishes war" (*TI* V:3; *KSA* 6:84), the dialectic still ends up promoting life, even in a disguised and less effective form. Second, the goal of the dialectic is not the eradiation of the passions but their taming. While Socrates thinks the passions are markedly inferior to reason and constantly lead it astray, he does not advocate their complete removal. In effect, Christianity follows Socratism and goes a step beyond: "the Christian proves himself to be an exaggerated form of self-control" (*WP* 228; *KSA* 11:44 [6]).

Whereas the practitioner of dialectic engages in a new kind of *agôn* and so exhibits a certain kind of strength, the castration performed by Christianity is only a last resort, something appropriate only for those "who are too weak-willed, too degenerate to moderate their own desire" (*TI* V:2; *KSA* 6:83). Thus, it is not for ascetics but for those who are unable even to muster the strength needed to be an ascetic. Although Nietzsche writes the following when speaking about Wagner, the point applies equally to Christianity: "To sense what is harmful is harmful, to be *able* to forbid oneself something harmful, is a sign of youth and vitality. The exhausted are *attracted* by what is harmful: the vegetarian by vegetables. Sickness itself can be a stimulant to life: only one has to be healthy enough for this stimulant" (*CW* 5; *KSA* 6:22). To be sure, as a revolt of slaves, Christianity is fundamentally a war fueled by revenge—and that has a certain kind of power. Indeed, one of the cleverest aspects of Christianity is its fundamental deception. It claims to be in favor of love, but it instead operates by way of hate. Yet its explicit *telos* is the end of all agonistics. Instead of fighting with the passions, the *pharmakon* is castration.

The result is that, while the Socratic *pharmakon* is ultimately deadly, it still proves a stimulant to life. In contrast, the Christian *pharmakon* is far more poison than cure. Although both Socrates and Paul are decadents, Paul is an example of a "weak" decadent, one who gives in to his decadence. Even though Socrates chooses the wrong method to deal with decadence, at least he actively attempts to deal with it. Here it is helpful to note Nietzsche's distinction between what he terms "active" and "passive" nihilism. Whereas the former is "a sign of increased power of the spirit," the latter represents the "decline and recession of the power of the spirit" (*WP* 22; *KSA* 12:9 [35]). We have already noted that, since nihilism is the recognition of the meaninglessness of life and decadence is a turning against life, it seems appropriate to consider nihilism to be a subcategory of decadence. With that in mind, one can speak of an active and passive decadence.[27] Active decadents recognize that decadence is simply part of the growth and decay that constitutes life (ibid.). With that recognition comes the recognition that decadence cannot really be "fought" but only "resisted." While Socrates unwisely chooses to fight against decadence,[28] Paul—and Christianity in general—simply gives in by negating life. Christianity, then, is only for the truly sick. Nietzsche claims that "nobody is free to become a Christian: one is not 'converted' to Christianity—one has to be sick enough for it. . . . At the bottom of Christianity is the rancor of the sick, instinct directed *against* the healthy, *against* health itself" (*AC* 51; *KSA* 6:231–32). Understandably, then, Nietzsche claims "life ends where the 'kingdom of God' begins" (*TI* 5:4; *KSA* 6:85).

Rereading Paul, Rereading Nietzsche

All of Nietzsche's theorizing about Paul requires some careful examination. To paraphrase Nietzsche, "one cannot read Nietzsche cautiously enough" (*AC* 44: *KSA* 6:218). Certainly not when it comes to Paul—and certainly not when it comes to Jesus, either. Even in the midst of his radical rereading of Paul, Nietzsche himself admits that, when reading the Bible, "one reads oneself into and out of it" (*D* 68; *KSA* 3:64). So Nietzsche has an idea of what he's up to. Moreover, what complicates Nietzsche's read of Paul is that it is a very strange concoction (not unlike Nietzsche's read of Jesus) composed of various elements. John Andrew Bernstein well sums up this mixture:

> One of the curious features of this account is that it is in part based upon what Paul wrote, in part on a travesty of what Paul wrote, and in part on Nietzsche's own psychologizing, from someone who did not disclaim an intimate acquaintance with the "lust for power." By not making any distinction between these, however, Nietzsche obscured the difference between confessions by Paul, made with a purpose, and that which seems to penetrate beneath what Paul himself thought and can serve to cast aspersions on him and his thought in their entirety. And by obscuring this distinction Nietzsche could avoid raising the question whether Paul's struggle with the law was at all related to the most legitimate aspects of his own "immoralism," if aspects that were often obscured by Nietzsche himself.[29]

Nietzsche's portrait of Paul is thus composed of (1) a more or less "orthodox" reading of writings of Paul, (2) a highly distorted reading of those writings, and (3) Nietzsche's own invented "psychology" of Paul. The result is not simply that one is unable to trust what Nietzsche says about Paul but also that one begins to wonder how much of Nietzsche's account of Paul is really about *himself*. Of course, one could read Nietzsche as simply following Paul's pattern of taking an event and developing an entire story to go with it. Yet one could just as easily see Nietzsche inventing a pattern and then attributing it to Paul.

As an interpretational corrective to Nietzsche, Badiou provides not merely a penetrating analysis of Paul but also a penetrating critique of Nietzsche that pinpoints exactly where Nietzsche goes wrong in reading Paul. Badiou is a particularly useful reader of Paul because, although he has his own distinct purposes in interpreting Paul, they are hardly *Christian:* "For me, truth be told, Paul is not an apostle or a saint. I care nothing for the Good News he declares, or the cult dedicated to him." And Badiou makes it amply clear that, for him, the resurrection is merely "a fable."[30]

Earlier we noted Nietzsche's account of what really transpired on the road to Damascus—that Paul suddenly discovered a way to overcome the law and to seize power. Yet Nietzsche gives us yet another account, this one being about Paul's desire to take revenge on life:

> Paul, the chandala hatred against Rome, against "the world," become flesh, become genius, the Jew, the *eternal* Jew par excellence. . . . This was his moment at Damascus: he comprehended that he *needed* the belief in immortality to deprive "the world" of value, that the concept of "hell" would become master even over Rome—that with the "beyond" one *kills life*. Nihilism and Christianity: that rhymes, that does not only rhyme. (*AC* 58; *KSA* 6:246–47)

As Badiou rightly notes, "nothing in this text fits."[31] Even though Badiou is no doubt wrong when he goes on to say that "'belief in immortality' is no concern of Paul's," there is every reason to think that Paul is strongly in favor of life. Paul has made it very clear that it is the *law* that kills, whereas the resurrection is an *affirmation of life*. Badiou is undoubtedly right when he claims that "the hatred against Rome is Nietzsche's invention,"[32] though Paul is clearly juxtaposing his claims to those of the Roman Empire. If anything, it is *Rome* that symbolizes death, not the resurrection. To the Roman Empire—with its *pax Romana* of never-ending war—Paul juxtaposes the peace of Christ. In place of an empire of death, Paul teaches the kingdom of life. Indeed, Badiou rightly points out that Paul's message is strongly affirmative, for Paul writes: "For the Son of God, Jesus Christ, whom we proclaimed among you, Silvanus and Timothy and I, was not 'Yes and No'; but in him it is always 'Yes.' For in him every one of God's promises is a 'Yes'" (II Cor. 1:19–20).

The resurrection is all about the eternal "Yes." It is God's "Yes" to the world. Thus, Norman Wirzba is right when he says, "Nietzsche is united with Christianity in his quest to affirm life," though Nietzsche is clearly unable to see that connection.[33] That Jesus is resurrected *bodily* is an especially strong affirmation of the body.[34] Further, what Nietzsche misses is that the Christian notion of redemption is not *merely* about the world to come; it is just as much about *this* world. As the theologian N. T. Wright puts it:

> The resurrection of Jesus, in the full bodily sense . . . supplies the ground work for this: it is the reaffirmation of the universe of space, time, and matter, after not only sin and death but also pagan empire (the institutionalization of sin and death) have done their worst. The early Christians saw Jesus' resurrection as the action of the creator god to reaffirm the essential goodness of creation. . . . To imply that Jesus "went to heaven when he died," or that he is now simply a spiritual presence, and to suppose that such ideas exhaust the referential meaning of "Jesus was raised from the dead," is to miss the point, to cut the nerve of the social, cultural, and political critique. . . . The resurrection, in the full Jewish and Christian sense, is the ultimate affirmation that creation matters, that embodied human beings matter.[35]

Nietzsche is certainly welcome to his "otherworldly" interpretation of the resurrection—and there have been plenty of theologians and believers throughout the past two millennia who have tended in that direction—but his interpretation clearly goes against orthodox Christianity. To say that the cross is the condemnation of life on earth is simply a gross misunderstanding. Whether it is likewise for Nietzsche a *willful* misunderstanding is a question that cannot be answered, even though it must be posed. For Nietzsche has his own agenda in "reading" Paul as he does, one that is at least as "sinister" as the one he attributes to Paul.

In any case, Nietzsche *must* read Paul in this way, for Paul turns out to be not merely his chief rival but also the exemplar for what Nietzsche wishes to accomplish. Consider how Nietzsche describes Paul:

> The life, the example, the doctrine, the death, the meaning and the right of the entire evangel—nothing remained once this hate-inspired counterfeiter realized what alone he could use. *Not* the reality, *not* the historical truth! . . . Paul simply transposed the center of gravity of that whole existence *after* this existence—in the *lie* of the "resurrected" Jesus. At bottom, he had no use at all for the life of the Redeemer—he needed the death on the cross *and* a little more. (*AC* 42; *KSA* 6:216)

On Nietzsche's read, Paul was the master of taking from Jesus exactly what he needed and leaving the rest behind. Of course, Nietzsche's account of

136

Paul is itself highly selective. It is true that Christ's death and resurrection are the prime focus of Paul's doctrine, but it is too much to say that Christ's life was simply left behind. What is the case—as we will consider in the following chapter—is that Nietzsche *himself* presents us with the most carefully manipulated portrait of Jesus, one that just happens to come very close to the Dionysian Pietism that Nietzsche wants to affirm.

It is Nietzsche *himself* who is so desperately trying to "shift the center of gravity": "I know my fate. One day my name will be associated with the memory of something tremendous—a crisis without equal on earth, the most profound collision of conscience, a decision that was conjured up *against* everything that had been believed, demanded, hallowed so far. I am no man, I am dynamite" (*EH* "Destiny" 1; *KSA* 6:365). How does Nietzsche think he will accomplish such a feat? To do so, as Badiou notes, Nietzsche simply follows Paul's playbook. First, whereas Paul uses the resurrection as the "self-legitimating subjective declaration," Badiou suggests that the equivalent for Nietzsche is Zarathustra.[36] *Pace* Badiou, I would instead claim that it is *amor fati* (love of one's fate). For Zarathustra is merely the bearer of the tidings of *amor fati*. In that sense, there is not a one-to-one correspondence between Jesus and Zarathustra, even if there are important parallels. By a "self-legitimating subjective declaration," Badiou means a truth that establishes *itself* (what we earlier noted as a "truth procedure"). Such is how Nietzsche treats the doctrine of *amor fati*. He never provides a rationale for it: instead, he simply puts it forth as an alternative value. Nietzsche opens book four of *The Gay Science* with a New Year's resolution (that we have already noted): "*Amor fati:* let that be my love from now on! . . . some day I want only to be a Yes-sayer!" (*GS* 276; *KSA* 3:521). Whether Nietzsche ever reaches that point is doubtful, but it is certainly his goal. Yet it is not a goal for which Nietzsche provides any justification—it is simply posited.

Oddly enough, though, we earlier noted that Nietzsche criticizes Paul for making the same move that he makes himself. Perhaps the difference between Paul and Nietzsche is that, whereas Paul didn't recognize the fallacy of reinterpreting the death of Christ as the propitiation for sins (which is what Nietzsche himself says), Nietzsche is well aware of what he is doing. However, here we come to a much more significant difference between Paul and Nietzsche. Whereas *amor fati* is a doctrine of Nietzsche's Dionysian Pietism that Nietzsche fully recognizes has no basis in "truth," that is rather hard to argue in the case with Paul—and the burden of proof is clearly on Nietzsche. Nietzsche's claim that Paul is simply "reinterpreting" the crucifixion for his own purposes is not only unique to Nietzsche, but it also goes squarely against orthodox Christian tradition. While Nietzsche is free to make such a claim, it is a psychological read of Paul that has little or no basis in what Paul writes. If anything, it is that Nietzsche has taken Paul—"a mere 'motif'"—and made out of him what he *needs* to discredit the central claims of Christianity. As an interpretative move, it is brilliant. But it is a concoction not cooked up by Paul but by *Nietzsche.*

Second, Nietzsche needs to break history, once again. For this he requires the revaluation of all values. Badiou perceptively suggests that Nietzsche's substitution would be "grand politics,"[37] a kind of politics designed to shape a rugged and aristocratic people of the future that would replace the "petty politics" of any given nationalism. But the challenge that faces Nietzsche—and modernity in general—is finding a way to develop beyond nihilism to the point of creating new values. Nietzsche writes: "We children of the future—how *could* we be at home in this today. . . . We 'conserve' nothing; neither do we want to return to any past" (*GS* 377; *KSA* 3:628–29). While Nietzsche envisions a society of severe self-discipline ruled by aristocrats, he is remarkably vague regarding the contours of that society.[38]

Third, in place of Paul's "new man," Badiou suggests the overman. Whether this is really the right figure is open to question. Not only does Nietzsche gives us so little to go by in defining *Übermenschlichkeit,* it would seem that he also comes to prefer the conception of the "free spirit" best illustrated by Goethe (as we noted in chapter 5).[39]

As this point exactly how all of this should work out is considerably less important than realizing how much Paul serves as a model for Nietzsche—and how much Nietzsche has to distort Paul for his own purposes. In the final chapter, I turn to the question of the extent to which Nietzsche effectively reverses the course of history, as well as Nietzsche's ultimate relation to Christianity. In the chapter that follows, though, I turn to Nietzsche's method of reading of Jesus. In one important respect, it mirrors Nietzsche's read of Paul: for Nietzsche takes what (to quote him) is "a mere motif" and turns him into something distinctly of his own making.

PART 3

Nietzsche's New Pietism

EIGHT
Deconstructing the Redeemer

> *I confess that I read few books with as many difficulties as the Gospels.*[1]

> *One cannot read these Gospels cautiously enough; every word poses difficulties. I confess—one will pardon me—that precisely on this account they are a first-rate delight for a psychologist—as the opposite of all naïve corruption, as subtlety par excellence, as artistry in psychological corruption. The Gospels stand apart.*[2]

> *I go back, I tell the genuine history of Christianity. The very word "Christianity" is a misunderstanding.*[3]

What Nietzsche alternately calls the "Redeemer" or the "evangel" must be carefully disentangled from the "Crucified," since what Jesus taught and lived are quite different from what Christianity has made him out to be—or so Nietzsche would have us believe. Given that discontinuity, Nietzsche insists that one must exercise extreme caution in explicating the Gospels. But, fortunately for us, Nietzsche will *finally* tell us "the *genuine* history of Christianity." Of course, Nietzsche is hardly the first to engage in this project of deconstruction and reconstruction. Nineteenth-century Europe was awash in a sea of such projects. Gary Shapiro is right when he claims: "In one sense the *Antichrist* is a very conventional nineteenth-century book which can be viewed, without great distortion, as part of a genre of the time: a contemporary life of Jesus, written by a philologist, which claims to investigate its subject without the aid of revelation and to articulate its implications for contemporary religion and secular life."[4] Of course, Nietzsche's purpose in writing his own little *Leben Jesu* is hardly that of an even-handed philologist just attempting to divide the wheat from the tare. In that respect, he is probably not alone: one can question whether others involved in the "quest for the historical Jesus," such as David Friedrich

141

Strauss or Ernest Renan, have their own axes to grind. For instance, Strauss is clearly after a fully rationalistic picture of Jesus, without anything supernatural. His first "rule" of interpretation is that a narrative is to be rejected if it is "irreconcilable with the known and universal laws which govern the course of events." Miracles are obviously the target here. Moreover, Strauss wants to set up his own "Christian system."[5] In contrast, Renan is probably more correctly characterized as a careful philologist who simply wants to set the record straight. But such is hardly Nietzsche's goal, nor is Nietzsche's goal that of Strauss.

I contend that Nietzsche's goal is twofold: (1) to render Jesus harmless, as opposed to the fiery leader portrayed in the Gospels and (2) to read Jesus through the lens of a "this-worldly" Pietism, with the result that Nietzsche seems in certain respects more the true heir of Jesus' message than Christians themselves. Although this second claim may sound strange, the Jesus that Nietzsche presents seems remarkably *Nietzschean* in important respects. Of course, Nietzsche's version of the teachings of Jesus is hardly going to be *exactly* the same as Nietzsche's Dionysian Pietism. Still, there are remarkable points of similarity (even despite sharp dissimilarities). But what *are* those teachings of the evangel? Nietzsche thinks that the "glad tidings" have *never* been truly presented, only what he calls the "dysangel." Certainly, those "bad tidings" are what Nietzsche thinks have counted as "Christianity" through the centuries. However, as we saw in chapter 3, Nietzsche identifies a "positive" form of Christianity, which he describes by saying: "Such a life is still possible today . . . genuine, original Christianity will be possible at all times. Not a faith, but a doing; above all, a *not* doing of many things, another state of *being*" (*AC* 39; *KSA* 6:211). Elsewhere (as we have noted) he praises Christianity (presumably of this pietistic sort) by saying that it is "the best example of the ideal life I have really come to know" (*KSB* 6:109). If such a life has been—and continues to be—possible, then at least *some* sort of "glad tidings" must have somehow been available, even if one must "read between the lines" of the Gospels to discover them.

At this point it is important to make one thing clear. Even though many commentators have read Nietzsche's comments regarding Jesus as overwhelmingly positive, that reading is far too simple. For instance, Michael Tanner writes that, when Nietzsche begins to describe Jesus, "the tone becomes ever warmer and even ecstatic. The portrayal of Nietzsche's (or Dionysos's) antipode becomes, bizarrely, one of the most moving passages in the whole of his writings. With the occasional omission, it could be used as a magnificent sermon addressed to a devout congregation."[6] These passages are indeed moving, and Nietzsche does evidence a certain kind of respect for Jesus. However, any "devout congregation" would no doubt realize that Nietzsche's description of Jesus bears only partial resemblance to the Jesus of historic Christian orthodoxy—mixed with a heavy of dose of heterodoxy. Further, Nietzsche is able to portray Jesus in such a positive way precisely because it is his *own* Jesus, one reinterpreted in light of Nietzsche's new Pietism. Yet Eugen Biser is still right when he says the following: "Nietzsche's criticism of Jesus is much more reserved because in his rejection he is continually stumbling over the traces of a connection he has never totally given up."[7] Nietzsche has *not* simply left all of Christianity behind: not only are there still residual traces of his earlier commitment to it but those traces have become part of his new religion. So it is not at all surprising that he is able to read Jesus in a somewhat sympathetic way.

The Quest for the Psychological Jesus

We noted that Nietzsche accuses Paul of treating Jesus as "a mere 'motif'" to which "*he* then wrote the music" (*WP* 177; *KSA* 13:15 [108]). Whether that is true, of course, is open to debate. But *Nietzsche* is certainly playing such a game. Nietzsche is writing his own melody, using both biblical and other sources to work his magic. The result is a strange distortion/creation that easily rivals any bizarre story Wagner ever dreamed up. Of course, we also noted earlier that Nietzsche admits that, when reading the Bible, "one reads oneself into and out of it" (*D* 68; *KSA* 3:64). So there is both exegesis and eisegesis at work in Nietzsche's reading. In the end, then, Nietzsche's "portrait" of Jesus ends up telling us a great deal about Nietzsche—both about who he *is* and about who he hopes to *become*.

Even Nietzsche's promise of finally getting to the bottom of just who Jesus is presents us with a problem. Supposedly, Nietzsche is going to give us a Jesus without any added facts or interpretation. That means we are going to get a picture of Jesus *prior* to his "makeover" by Paul, the disciples, and others who create "Christianity." But one rapidly loses faith in Nietzsche's "retelling" as soon as he in effect *repudiates* "the quest for the historical Jesus." After writing "I confess that I read few books with as many difficulties as the Gospels," he goes on to say:

> The time is long past when I too, like every young scholar, slowly drew out the savor of the work of the incomparable Strauss, with the shrewdness of a refined philologist. I was twenty years old then: now I am too serious for that. What do I care about the contradictions in the "tradition"? How can one call saints' legends "tradition" in the first place? The biographies of saints are the most ambiguous kind of literature there is: to apply scientific methods to them, *in the absence of other documents,* strikes me as doomed to failure from the start—merely scholarly idleness. (*AC* 28; *KSA* 6:199)

And this repudiation of using any kind of "philological tools" is only strengthened by what Nietzsche writes to Overbeck, who happens to be a historian: "This winter I have also read Renan's *Origines* [*de la Chrétienté*], with much spite and—little profit. This whole history of conditions and *sentiments* in Asia Minor seems to me to hang comically in the air. At root, my distrust goes so far as to question if history is really *possible*. What is it that people want to establish—something that was not itself established at the moment when it occurred?" (letter of February 23, 1887; *SL* 261; *KSB* 8:28).

I have to confess that, while I'm not particularly worried about difficulties in the Gospels, I completely agree with Nietzsche that the enterprise of picking and choosing from them is itself fraught with difficulties. And that enterprise seems to me to have gotten no easier—or more sensible—with the *addition* "of other documents." I have no more faith in the Jesus Seminar with their black beads than I do in the "incomparable Strauss."

But let us leave that point aside and instead concentrate on the move Nietzsche is making. For Nietzsche is telling us that (1) the Gospels are unreliable as accounts of Jesus' life; (2) standard philology is unreliable as a tool when it comes to accounts of lives of saints; (3) he has questions about the very enterprise of history itself; and (4) he is going to tell us "the truth" about Christianity *anyway* by way of a "psychological" account. Such a project would seem to be simply a nonstarter, at least as configured. Nietzsche might have *some* credibility were he to lay down some philological principles of his own. But that is exactly what he refuses to do, given the genre with which he is working. For Nietzsche, there are no philological principles that would enable the contemporary scholar to separate the wheat from the tare in the Gospels. So Nietzsche's quest is not really for the "historical Jesus" but what he calls "the psychological type of the redeemer." Given the range of portraits of Jesus that are available, Nietzsche tries to conjecture what Jesus must have been like—in a psychological sense—to give rise to such varied depictions. So his method is something like the following: in light of all the conflicting pictures we have of Jesus, what kind of person would someone like Jesus have been to result in this particular collection of narratives? To assure us that such a route is possible, he says, "after all, this could be contained in the Gospels despite the Gospels, however mutilated or overloaded with alien features: as Francis of Assisi is preserved in his legends, despite his legends" (*AC* 29; *KSA* 6:199). Here we have a version of "the truth is there; we just need to pick out the false bits." But how *does* one pick out the false bits, especially if one has no guideline by which to determine what is *false* and one has explicitly ruled out philological principles? How does one determine the "psychology of the redeemer"?

Shapiro thinks Nietzsche's move can be justified—at least to some extent—by understanding Nietzsche's view of Jesus: "According to Nietzsche, Jesus was a blissful naif with no interest in belief, the other world, rewards. Jesus, then, was simple and ahistorical. He is not to be understood narratively, because he remained the same and had no development. Nietzsche's affirmations of Jesus' simplicity and ahistoricity are formulated often as denials of the complexity and development found in Renan's *Life*."[8] Shapiro seems correct in saying that this is what Nietzsche is doing, but it is hard to see how this *justifies* the project. Even if we were to agree that Jesus is "simple" (and there are, of course, a number of ways in which that adjective could be read), it is hard to see how Jesus could be "ahistorical." Unless there simply was no Jesus at all, not even "a mere 'motif.'" A truly "invented" Jesus—from the ground up—might (though not necessarily) make such an interpretation possible. But not a living one. Thus, in order to make this move, Nietzsche has to resort to his own strange form of "Egyptianism"—the mummification of Jesus in which there is no "history" and no "development."

Tim Murphy's answer to how Nietzsche intends to negotiate this difficulty is that Nietzsche applies two metaphors to Jesus' life: "Jesus as idiot" and "Jesus as Buddha," the result being that Nietzsche's account moves from "fifth-century B.C.E. India to nineteenth-century C.E. Russia."[9] A truly impressive journey, to say the least. Of course, Murphy is hardly the first to suggest that the conceptions of "idiot" and "Buddha" are part of how Nietzsche reads Jesus.[10] Moreover, although the connection of them with Jesus is often mentioned, the exact details of those connections are often only superficially mentioned and seldom critiqued as to whether they are appropriate interpretational lenses for Jesus. But there is much more to this very complicated, twisted story than merely the conceptions of "idiot" and "Buddha"—and for at least two reasons, both of which concern Nietzsche *himself*.

On the one hand, if one examines the lenses by which Nietzsche reads not just Jesus but also Socrates and Paul, they usually turn out to be recent discoveries of Nietzsche's. For instance, once Nietzsche reads Paul Bourget's essay on decadence in 1885, Socrates, Paul, western society, modernity, Christianity, and Jesus (and much else) all come to be labeled "decadent." Then, in early 1887 (or late 1886),[11] he discovers a French translation of Dostoevsky's *L'esprit souterrain* in a Nice bookstore, which leads him to read a number of that author's books.[12] Not surprisingly, little more than a year later, Christianity becomes "a *souterrain* kingdom" (*AC* 17; *KSA* 6:184) and Jesus is interpreted as an idiot (*AC* 29; *KSA* 6:200). Again, when Nietzsche discovers the "Law of Manu" in May 1888, it suddenly becomes a way of framing Christianity in *The Anti-Christ(ian)*.[13] So Nietzsche's interpretive lenses are very much connected to what he happens to have read at the moment. On the other hand, Nietzsche finds it convenient to include two important features about *himself* in order to deconstruct the Crucified to fit his own needs. First, Jesus turns out to be a decadent. Not only does this fit best with how Nietzsche ends up reading anyone to whom he is "close" (and Nietzsche is clearly close to Jesus in important ways), but it also enables Nietzsche to dismiss him. True, Nietzsche is a decadent too, but he has the advantage of knowing the right means to "resist" (an advantage that he reserves for himself alone). Second, Jesus turns out to embody the kind of piety that Nietzsche wants to champion. In other words, for Jesus to be "useful" to Nietzsche—in Nietzsche's own quest to "resist" decadence and promote his Dionysian Piety—he needs to both uphold Jesus as exemplary and have grounds for dismissing him. That way Nietzsche appears—at least in some respects, that is, in the respects about which he cares—superior to the other decadents and a kind of inheritor of the true Christian legacy.

To put that last point another way, Nietzsche is less "anti-Christ" than "anti-Christian." Of course, the title of the book can be read either way. It also depends upon what one means by "Christ" (as opposed to "Jesus" or, to use Nietzsche's terminology, the "evangel" or the "Redeemer"). Moreover, there are passages in *The Anti-Christ(ian)* in which the term can *only* be translated as "anti-Christian." For example, Nietzsche speaks of "false" believers as "anti-Christians":

> All the concepts of the church have been recognized for what they are, the most malignant counterfeits that exist, the aim of which is to devalue nature and natural values. . . . We know, today our *conscience* knows, what these uncanny inventions of the priests and the church are really worth. . . . Everybody knows this, *and yet everything contin-ues as before.* Where has the last feeling of decency and self-respect gone when even our statesmen, an otherwise quite unembarrassed type of man, anti-Christians [*Antichristen*] through and through in their deeds, still call themselves Christians today and attend com-munion. (*AC* 38; *KSA* 6:210–11)

So there are actually at least two senses in which one could be an "anti-Christian." First, one could oppose what "Christians" did to Christ's teach-ings. Certainly Nietzsche fits that category. He maintains "in truth, there was only *one* Christian, and he died on the cross," which leads Nietzsche to go on to say: "*In fact, there have been no Christians at all*" (*AC* 39; *KSA* 6:211–12). Second, one could—in what might at first seem a strange reversal—be against the "anti-Christians" for being disingenuous. In other words, they call themselves Christians, and thus taking a stand against them means styling oneself as "anti-Christian." Nietzsche turns out to be an anti-Christian in both these senses.

Simply in terms of terminology, we already have a problem in *The Anti-Christ(ian)* with Nietzsche's identification of Jesus. Robin A. Roth suggests that "the fundamental distinction" is "between the man Jesus and the Redeemer-type."[14] Were it only so simple. When Nietzsche says he is going to give us "the psychological type of the Redeemer" (*AC* 29; *KSA* 6:199), one might reasonably assume that he is going to describe the Crucified. However, Nietzsche goes on to say "what concerns *me* is the psychological type of the Redeemer. After all, this could be contained in the Gospels despite the Gospels" (*AC* 29; *KSA* 6:199). In the following sec-tion, he claims "the Redeemer type is preserved for us only in extensive distortion" (*AC* 30; *KSA* 6:201). Here we have what sounds like a quest for the historical Jesus. As it turns out, Nietzsche basically equates the "evangel," the "redeemer," and the historical Jesus. That he slips back and forth between these terms makes that evident. Given Nietzsche's infamous ending for *Ecce Homo*—"*Dionysus versus the Crucified*"—it is strange that the term "Crucified" doesn't even make it into *The Anti-Christ(ian)*. This is all the more strange in that Nietzsche contrasts the two "types"—Dionysus and the Crucified—in a very revealing unpublished fragment, which we will take up later. However, the Crucified is clearly the alternative pole to the historical Jesus/evangel/Redeemer.

In any case, Nietzsche promises to give us a psychology of the Redeemer that can be worked out in the following terms: decadence, nihilism, sublimity, sickliness, idiocy, childlikeness, free spiritedness, and freedom from *ressentiment*. He also gives us a psychology of the evangel, though that works out in terms of a piety that bears an uncanny resemblance to Nietzsche's own. Since Nietzsche's account of the Redeemer is a complicated one, we need to consider each of these terms carefully. We noted that Nietzsche questions what it is that people hope to establish in writing "history." What will become clear is that Nietzsche is after "something which was not itself established at the moment when it occurred," that is, his own *version* of "history."

"This Most Interesting of All Decadents"

Nietzsche describes the "psychological type of the Redeemer" in two respects:

> *The instinctive hatred of reality:* a consequence of an extreme capacity for suffering and excitement which no longer wants any contact at all because it feels every contact too deeply. *The instinctive exclusion of any antipathy, any hostility, any boundaries or divisions in man's feelings:* the consequence of an extreme capacity for suffering and excitement which experiences any resistance, even any compulsion to resist, as unendurable *displeasure* . . . and finds blessedness (pleasure) only in no longer offering any resistance to anybody, neither to evil nor to him who is evil—love as the only, as the *last* possible, way of life. (*AC* 30; *KSA* 6:200–201)[15]

So the Redeemer type (1) is characterized by acute sensitivity to pain and (2) thus wishes to avoid any contact with reality or any kind of resistance.

Nietzsche goes on to tell us that this (supposedly "pure") type "could not remain pure, whole, free from accretions" and that "the queer and sick world" of the Gospels could only have "*coarsened* the type" (*AC* 31; *KSA* 6:201–2). So this begs the question of whether what Nietzsche goes on to describe is the "coarsened type" or one that has been "philologically purified." Although Nietzsche does not give us an answer to this question, we can assume that his is *supposed* to be the "pure" version.

Yet, if it's a pure version, it is amazing how much it resembles Buddhism. To be sure, Nietzsche actually begins his remarks by *distancing* Buddhism from Christianity. "Buddhism is a hundred times more realistic than Christianity" because "it stands *beyond* good and evil" and so is a "struggle against *suffering*" rather than against *sin* (*AC* 20; *KSA* 6:186). Buddhism is also more realistic in that it makes few promises regarding being able to avoid suffering. Yet the psychology of Buddhism sounds remarkably similar to that of the Redeemer. Nietzsche says that there are two basic "physiological facts" that form the basis of Buddhism: "*First,* an excessive sensitivity, which manifests itself in a refined susceptibility to pain; and *second,* an overspiritualization" (ibid.). The first of these is virtually identical to the psychology of the Redeemer: an acute sensitivity to pain. While the second feature of Buddhism sounds less like that of the Redeemer, they are actually remarkably close. The Buddhist strategy of "overspiritualization" takes the form of damaging "the instinct of personality by subordinating it to the 'impersonal'" (ibid.). Jesus' strategy of "overspiritualization" is "spiritualizing away" anything that is "solid": "He does not care for anything solid: the word kills, all that is solid kills. The concept, the *experience* of 'life' in the only way he knows it, resists any kind of formula, law, faith, dogma. He speaks only of the innermost: 'life' or 'truth' or 'light' is his word for the innermost—all the rest, the whole of reality, the whole of nature, language itself, has for him only the value of a sign, a simile" (*AC* 32; *KSA* 6:204).

Nietzsche even goes on to call him "a symbolist par excellence." Hence, the strategy that Jesus invokes is that of removing himself from anything "solid" that could do him damage. In effect, he takes refuge in the symbolic, which is why Nietzsche terms him an "anti-realist" (ibid.). Precisely because he is able to do so, he makes himself invulnerable to pain: "nothing" can hurt him, since "nothing" exists. But this is remarkably similar to the Buddhist strategy of renouncing the individuality of the self and taking refuge in the nonpersonal.

Nietzsche makes it clear that both Buddhism and Christianity are decadent and nihilistic. Both are clearly against the instincts, certainly the instinct of ascending life that is characterized by the will to power. Neither is in favor of gaining power. Moreover, Christianity even teaches equality: "The poison of the doctrine of 'equal rights for all'—it was Christianity that spread it most fundamentally" (*AC* 43; *KSA* 6:217). As to nihilism, the goal of Buddhism is to escape this world and become one with the world soul. Although Christianity is not about a loss of personal identity, it is aimed at escaping from this world. Where they differ, according to Nietzsche, is in how they treat the individual: "In the Buddha's doctrine, egoism becomes a duty: 'the one thing needful,' the question 'how can *you escape* from suffering?'" (*AC* 20; *KSA* 6:187). This results in a strong emphasis on diet, "hygienic measures," "wariness of all intoxicants," inventing "ideas which are either soothing or cheering." There is no prayer and no asceticism. There is also "nothing to which [Buddha's] doctrine is more opposed than the feeling of revenge, antipathy, *ressentiment*" (*AC* 20; *KSA* 6:186–87).

Christianity, at least according to Nietzsche, presents a remarkable contrast to this way of life. It is almost as if Nietzsche simply takes Buddhism and reverses it, which is as likely an explanation for his description of Christianity as any:

> In Christianity the instincts of the subjugated and oppressed come to the fore: here the lowest classes seek their salvation. The casuistry of sin, self-criticism, the inquisition of the conscience, are pursued as a *pastime*. . . . The body is despised, hygiene repudiated as sensuality; the church even opposes cleanliness. . . . Christian too is a certain sense of cruelty against oneself and against others; hatred of all who think differently; the will to persecute. Gloomy. . . . Christianity, finally, is the hatred of the *spirit*, of pride, courage, freedom, liberty of the spirit; Christianity is the hatred of the *senses*, of joy in the senses, of joy itself. (*AC* 21; *KSA* 6:188)

We need to examine this collection of characteristics of Christianity one by one, and then consider just how accurate they are. First, it is certainly true that Christianity has extremely humble origins. To be sure, there were early followers whose standing was significant. But it is a religion of what Nietzsche would call "slaves"—the outcasts of society. Despite the genealogy of Jesus found in Matthew (that traces his lineage to King David, something that Nietzsche would no doubt discount as an invention by his followers), Jesus' origins were humble enough: the son of a carpenter who lived in insignificant Nazareth. But these humble origins have a particular result for Nietzsche. Since Christianity is a slave religion—that is, a religion created by those out of power—it is characterized by *ressentiment*. As Nietzsche makes clear, *ressentiment* is the result of weakness. The slaves are not in a position to have a "true reaction," thus they "recover their losses only through an imaginary revenge," a no-saying to all that is different from them (*GM* I:10; *KSA* 5:270). What Christianity most needs to survive are "enemies" rather than friends (*TI* V:3; *KSA* 6:84). They need something to be *against* in order to have a purpose to being. This is why Nietzsche thinks Christianity is "created by eternal *hate*" (*GM* I:15; *KSA* 5:284).

Yet this *ressentiment* also gets turned *inward:* one becomes obsessed with sin and is constantly inspecting one's conscience. Nietzsche speaks of a "self-destruction" which engages in "self-vivisection" (*WP* 55; *KSA* 12:5 [71]). It is a form of *spiritual* hygiene that turns out to be very destructive. For it can result only in continual self-criticism *that weakens one further.* Moreover, since the nobles are powerful in a bodily sense, the body is then denigrated. The result is all-around hatred—of oneself and of the other. When Nietzsche speaks of the "will to persecute," he means a general sense of wanting to do injury—whether to others or to oneself. And that will stems from a deep-seated desire for revenge. The result is that Christianity says "No to everything on earth that represents the ascending tendency of life" (*AC* 24; *KSA* 6:192). As to the idea that Christianity is against the hatred of "pride, courage, freedom, liberty of the spirit" and "the senses" and "joy itself," the reason is simple: these are all denied the slaves. They have nothing in which to take pride; there are little or no opportunities for courage or freedom; and what they experience by way of the senses is hardly joyful. So they take these virtues of the nobles and turn them into vices in the greatest act of revenge possible. What once was good now becomes not just bad but *evil.*

What are we to do with this as a description of Christianity? If one considers the logic Nietzsche puts forth, it is quite clear: one begins with humble origins, and that leads to a desire for salvation, a belief that one is somehow "responsible" for one's situation, a creation of another world "in which to escape," a hatred of this world and its virtues and everything associated with it (even the senses themselves). But, while this logic makes sense, the question is whether it actually describes how Christianity develops. One could equally work out the logic as follows: one recognizes that there are "bad" (or even "evil") aspects of the world, one despises those aspects and wishes for salvation from them, one takes bodily things to be less important than spiritual things, one sees certain virtues are sometimes good and sometimes bad (courage being a good example here, even pride if properly defined), and one sees the senses as valuable but not ultimate. That strikes me as a much more plausible genealogy of Christianity than that of Nietzsche's. But, of course, one can only counter a genealogy with another genealogy and then argue as to which one fits best. Nietzsche's works well if one considers certain elements of Christian history and not others.

Speaking of Nietzsche, the German satirist Kurt Tucholsky joked: "Tell me what you need, and I'll supply you with the right Nietzsche quotation."[16] Similar things are often said about the Bible—and everything becomes far more complicated once we talk about the entity "Christianity" and its history. For there have been "Christians" who could fit just about any description. Paraphrasing only slightly, one could say: "Tell me how you want to portray Christianity, and I'll provide you with the right examples." Have there been "Christians" obsessed with sin, unconcerned about the body, cruel to themselves and others because of *ressentiment*, gloomy, against pride, freedom, and courage, and even the joy of the senses? Of course. When it comes to guilt and self-criticism, one need only think of Augustine. When it comes to hatred against the enemy, one can hardly outdo Nietzsche's quotes from Aquinas and Tertullian. Aquinas: "The blessed in the kingdom of heaven will see the punishments of the damned, *in order that their bliss be more delightful to them*."[17] Tertullian, also speaking on the view from heaven looking down toward hell: "What variety of sights then!" Former kings "now groaning in deepest darkness"; persecutors "being liquefied by flames fiercer than those which they raged against the Christians"; "philosophers reddening [literally] before their disciples as they blaze together." Just to make clear how he feels about these sights, Tertullian adds that he will *"laugh," "feel joy,"* and *"exult."*[18] To all this one can add Nietzsche's sarcastic retort to the rather exhaustive list of sayings that he claims were *"put into the mouth"* of Jesus (about judgment, forgiveness, etc.): "How *evangelical!*" (*AC* 45; *KSA* 6:221).[19]

But one can just as easily come up with other examples of Christians who do not hate themselves or their bodies or those who are not Christians, or courage or the senses or joy. Nietzsche has deliberately painted a rather radical picture of hatred and self-denial. While painting such a vivid portrait works well in communicating failings of a religion, its great disadvantage is that it is a portrait that is so easy to pillory. That Nietzsche is able to find some examples that fit the description lends at best partial credence to it. Otherwise, he provides remarkably little support. If his is to be a convincing revisionist history, he needs considerably more examples—and better ones than those he has. For instance, his "support" for the church's opposing cleanliness is that "the first Christian measure after the expulsion of the Moors was the closing of the public baths, of which there were two hundred and seventy in Cordova alone" (*AC* 21; *KSA* 6:188). An interesting little fact, to be sure, but hardly very decisive in establishing a Christian aversion to cleanliness. There are all sorts of reasons why one might close down public baths that would have nothing to do with cleanliness (not to mention the fact that this example covers only one city and one vignette in time). To counter Nietzsche, one could easily set up such an example as Mother Theresa. However, Nietzsche has a way of dealing with any and all such positive examples: for all he needs to claim is that their "real" motives are hatred and *ressentiment,* and he seemingly has won the game. However, at this point, there can be no game. Either one thinks that people can be in touch enough with their motives to claim that they are not *totally* selfish or else one does not. Of course, this cuts both ways: for, if Nietzsche were to claim that one could never really *know* one's own selfishness, then he would be in the same epistemological predicament. In any case, the claim of self-deception does not stick simply because it is made.

Nietzsche's description of Christianity provides the perfect foil for him to set against the evangel. For the evangel is quite different from the above, and also quite Buddhist. Nietzsche speaks of "the sermonizer on the mount, lake, and meadow, whose appearance seems like that of a Buddha on soil that is not at all Indian" (*AC* 31; *KSA* 6:202). In the same way that Buddhism rules out "the feeling of revenge, antipathy, *ressentiment*" (*AC* 20; *KSA* 6:187), so Jesus exemplifies "the superiority over any feeling of *ressentiment*." Nietzsche prefaces that statement by saying "this warlike, this No-saying, No-doing trait had been *lacking* in his image; even more, he had been its opposite" (*AC* 40; *KSA* 6:213). Quite in opposition to Renan, who had used the concepts "genius" and "hero" as interpretive lenses for Jesus, Nietzsche contends that these are both utterly inappropriate to make sense of Jesus.[20] Genius seems inappropriate, not least because the term "idiot" is for Nietzsche much more fitting. Earlier, Nietzsche had written: "Socrates excels the founder of Christianity in being able to be serious cheerfully and in possessing that *wisdom full of roguishness* that constitutes the finest state of the human soul. And he also possessed the finer intellect" (*HH* II:86; *KSA* 2:592). But the concept of hero is just as problematic, as Nietzsche makes clear by appealing to Jesus' basic character: "If anything is unevangelical it is the concept of the hero. Just the opposite of all wrestling, of all feeling-oneself-in-a-struggle, has here become instinct: the incapacity for resistance becomes morality here ('resist not evil'—the most profound word of the Gospels, their key in a certain sense), blessedness in peace, in gentleness, in not *being able* to be an enemy" (*AC* 29; *KSA* 6:199–200). Jesus is weak, and his way of dealing with life is by offering no resistance. It is this very formula of "no resistance" that virtually constitutes the Gospel for Nietzsche.

As it turns out, Jesus is actually practicing Nietzsche's remedy for *ressentiment*. Quoting (or, rather, paraphrasing) from the Buddha, Nietzsche writes: "'Not by enmity is enmity ended; by friendliness enmity is ended': these words stand at the beginning of the doctrine of the Buddha" (*EH* "Wise" 6; *KSA* 6:273).[21] Loving even his enemies, Jesus avoids *ressentiment*. Instead of participating in the reactionary logic of *ressentiment*, Jesus in effect practices what Nietzsche terms "Russian fatalism":

> Against all this the sick person has only one great remedy: I call it *Russian fatalism*, that fatalism without revolt which is exemplified by a Russian soldier who, finding a campaign too strenuous, finally lies down in the snow. No longer to accept anything at all, no longer to take anything, no longer to absorb anything—to cease reacting altogether. This fatalism is not always courage to die; it can also preserve life under the most perilous conditions. . . . Because one would use oneself up too quickly if one reacted in *any* way, one does not react at all any more: this is the logic. Nothing burns one up faster than the affects of *ressentiment*. (*EH* "Wise" 6; *KSA* 6:272)

Nietzsche tells us that "during periods of decadence I forbade myself such feelings [of *ressentiment*] as harmful" and that he "displayed the 'Russian Fatalism' . . . by clinging for years to all but intolerable situations" (*EH* "Wise" 6; *KSA* 6:273). Moreover, this practicing of fatalism is something that Nietzsche endorses. As he says, Goethe had envisioned a "human being who was strong, highly cultivated, skilled in everything bodily, with self-control and self-respect" who also exhibits a "glad and trusting fatalism" (*TI* IX:49; *KSA* 6:151–52). So Jesus instinctively does what keeps one from *ressentiment*. He accepts all that comes his way, even crucifixion. In Jesus, love becomes "the only, as the *last* possible, way of life." In effect, Jesus brings about a "sublime further development of hedonism. . . . The fear of pain, even of infinitely minute pain, that can end in no other way than in a *religion of love*" (*AC* 30; *KSA* 6:201). This is Jesus' sublimity.

Clearly, Nietzsche is against this development of a "religion of love." Yet, given that Nietzsche finds the passiveness of Russian fatalism to be an effective measure against decadence in times of extreme weakness but then goes on to take "active" measures, the question might be asked: could Jesus have followed Nietzsche's path and become an "active decadent"? Nietzsche thinks that such would have been a possibility, if he had only lived long enough.

> Verily, that Hebrew died too early whom the preachers of death honor; and for many it has become a calamity that he died too early. As yet he knew only tears and the melancholy of the Hebrew, and hatred of the good and the just—the Hebrew Jesus: then the longing for death overcame him. Would that he had remained in the wilderness and far from the good and the just! Perhaps he would have learned to live and to love the earth—and laughter too. Believe me, my brothers! He died too early; he himself would have recanted his teaching. But he was not yet mature. (*Z* I "Free Death"; *KSA* 4:95)

However, a further question at this point arises: assuming Jesus would have recanted had he only had the possibility of living long enough to do so, would he have thought that a *good idea*? For Nietzsche himself thinks that passivity is the way to avoid the reactive logic of *ressentiment* and thus decadence. I consider this question in the final chapter.

Whatever the answer to that question may be, we are not at all through with Nietzsche's descriptions of Jesus. The next primary descriptor is "idiot," to which is added sickliness and childlikeness.

Jesus as Idiot

As soon as Nietzsche introduces the term "idiot," Kaufmann immediately informs us that Nietzsche had Dostoevsky's *The Idiot* in mind (note to *AC* 29). Although Miller claims only that Nietzsche had "perhaps" read *The Idiot,* Bruce Ward contends that Nietzsche had indeed read it.[22] That Nietzsche has a section in the *Nachlass* titled "Jesus: Dostoevsky" in which he claims that Dostoevsky provides us with a psychological analysis of Jesus (*KSA* 13:15 [9]) is telling. In that passage Nietzsche explicitly contrasts the depiction of Christ as an idiot with Renan's portrait of him as a hero, affirming the former over the latter. Moreover, Nietzsche speaks of the Gospels as introducing us to a world like that "in a Russian novel, a world in which the scum of society, nervous disorders, and 'childlike' idiocy" abound and says "it is regrettable that a Dostoevsky did not live near this most interesting of all decadents" (*AC* 31; *KSA* 6:201–2).[23] So a close examination of *The Idiot* would be in order. William Hamilton provides a particularly useful account of how Prince Myshkin relates to the evangel, and I follow it here. However, the crucial difference between Hamilton's account and mine is that I go beyond mere reconstruction and ask whether the supposed parallels that he draws are convincing.

Although Prince Myshkin first took shape in Dostoevsky's mind as a morally contradictory figure, he eventually developed into a human version of Christ.[24] Describing Christ as the "only positively good figure in the world," Dostoevsky's vision was that of writing a novel that would *"portray a perfectly good man."* But, as he admits, "there can be nothing more difficult than this, especially in our time."[25] Yet, as Hamilton notes, Myshkin does not simply give up being evil; rather he causes evil that is "inadvertent and unintended."[26] The parallel to Jesus here is obvious: just as Myshkin doesn't intend (and often doesn't even realize) the trouble he causes, so Jesus is well intentioned but ends up stirring up trouble wherever he goes. Of course, one has to assume that Jesus neither intends this trouble nor necessarily recognizes that he routinely wreaks havoc. That, for instance, Jesus routinely cautions people he heals not to spread the news would seem to indicate someone who is very well aware of what he's doing. Yet Nietzsche would likely counter that these were mere additions by the writers of the Gospels. He maintains that Jesus' faith "does not bring 'the sword'—it simply does not foresee how it might one day separate" (*AC* 32; *KSA* 203). Of course, here Nietzsche is explicitly denying that Jesus would have said the following: "Do not think that I have come to bring peace to the earth; I have not come to bring peace, but a sword" (Mt. 10:34). Such a verse would have to be written off as merely an addition that doesn't happen to *fit* with the picture Nietzsche is attempting to paint of Jesus.

Hamilton points us to three vignettes in *The Idiot* that give us particular insight into his character. The first of these comes when Myshkin admits that he indeed sees himself as a child: "I really don't like being with adults, with people, with grown-ups—and I noticed that long ago— I don't like it because I don't know how. Whatever they say to me, however kind they are to me, still I'm always oppressed by them for some reason, and I'm terribly glad when I can go quickly to my comrades, and my comrades have always been children—not because I'm a child myself, but simply because I'm drawn to children."[27] Myshkin gives this account when his doctor accuses him of being a child. At first, he denies it, but then provides the admission above. Yet he denies being an idiot, for "what sort of idiot am I now, when I myself understand that I'm considered an idiot? . . . I'm intelligent all the same, and they don't even suspect it."[28] So Myshkin does not see himself as an idiot, but he admits to having reverted to the world of a child. He prefers the world of children because he is threatened by the world of adults.

How, though, does all of this relate to Jesus? One of the adjectives used by Nietzsche for Jesus is "childlike." So understanding Myshkin's childlikeness should—assuming Nietzsche is right—be instructive for understanding that of Jesus. Hamilton claims that being like a child is the first aspect in which Myshkin and Christ are alike. He quotes two things Jesus says regarding children. First, "whoever welcomes one such child in my name welcomes me" (Mk. 9:37). Hamilton goes on to say, "child and Jesus are identical, interchangeable."[29] But this passage in no way makes any such identification. It only establishes that Jesus—and, for that matter, God the Father—is always on the side of those who are powerless. Such was a basic belief of Judaism that goes back to the Old Testament. Thus, Jesus also speaks of being thirsty and receiving drink, hungry and receiving food, a stranger and being welcomed, naked and being clothed, sick and being cared for, in prison and being visited (Mt. 25: 35–36). When the righteous respond, "Lord, when was it that we saw you hungry and gave you something to drink?" the response is "just as you did it to the least of these who are members of my family, you did it to me" (Mt. 25:37, 40). So here we have merely the strong identification of Jesus with all who are powerless, not merely with children. Second, Jesus does indeed say "whoever does not receive the kingdom of God as a little child will never enter it" (Mk. 10:15). But receiving the kingdom as a child in no way requires *becoming* a child; rather, it is emulating a certain kind of reception to the Gospel, one open to receiving rather than skeptical and suspicious. So neither of these two passages establishes any connection between Jesus and Myshkin, nor do they establish any sense in which Jesus is "like a child" other than being on the side of the powerless and seeing faith as requiring a childlike reception.

Nietzsche's own connection of Jesus to childlikeness comes when he claims "the kingdom of heaven belongs to the *children*." Moreover, he goes on to characterize the "glad tidings" as being not the result of a "struggle" but instead the result of "an infantilism that has receded into the spiritual." He classifies this as a "case of puberty being retarded and not developing in the organism, as a consequence of degeneration, . . . well known, at least to physiologists" (*AC* 32; *KSA* 6:203). So Jesus is the result of a spiritual puberty "being retarded." In *that* sense, he is childlike. But the evidence for this charge is lacking. When Nietzsche goes on to say that "such a faith is not angry, does not reproach, does not resist," it is difficult to see what is particularly "childlike" about that. Children are just as prone to anger and resistance as adults (just ask the mother of a two-year-old). Moreover, all one has to do is consider the people with whom Jesus spends his time to determine that he is clearly *not* childlike as in the case of Myshkin. They are quite a cast of characters—prostitutes, tax collectors, etc.—but they are not *children*. In fact, they would seem to be anything but. Instead, prostitutes and tax collectors would likely qualify as jaded and cynical—hardly childlike. And Jesus seems to be quite at home in their company, unlike Myshkin.

The second aspect of Myshkin's "idiocy" is his being out of place. This meaning goes back to the Greek term *idios,* which has the idea of being in a private station (as opposed to holding public office) or to be a "peculiar" person.[30] Given that Myshkin is a prince, that former meaning would be inappropriate, though the latter meaning certainly fits. At one point, Lizaveta Prokofyena says of Myshkin that "he's a fool, who neither knows society nor has any place in society."[31] That describes Myshkin perfectly, though it seems only partly applicable to Christ. Kee interprets Nietzsche's use of "idiot" for Christ as follows: "In classical Greek *idios* meant 'private' as opposed to 'public.' Jesus would therefore appeal to [Nietzsche] as a man who goes his own way, by his actions and demeanour exposing and thereby judging the unworthy judges."[32] And Nietzsche *does* interpret Christianity in this "private" sense: "Christianity is possible as the most *private* form of existence; it presupposes a narrow, remote, completely unpolitical society—it belongs in the conventicle" (*WP* 211; *KSA* 12:10 [135]). Certainly Jesus does not have much of a place in society: in effect, he's a rabbi who isn't part of the establishment. As Nietzsche puts it, "*Culture* is not known to him even by hearsay" (*AC* 32; *KSA* 6:204). Moreover, although Nietzsche explicitly says that "to negate is the very thing that is impossible for him" (ibid.), he seems to celebrate Jesus' "radicality" when he notes that "the whole Jewish *ecclesiastical* doctrine was negated in the 'glad tidings'" (*AC* 33; *KSA* 6:206). Here the negation is not intentional, as if it were motivated by some kind of act of *ressentiment*. Rather, the glad tidings simply overturn the whole ecclesiastical system in a positive way.

As to being a fool who didn't know his place in the world, Nietzsche never makes this charge against Jesus. It would certainly be hard to support the idea that Jesus is simply unaware of what he is doing. Jesus seems remarkably self-aware—in a way that Myshkin simply isn't—and his clever answers to questions designed by the scribes and Pharisees to trip him up are indicative of both how aware and in control of things he is. So a childlike innocence actually seems quite foreign to Jesus, at least in one sense. Later we turn to a sense in which "childlikeness" *does* seem to fit.

A third way of characterizing Myshkin that Hamilton employs is by pointing to his epilepsy and how it results in a kind of mystical vision of serenity:

> He fell to thinking, among other things, about his epileptic condition, that there was a stage in it just before the fit itself (if the fit occurred while he was awake), when suddenly, amidst the sadness, the darkness of the soul, the pressure, his brain would momentarily catch fire, as it were, and all his life's forces would be strained at once in an extraordinary impulse. The sense of life, of self-awareness, increased nearly tenfold in these moments, which flashed by like lightning. His mind, his heart were lit up with an extraordinary light; all his agitation, all his doubts, all his worries were as if placated at once, resolved in a sort of sublime tranquility, filled with serene, harmonious joy, and hope, filled with reason and ultimate cause.[33]

Hamilton associates this passage with Myshkin's belief that one can live truly only in the moment, without worrying about tomorrow ("'reckoning up' every minute," as Myshkin puts it).[34] Even though the connection between Myshkin's epilepsy and his ability to live in the moment is tenuous at best (which is to say that Hamilton does little to establish that connection), the implication would be that Myshkin is like Jesus in that he is able to follow Jesus' advice, "do not worry about tomorrow" (Mt. 6:34). Yet Murphy takes this point in a very different direction, focusing on Nietzsche's association of epilepsy with religion, in which the latter may cause the former.[35] Specifically, Nietzsche says that "in the wake of penitence and redemption training we find enormous epileptic epidemics" (GM III:21; KSA 5:391). The problem with this interpretation is that it is simply irrelevant: Nietzsche nowhere makes any such epileptic connection to Jesus, so his discussion of epilepsy elsewhere simply has no bearing on Nietzsche's account of him in The Anti-Christ(ian). Moreover—and more important—Jesus neither advocates penitence nor promotes redemption, at least according to Nietzsche's version in The Anti-Christ(ian).

However, sickness is surely a central component of Nietzsche's psychology of the Redeemer type, manifested in terms of no longer wanting contact with reality (because of feeling everything so deeply) and unable to offer resistance. Dostoevsky ascribes this first quality to Myshkin when he says "the idiot sees all afflictions."[36] The assumption would be that he likewise *feels* them. And that assumption is what Nietzsche is working with in regard to Christ. Here the connection with Buddhism is important, for Nietzsche once again describes the psychology of the Buddha and simply imports this into the psychology of the Redeemer. However, Nietzsche neither points to any accounts in the Gospels to support such an assertion, nor would he be *able* to find such examples.

Having seen just how many problems there are in reading Jesus as an idiot, we need to turn to one last way in which Nietzsche reads Jesus. It is this account that comes closest to Nietzsche's own Dionysian faith.

Jesus as Pietistic Model for Nietzsche

We have already seen that, though Jesus is a decadent (due to his *"instinctive hatred of reality"* [AC 30; KSA 6:200]), he is free from *ressentiment*. Although Nietzsche portrays Jesus as a "weak" figure, that very weakness is what enables him to be a "free spirit." While Nietzsche somewhat grudgingly acknowledges this (as he puts it: "using the expression somewhat tolerantly" [AC 32; KSA 6:204]), becoming a free spirit is what he wants for himself. And, so far, it seems to have eluded his grasp.

So Jesus proves a kind of model for Nietzsche—reluctant as he would be to admit that—both in being free and being a child. As it turns out, the two go together.

Consider how Nietzsche describes Jesus. What marks Jesus is how he *lives:* his faith *"lives, it resists all formulas"* (*AC* 32; *KSA* 6:203):

> It is not a "faith" that distinguishes the Christian: the Christian *acts,* he is distinguished by acting *differently:* by not resisting, either in words or in his heart, those who treat him ill. . . . The life of the Redeemer was nothing other than *this* practice—nor was his death anything else. He no longer required any formulas, any rites for his intercourse with God—not even prayer. He broke with the whole Jewish doctrine of repentance and reconciliation; he knows that it is only in the *practice* of life that one feels "divine," "blessed," "evangelical," at all times a "child of God." Not "repentance," not "prayer for forgiveness" are the ways to God: *only the evangelical practice leads to God, indeed, it is "God"!* (*AC* 33; *KSA* 6:205–6)[37]

And Nietzsche thinks that such a way of life is still possible:

> Christianity is still possible at any time. It is not tied to any of the impudent dogmas that have adorned themselves with its name: it requires neither the doctrine of a personal God, nor that of sin, nor that of immortality, nor that of redemption, nor that of faith; it has absolutely no need of metaphysics, and even less of asceticism, even less of a Christian "natural science." Christianity is a *way of life,* not a system of beliefs. It tells us how to act; not what we ought to believe. (*WP* 212; *KSA* 13:11 [365])

All of this, of course, is precisely what *Nietzsche* wants. Of course, anyone familiar with the New Testament will realize that Nietzsche is giving us a radical rereading of the Gospels (and an even more radical reading when one takes into account Paul's epistles). But why this *particular* read? One reason is due to yet another of Nietzsche's recent discoveries: Leo Tolstoy's *My Religion.* There Tolstoy gives us a very similar read of Jesus, in which being a Christian means following Christ's teaching and example rather than subscribing to a set of doctrines.[38] One could also point to Renan, who makes the same kind of distinction between the blissfulness of Jesus and the revenge that characterizes Christianity. However, Nietzsche likewise reads Jesus this way not simply because he was brought up as a Pietist—in which how one lives and how one feels in one's heart trumps doctrine—but also because all of this so closely mirrors his own refigured Pietism. As he says, "the 'kingdom of heaven' is a state of the heart" (*AC* 34; *KSA* 6:207). We could just as easily rewrite that as "Dionysian Pietism is a state of the heart." Nietzsche insists "only we, we spirits who have *become free,* have the presuppositions for understanding something that nineteen centuries have misunderstood" (*AC* 36; *KSA* 6:208). It has taken nineteen centuries for a Nietzsche to come along and finally understand the meaning of the "glad tidings." They are truly *glad,* for they abolish all of the "*ecclesiastical crudities*" that have been taken to be the substance of Christianity (*AC* 34; *KSA* 6:206). Yet, if Nietzsche's deconstructed Jesus actually comes remarkably close to Nietzsche's Dionysian Pietism, can Nietzsche *himself* become a true Dionysian Pietist? To be sure, Jesus has the strike against him in that he's decadent by way of his "*instinctive hatred of reality.*" Yet he does not—unlike Nietzsche—suffer from *ressentiment.*

There is yet a further problem with Nietzsche's read of Jesus. What Nietzsche gives us is a very "weak" version of Jesus. To do that, of course, he has to ignore all sorts of aspects of Jesus' life recorded in the Gospels that would seem to give us a very "strong" character (such as Jesus' repeatedly breaking rules regarding the Sabbath or his habit of saying "you have heard it said" and then saying "but I say to you").[39] But, for the sake of argument, let us allow Nietzsche's version to stand (at least momentarily). What is *not* clear is that Jesus' "weakness" is *necessarily* a mark of "declining" rather than "ascending" life. Nietzsche, of course, thinks that the virtues of nobility (courage, pride, etc.) are what mark ascending life. But Nietzsche's account is far too simple. Dostoevsky puts the problem well when he exclaims: "Humility is the most terrible force that can ever exist in the world!"[40] Nietzsche assumes that humility is a mark of weakness, but it can just as easily be conceived as a mark of strength. The kind of quiet strength exuded by, say, Gandhi is simply off Nietzsche's strength spectrum. And so is the kind of strength exuded by Jesus. As Stephen N. Williams well puts it: "*Amor patris* actually requires more strength than *amor fati.*"[41] So Nietzsche would simply read Jesus as an example of declining life. Of course, as I have argued, Nietzsche *needs* this weak read of Jesus in order for *Nietzsche* to come off looking the superior of the two.

Unfortunately for Nietzsche, this reading of both Jesus and Nietzsche is possible only on the basis of self-deception, using Nietzsche's own definition: "By lie I mean: wishing *not* to see something that one does see; wishing not to see something *as* one sees it. Whether the lie takes place before witnesses or without witnesses does not matter. The most common lie is that with which one lies to oneself; lying to others is, relatively, an exception" (*AC* 55; *KSA* 6:238). It is hard to see Nietzsche as anything other than self-deceived. Of course, self-deception is not simple ignorance. One must have some inkling, some nagging sense, that the story one tells oneself is not completely true. Or else there would be no self-deception. Nietzsche is, I think, too self-aware—too little of an "idiot"—to be simply ignorant of his own situation. So one can only see him as deceiving himself. Yet, if such is the case, then is there any reason to think that Nietzsche really "resists" decadence and *ressentiment*? How seriously are we to take his accounts of having successfully "resisted" decadence in *Ecce Homo*? Indeed, how seriously are we to take any of his accounts of having moved beyond Christianity and having truly *embraced* a Dionysian Pietism? In the final chapter, I argue that Nietzsche's Pietism remains Christian, all too Christian.

But first we need to examine Nietzsche's musical *askêsis* and see how it might help him resist decadence, and truly embrace a Dionysian Pietism.

NINE

Nietzsche's Musical *Askêsis*

> *Was there anything more useful than rhythm to the old super-*
> *stitious type of human being? One could do everything with it:*
> *promote some work magically; compel a god to appear, to be near,*
> *to listen; mould the future according to one's own will; discharge*
> *some excess (of fear, of mania, of pity, of vengefulness) from one's*
> *soul, and not only one's own soul but also that of the most evil*
> *demon. Without verse, one was nothing; through verse one almost*
> *became a god. Such a basic feeling cannot be eradicated—and*
> *still today, after millennia of work at fighting superstition, even*
> *the wisest of us occasionally becomes a fool for rhythm, if only*
> *insofar as he feels a thought to be truer when it has a metric form*
> *and presents itself with a divine hop, skip, and a jump.*[1]

How does one become a fool for rhythm, not just any old rhythm but the rhythm of life—which is not only as old a rhythm as there is (at least for Nietzsche) but also the one rhythm that is *not* decadent? Such is not merely a theoretical question but Nietzsche's very practical *pursuit*. To escape from the rhythm of decadence, one must put a new rhythm in its place. To that end, Nietzsche needs an *askêsis* that is *musical* in nature.

This last claim—that Nietzsche needs a musical *askêsis*—immediately raises two central questions. First, if falling back into rhythm is Nietzsche's goal, then why does he require an *askêsis*? Second, what makes this *askêsis* distinctly *musical*? The answers to both of those questions are hardly immediately apparent, largely because the usually accepted definitions of both "music" and *askêsis* are both too simple and too narrow.

To answer these two questions, I suggest four factors, which this chapter will develop in detail. First, as we've already noted, music proves an immensely important part of both life and *thought* for Nietzsche. Strong goes so far as to claim that "music provides Nietzsche with both a paradigm of philosophical activity and an insight into the workings of a healthy culture."[2] So music is not just about tones or even rhythm: it has to do with both philosophy and culture—in short, life itself. Second, Nietzsche himself frequently speaks of music as a catalyst for change, a belief fully in line with that of the ancient Greeks. The citation that opens this chapter provides us with a rather remarkable list of what music used to be able to accomplish. And it is clear that Nietzsche thinks some of these uses are still possible. Most specifically, it is in the practicing of *mousikê*—and the *ekstasis* that it engenders—that allows Nietzsche to become what he most wants to become: a "free spirit" [*freie Geist*]. As Valadier puts it, "The Dionysian ideal . . . aims at a *real* overcoming of the individual by way of a metamorphosis, a self-transformation by steadfast affirmation."[3] Music is transformative in precisely this sense. Third, the model that Nietzsche gives us of the "music-practicing Socrates" in *The Birth of Tragedy* is not only never abandoned but also later indirectly affirmed. To be a philosopher who is able to practice music represents a quantum leap forward from the philosopher as represented by Socrates. Finally, Nietzsche styles himself as "a disciple of the philosopher Dionysus" (*EH* "Books" P 2; *KSA* 6:258). To follow Dionysus—the god of music—would, at the very least, mean privileging music to an unprecedented degree. Such is precisely what Nietzsche does. As Claudia Crawford puts it, "Nietzsche began his published works with praise of the languages of the Dionysus dithyramb: dance and song. And he ended his works with the singing of the *Dionysus Dithyrambs* and his dancing, singing and shouting utterances in Turin."[4] Music, then, plays a key role throughout the entire Nietzschean corpus.

The Music-Practicing Nietzsche

To trace the pivotal role that music has in Nietzsche's thought, it is helpful to turn back to one of Nietzsche's earliest models—the "music-practicing Socrates." How does this Socrates—one hinted at rather than truly instantiated—become the model for the "music-practicing Nietzsche"? To answer that question, we need to return to Socrates' death scene once again:

> It is like this, you see. In the course of life I have often had the same dream, appearing in different forms at different times, but always saying the same thing, "Socrates, practice and cultivate the arts" [the Greek word here is *mousikê*]. In the past I used to think that it

was impelling and exhorting me to do what I was actually doing; I mean that the dream, like a spectator encouraging a runner in a race, was urging me on to do what I was already doing, that is, practicing the arts, because philosophy is the greatest of the arts, and I was practicing it. But ever since my trial, while the festival of the god has been delaying my execution, I have felt that perhaps it might be this popular form of art that the dream intended me to practice, in which case I ought to practice it and not disobey. I thought it would be safer not to take my departure before I had cleared my conscience by writing poetry and so obeying the dream. I began with some verses in honor of the god whose festival it was. When I had finished my hymn, I reflected that a poet, if he is to be worthy of the name, ought to work on imaginative themes, not descriptive ones, and I was not good at inventing stories.[5]

Such is what Socrates tells us only moments before his death. He thought he had been practicing *mousikê* by doing philosophy, but now he isn't so sure after all. To our ears, of course, that admonition to practice music seems plain enough: Socrates should have been composing or singing songs. Yet the ancient Greek conception of *mousikê* is much more complex than our conception of "music." Thus, for example, Lydia Goehr rightly describes the "Socratic concept of *mousikê*" as "a philosophical quest for the cultivation of the soul and political quest for freedom."[6] As strange as that claim may sound to us, it would have made perfect sense to Socrates.

To make sense of Socrates' confusion—or to see why he *should* be confused—we need to consider the scope of *mousikê* for the ancient Greeks.[7] First, unlike our conception of music, *mousikê* includes tones, rhythm, dance, and words. The idea of "absolute music" (i.e., music without words) is simply foreign to the ancient Greeks, who normally thought of poetry being sung with accompanying movement as *mousikê*. So, whereas we would tend to make a distinction between *logos* and *mousikê*, the Greeks simply would not have made this distinction.[8] Music, then, is not some other *thing* than "reason" (even though it is something *more* than reason defined as logic or dialectic). Second, *mousikê* is defined even more broadly than that, for in ancient Greece "people described as μουσικοι, *musici,* are often not musicians but students of musical theory and philosophy."[9] One need only think of Pythagoras as an example of a philosopher whose philosophy and mathematics were both dependent upon musical theory. However, simply being a philosopher would already be enough to identify one as a *mousikos*—a musician. Indeed, any sort of endeavor in which one depended upon the muses—originally poets, but later artists in general, philosophers, and intellectuals—would have counted as *mousikê*. So, while a *principal* definition of the *mousikos* would be of a person "skilled in music," a *secondary* definition would be "man of letters and accomplishments, scholar."[10] Socrates' confusion should now be clear: he thinks he *is* practicing *mousikê*. Moreover, given his elitist dismissal of not just music but also all of what we would today call the "arts," he sees himself as practicing "the greatest of the arts"— philosophy. So, when he finally takes time to write a hymn to Apollo (given that it happened to be the time of Apollo's feast day), he thinks he has lowered himself to significant depths of vulgarity.

Yet Nietzsche reads this passage quite differently. And that fundamental ambiguity in the ancient Greek notion of *mousikê* is what makes his reading not only possible but also somewhat plausible. On Nietzsche's account, Socrates was indeed confused, and that confusion stems from his elevation of philosophy—or more specifically logic—over the *other* arts. In the wake of Platonic philosophy, we in the western tradition are inclined to accept that difference in valuation without question. Yet that hierarchy is one that is distinctly Platonic but also deeply at odds with "truly ancient" Greek thought. In privileging philosophy over rhetoric, Plato and Socrates were making a bold new move. So Nietzsche hints at the possibility of *another* Socrates, one who goes back on that distinction and finally begins to take the muse seriously. Even though Nietzsche invokes this *musiktreibende Sokrates* in a work that he later renounces in some fairly significant ways—and we have seen that *Twilight of the Idols* has a rather different ending for Socrates—there is no reason to think that Nietzsche ever gave up on the idea of a *musiktreibende Nietzsche*. Indeed, what he writes in *Ecce Homo* about *The Birth of Tragedy* would seem to keep this hope alive: "A tremendous hope speaks out of this essay. In the end I lack all reason to renounce the hope for a Dionysian future of music" (*EH* "Books" BT 4; *KSA* 6:313).

At least two closely related confusions should now be cleared up. First, we have seen that the Greek conception of music includes more than just tones and rhythm. Not only would music without words have been unthinkable but also music is not something *other than* rationality (even though it goes *beyond* any narrow conception of rationality). But here Nietzsche is not *simply* working with the ancient Greek conception of music. Given the role he accords music, it is clear that he holds to a view that was common among the German Romantics. As Goehr puts it, for the German Romantics, "the purely musical" serves "as a repository for all that which could not be captured by a philosophical theory constrained solely by the authority of reason" and "as a general metaphor symbolizing a repository for all that was unknowable by ordinary cognitive or logical means."[11] This broader sense of "music" leads to a second point, namely, that "practicing music" would have been broad enough to include any art that required skill and practice. So, when Nietzsche speaks of practicing music, we should think much more broadly than someone playing the piano or listening to an orchestra. Indeed, we should think of practicing the very kinds of skills that are part of *living life,* since doing so is exactly what constitutes "practicing music" for Nietzsche.

This latter point also helps flesh out the meaning of a musical *askêsis.* For, if *askêsis* is a spiritual exercise that is designed to transform one's being (as we saw in chapter 4), then the phrase "musical *askêsis*"—at least in its broadest form—is almost redundant. Given that someone who is accomplished and skilled is a *mousikos*—and given that "practicing music" is likewise synonymous with cultivating the soul—then practicing music in this broad sense necessarily is engaging in an *askêsis* (a spiritual exercise). That the Greeks—and certainly Nietzsche—thought that music had an enormous effect upon one's very being only makes this connection more obvious. Of course, there is one complication that—in an important sense—not only remains but actually becomes more problematic: Nietzsche constantly moves back and forth between music in the narrow sense and music in the broad sense (sketched above). Here we could attempt to sort out these senses. Yet, since Nietzsche clearly thinks that they are fundamentally connected, such a move would seem to be truly un-Nietzschean. Thus, I will follow Nietzsche's lead here and refrain from disentangling these senses. In most cases it is relatively clear which sense (or senses) Nietzsche has in mind.

So what would a *musiktreibende Nietzsche* be like? At the most basic level, he would be truly *musical* in both practice and theory. But, of course, "musical" here would be used in the richest possible sense of *mousikê,* which includes thinking, writing, composing music, dancing, and singing—or *living life* in a way in which one is utterly "in tune" or in harmony with life. One would be a *mousikos* in the complete sense: musician and scholar, writer and dancer, one fully developed. Although it might sound like hyperbole when Nietzsche claims the following, I take it as indicative of the absolute centrality of music for Nietzsche—as a person and as a thinker. Writing to an accomplished musician (who happened to be the conductor of the premiere of *Parsifal*), Nietzsche says: "Perhaps there has never been a philosopher who was so very much a musician at bottom as I am" (letter to Hermann Levi, October 20, 1887; *KSB* 8:172). This inherent musicality is what makes Nietzsche and Socrates so different. Whereas Socrates needed to be persuaded to practice music—and then only does so rather begrudgingly—Nietzsche takes such a practice as central to life. In the same way that Socrates is "destined" to turn to dialectic as his method against decadence, Nietzsche would see himself as "destined" to be a musical philosopher. If previous philosophers had closed their ears to music, Nietzsche is finally able—and willing—to *listen*. As it turns out, music is central to Nietzsche's life and philosophizing in several ways.

The Centrality of Music

First, Nietzsche thinks that music allows us to face the tragedy of human existence, not so much in the sense of a diversion but as a means of "speaking" about life.[12] There are things that can be "said" musically—or perhaps *sung*—that cannot be said philosophically. Leiner puts that as follows: "[Music] made possible a non-discursive direct experience of life far different from the highly analytical, scholarly reflections of professional academic scholarship of late 19th century Europe."[13] Such a claim can be parsed out in two different ways. On the one hand, music speaks to us with a directness, honesty, and truth that is simply unmatched by words. In a fragment titled "On Music and Words" (probably from 1871) Nietzsche maintains that "The multiplicity of languages immediately reveals the fact that word and thing do not completely and necessarily coincide and that words are symbols. But what do words symbolize? Surely, only representations. . . . For how could a word-symbol correspond to that inmost essence whose images we ourselves are along with the world? It is only through representations that we know this kernel" (*OMW* 107; *KSA* 7:12 [1]).

Here it sounds as if Nietzsche is still under the Kantian-Schopenhauerian spell (in which there really *is* a *Ding-an-sich*). Yet the point he makes stands with or without the phenomenal/noumenal distinction. Precisely because words are representations—and so "stand in" for something else—they never give us reality (so to speak) "as it is." So the problem is that language never "gives us" anything directly—and it seems that Nietzsche is uncertain about exactly how much it gives us *indirectly*. He claims: "Every concept arises from the equation of unequal things. Just as it is certain that the concept 'leaf' is never totally the same as another, so it is certain that the concept 'leaf' is formed by arbitrarily discarding these individual differences and by forgetting the distinguishing aspects" (*PT* 83; *KSA* 1:880).

Since language is always metaphorical—and so never delivers to us the "thing itself"—music is all the more significant. For Nietzsche (like the German Romantics) thinks it has a directness that is unlike language. When Nietzsche contrasts the value to the words of a lyrical poem (and thus the images it conjures up) to the music to which it is set, he makes it clear that music has a revelatory power that language and its images simply cannot have: "Confronted with the supreme revelations of music, we feel, willy-nilly, the *crudeness* of all imagery and of every emotion that might be adduced by way of an analogy [i.e., precisely the way language functions for Nietzsche]. Thus Beethoven's last quartets put to shame everything visual and the whole realm of empirical reality" (*OWM* 112; *KSA* 7:12 [1]). So music has a significant edge over words. Of course, whatever it is that music conveys cannot be conveyed by words. So, at a certain point, we are—by definition—unable to "describe" exactly what it is that music *says*. If it could be put into words, we wouldn't need music.

On the other hand, music likewise has a significant edge over science —which would include logic and dialectic. In *The Birth of Tragedy*, Nietzsche's conclusion regarding Socrates' claim on his deathbed that he has often been called to "practice music" is that Socrates is actually called to *honesty*. Nietzsche suggests that art may have something to add that makes *logos* more truthful: "The words spoken by the figure who appeared to Socrates in a dream are the only hint of any scruples in him about the limits of logical nature; perhaps, he must have told himself, things which I do not understand are not automatically unreasonable. Perhaps there is a kingdom of wisdom from which the logician is banished? Perhaps art may even be a necessary correlative and supplement of science?" (*BT* 14; *KSA* 1:96).

Here the problem is clear enough for Nietzsche. Socrates has failed to listen to the muse (who has spoken over and over again), and the result is that he has fundamentally not only misunderstood his role as philosopher but also fails to understand what true knowledge is. Nietzsche accuses Socrates of having used philosophy to mask the truth: "The optimistic dialectic drives *music* out of tragedy under the lash of its syllogisms" (*BT* 14; *KSA* 1:95). In other words, the truth is obscured by the optimism of the dialectic, which operates with the assumption that we can "make sense" of the world in general and life in particular. So Nietzsche clearly thinks that Socrates has not heard the truth that music—defined both narrowly and also more broadly in the sense of poetry and rhetoric—has to offer. Given that "music" stands for all that cannot be grasped by logic or dialectic, then the unmusical Socrates has missed the entire wealth of meaning that extends beyond logic and dialectic.

A second reason why music is so important to Nietzsche has to do with Nietzsche's great emphasis on the body. Since words speak to "little reason" and music to "great reason," music trumps words—immeasurably. Music is thus much more effective in bringing about a change in us. We noted in chapter 5 that Nietzsche thinks dialectic—providing intellectual reasons for one's beliefs—is relatively unconvincing. On his account, as soon as one has to provide reasons, the suspicions of the listener are already raised. The most convincing views are ones that are simply presented and accepted as true, without any kind of "grounding" by way of reason. Further, since the intellect or consciousness is one of the least developed aspects of our body, it is one of the least important things in causing a change in us. Frederick R. Love notes that the ability accorded music actually grows *stronger* in Nietzsche's later thought. As he puts it, there is a growing "willingness to recognize the increased therapeutic effect of musical enjoyment."[14] In support of that claim, Love cites what Nietzsche says in a letter to Gast (January 15, 1888), in which one of Nietzsche's most famous statements regarding music appears (though, quite surprisingly, Love does not include that statement in his citation): "Music now gives me sensations, as never before. It detaches me from myself, it sobers me, as if I were observing myself from afar, overfilled; in this, it strengthens me, and every time after an evening of music (I have heard *Carmen* four times) comes a morning full of resolute insights and ideas. This is very strange. It is as though I had been bathing in a more natural element. Life without music is simply an error, a strain, an exile" (*KSB* 8:231–32).

These are remarkably strong claims. For Nietzsche, music proves capable of sharpening his mind, which in turn gives him critical distance, new insights, and ideas—to the bursting point. Moreover, life becomes more natural, which is precisely what Nietzsche seeks. One could easily paraphrase Wagner—who writes, "in the drama, we must become *knowers* through *the feeling*" [Im Drama müssen wir *Wissende* werden durch *das Gefühl*]—to describe Nietzsche's view of music: "in music we must become *knowers* through the feeling."[15] Consider these claims in relation to a very similar one from *Twilight of the Idols*. There Nietzsche says: "How little it takes to make us happy! The sound of a bagpipe.—Without music, life would be an error. The German even imagines God as singing songs" (*TI* I:33; *KSA* 6:64). Here the claim is that music provides happiness.[16] However, in light of the previous citation, that "happiness" needs to be interpreted in a both a broad and a deep sense. The happiness that accrues to us by way of music is that which makes us "overflow" with insights and joy. Music gives us "*joy. A Trinity of Joy:* elevation, illumination, calm, a unity of the three" (*KSA* 8:40 [16]). It also sets us aright in our relation to nature.[17]

Third, music also proves ecstatic for Nietzsche. It has the power to take us out of ourselves, allowing us both to see the world in a different way *and also* to transform us. Personally, Nietzsche experienced this *ecstasis* in his own improvising at the piano: when he improvised, it was often as if a frenzy overcame him.[18] Moreover, Nietzsche is convinced that "music *liberates* the spirit" (*CW* 1; *KSA* 6:14). He writes to conductor Hans von Bülow that he is "cured" by good music (July 20, 1872; *KSB* 4:27) and, later, that music is "a great refreshment" (*KSA* 11:40 [65]). So music is an ingredient to his self-overcoming [*Selbstüberwindung*] or transformation. Nietzsche believes that music has a "swaying" power over us, not merely emotionally but even intellectually. "With tones," he writes, "one can seduce people into every error and every truth" (*GS* 106; *KSA* 3:463). Nietzsche's claim can be validated once we realize how much of what we believe—and even hold dear—has been driven into us by way of rhyme and song. Singing hymns, for instance, is even more a theological conditioning than is preaching. Nietzsche is convinced—as were the ancient Greeks—that words sung in rhythm had a *special* effect upon one that simply was not matched by the bare spoken word. This is why Leiner goes so far as to say we get a better idea of Nietzsche's idea of self-overcoming precisely within the context of music, since it "makes possible a more direct and vivid experience of self-overcoming in its fullest existential dimension." He goes on to add that (as we noted in the introduction) "there must be a rhythm, a rhyme, a meter to the lives of those who would overcome themselves."[19] It is precisely this rhythm that can counter decadence.

Fourth, and most important, music can restore the order of the soul. Here we need to return to the quotation that opened this chapter:

> When one had lost the proper tension and harmony of the soul, one had to *dance* to the beat of the singer—that was the prescription of this healing art. . . . In short: was there anything more *useful* than rhythm to the old superstitious type of human being? One could do everything with it: promote some work magically; compel a god to appear, to be near, to listen; mould the future according to one's own will; discharge some excess (of fear, of mania, of pity, of vengefulness) from one's soul, and not only one's own soul but also that of the most evil demon. Without verse, one was nothing; through verse one almost became a god. (*GS* 84; *KSA* 3:442)

Although Nietzsche goes on to speak of this as a "superstition," he admits that "even the wisest of us occasionally becomes a fool for rhythm." If escape from decadence is not possible by waging war against it (as we have seen), then perhaps becoming "a fool for rhythm" *might* be a way of resisting decadence. The "healing art" is found precisely in the dance that brings the soul into a "proper tension and harmony." For Nietzsche, that dance is both literal and metaphorical.

Since Nietzsche has fallen out of rhythm with life, he needs to finds this new rhythm to overcome himself. In chapter 5 we noted that decadence for Nietzsche can be described in terms of the instincts either being suppressed or else in disarray. For Nietzsche, our instincts *are* life itself. Thus, when they are suppressed or disordered (or, as Nietzsche puts it, we "fight the instincts"), we are simply out of step with life. Properly ordered, our instincts and drives provide our lives with vitality. We noted that, with Socrates, the instinct of reason (which Nietzsche sees as just as "bodily" as any other instinct) is given a place above the other instincts. But, contrary to what Socrates believes, the instinct of reason is less developed that other instincts—and less important to our living in an ordered fashion. So the instincts need to be reordered in such a way that the most "natural" drives (rather than the much more contrived drive of reason) are in charge of our being. Nietzsche identifies these more "natural" drives (as we noted in chapter 5) as will, power, strength, energy, and force.

Of course, exactly *how* these instincts are to be arrayed is somewhat unclear, as is the precise meaning of each of these terms. Yet, in an early essay titled "On Moods," Nietzsche does give us a helpful way of describing the organization of the instincts. Drawing on Plato's view of the soul, he uses the metaphor of an *oikos* [household] to describe the relation of forces within the soul.[20] Socrates speaks of the one who "sets his own house [*ta oikeia*] in order and rules himself; he arranges himself, becomes his own friend, and harmonizes the three parts, exactly like three notes in a harmonic scale."[21] Although Nietzsche's conception of proper harmonization is significantly different from that of Plato (given that Plato makes *reason* the dominant part and Nietzsche seeks to reverse that order), he is clearly working with a conception of "harmony" of the soul. Decadence occurs either when this harmony is lacking *or* when the harmony is achieved with reason in control (as in the case of Socrates). True harmony, then, is achieved when the most important instincts—those that are most in tune with our earthly, this-worldly nature—are dominant. Harmony, though, is achieved by way of *tension,* precisely what puts strings on a lute or a piano in tune. With that in mind, Nietzsche maintains that "conflict is the constant nourishment of the soul, and the soul knows how to extract from it much that is sweet and fine" (*OM* 8; *KGW* I/3, 17 [5]). We noted in chapter 5 that a certain degree of jostling of the instincts is simply part of life. But that conflict must be kept under control; otherwise, there is a "disgregation of the will" (*CW* 7; *KSA* 6:27). "Unless one passion at last becomes master," there is an increasing "inner conflict and anarchism" (*WP* 778; *KSA* 13:14 [157]. Whereas conflict in the healthy soul leads to flourishing and development, it leads to exhaustion in the unhealthy soul.

Musical *Askêsis*

Given just how important music is for Nietzsche, how might he put the power of music to work in the service of overcoming his own decadence? In the fall of 1887 (while composing *On the Genealogy of Morality*), Nietzsche writes the following in one of his notebooks: "I want to make asceticism natural once again: in place of the aim of denial [*Verneinung*], the aim of *strengthening* [*Verstärkung*]; a gymnastics of the will; abstinence and periods of fasting of all kinds, in the most spiritual realm, too . . . an experiment [*Versuch*] with adventures and arbitrary dangers" (*WP* 915; *KSA* 12:9 [93]).

On his own admission, then, Nietzsche is an ascetic—or at least wants to be one. So what would be the most "natural" asceticism?[22] If Nietzsche wants a "gymnastics of the will," then music would seem to be the most logical choice. In commenting on the ancient Greeks and music, Walter Lippman notes that "gymnastics affect the spirited part of the soul and music its rational or philosophic art."[23] Nietzsche actually believes that music "reaches out" to us and takes the form of "*gymnastics*" (*UM* IV:5; *KSA* 1:458). So music can be considered the gymnastics of the will. Moreover, consider how Nietzsche defines life: "life *is* music" (*GS* 372; *KSA* 3:623, my italics). If music *is* life for Nietzsche, then the most "natural" *askêsis* would be musical in nature. Finally, note why Nietzsche claims that philosophers have always attempted to *silence* music: "a true philosopher didn't listen to life insofar as life is music" precisely because listening was considered too *dangerous* in that it exposed one to the ultimate truth (ibid.). Whereas dialectic is (at least for Nietzsche) all about avoiding the complications and unpleasant aspects of life, listening to music means that one is fully aware of those complications and unpleasant aspects—which is what it means to understand *life*.

How, exactly, does this work out in practice? As not only a musical improviser but also an improviser upon himself, Nietzsche certainly "practices music." Composing, playing, and listening to music are central to Nietzsche's *askêsis,* in the sense of being "spiritual exercises" for him. Although Nietzsche felt particularly free while improvising at the piano, we noted earlier that he also speaks of music as providing liberation of and a catalyst for *thought*. That passage is worth quoting in full: "Has it been noticed that music liberates the spirit? gives wings to thought? that one becomes more of a philosopher the more one becomes a musician?— The gray sky of abstraction rent as if by lightning. . . . And unexpectedly answers drop into my lap, a little hail of ice and wisdom, of *solved* problems" (*CW* 1; *KSA* 6:14).

It is not *merely* that music and philosophy *complement* one another but that thinking improves when it *becomes* musical in nature. Given what we noted earlier regarding the importance of the body's "reason" over the mind's reason and also the fact that music "speaks" to the body in a special way, this statement should come as no surprise. Nor should Nietzsche's remedy for helping Germans by learning how to dance. "Thinking," writes Nietzsche, "wants to be learned as dancing wants to be learned, *as* a kind of dancing" (*TI* VIII:7; *KSA* 6:109). While it might first appear as if Nietzsche is merely making an analogy between learning to dance and learning to think, when he goes on to say "*as* a kind of dancing," it becomes clear that "thinking" really *is* a kind of dancing for him. In other words, it is not as if Nietzsche is merely claiming that learning how to dance will somehow help one think; rather, he is making the radical claim that thinking simply *is* dancing. To be sure, this is an unusual claim. But Nietzsche is quite adamant about it. Accordingly, becoming a good philosopher is the same as becoming a good dancer. Not surprisingly, then, Nietzsche writes: "I wouldn't know what the spirit of a philosopher might more want to be than a good dancer. For the dance is his ideal, also his art, and finally also his only piety, his 'service of God'" (*GS* 381; *KSA* 3:635). If the philosopher's *ideal* and *art* is dance, then philosophy must be a kind of dance for Nietzsche.[24]

But why is music—and in particular dance—so important to liberated thinking? Since thinking for Nietzsche has its locus in the body (rather than the fictional entity "mind"), music holds great sway over us. Nietzsche thinks "our most sacred convictions, our most unalterable faith in the matter of supreme values, are *judgments of our muscles*" (*KSA* 13:11 [376]). Accordingly, "first one must convince the *body*" (*TI* IX:47; *KSA* 6:149). So change in "thought" comes about by means of change in the body. Although Nietzsche uses such terms as "soul" and "spirit," he makes it clear that "body am I entirely, and nothing else; and soul is only a word for something about the body" (Z I "Despisers of the Body"; *KSA* 4:39). In recounting his experience of composing *Zarathustra,* Nietzsche writes that "the *body* is inspired; let us keep the 'soul' out of it." It is no accident that he goes on to relate that, during this fertile time, "often one could have seen me dance" (*EH* "Books" Z 4; *KSA* 6:341). The body, then, is the locus of change. Given that bodily emphasis, it is not surprising that, in *Ecce Homo,* Nietzsche proudly tells us of his accomplishments with such bodily things as "nutrition, place, climate, recreation." He characterizes these aspects as "inconceivably more important than everything one has taken to be important so far. Precisely here one must begin to *relearn*" (*EH* "Clever" 10; *KSA* 6:295). In true ascetic fashion, then, bodily exercises for Nietzsche are important influences on what we call "mind" or "soul." Likewise, since the body is so central to *who* we are, *how* we act, and *what* we think, it makes sense that Nietzsche's criticism of Wagner is *physical* rather than *intellectual* or *aesthetic* in nature:

> My objections to Wagner's music are physiological objections: why disguise them with aesthetic formulas? My "fact" is that I stop

> breathing easily once this music starts affecting me; that my *foot* immediately gets angry at it and revolts—it has need for tempo, dance, march; it demands chiefly from music the raptures found in *good* walking, striding, leaping, and dancing—but doesn't my stomach protest, too? My heart? My circulation? My intestines? (*GS* 368; *KSA* 3:616–17)

Even more important, though, music pushes us beyond thought to a place in which we can *live*. To be caught up in the rapture of music's ecstasy is the ultimate goal. Thus, a Dionysian Pietism places us "into the flow" of life, rather than removes us from it (as logical or dialectical thinking would do—at least according to Nietzsche). The "thinking" that takes place from that "point of view" is far more able to "grasp" (to whatever extent this is truly possible) what is truly "real" about life. It is from this ecstatic place that we are able to "see" in a more profound way. Given that it is so difficult to put into words whatever "insights" are available by way of being enraptured, probably the easiest way to think about these "thoughts" from the viewpoint of *ecstasis* is to compare them to what it is the Christian mystic would be able to "see" or understand from having an enrapturing mystical experience. Much the same as the Christian mystic claims that ecstatic rapture enables one to "see" in a way that is simply not available to one who has never had such an ecstatic experience, so Nietzsche would claim such a viewpoint as simply beyond communication. One must experience this state of being for oneself.

Having established that Nietzsche believes that thinking is at its best when it is "musical" in nature and that the locus of change in one's thought is the body, we can now examine how one can "become a fool" for a new sort—or rather the *old* sort—of rhythm. One moves from not only decadence but also the "no-saying" part of Nietzsche's *askêsis* to Nietzsche's affirmative "yes-saying" by way of a musical *askêsis* that requires that one learn (1) to listen, (2) to be swayed by life's music, (3) to sing, and (4) to dance. One changes precisely by *practicing* a new set of spiritual exercises that have a distinctly musical form to fit a distinctly musical way of life.

Putting Music into Practice

First, listening—one of the exercises listed by Philo of Alexandria. Babich puts it well when she says: "It is music that invites one to think by hearing what is said both in the words and between the lines in the style of expression, attending to the unsaid in what is said at the end of philosophy."[25] One reason for learning to listen in Nietzsche's case is *"sounding out idols,"* using a hammer doubling as a tuning fork to reveal all that which is hollow. Nietzsche gives us this metaphor in *Twilight of the Idols,* where he writes: "To pose questions here with a *hammer* for once, and maybe to hear in reply that well-known hollow tone which tells of bloated innards—how delightful for one who has ears even behind his ears" (*TI* P; *KSA* 6:57–58). While Nietzsche particularly has the idols known as Plato's Forms in mind, there are many other idols. To hear those idols *as* idols, though, one must develop "ears even behind his ears," a kind of supersensitive hearing that hears between the lines. Before one can rid oneself of idols, one must first *detect* them—a rather difficult thing to do. All of *Twilight of the Idols* is the practicing of listening for Nietzsche, and so part of his *askêsis.*

A second reason for listening is to hear what philosophers have long tried to tune out. Nietzsche writes: "'Wax in the ear' was virtually a condition of philosophizing; a true philosopher didn't listen to life insofar as life is music; he *denied* the music of life—it is an old philosopher's superstition that all music is siren music" (*GS* 372; *KSA* 3:623–24). Taking the wax out of one's ear symbolizes that one is no longer attempting to deny aspects of life that one might rather not acknowledge. We might say that part of Nietzsche's *askêsis* is an honest reflecting upon what philosophers have tried to deny—viz., that life *doesn't* make rational sense. But there is further benefit of this sort of listening. If one gives in to siren music, one can allow oneself to become a fool for its rhythm. For that to happen, we must be willing (and also able) to *listen.* Usually, like any *askêsis,* this change takes place over time. Yet Nietzsche surprisingly speaks of having "a sudden and profoundly decisive change in my taste, especially in music" at the time of writing *Zarathustra.* He goes on to say: "Perhaps the whole of *Zarathustra* may be reckoned as music; certainly a rebirth of the art of *hearing* was among its preconditions" (*EH* "Books" Z 1; *KSA* 6:335). Of course, listening for Nietzsche would also naturally involve three other exercises from that list by Philo: research, investigation, and reading. For instance, Nietzsche's "listening"—in effect, "being attentive"—takes place in regard to his investigation regarding Jesus. That reading of Jesus is designed precisely to get past the usual story and "hear" what has gone unsaid. If (as Nietzsche claims) "one cannot read these Gospels cautiously enough" (*AC* 44; *KSA* 6:218), then the kind of reading necessary for the Gospels is one that is extremely attentive to both what is said and unsaid.

Second, we *"must learn to love."* Nietzsche claims "this happens to us in music" when we first *"learn to hear* a figure and a melody." Simply learning to recognize a new melody is already an accomplishment. But the next step is to be able to *"stand* it despite its strangeness." That life cannot be controlled or explained is a *countermelody* to the one we know (and love) so well. This new melody is not one that we immediately love. In fact, to love it requires a sacrifice on our part—we must let go of the old melody (in which life makes sense or "reason = virtue = happiness"). Yet, finally, we reach the stage when "we have become [the new melody's] humble and enraptured lovers, who no longer want anything better from the world than it and it again." Of course, Nietzsche realizes that this is not merely a phenomenon of music but the "way that we have *learned to love* everything we now love" (*GS* 334; *KSA* 6:559–60). So, if we want to love life, we must learn to listen to it and let ourselves become "its humble and enraptured lovers." There is a sense in which we step into rhythm with what we come to love. At first, it is dissonant and foreign. But then we come to be at home with its harmony and rhythm. It is the arrival at not merely familiarity with the rhythm of life but also *loving* that rhythm that Nietzsche seeks.

Third, we must learn to sing new songs. On the one hand, Nietzsche is well aware how much is communicated to us by way of songs and rhymes. Already in *Aus meinem Leben,* Nietzsche had written: "God has given us music, so that first of all we would be led by it upwards. . . . [Music] can elevate, it can flirt, it can cheer us up. . . . The musical art often speaks to us in tones more insistently than poetry in words and seizes the most secret folds of the heart" (*KGW* I/1, 4 [77]). As Higgins notes, "strong rhymes and regular rhythms emphasize and render memorable the messages with which they are conjoined."[26] And we are given these messages from early on: Zarathustra reminds us that "we are presented with grave words and values almost from the cradle" (*Z* III "Spirit of Gravity"; *KSA* 4:242). Since we learned so many of our current values by way of song and rhyme, we can best unlearn them by substituting new songs and rhymes.

Singing also proves therapeutic, as Zarathustra discovers when he is overcome by his own teachings. Zarathustra/Nietzsche copes with this inability by emulating the saint whom Zarathustra discovers when he first goes down from the mountain: with "singing, weeping, laughing, and humming." When Zarathustra is overcome by his own teachings, the animals remind him that "singing is for the convalescent; the healthy can speak." Zarathustra admits that this singing cure is the very "comfort and convalescence I invented for myself."[27] The animals admonish him: "O convalescent, fashion yourself a lyre first, a new lyre! For behold, Zarathustra, new lyres are needed for your new songs. Sing and overflow, O Zarathustra: cure your soul with new songs that you may bear your great destiny, which has never yet been any man's destiny. For your animals know well, O Zarathustra, who you are and must become: *you are the teacher of the eternal recurrence*—that is your destiny" (*Z* III "Convalescent" 2; *KSA* 4:275).

There are two important points in this text. First, singing proves both a cure for Zarathustra's illness and a means of self-overcoming that pushes him on to something greater. It does what thinking alone could not do. So singing is part of or contributes to yet another one of the spiritual exercises listed by Philo: self-mastery. Singing enables Zarathustra to "bear [his] great destiny" and thus become master over himself. Second, for the cure to work, Zarathustra needs *new* lyres, and not just new songs. The implication is that these new songs are so different that they simply cannot be played on the old lyres. It is new *sort* of music that goes along with a new sort of *being*.

As Nietzsche tries to move toward a view of life that both acknowledges its inherent tragedy and yet rejoices in life, he wants new music, new songs to sing. Earlier he had spoken pejoratively of operas that expressed a "longing for the idyll" (*BT* 19; *KSA* 1:122). But now he says, "I should not know how to get along without Rossini" and that he wants his music to be "cheerful and profound like an afternoon in October" (*EH* "Clever" 7; *KSA* 6:290–91). Instead of the "'German seriousness' in music," he wants "the genius of gaiety" (letter to Gast, November 10, 1887; *KSB* 8:191). One finds this, for instance, in Mozart. Nietzsche speaks of "the cheerful, enthusiastic, tender, enamored spirit of Mozart, who was happily no German and whose seriousness is a gracious, a golden, seriousness, and *not* the seriousness of a German Philistine" (*NCW* "Wagner as a Danger" 2; *KSA* 6:423).[28] Although Nietzsche says that he "shall never admit that a German *could* know what music is," he does make exceptions for either Germans who were actually foreigners or else "*extinct* Germans, like Heinrich Schütz, Bach, and Handel" (*EH* "Clever" 7; *KSA* 6:290–91).[29] Other German composers, however, are simply inferior. Nietzsche proclaims: "The Germans are *incapable* of any notion of greatness; proof: Schumann" (*EH* "Clever" 4; *KSA* 6:286). Although much of Nietzsche's own music bears a striking resemblance to that of Robert Schumann, Nietzsche accuses him of having "a *small* taste (being a dangerous tendency towards calm lyricism and a drunkenness of feeling, which is twice as dangerous among Germans)" (*BGE* 245; *KSA* 5:188). This critique of a lack of "greatness" is one that Nietzsche also levels against Johannes Brahms, claiming that "he does *not* create out of an abundance, he *languishes* for abundance" (*CW* 2nd Postscript; *KSA* 6:47). German music also ends up being decadent for Nietzsche, for "in all German music one can hear a deep bourgeois envy of nobility" (*GS* 103; *KSA* 3:459). And, of course, Wagner is the worst of all, for he "makes sick whatever he touches—*he has made music sick*" (*CW* 5; *KSA* 6:21). It is understandable, then, that Nietzsche cautions against the influence of German music:

> I recommend taking a number of precautions against German music. Suppose that someone loves the south like I do, as an immense school for convalescence of both the most spiritual and the most sensual kind, as an unbridled, sun-drenched, sun-transfiguration that spreads across a high-handed, self-assured existence: such a person will learn to be somewhat careful with German music, because, along with ruining his taste, it will ruin his health again too. If someone like this (who is southern not by descent but by *belief*) dreams about the future of music, he will also have to dream about music being redeemed from the north, and have the prelude to a more profound and powerful, perhaps more evil and mysterious music in his ears. (*BGE* 255; *KSA* 5:200–201)

Who might provide this music that is "more profound and powerful," as well as "more evil and mysterious"? The answer for Nietzsche is simple: Bizet. In place of music that makes one sick, Nietzsche prefers music that tempts us to love life. Thus, when criticizing Wagner he exclaims: "Bizet makes me fertile. Whatever is good makes me fertile. I have no other gratitude, nor do I have any other *proof* for what is good." Even though Nietzsche elsewhere tempers his comments regarding Bizet, *Carmen* evidently achieves something that Wagner's operas cannot achieve—a new song that "liberates the spirit."[30] Nietzsche finds that "every time I heard *Carmen* I seemed to myself more of a philosopher, a better philosopher" and that "improvement" is characterized by a state in which he becomes "patient" and "settled." Bizet's music proves to be a model of what Nietzsche wishes to become: "This music seems perfect to me. It approaches lightly, supplely, politely. It is pleasant, it does not *sweat*. 'What is good is light; whatever is divine moves on tender feet': first principle of my aesthetics. This music is evil, subtly fatalistic. . . . Have more painful tragic accents ever been heard on the stage? How are they achieved? Without grimaces. Without counterfeit. Without the *lie* of great style" (*CW* 1; *KSA* 6:13–14).

Bizet is able to be strikingly *honest* about the wretched lot that is human life. Indeed, *Carmen* the opera and Carmen the character exemplify *amor fati*. And, yet, Bizet's music is light, subtle, and even cheerful. Its subtlety partakes of what Nietzsche elsewhere terms *la gaya scienza*— the gay science. In speaking of *la gaya scienza*, Nietzsche refers to the last poem ("To the Mistral") in "*Songs of Prince Free-as-Bird* [*Vogelfrei*]" as "an exuberant dancing song in which, if I may say so, one dances right over morality" and so "is a perfect Provençalism" (*EH* "Books" GS; *KSA* 6:334).[31] Elsewhere, Nietzsche characterizes *la gaya scienza* as "light feet, wit, fire, grace; the great logic; the dance of the stars; the exuberant spirituality; the southern shivers of light; the *smooth* sea—perfection" (*CW* 10; *KSA* 6:37). Such freedom, lightness, and honesty as found in *Carmen* and *la gaya scienza* is what Nietzsche finds that changes him: "You begin to see how much this music improves me? . . . The return to nature, health, cheerfulness, youth, *virtue!*" (*CW* 3; *KSA* 6:16). That Bizet is able to bestow both health and cheerfulness is because he returns Nietzsche to "nature," which is to say the rhythm of life. It is precisely the ability to be cheerful—with grace and exuberance—in the midst of all the difficulties life has to offer that means one has left decadence behind.

Finally, we must learn to dance. For Nietzsche, dancing is the most important of the musical arts. It is telling that he ends his 1886 preface to *The Birth of Tragedy* with these lines from *Thus Spoke Zarathustra*: "Lift up your hearts, my brothers, high, higher! And do not forget your legs! Lift up your legs, too, you fine dancers! Even better, stand on your heads! . . . Zarathustra the dancer, Zarathustra the light one, he who beckons with his wings, he who is ready to fly, beckoning to all the birds, prepared and ready, he who is blissfully frivolous" (*BT* P 7; *KSA* 1:22). As we have noted, dancing changes us for it moves our bodies, which are our first and greatest reason. While *Thus Spoke Zarathustra* is filled with dancing, there are a few particularly important dance scenes.

One use of dance turns out to be part of Nietzsche's "no-saying" *askêsis* that leads to his "yes-saying" *askêsis* (in "The Seven Seals"). In "The Tomb Song," Zarathustra dances against everything he wishes to leave behind. Although Nietzsche does not use the phrase, it is hard not to have the image of one dancing over the graves of one's enemies in mind. Zarathustra opens "The Tomb Song" by singing: "'There is the isle of tombs, the silent isle; there too are the tombs of my youth. There I wish to carry an evergreen wreath of life'" (*Z* II "Tomb Song"; *KSA* 4:142). Zarathustra's enemies are those from his youth who wished to deprive him of his will by entrapping him in morality and all of the notions of the weak (neighbor love, pity, guilt, etc.). It is only Zarathustra's *will* that allows him to stand firm: "Indeed, for me, you are still the shatterer of all tombs. Hail to thee, my will! And only where there are tombs are there resurrections" (*Z* II "Tomb Song"; *KSA* 4:145). Only if Zarathustra holds fast—and these enemies remain dead—can there be a "resurrection." Of course, that resurrection is not that of these old enemies, but that of the more original values that Nietzsche associates with the truly ancient Greeks—pride, self-certainty, and nobility. Thus, Zarathustra dances against all that is heavy, all that attempts to imprison him. Simply dancing proves to lighten one's being and render powerless the spirit of gravity. In this dance, Zarathustra says, "all the visions and consolations of my youth died" (Z II "Tomb Song"; *KSA* 4:144).

Second, in "The Other Dancing Song," Zarathustra is faced with learning to dance with life, which means learning to dance with uncertainty and tragedy. In effect, learning to dance is learning to embrace life with all of its dangers and vicissitudes. In other words, dancing requires that one be willing to play the rough game. As we noted in chapter 5, "to the rabble, wisdom seems like a kind of escape, a device or trick for pulling yourself out of the game when things get rough." But, for Nietzsche, the true philosopher does the exact opposite: "The real philosopher . . . lives 'unphilosophically,' 'unwisely,' in a manner which is above all *not clever,* and feels the weight and duty of a hundred experiments [*Versuchen*] and temptations [*Versuchungen*] of life:—he constantly puts *himself* at risk, he plays *the* rough game" (*BGE* 205; *KSA* 5:133).

Instead of playing it safe, the real philosopher risks it all. Moreover, if Zarathustra is truly to affirm life, it is Life who must *lead* in the dance. Yet Zarathustra turns out to be rather poor at dancing with Life—and *unfaithful*. To make up for his lack of skill, he keeps cracking his whip. Surely this is the whip of "the optimistic dialectic" that operates by way of the "lash of its syllogisms" (*BT* 14; *KSA* 1:95). In the first dancing song, Life had said: "But I am merely changeable and wild and a woman in every way, and not virtuous" (*Z* II "Dancing Song"; *KSA* 4:140). Zarathustra recognizes *intellectually* that Life is changeable and wild, but he finds it difficult to *feel differently*. For, like Socrates, he had always felt that Life could be tamed by reason. But, in the other dancing song, Life acknowledges to him their similarities, and the fact that they had better learn to get along: "We are both two real good-for-nothings and evil-for-nothings. Beyond good and evil we found our island and our green meadow—we two alone. Therefore we had better like each other. And even if we do not love each other from the heart—need we bear each other a grudge if we do not love each other from the heart?" (*Z* III "Other Dancing Song" 2; *KSA* 4:284).

Zarathustra should at least like Life, if not love Life. After all, what else would *amor fati* be, if not loving Life? Yet Zarathustra's love is an unfaithful love. Life realizes that Zarathustra is not so true to her after all. For she goes on to say: "O Zarathustra, you are not faithful enough to me! You do not love me nearly as much as you say. I know that you are thinking of leaving me soon" (*Z* III "Other Dancing Song" 2; *KSA* 4:484–85). What would it mean for Zarathustra to "leave Life"? It would be to take refuge in the metaphysical comfort of philosophy, art, and religion—all that is "otherworldly"—and thus to take a stand *against* Life.

At this point—having been charged with infidelity—Zarathustra resorts to song. In effect, Zarathustra attempts to affirm his fidelity to Life by singing a new song:

> If my virtue is a dancer's virtue and I have often jumped with both feet into golden-emerald delight; if my sarcasm is a laughing sarcasm, at home under rose slopes and hedges of lilies—for in laughter all that is evil comes together, but is pronounced holy and absolved by its own bliss; and if this is my alpha and omega, that all that is heavy and grave should become light; all that is body, dancer; all that is spirit, bird—and verily, that is my alpha and omega: Oh, how should I not lust after eternity and after the nuptial ring of rings, the ring of recurrence. Never yet have I found the woman from whom I wanted children, unless it be this woman whom I love: for I love you, O eternity. *For I love you, O eternity!* (*Z* III "Seven Seals" 6; *KSA* 4:290–91)[32]

Here we have expressed all that Nietzsche longs for. He wants to be a dancer, to dance lightly with laughter over all that is grave and "good." His "no-saying" effectively becomes "yes-saying." He says that he *lusts* after eternity, the doctrine of eternal recurrence, which is to say Life her-self. Here he pledges his love and fealty, as strongly as it could be pledged. As David B. Allison notes, for Nietzsche "musical harmony symbolizes the world."[33] If such is the case, then Nietzsche is certainly going to want to be part of that harmony with the world.

So how might we summarize what Nietzsche's *askêsis* is ultimately designed to accomplish? Strong claims that Nietzsche's *askêsis* can be found in the Preface to *Human, All Too Human*.[34] Although the aspects that Nietzsche mentions there are certainly not exhaustive of all that he hopes to become—nor does Nietzsche speak of them in terms of an *askêsis* per se—they *do* provide a kind of summary of the free spirit's basic characteristics, which can be enumerated as follows.[35]

First, Nietzsche hopes to attain an "overflowing health and certainty" that is so vibrant and certain of itself (which is to say *not* decadent) that it is even able to use "illness" [*Krankheit*] to its own advantage.[36] Implied here (even if not specifically stated) is the idea that Nietzsche sees himself as capable of using precisely what ails him as a kind of cure: "Sickness itself can be a stimulant to life: only one has to be healthy enough for this stimulant" (*CW* 5; *KSA* 6:22). The ability of incorporating his decadence to his own advantage is at least part of what a free spirit should possess. Thus, Nietzsche makes it clear that he has a special ability to take pre-cisely what ails him and incorporate it into his cure for health. He claims: "For a typically healthy person . . . being sick can even become an ener-getic *stimulus* for life, for living *more*. . . . what does not kill him makes him stronger" (*EH* "Wise" 2; *KSA* 6:267).[37]

Second, we noted that music allows for a kind of self-mastery, and this is one of the aspects of the free spirit Nietzsche mentions here. Specifically, this "*mature* freedom of spirit" is "equally self-mastery and discipline of the heart" that "permits access to many and contradictory modes of thought." In *Ecce Homo*, Nietzsche tells us that his ability to resist deca-dence is due (at least partly) to his ability to "*reverse perspectives*" (*EH* "Wise" 1; *KSA* 6:266). As we noted in chapter 4, Nietzsche confidently tells us that he is able to resist decadence because of his two-sided nature and certain skills that he at least thinks he possesses. He says that he is "at the same time a *décadent* and a *beginning*," both "a *décadent*" as well as "the opposite." His "proof" for being the opposite is that he has "always instinctively chosen the *right* means against wretched states" (*EH* "Wise" 1–2; *KSA* 6:264–66). But it is also this ability to master oneself—and even discipline one's heart—that enables one to be a free spirit. As he puts it elsewhere: "*True philosophers are commanders and legislators:* they say, that is how it *should* be" (*BGE* 211; *KSA* 5:145). Of course, disciplining the heart is a crucial part of any *askêsis*.

Third, Nietzsche speaks of "an inner spaciousness and indulgence of superabundance." That one could allow oneself to "indulge" in abundance and yet (as Nietzsche goes on to say) not succumb to the "danger" of the free spirit losing itself shows just how strong such a spirit would be. Clearly, one must have one's soul in proper order to be able to control superabundance. The right instincts must be at the helm to keep one from falling into disarray.

Finally, the free spirit would have a "superfluity of formative, curative, moulding and restorative forces which is precisely the sign of *great* health." This "superfluity" means that the free spirit is able to live "*experimentally*" and partake in "adventure." Earlier, we noted that Nietzsche characterizes his "natural" asceticism as "an experiment [*Versuch*] with adventures and arbitrary dangers." Note that the superfluity of the free spirit both allows for those adventures, and those adventures, in turn, make the free spirit even more free.

Of course, this set of characteristics is one that fits well with what we have seen that music is supposed to be able to accomplish. Music has the ability to change us, to enable us to go beyond the limited sort of thinking found in dialectic and logic, to help us face the very tragedy of human existence, to restore the "proper tension and harmony of the soul," to liberate the spirit, and to affirm life from a position of strength. In short, the power of music for Nietzsche is quite remarkable.

Just how far, though, does Nietzsche get in terms of these goals? Such will be the primary question of chapter 10, but it is worth considering briefly here. If we return to the dance of Nietzsche/Zarathustra at the end of book 3 of *Thus Spoke Zarathustra,* we are confronted with a question. Life has just before this said to Zarathustra that she knows that he isn't truly faithful to her. So, does this song that follows life's negative assessment of Nietzsche/Zarathustra suddenly mean that, *now,* all is right—that Nietzsche/Zarathustra has reached true Dionysian Piety, in the sense of having fallen back into rhythm with life? Or does it instead mean that Nietzsche/Zarathustra is *practicing* (perhaps somewhat desperately) his *askêsis* toward that result? In the final chapter, we consider how far Nietzsche's *askêsis* actually takes him toward truly embracing and *living* his Dionysian Pietism.

TEN

We, Too, Are Still Pious

In what way we, too, are still pious. . . . We see that science, too, rests on a faith; there is simply no "presuppositionless" science. . . . "will to truth" does not mean "I do not want to let myself be deceived" but—there is no alternative—"I will not deceive, not even myself"; and with that we stand on moral ground. . . . But you will have gathered what I am getting at, namely, that it is still a metaphysical faith upon which our faith in science rests— that even we knowers of today, we godless anti-metaphysicians, still take our fire, too, from the flame lit by the thousand-year-old faith, the Christian faith which was also Plato's faith, that God is truth; that truth is divine. . . . But what if this were to become more and more difficult to believe, if nothing more were to turn out to be divine except error, blindness, the lie—if God himself were to turn out to be our longest lie.[1]

There is a complicated logic at work in this passage, not to mention in Nietzsche and his relation to faith and piety in general. Nietzsche *admits* to being pious. Even though he calls himself a "godless anti-metaphysician" (a phrase that turns out to be ironic precisely because Nietzsche is *not* godless), he still believes in truth, which has for millennia been equated with the divine. He realizes that his belief in truth signals a vestigial Christian piety. Yet Nietzsche holds out the possibility of taking Christian morality to its furthest degree—the degree we noted in chapter 2. Precisely because of an absolute commitment to *truth*, perhaps belief in God will be exposed as a "lie." It would be the triumph of Christian morality *over* God. But, if we were to go one step further, the commitment to truth might even be overcome. Admittedly, this would be a strange overcoming. For, although it would have to be *in the name of truth*, it would result in a view of "truth" in which the word "true" was really just a way of talking, not a way of expressing something truly "True." Yet, more important, if God turns out to be "our longest lie," would the death of such a God—the God who is equated with truth—allow for the possibility of the creation of a *new god*? Nietzsche admits that—so far—"at bottom, it is only the moral god that has been overcome." And then he goes on to ask: "Does it make sense to conceive a god 'beyond good and evil'?" (*WP* 55; *KSA* 12:5 [71]). Such, I contend, is exactly what Nietzsche desires and toward which he strives. Yet what exactly does Nietzsche actually *reach*? Moreover, is Nietzsche's project ultimately even *coherent*?

The formula for Nietzsche's new "faith" turns out to be remarkably like that of Gianni Vattimo—who happens to teach at the University of Turin, where Nietzsche spent his final months of sanity and wrote both *The Case of Wagner* and *Ecce Homo*. When asked by an old professor of philosophy whether he still believes in God, Vattimo's answer is: "Well, I believe that I believe."[2] I think that Nietzsche would say that he "believes that he believes" not, of course, in the God of Christianity but in the god of his Dionysian Piety. For Nietzsche, living out his Dionysian Piety is a project begun but never truly completed. Moreover, that "belief" is significantly complicated. First, Nietzsche is *not* truly godless. In fact, his announcement of the death of God allows for a new space for new gods. He himself says: "how many new gods are still possible!" (*WP* 1038; *KSA* 13:17 [4] 5). For Nietzsche, this new god is actually a very old one—Dionysus. Exactly *who* this refigured Dionysus is never becomes fully clear in Nietzsche. But, of course, Dionysus has always been the god of masks, change and metamorphosis, and deception. Second, the extent to which Nietzsche remains connected to the logic—and perhaps even the substance—of Christianity is more significant than he realizes. In other words, he has not *simply* left it all behind. Third, and closely connected, the extent to which Nietzsche is still a decadent means that he is enmeshed not only in the logic of *ressentiment* but also in all that is decadent—including Christianity's supposed denunciation of life.

The Emergence of Dionysian Piety

Haar points out that "the famous phrase 'God is Dead,' however one interprets it, does not put an end to questions about God, gods, or the divine, but rather raises anew the question of the very essence of divinity."[3] Nietzsche can hardly be relegated to the realm of the "confirmed atheist," for the question of God or gods or divinity remains very much alive in his writings. When Nietzsche writes, "I would believe only in a god who knew how to dance" (*Z* I "Reading and Writing"; *KSA* 4:49), it seems as if he has found his "god" in Dionysus. For Zarathustra's encounters with Life (who represents Dionysus) are usually *dancing* encounters. Or, put another way, Life seems in Nietzsche to be the very incarnation of Dionysus, who is also the god of *mousikê*—and thus dance. While it is true that Nietzsche remains silent regarding Dionysus between *The Birth of Tragedy* and *Beyond Good and Evil,* I think that Adrian del Caro is right in claiming that Nietzsche never leaves Dionysus behind: "The Dionysian as a principle, and as a symbol infused with new meaning at various stages in Nietzsche's writing, is in fact quite constant, so that one might say the Dionysian transformed along with Nietzsche, and he was helped in his own transformation from a philologist to a philosopher to the extent that he steered by the Dionysian."[4] For Nietzsche, the Dionysian is slowly transformed from being the opposition to the Apollonian into being the principle or "god" of Life.

Thus, from *The Birth of Tragedy* to the *Dithyrambs of Dionysus,* the presence of Dionysus is always felt—whether explicitly or implicitly. That Dionysus is not always explicitly mentioned is perfectly appropriate, for Dionysus is perhaps the most amorphous of all Greek gods, one who appears in various forms and is both human and divine. Dionysus turns out to be a particularly good replacement for the *Unbekannter* of whom Nietzsche spoke as early as "Dem unbekannten Gott" (1864). As the god of becoming, Dionysus is described as *polumorphos* (polymorphous) and *polueidēs* (appearing in many ways).[5] Moreover, not only is Dionysus "the most versatile and elusive of all Greek gods" but his myths and cults had always been "a challenge to the established social order."[6] Since Nietzsche himself wants to challenge particularly the philosophical and theological order, doing so in the name of Dionysus is particularly appropriate.

Early on in *The Birth of Tragedy,* Nietzsche speaks of "the mysterious primordial One" [*das geheimnissvolle Ur-Eine*] (*BT* 1; *KSA* 1:30). Given the influence of Schopenhauer on Nietzsche at this point (1871–72), it is natural to equate the *Ur-Eine* with Schopenhauer's *Wille* (remarkably like the *Unbekannter*—unknown, unpredictable, and incomprehensible).[7] But, in his "Attempt at Self-criticism" (1886) Nietzsche implies that it is rather Dionysus who is this One.[8] The reason for the emphasis on Dionysus in this early work is clear: Nietzsche sees himself as "a disciple of his god [Dionysus]," and he envisions a new world that is a result of "the release and redemption" of that god. In response to Christianity (which, as Nietzsche notes, is never mentioned in *The Birth of Tragedy*), Nietzsche invents "a fundamentally opposed doctrine and counter-evaluation of life" that he says he "baptized," "not without a certain liberty—for who can know the true name of the Antichrist?—by the name of a Greek god: I called it *Dionysiac*" (*BT* P 4–5; *KSA* 1:15–19). Of course, this interpretation is that of Nietzsche looking back about fourteen years later. By this point he is keenly aware of where *The Birth of Tragedy* went strikingly wrong: it radiated a Romantic pessimism that sought redemption of the world through art. But Nietzsche has now adopted a "Dionysian pessimism," one he associates with a *"superabundance of life"*:

> What is romanticism? Every art, every philosophy can be considered a cure and aid in the service of growing, struggling life: they always presuppose suffering and sufferers. But there are two types of sufferers: first, those who suffer from a *superabundance of life*—they want a Dionysian art as well as a tragic outlook and insight into life; then, those who suffer from an *impoverishment of life* and seek quiet, stillness, calm seas, redemption from themselves through art and insight, or else intoxication, paroxysm, numbness, madness. (*GS* 370; *KSA* 3:620)

That Nietzsche has a Dionysian "tragic outlook" is clear from his preface to the second edition of *The Birth of Tragedy*, which ends with his writing: "You should first learn the art of comfort *in this world*" (*BT* P 7; *KSA* 1:22). It is what Nietzsche elsewhere calls a *"pessimism of strength"* that leads to "a total affirmation of the world" (*KSA* 12:10 [21]). It is "the Dionysian man," writes Michael Allen Gillespie, who is "able to affirm the chaos and contradiction of existence absolutely."⁹

Further, that Nietzsche is at least *attempting* to adopt this "god" Dionysus/Life is evidenced by various claims he makes. Nietzsche styles himself as "the last disciple and initiate of the god Dionysus," who he describes as "that great ambiguity and tempter god" (*BGE* 295; *KSA* 5:238). The "ambiguity" of Dionysus is what enables Nietzsche to reinterpret Dionysus as a *philosopher:* "Even the fact that Dionysus is a philosopher and that, consequently, even gods philosophize, seems to me something new and *not* without its dangers, something that might arouse mistrust precisely among philosophers,—among you, my friends, it has less opposition, unless it comes too late and at the wrong time: I have been told that you do not like believing in God and gods these days" (ibid.). Nietzsche recognizes that it is strange to speak of a god who philosophizes, and yet he affirms this. Just how, though, is he able to make this affirmation? Perhaps the simplest answer is that Nietzsche follows a long tradition. He is certainly wrong when he claims "I was the first to take seriously that wonderful phenomenon that bears the name of Dionysus" (*TI* X:4; *KSA* 6:158).[10] It is all the more odd that this claim comes in a section titled "What I Owe to the Ancients," for it turns out that Nietzsche owed a great deal to the *Romantics.* Long before Nietzsche, Johann Joachim Winckelmann, Johann Georg Hamann, and Johann Gottfried von Herder had already appropriated the Dionysian in their own ways. In fact, "Novalis and Hölderlin united it with Christian elements in the form of poetic inspiration; Heinrich Heine and Robert Hamerling, a much-read novelist in Nietzsche's time, anticipated his famous antithesis 'Dionysus versus the Crucified One.'"[11] So appropriating the Dionysian was well established in the German scholarship of Nietzsche's day.

Moreover, given that these earlier writers had been able to appropriate Dionysus in various ways, it is not hard to explain how Nietzsche does so: he simply "maps" his interpretation of Dionysus as philosopher onto the god Dionysus. This is why I think del Caro is incorrect when he says: "Since no god can 'become' a philosopher, but a man indeed can, Nietzsche effectively becomes his own first disciple."[12] Nietzsche does not claim to *be* Dionysus but rather to be Dionysus's *disciple,* calling himself "the final follower of the philosopher Dionysus" (*TI* X:5; *KSA* 6:160). But, if Nietzsche does not become Dionysus, can Dionysus become a philosopher at Nietzsche's command? Probably the simplest way to explain how this change might be possible is by way of Dionysus's two natures. Since Dionysus has always been figured as both human and divine, that "human side" could simply be designated as the part that does the philosophizing. To be sure, Nietzsche does "style" himself as Dionysian. Indeed, Nietzsche signs a number of his letters as *"Dionysos"* both *before* and just after his mental collapse. The tendency among commentators has been simply to dismiss this as a symptom of his lunacy (especially since nearly as many of the letters are signed *"Der Gekreuzigte"* [the Crucified] as are signed *"Dionysos"*).[13] That interpretation is certainly a possibility. Yet one could also interpret the signing of those letters as "Dionysos" as a sign that Nietzsche has identified himself so strongly with Dionysus that he can even appropriate that label for himself. The only question, then, would be how he could sign the other letters as "Der Gekreuzigte." I turn to an explanation for that later.

Second, Nietzsche in effect recognizes that his speaking of Dionysus—a god—is going to be unpopular with philosophers. But this does not deter him. In fact, elsewhere Nietzsche explicitly applies the term "faith" to his view. We earlier considered Nietzsche's portrait of Goethe, but here we need to consider the further element of *faith* that Nietzsche adds to that portrait:

> Goethe conceived of a human being who was strong, highly cultivated, skilled in everything bodily, with self-control and self-respect—a human being who is allowed to dare to accept the entire scope and wealth of naturalness, who is strong enough for this freedom; a tolerant human being, not out of weakness but out of strength, because he knows how to use to his own advantage even what would make an average nature perish; the human being for whom nothing is forbidden anymore, with the exception of *weakness,* whether it be called vice or virtue. . . . Such a spirit who has *become free* stands with a glad and trusting fatalism in the midst of the universe, with a *faith* that only the particular is to be rejected, that as a whole, everything redeems and affirms itself—such a spirit *does not negate anymore.* . . . But such a faith is the highest of all possible faiths: I have baptized it with the name of *Dionysus.* (*TI* IX:49; *KSA* 6:151–52)

All of the parts of this passage are necessary to comprehend the exemplar of Dionysian faith. That one is able to accept all that happens is *only possible* on the basis of this Dionysian faith. Such a faith is characterized by a "glad and trusting fatalism." It is a complete trust in life, in which all of life is sacred.

Here it is important to be clear as possible regarding what Nietzsche means by "faith," for it might seem that he is simply against faith of any kind. He is certainly against *Christian* faith and notes (positively) that "the greatest recent event—that 'God is dead'"—means that "faith has been undermined" (*GS* 343; *KSA* 3:573). In the *Anti-Christ(ian),* he provides an even stronger statement against faith:

> Great spirits are skeptics. Zarathustra is a skeptic. Strength, *freedom* which is born of the strength and overstrength of the spirit, proves itself by scepticism. . . . A spirit who wants great things, who also wants the means to them, is necessarily a skeptic. Freedom from all kinds of convictions, to be able to see freely, is part of strength. . . . Conversely: the need for faith, for some kind of conditional Yes and No, this Carlylism, if one will forgive me this word, is a need born of

weakness. The man of faith, the "believer" of every kind, is necessarily a dependent man—one who cannot posit *himself* as an end, one who cannot posit any end at all by himself. The "believer" does not belong to *himself.* (*AC* 54; *KSA* 6:236)

Of course, Nietzsche does not criticize just any kind of faith in this passage; rather, he criticizes faith that is the product of "weakness" and a need for "dependence." The problem with such a person is that he "cannot posit *himself* as an end." So the result of this kind of faith is that one "loses" oneself to faith. Yet Nietzsche makes it clear that such is *not* the only kind of faith. The ancient Greeks, for instance, had a religiosity that was found in the "very noble type of person" who was able "to face nature and life" without fear (*BGE* 49; *KSA* 5:70). Clearly, the kind of "faith" that Nietzsche has in mind here is a faith of *strength.* Such is Dionysian faith. It is in light of this faith that one is able to be strong, have self-control, accept that which is natural, be tolerant, and even have nothing forbidden to oneself anymore. Rather than restrict, Dionysian faith enables and emancipates. Of course, there is a sense here in which this faith is *dependent,* though the dependency is upon life itself. One may be a skeptic regarding everything *but* life. Upon life, one is wholly dependent.

This dependency clearly represents a *religious* move for Nietzsche, what he terms the "*holy way*":

> *Eternal* life, the eternal recurrence of life; the future promised and made sacred by the past; the triumphant yes to life beyond death and change; *true* life as collective survival through reproduction, through the mysteries of sexuality. . . . In the teachings of the mysteries, *pain* is declared holy; the "pangs of the childbearer" make pain in general holy—all becoming and growth, everything that vouches for the future *requires* pain. . . . For there to be the eternal joy of creation, for the will to life to affirm itself eternally, there *must* also eternally be the "torment of the childbearer." . . . All this is signified by the name Dionysus: I know no higher symbolism than this *Greek* symbolism, the symbolism of the Dionysian rites. In them, the deepest instinct of life, the instinct for the future of life, for the eternity of life, is experienced religiously—the very way to life, reproduction, as the *holy way.* (*TI* X:4; *KSA* 6:159–60)

One cannot read this text without seeing that Nietzsche is very serious about his faith. It is a new sense of "holiness," not a Christian but a

Dionysian holiness. Although Nietzsche elsewhere says "I *want* no believ-ers," that he goes on to say "I have a terrible fear that one day I will be pronounced *holy*" is telling (*EH* "Destiny" 1; *KSA* 6:365). Indeed, how could Nietzsche *not* be taken as setting up something very much akin to a religion?[14] Again, del Caro is incorrect when he writes: "In all fairness to Nietzsche, however, it must be conceded that the Dionysian is not a religion in the sense that it requires religious faith or needs a dogma to defend it."[15] What else is *trusting* fatalism than a profound faith in life? Although Nietzsche does not need "a dogma to defend" his faith, his faith certainly is *founded upon* a dogma—the eternal recurrence that should provoke an *amor fati*. One may choose or not choose to believe it, but it is a dogma that is central to Nietzsche's faith.[16] Moreover, since Nietzsche thinks that such notions as God can be replaced only by what he terms "other metaphysical plausibilities (at bottom likewise untruths)" (*HH* I:109; *KSA* 2:108), then Nietzsche needs alternative "metaphysical plausibilities." The eternal recurrence is just such a "plausibility" (how-ever implausible it may be).

That Nietzsche sees himself as "religious" becomes even more clear when he contrasts the two types, "Dionysus" and the "Crucified": "To determine: whether the typical *religious* man [is] a form of decadence . . . but are we not here omitting one type of religious man, the *pagan*?" (*WP* 1052; *KSA* 13:14 [89]). In this passage Nietzsche goes on to identify with the pagan (i.e., Dionysian) cult that is "a form of thanksgiving and affir-mation of life." Being a pagan for Nietzsche does not signify the *lack* of religion but *another form* of religion, a form that Nietzsche thinks actually embodies the highest possible religion. In the end, Nietzsche does what he accuses Paul of doing: create "a pagan mystery doctrine" (*WP* 167; *KSA* 13:11 [282]).

Is Nietzsche's new religion like Derrida's "religion without religion"? Derrida proposes a "nondogmatic doublet of dogma, a philosophical and metaphysical doublet, in any case a *thinking* that 'repeats' the pos-sibility of religion without religion."[17] I think Nietzsche's religion is *not* like that of Derrida, in at least three senses. First, Nietzsche's religion *is* dogmatic: it may have very few tenets at its core, but they are held dogmatically—and simply *must* be held in that fashion precisely because they cannot be given any "rational" or "scientific" justification. As we have seen, Nietzsche admits that one can only have "metaphysical plau-sibilities." Second, Nietzsche is explicit in calling it both a "faith" and a "*holy way,*" whereas Derrida attempts to think a "religion without religion." Third, Nietzsche may not be certain exactly as to "who" Dionysus *is,* but Dionysus is clearly his god. Here there may be somewhat of a parallel between the two. Although Derrida claims "I quite rightly pass for an atheist," he also takes Augustine's question "Quid ergo amo, cum Deum meum amo [What then do I love when I love my God?]" quite seriously.[18] We have already noted that this question is one that Nietzsche has been asking all along. First, it would have been a question regarding the identity of the *Unbekannter,* and then it would have been a question regarding the identity of Dionysus.

However unclear Nietzsche may be regarding the exact identity of Dionysus, in adopting him as his god—instead of the Crucified—Nietzsche makes it clear for which each stands:

> Dionysus versus the "Crucified": there you have the antithesis. It is *not* a difference in regard to their martyrdom—it is a difference in the meaning of it. . . . One will see that the problem is that of the meaning of suffering: whether a Christian meaning or a tragic meaning. In the former case, it is supposed to be the path to a holy existence; in the latter case, being is counted as *holy enough* to justify even a monstrous amount of suffering. The tragic man affirms even the harshest suffering: he is sufficiently strong, rich, and capable of deifying to do so. The Christian denies even the happiest lot on earth: he is sufficiently weak, poor, disinherited to suffer from life in whatever form he meets it. The god on the cross is a curse on life, a signpost to seek redemption from life; Dionysus cut to pieces is a *promise* of life: it will be eternally reborn and return again from destruction. (*WP* 1052; *KSA* 13:14 [89])

The death of Dionysus is all about the *affirmation of* life. In contrast, the death of the Crucified is all about *redemption from* life.[19] As we have observed previously, when Nietzsche uses the term "redemption" he means something quite different from what Wagner or Christianity means. Nietzsche makes a joke out of the phrase "redemption for the redeemer." Evidently someone had hung a wreath on Wagner's tombstone with that inscription. But Nietzsche suggests that many would have made the same small "correction" to that inscription: "redemption *from* the redeemer" (*CW* Postscript; *KSA* 6:41–42). That is virtually the formula for Nietzsche's own sense of redemption: redemption *from* redemption. Nietzsche defines redemption as "*redemption from all guilt*" (*WP* 765; *KSA* 13:15 [30]). This is the opposite of redemption from all *sin*. To be redeemed from guilt means—for Nietzsche—that there was no "sin" in the first place. Earlier, we noted that Nietzsche writes: "To redeem those who lived in the past and to recreate all 'it was' into a 'thus I willed it'—that alone should I call redemption" (*Z* II "On Redemption"; *KSA* 4:179). To will the past to be *different* is redemption in the Christian and Wagnerian sense; to will that it be the *same* is redemption in Nietzsche's sense.

Despite Nietzsche's clarity in defining his notion of redemption, Fraser insists that Nietzsche's project is still redemptive, citing the following admittedly problematic passage:

> But someday, in a stronger time than this decaying, self-doubting present, he really must come to us, the *redeeming* human of the great love and contempt, the creative spirit whose compelling strength again and again drives him out of any apart or beyond, whose loneliness is misunderstood by the people as if it were a flight *from* reality—: whereas it is only his submersion, burial, absorption *in* reality so that one day, when he again comes to light, he can bring home the *redemption* of this reality: its redemption from the curse that the previous ideal placed upon it. This human of the future who will redeem us from the previous ideal as much as from that *which had to grow out of it,* from the great disgust, from the will to nothingness; this bell-stroke of noon and of the great decision, that makes the will free again, that gives back to the earth its goal and to man his hope; this Anti-Christ and anti-nihilist; this conqueror of God and of nothingness —*he must one day come.* (*GM* II:24; *KSA* 5:336)

Fraser asks, not surprisingly: "How is it possible to square a passage such as this with the idea that Nietzsche's fundamental insight is that those who speak of salvation are being disloyal to their humanity?"[20] Fraser points us to a number of commentators who have attempted to deal with this problem. For instance, Ansell-Pearson claims that "Nietzsche's yearning for a new humanity can itself be seen as an expression of the nihilistic condition he wishes us to overcome."[21] On this read, then, while Nietzsche doesn't *really* want anything like "salvation" or "redemption," he occasionally lapses into "redemptive" thinking. In one sense, Salomé confirms this when she writes (as we have noted) that Nietzsche's "impassioned battle against religion, belief in God, and the need for salvation" is due to the fact that "he came precariously close to them."[22] Here we have an example of Nietzsche coming so close to salvific thinking that he actually lapses into it.

Given Nietzsche's admissions of his own decadence, one *could* certainly interpret this passage in this light, viz., that he is simply betraying his own decadence in these moments of hoping for a redeemer. Since I have been arguing all along that Nietzsche both sets out a goal that he wishes to reach (i.e., to become a disciple of Dionysus) and fails to reach it, the explanation that this is merely a decadent lapse is not only plausible but also quite likely true. Moreover, Conway suggests that perhaps Nietzsche is being ironic in such passages and in effect criticizing the human search for redemption.[23] Yet it is difficult to read the quotation above as an ironic text, since it *seems* so serious. True, irony can take such a serious form, but Nietzsche usually provides the reader with some clue when he is being ironic.

However, it seems to me that another explanation may be more plausible than either of the two mentioned above. Depending on how we read this passage, it could actually be read as *fully in line* with how Nietzsche defines redemption. First, we have to ask who this person might be. Although it could be the *Übermensch*, Nietzsche certainly doesn't use that term. Instead, he uses the term "creative spirit" [*schöpferische Geist*], which suggests a connection with what he elsewhere terms a "free spirit" [*freie Geist*]. While Nietzsche continues to use the term "*Übermensch*," we noted in chapter 7 that the notion of the "free spirit" eclipses that of the *Übermensch* in Nietzsche's late thought. So "free spirit" is the more likely candidate here. One obvious characteristic of the free spirit is that of affirmation of *this* life. Second, this "*redeeming* human" comes with a message that has been Nietzsche's message all along. In fact, his role is to "bring home [*heimbringe*] the *redemption* of this reality," that this world has *already* been "redeemed." If anything, there is the sense here that Nietzsche himself has been ineffective in bringing that message "home" and looks forward to someone who will be able to accomplish what he has so far not accomplished. *Heimbringen* suggests the idea of wooing or winning, something Nietzsche has clearly been unsuccessful in doing regarding his ideas.[24] In this respect, Nietzsche elsewhere says something quite similar: "'I am thirsting for a master composer,' said an innovator to his disciple, 'who can learn my thoughts from me and hereafter speak them in his language: that way I will better penetrate into people's ears and hearts'" (*GS* 106; *KSA* 3:463). So such a "master composer" would not redeem in any Christian sense, but rather spread the "good news" in such a way that it can be more effectively heard. Third, in *Ecce Homo* (which Nietzsche writes the following year), he once again repeats his definition of redemption—word for word—that he gives in *Thus Spoke Zarathustra*. Clearly, then, Nietzsche has not abandoned that definition—and everything in the passage cited above can be read as affirming his own distinctive notion of "redemption" in which the earth and all that has taken place is affirmed.

If one continues to insist, as does Fraser, that Nietzsche is still engaged in a project of redemption or soteriology, then it must be admitted that this is a very strange soteriology indeed. For it is a soteriology *from* soteriology, a soteriology that insists on abandoning soteriology. Nietzsche is willing only to call *that* "redemption"—a redemption *from* redemption. If Nietzsche truly falls into some kind of soteriology (such as in the passage from *On the Genealogy of Morality* cited above), then it would have to be stated as follows: Nietzsche hopes for some kind of figure of the future who would lead us to realize that our wish for redemption (as normally defined) is misguided and disloyal to the earth. Such a "redemption" would be in effect a change of mind and heart so that we would no longer long for such "redemption." In effect, "redemption" would be a permanent move beyond any desire for redemption.[25] It is this sort of redemption that Nietzsche finds in Bizet. He remarks (regarding *Carmen*): "This work, too, redeems; Wagner is not the only 'redeemer.'" Yet how does *Carmen* "redeem"? By a cheerful examination of "love as *fatum,* as fatality, cynical, innocent, cruel" (*CW* 2; *KSA* 6:15). In short, we are redeemed from all hope of redemption. Further, Fraser incorrectly reads the point of Nietzsche's "redemption" as being simply about the hereafter. In light of Nietzsche's own definition of redemption as "to redeem those who lived in the past and to recreate all 'it was' into a 'thus I willed it,'" the emphasis is instead on how one looks at *this* life. Either there is something wrong with this life that needs to be "fixed," or else it is just fine as it is. When Fraser says "like the Psalmist, Nietzsche seeks redemption from the pit,"[26] he should instead say that, quite unlike the Psalmist, Nietzsche wants to *affirm* the pit.

Yet, while Nietzsche has given up the redemptive project, he clearly has a faith and has a god whom he serves. Long ago, he had written:

> I want to know you, Unknown One,
>
> you who have reached deep into my soul,
>
> into my life like the gust of a storm,

you incomprehensible yet related one!
I want to know you, even serve you.[27]

And such is *still* Nietzsche's wish. He has not left faith behind; he has merely moved to *another* faith. Heidegger (rightly) calls Nietzsche "that passionate seeker of God," and Nietzsche ultimately finds him in Dionysus.[28] But, then, what kind of god is Dionysus? As the ultimate affirmer of *this* life, Dionysus would seem to be an *immanent* rather than a transcendent god. Citing Husserl's assertion that "a world-god [*ein mundaner Gott*] is evidently impossible" and that "the immanence of God in absolute consciousness cannot be grasped as immanence in the sense of being as experience—which would be no less absurd," Haar notes that "for Nietzsche, neither the immanence of a god in the world nor the coincidence of the lived experience and of the divine are [*sic*] absurd."[29] Haar sees Nietzsche as the inheritor of both the tradition of the Greek gods as immanent and of a mystical tradition in which there is the possibility of a kind of mystical union.

Regarding the first of these claims, the complication with the Greek gods is that they are *simultaneously* immanent and transcendent—and very strangely so. They have human characteristics, but also *divine* characteristics. Although the twelve gods found on the Parthenon frieze were traditionally thought to reside on Mt. Olympus—and so are *this-worldly* gods—they still transcend the realm of the *human*. In that sense, at least, they are transcendent. There is still a distinction here between the divine and the human, even though that distinction is considerably weaker than in Christianity. We should instead say that Nietzsche gives us a "weak" sense of transcendence, but it is still a *kind* of transcendence. As to the second of Haar's claims, that Nietzsche is able to identify so strongly with Dionysus, that in no way reduces the Dionysian to a strict immanence. Even in the Christian tradition one finds certain church fathers—such as Gregory of Nyssa—who speak of believers as "becoming divine"— what is usually termed *theosis*.[30] Thus, *theosis* in no way undercuts the Christian doctrine of the transcendence of God. Moreover, the kind of mystical union Haar ascribes to Nietzsche does not necessarily presuppose immanence but is perfectly compatible with transcendence. In the end, by adopting Dionysus as his god, Nietzsche in effect *refigures* transcendence into a kind of "immanent transcendence." Yet he also refigures Dionysus. Nietzsche speaks of his "religious . . . god-building instinct" that enables him to create a god (*WP* 1038; *KSA* 13:17 [4]). Of course, it is worth noting that Nietzsche's Dionysus turns out to be made in his own image (not that such a claim would bother him).

Becoming Dionysian

Having laid down the "doctrines" of his Dionysian faith, how faithful a follower does Nietzsche prove to be? For, rather than merely postulating Dionysus and his Dionysian Piety, Nietzsche actually needs to *become* Dionysian. Such is a project to be accomplished, rather than something already completed. Speaking of *Thus Spoke Zarathustra,* Nietzsche says: "It contains an image of myself in the sharpest focus, as I am, *once* I have thrown aside my whole burden" (letter to Franz Overbeck, February 1883, *SL* 207; *KSB* 6:326). That small word "once" is the crux of this passage: that Nietzsche realizes this is indicated by the fact that he italicizes the word. There is no reason to think that Nietzsche has truly reached the place of having completely internalized Zarathustra's teachings to such an extent that he is finally "free," if for no other reason than that—as late as 1888—he recognizes that he is a decadent. Instead, Nietzsche needs the Dionysian *ekstasis* to become a free spirit who says the ultimate "Yes" to life. At the end, the question is whether Nietzsche is a faithful follower of Dionysus—or a decadent follower who is still caught in the logic of *ressentiment*. For, as long as Nietzsche is caught up in the logic of *ressentiment,* he cannot be truly Dionysian. Rather, he follows the rhythm of decadence, still out of step with life.

How does Nietzsche think that he can reach the Dionysian? The answer lies in the very nature of Dionysus. Not only is Dionysus himself able to take on multiple appearances; those whom he inspires are likewise enabled to become "other" in two ways. First, the actor in Greek tragedy—the *hupocritēs*—puts on masks, allowing him to take on a different persona. The wearing of masks is an important part of Nietzsche's transformation. He writes: "We, too, deal with 'people'; we, too, modestly don the cloak in which (*as* which) others know us, respect us, seek us, and so we appear in company, i.e. among others who are disguised but don't want to admit it. Like all clever masks we, too, politely prop up a chair against the door when confronted with curiosity about anything but our 'cloak'" (*GS* 365; *KSA* 3:613). The goal of wearing a mask is twofold: on the one hand, a mask hides things we don't want others to see and, on the other hand, a mask enables us to transform ourselves—or at least see ourselves differently. Nietzsche resorts to this strategy at key points (such as in various comments he makes about himself in *Ecce Homo*). Second, the *Rausch*—frenzy or rapture—that one experiences when under the spell of Dionysus brings about an "ecstasy"—an *ekstasis* that removes one beyond normal existence. Dionysus is associated with a kind of intoxication that allows for change of one's persona. The substitution, then, of Dionysus for the God of Christianity not only changes the identity of God for Nietzsche but also enables Nietzsche to change his own identity (from the follower of Christ to the follower of Dionysus).

We have seen that Nietzsche's goal is that of becoming a free spirit. Of course, Nietzsche does not claim to be a free spirit, at least not early on. Not only does he say "'free spirits' of this kind do not exist," but he also makes it clear that one *becomes* a free spirit: "One may conjecture that a spirit in whom the type 'free spirit' will one day become ripe and sweet to the point of perfection has had its decisive experience in a *great liberation* and that previously it was all the more a fettered spirit and seemed to be chained for ever to its pillar and corner" (*HH* P 2–3; *KSA* 2:15–16). Even the arrival of the free spirits does not signal that they have truly arrived. Nietzsche characterizes free spirits as *"those who attempt"* [*Versucher*], not those who necessarily succeed (*BGE* 42; *KSA* 5:59). So Nietzsche is still a *Versucher,* an experimenter in the project of self-overcoming. But the goals of becoming a free spirit are that one "will be free, *very* free" and achieve a level of existence that is "something more, higher, greater, and fundamentally different" (*BGE* 44; *KSA* 5:60). Nietzsche has set his sights high.

We have already noted Nietzsche's New Year's resolution: "Some day," he says, "I want to be a Yes-sayer" (*GS* 276; *KSA* 3:521).[31] Nietzsche wants to be able to say "Yes and Amen" to all that comes his way. He defines the "Dionysian" as "an ecstatic affirmation of the total character of life" (*WP* 1050; *KSA* 13:14 [14]). Of course, a major—perhaps *the* major—problem facing Nietzsche is that to accept *all* of life would mean accepting *everything,* and that "everything" would have to include Christ, the whole history of Christianity, and even the doctrine of redemption as interpreted by Christians. Can Nietzsche *really* accept all of this—and *love* it?

As it turns out, Jesus proves—in many ways—the exemplar for Nietzsche. In *The Anti-Christ(ian),* Nietzsche reads Jesus as living out a sense of "blessedness." It is in that *practice* that one finds blessedness. On Nietzsche's (admittedly unorthodox) read, Jesus does not care about repentance or reconciliation, for there is no sin for which to feel guilty. Nietzsche says that the *"glad tidings"* finally "dispose" of the notion of "redemption through faith." Instead, one can "feel oneself 'in heaven'" simply by this "new way of life" (*AC* 33; *KSA* 6:205–206). So Jesus' life (as Nietzsche reads him) is a radical affirmation of life. All of this is what Nietzsche wants. His Dionysian faith is nothing other than a way of "acting," a way of being in the world. It has given up on sin, immortality, and redemption. By adopting the *amor fati,* there is no resistance to what happens. Instead, one affirms all that happens. Even Nietzsche's own conception of "blessedness" is one in which there is *no longer* any need for "repentance and reconciliation." Moreover, Jesus is also free from *ressentiment* and seems to be able to say "Yes" to life in a way that Nietzsche does not seem free to do. Here the difference is probably best put in terms of "The Three Metamorphoses" in *Thus Spoke Zarathustra*. While the camel can bear heavy burdens and the lion can destroy, only the child can say yes: "Why must the preying lion still become a child? The child is innocence and forgetting, a new beginning, a game, a self-propelled wheel, a first movement, a sacred 'Yes.' For the game of creation, my brothers, a sacred 'Yes' is needed" (*Z* I "Three Metamorphoses"; *KSA* 4:31).

Jesus is like a child in *this* respect (rather than the ones we considered in chapter 9), but can *Nietzsche* become like Jesus? Even though Nietzsche speaks of himself as one of the "spirits who have *become free,*" it is not at all clear that he is being honest with himself. If anything, he still seems mired in *ressentiment,* and so not an active nihilist but a passive, decadent nihilist. Luce Irigaray puts that charge as follows: "To overcome the impossible of your desire—that surely is your last hour's desire. Giving birth to such and such a production, or such and such a child is a summary of your history. But to give birth to your desire itself, that is your final thought. To be incapable of doing it, that is your highest ressentiment. For you either make works that fit your desire, or you make desire itself into your work. But how will you find the material to produce such a child?"[32] Irigaray realizes just how desperate the predicament is in which Nietzsche finds himself. Nietzsche wants to become a child—and so be free from *ressentiment*—but what he finds himself left with is simply a *desire,* rather than fulfillment of that desire. At best, then, it seems like Nietzsche can give birth to a desire, rather than to a child. So is that the "substance" of Nietzsche's Dionysian Piety—a "desire" rather than a child? A further way in which Jesus excels Nietzsche is that he provides the key to Nietzsche's own project of a revaluation of all values: "Jesus said to his Jews: 'The law was for servants,—love God as I do, as his son! Why should we care about morals, we sons of God?'" (*BGE* 164; *KSA* 5:101). In a text titled *Beyond Good and Evil*, Jesus is depicted as already *being* beyond! So Jesus, once again, provides the example of what Nietzsche hopes to accomplish.

Nietzsche's Dionysian Pietism, then, is remarkably like his conception of Christian Pietism.[33] For example, consider Nietzsche's early prayer from *Aus meinem Leben* rewritten as a Dionysian prayer. As is clear, it can be relatively easily transformed into a prayer to Dionysus:

> I have firmly resolved within me to dedicate myself forever to Dionysus's service. May dear Dionysus give me strength and power to carry out my intention and protect me on life's way. Like a child I trust in Dionysus: Dionysus will preserve us all, that no misfortune may befall us. But Dionysus's holy will be done! All Dionysus gives I will joyfully accept: happiness and unhappiness, poverty and wealth, and boldly look even death in the face, which shall one day unite us all in eternal joy and bliss. Yes, dear Dionysus, let Thy face shine upon us forever! Amen!

To be sure, some aspects of this prayer would need to be modified. Nietzsche is not going to expect that Dionysus "protect [him] on life's way," nor that "Dionysus will preserve us all, that no misfortune may befall us." Of course, given Nietzsche's desire to affirm all that happens, one might question what would count as a "misfortune," and whether it wouldn't end up being affirmed by the *amor fati* anyway. Also, Nietzsche no longer expects anything like "eternal joy and bliss." He is quite content with a this-worldly joy (though it is worth mentioning that, classically, Dionysus is also associated with the afterlife). Yet other aspects of the prayer sound positively Dionysian in their affirmation. "I have firmly resolved within me to dedicate myself forever to Dionysus's service" and "All Dionysus gives I will joyfully accept" sound reminiscent of Nietzsche's "faith" character-ized by a "glad and trusting fatalism" (*TI* IX:49; *KSA* 6:152). So Nietzsche can pray much of this same prayer—just to another God.

While Nietzsche hopes and prays to become a child, he portrays the evangel—at least in two crucial respects—as someone like the person he himself wishes to be—a child and a free spirit. Thus, the evangel is *not* a *Versucher* but already a free spirit, rather than merely an aspiring one like Nietzsche. He is *already* the perfect child, not one who has to undergo the difficult metamorphoses that lead to the child. He is able only to say "yes." Even though Nietzsche goes on to speak of "we spirits who have *become free*" (*AC* 36; *KSA* 6:208), the kind of freedom manifested by the evangel is something that still seems beyond Nietzsche's grasp. Of course, Nietzsche considers the fact that he has to *work* to become a child a mark of his superiority over the evangel. But, if becoming a child is truly the goal, then why would it be important how one got there? Wouldn't simply *being* a child be all that truly matters? Further, Nietzsche is stuck in the stage of the lion (the stage of "no-saying"), which hardly seems preferable to being a child naturally.

Just how far, then, *does* Nietzsche get in becoming Dionysian? To answer that question, we need to consider Nietzsche's success in resisting decadence and his ability to fall into the rhythm of life. Theoretically, we can say that Nietzsche's *askêsis* has the potential to help one to *resist* decadence, though certainly not to "overcome" or "escape" it. If the alternative to decadence is "becoming a fool" for the rhythm of life, then the best one can do is to follow an *askêsis* of learning to listen, to sing and love new songs, and to dance new dances. To the extent that Nietzsche's *askêsis* "allows" him to be changed and live by the rhythm of life, it is nonreactive in nature (and thus does not reinstate the logic of decadence). More problematic, though, is the "no-saying" [*Verneinung*] that is designed to lead to "yes-saying." Nietzsche is clearly right that "negating *and destroying* are conditions of Yes-saying" (*EH* "Destiny" 4; *KSA* 6:368). But the crucial question is whether Nietzsche can go *beyond* "No-saying." True, Nietzsche admits that *Thus Spoke Zarathustra* was his period of "Yes-saying" and that it needed to be followed up by a period of "No-saying" (*EH* "Books" BGE; *KSA* 6:350). There is a sense, then, in which Nietzsche's role—not just in subsequent texts but in his life as a whole— is to provide this "no-saying" that is preliminary to the revaluation of all values. But this role proves problematic for Nietzsche's own development: is Nietzsche so enmeshed in no-saying that he cannot become the child who is "a sacred 'Yes'" or a truly "free spirit"? It would seem that his role of no-saying prevents these latter possibilities.

So what does Nietzsche say about *himself*? We have already noted that, in *Ecce Homo,* Nietzsche in effect gives us two different answers to the question of whether he truly "resists" decadence. On the one hand, in section 1 of "Why I Am So Wise" he says: "A long, all too long, series of years signifies recovery for me; unfortunately it also signifies relapse, decay, the periodicity of a kind of decadence" (*EH* "Wise" 1; *KSA* 6:265). Here we get a picture of *askêsis* as the continuing *practice* of spiritual exercises. Nietzsche's *Versuch* [experiment] according to this version is a continual process that is ever threatened by the temptation [*Versuchung*] of falling back into decadence. That *askêsis* is a *Versuch* is in line with what Nietzsche says about free spirits in *Beyond Good and Evil*, where he defines them as "those who attempt" [*Versucher*] (*BGE* 42; *KSA* 5:59). On the other hand, in section 2 of "Why I Am So Wise" Nietzsche makes a much stronger claim. He says: "I took myself in hand, I made myself healthy again" (*EH* "Wise" 2; *KSA* 266). Not only does this suggest a voluntarism that goes against the very notion of *askêsis* (which operates by allowing oneself to be changed rather than simply "taking oneself in hand"), it likewise suggests a voluntarism that goes against Nietzsche's own views regarding the freedom of the will.[34] It *does* fit, however, with what Nietzsche later says about himself in *The Anti-Christ(ian)*, where he speaks of "we spirits who have *become free*" (*AC* 36; *KSA* 6:208). Yet this statement is hard to take seriously. Even Nietzsche admits that the very idea of a free spirit is "*a relative concept*" (*HH* I:225; *KSA* 2:189). Moreover, we have already noted that only two years previously (1886, in his various prefaces), Nietzsche had acknowledged how far he had to go to become a free spirit. So how exactly has he suddenly made such progress in a mere two years?

To the extent, then, that Nietzsche "allows" himself to be changed by singing new songs and learning to dance with life—in short, of learning to live by a nondecadent rhythm—he "escapes" from the reactive logic of decadence. Conversely, the extent to which he "takes himself in hand" and makes war with decadence is the extent to which he is likewise guilty of merely altering decadence's expression. But this raises a further question: is waging war a *better* way of "resisting" decadence than "Russian fatalism"? We have seen that Nietzsche opposes the active waging of war to the weak response of what he terms "*Russian fatalism*" (*EH* "Wise" 6; *KSA* 6:272). For the truly sick, the *only* possibility is by simply giving in and refusing to fight. Fighting quickly exhausts the weak, for "nothing burns one up faster than the affects of *ressentiment*" (ibid.). Again, here Nietzsche's distinction between "active" and "passive" nihilism is appropriate (*WP* 22; *KSA* 12:9 [35]). Whereas active nihilism actively resists degeneration, "weary nihilism" doesn't even bother to fight back. While resisting degeneration is for Nietzsche superior to simply giving in, the weak have no choice. Since Nietzsche sees himself among the strong, he thinks he can resist by waging war.

Yet all of this talk of resistance raises the fundamental question of whether waging war is inherently connected to *ressentiment*. Is Nietzsche really right that active resistance is better than passive resistance? Given his increasingly negative outlook on the possibility of true resistance, is there anything to be gained by resisting? Moreover, if no real progress is possible by resistance, then might not admission of defeat—that is, Russian fatalism—be simply the wisest course of action, not to mention the most *honest*? Nietzsche himself says that he clung to Russian fatalism as a way of dealing with his own decadence (*EH*, "Wise" 6; *KSA* 6:273). So why exactly is waging war *better* than simply accepting Russian fatalism? Nietzsche's response would no doubt be that actively fighting decadence is better than passively allowing it to spread like a contagion. Moreover, Nietzsche seems to think that waging war does not partake of the logic of *ressentiment*.

But is that truly the case? True, waging war is at least *potentially* different from "anger, pathological vulnerability, impotent lust for revenge" (*EH* "Wise" 6; *KSA* 6:272). Yet might not the warrior *also* be harboring anger and the desire for revenge? Is revenge or *ressentiment* truly the *opposite* of warfare, in the sense that one acts *either* one way *or* the other? Or does warfare—*by its very nature*—partake at least to some degree of the logic of *ressentiment*? According to Nietzsche, acting out of *ressentiment* is when one is "denied the true reaction, *that of the deed*" (*GM* I:10; *KSA* 3:270, my italics). In other words, *ressentiment* is "reactionary," whereas true action simply acts. As Nietzsche goes on to say, the truly noble person is the one who acts out of "a triumphant yes-saying to oneself," whereas the weak person or the slave "says 'no.'" The one acts creatively; the other does not. But, having said all that, it is not at all clear that "waging war" is necessarily a true "deed," rather than something reactionary. *If* Nietzsche is right here (and that would be granting him quite a bit), then he is drawing an *extremely thin line*. For even Nietzsche admits that the "deed" is a "true *reaction*." Given that point, waging war at best seems to have negation as only a secondary effect rather than a primary quality. Yet the question is: does that distinction really matter? Perhaps it does. But, if so, it would seem to hold only *de jure*. *De facto*, the two seem almost indistinguishable.

Perhaps the best way of answering this question is by turning back to what Nietzsche himself says regarding Russian fatalism. After describing the free spirit, Nietzsche goes on to say that "such a spirit who has *become free* stands with a glad and trusting fatalism in the midst of the universe"

(*TI* IX:49; *KSA* 6:152). So it is the free spirit who is characterized by this glad and trusting fatalism, not by warlike ambitions.[35] Although Nietzsche himself seems not to be entirely clear about this, it would seem that only the one who has this "joyous/glad and trusting fatalism" can *truly* be a free spirit and thus freed from the logic of *ressentiment*. In contrast, the warrior is far too enmeshed in the logic of *ressentiment*.

But, in the end, which of the accounts in *Ecce Homo* better describes Nietzsche—the one who is still a *Versucher* or the one who has "arrived"? If we take *ressentiment* as having a similarly reactive structure to that of decadence, then the Nietzsche we find in the texts of 1888 seems to be the decadent par excellence. Nietzsche claims "one pays heavily for being one of Wagner's disciples" (*CW* Postscript; *KSA* 6:40). Yet one pays a heavier toll still for having so much *ressentiment* against Wagner—not to mention Socrates or Paul. Although Nietzsche says that Bizet makes him "a better *listener*" (*CW* 1; *KSA* 6:14), that improved listening may help him detect his own decadence but likewise fuels his *ressentiment* against Wagner. As part of the New Year's resolution, Nietzsche had said—in addition to "some day I want only to be a Yes-sayer"—"I do not want to accuse; I do not even want to accuse the accusers. Let *looking away* be my only negation" (*GS* 276; *KSA* 5:521). But he clearly has not reached that point by 1888: he is *full* of accusation. Whereas Tanner claims that at the time of *Thus Spoke Zarathustra* "the least convincing" aspects are those of "exaltation and affirmation," that could just as easily be said of Nietzsche's later philosophy.[36]

While Nietzsche speaks lovingly at times of Life in *Zarathustra,* that love is too often eclipsed by *ressentiment*—all the more so in his late texts. It is particularly telling that Nietzsche makes remarkably little headway on his projected *Revaluation of All Values* (i.e., a "positive" endeavor). He talks in the preface to that work of "new ears for new music" but we get little in the way of "new" music, just the vehemence of *The Anti-Christ(ian)*.[37] Nietzsche gives us some wonderful songs—in *Zarathustra,* his dithyrambs, and the "Hymn to Life." But, if Zarathustra's convalescence is to learn *new* songs, then Nietzsche seems to be still singing too many songs of deep *ressentiment* rather than songs of deep affirmation. Even though Nietzsche suggests—as we noted in the previous chapter— that music "can discharge some excess . . . of vengefulness" (*GS* 84; KSA 3:442), music seems to have failed in his case to bring about such a "discharge." Further, as Conway points out, by the time of *The Anti-Christ(ian)* and *Ecce Homo,* Nietzsche acts as if the numerous tasks which he has set out for himself only a year or two earlier have already been completed.[38] For example, Nietzsche opens *On The Genealogy of Morality* with the claim "We are unknown to ourselves, we knowers" (*GM* P; *KSA* 5:247). But, just a year later, he begins *Ecce Homo* with the seemingly contradictory claim: "Seeing that before long I must confront humanity with the most difficult demand ever made of it, it seems indispensable to me to say *who I am*" (*EH* P 1; *KSA* 6:257). How is it that Nietzsche has suddenly gotten such a good idea of himself, good enough in fact to write an extensive volume delineating "who I am"?

Moreover, to what extent is Nietzsche truly honest with *himself*? In chapter 8 I accused Nietzsche of self-deception regarding his reading of the evangel. But in *Ecce Homo* that self-deception extends to *himself*. Consider the following "self-assessment" Nietzsche offers in *Ecce Homo:* "Really *religious* difficulties, for example, I don't know from experience. . . . 'God,' 'the immortality of the soul,' 'redemption,' 'beyond'—without exception, concepts to which I have never devoted any attention, or time; not even as a child. Perhaps I have never been childlike enough for them" (*EH* "Clever" 1; *KSA* 6:278). At best, only *part* of this describes Nietzsche: true, he has not been concerned with immortality of the soul and the beyond. Yet he has been obsessed with God throughout his life. His problem is that he is not childlike enough, though in exactly the opposite sense he means here. And the self-deception hardly ends there: Nietzsche also claims to be of Polish ancestry, to have overcome *ressentiment,* and also never to have been guilty of adopting "a presumptuous and bombastic posture" (*EH* "Wise" 3, 6, "Clever" 10; *KSA* 6:268, 272, 296). Of course, we can read these claims as Nietzsche wearing a mask to help *make himself* into the person he so desperately wants to be. Making this claim turns out to be a strategy Nietzsche employs for overcoming his religious concerns, a way of viewing his life from a different perspective in order to reframe it and, ultimately, reshape it. Yet, as Young so appropriately points out, this is "not an exercise in *amor fati* at all" but rather its opposite.[39] If *amor fati* is "saying yes to life even in its most strange and intractable problems," then Nietzsche is unable to live up to that (*TI* X:5; *KSA* 6:160). In place of "yes-saying," he is full of denial.

Yet the problem is actually much worse than that, for Nietzsche seems to be engaged in a project that he explicitly renounces. Having given up on the project of redemption, it turns out that he *enacts* it in *Ecce Homo* precisely through his self-deception of "rereading" his life in nondecadent terms. This "redemption" is the *worst possible* kind of redemption:

for it is not merely redemptive in the sense from which Nietzsche so desperately wants to escape but it is also self-deceptive. At least Christianity is honest enough to admit that its project is redemptive. Alternatively, one might defend Nietzsche by arguing that he doesn't truly realize what he is doing. But then the problem is that he is utterly unaware of who he truly is, precisely what he claims he in fact knows so well in *Ecce Homo*. On either reading, Nietzsche seems guilty of falling back into the logic of redemption, which is exactly what Wagner had done.

Ultimately, the self that Nietzsche wishes to overcome is that of the pious young Fritz. But does Nietzsche really overcome this self? We have already seen that Nietzsche remains remarkably true to his Pietistic roots in important ways. True, he moves from his old faith in the God of Christianity to faith in Life, resulting in both a desire to serve Life and a willingness to say "Yes and Amen" to Life rather than God. But he has not left what Salomé terms the "mystical God-ideal" behind. And he seems quite unable to leave it behind. Further, even in his desire to serve Life he turns out to be a decadent. He attempts to resist that decadence, but it is a resistance that seems (on Nietzsche's *own* account) to grow more and more futile the more he becomes convinced that the ideas of "free will" and "human agency" are mere fictions.[40] Nietzsche realizes that he is not true to Life and he feels deep remorse for his infidelity. So he turns out to be a heretic in his own religion.

Part 4 of *Thus Spoke Zarathustra* (which Nietzsche later adds to the text) ends with Zarathustra's proclaiming "the lion came, my children are near, Zarathustra has ripened, my hour has come" (*Z* IV "Sign"; *KSA* 4:408). However, it is difficult to be convinced. Even if we were to accept that the lion has truly come, just how near are the children? We get a glimpse at Zarathustra's continuing vulnerability in the section titled "The Magician," who (surprisingly enough) represents *both* Wagner and Nietzsche. This magician prays to the *Unbekannter,* saying "Thou unknown *god!*" He asks: "What wilt thou, unknown—god?" and "Me thou wilt have? Me? / Me—entirely?" "Wouldst thou *enter* / The heart / climb in, deep into my / Most secret thoughts?" The Pietistic overtones of this prayer are unmistakable, as are the similarities with Nietzsche's earlier poetry/prayers. However, the speaker is clearly torn. On the one hand, he proclaims:

> Away!
> He himself fled,
> My last, only companion,

> My great enemy,
> My unknown,
> My hangman-god!

On the other hand, he goes on to say:

> No! Do come back,
> *With* all your torments!
> To the last of all that are lonely,
> Oh, come back!
> All my tear-streams run
> Their course to you;
> And my heart's final flame—
> Flares up for *thee*!
> Oh come back,
> My unknown God! My *pain*! My last—happiness![41]

Zarathustra responds by saying: "Stop it, you actor! You counter-feiter! You liar from the bottom!" (*Z* IV "Magician" 2; *KSA* 4:317). Yet the story turns out to be more complicated. For there is an undeniable tension in these last two stanzas. One possible interpretation is that the magician demands *both* that God leave *and* that God return precisely because each departure serves to make one harder. Still, there is something more at work here. The magician admits that he is acting out "*the penitent of the spirit*" and that "it took a long time" for Zarathustra to realize that it was an act. Why is Zarathustra so slow to see through the ruse? His own explanation is that he must "be without caution: so thus my lot wants it" (*Z* IV "Magician" 2; *KSA* 4:318). But, even if Zarathustra needs to throw caution to the winds, why does he so quickly take pity upon the magician and reach out to comfort him? A much more plausible explanation than the one Zarathustra gives is that the magician touches Zarathustra's heart. And he touches Zarathustra's heart because Zarathustra sees *himself* in the magician (in the same way that Nietzsche sees himself in Wagner). The magician's double gesture—of desiring God to depart and yet return— mirrors not just Nietzsche's early poetry but also the adult Nietzsche. So Nietzsche has not *simply* left that ambiguity behind.

However, the poem is even more complicated by the fact that Nietzsche transforms it into one of his dithyrambs with the title "Ariadne's Complaint." From an interpretational standpoint, this makes the poem highly problematic. As a poem from Wagner/Nietzsche, it can be seen as indicating a continuing temptation [*Versuchung*] to the decadent religion of Christianity. Yet, coming from the semidivine Ariadne and addressed to Dionysus, it takes on quite a different meaning. While Hollingdale is right that "the two contexts, both dramatic, in which the poem is employed are artistically irreconcilable with one another," I believe he is not quite correct when he goes on to say "the poem itself is irresolvably ambiguous" (*DD* 92). Instead, we might better say that the poem has two strikingly different meanings in its two contexts. The latter context now refigures that ambiguity in terms of his allegiance to Dionysus. Ariadne, daughter of Minos and Parisiphaë and wife of Dionysus, represents human suffering. Thus, she prays to the *Unbekannter* [Dionysus], saying, "Strike deeper! / Strike once again! / Sting and sting, shatter this heart!"[42] Clearly, this is an affirmation of suffering and pain. There are also the same Pietistic overtones in this dithyramb as in the poem of the magician. Moreover, that same wavering between wanting God to depart and return is just as strongly depicted. However, at the very end of *this* version, Dionysus *does* return and exhorts Ariadne: "Be wise, Ariadne! . . . / You have little ears, you have ears like mine: / let some wisdom into them!" He then adds: "*I am thy labyrinth*" (*DD* 65; *KSA* 6:401). No doubt, this is a highly unusual marriage relationship. But it also tells us something about Nietzsche's relation to his new god, assuming that we can read Nietzsche as expressing his own thoughts through Ariadne.[43] There is an equally deep ambiguity in that relationship, making Nietzsche's commitment to Dionysus a wavering commitment. Nietzsche needs to reach a point in which he is comfortable *being* in the labyrinth, in which one cannot see what is to come and has no explanation for what has come to pass. But it seems he has not reached that point.

Yet there is a further problem that Nietzsche faces. Not only does he wish to be free from the God of Christianity, we have seen that he also wishes to be free from the very hope of redemption. But—in the end—can Nietzsche make such a move? It would seem that to be saved from salvation—or redeemed from redemption—is once again to repeat the very logic from which one wishes to escape. Nietzsche *does* realize that one cannot escape decadence merely by making war against it, as is clear from what he says of Socrates. But how, then, can Nietzsche truly escape from escaping, overcome overcoming, redeem himself from redemption, or save himself from salvation? The *most* Nietzsche can do is what we've already noted: he makes a religious move, saying that all this can only be accomplished by *faith*. But is Nietzsche's faith *strong enough*? Has he actually fallen back into step with life and become at one with the rhythm of the earth?

He hopes and prays to be free. He hopes and prays to be a true follower of Dionysus. But he knows he is unfaithful. So Nietzsche's last of multiple autobiographies, *Ecce Homo,* is an attempt to reinterpret his life as a *faithful* follower of Dionysus. It is a confession of faith and a confession of unfaithfulness. When Nietzsche claims that *Ecce Homo* is designed to tell us *"who I am,"* that claim is only partly right (*EH* P 1; *KSA* 6:257). For it is also designed to tell us who Nietzsche *wishes* to be. "I am a disciple of the philosopher Dionysus," writes Nietzsche (*EH* P 2: *KSA* 6:258). Such is both what Nietzsche is and what he also wants to be. In effect, Nietzsche says: "I believe; help my unbelief." Nietzsche is rightly interpreted as giving us an aesthetic creation of himself in *Ecce Homo,* a self that is constructed by masks and the *Rausch* that takes one out of oneself. But *Ecce Homo* also fits with Nietzsche's long history of prayer: not the prayer of the weak but the prayer of the strong, the ones who use songs and rituals to reinforce that strength.

Despite his attempt to be strong, Nietzsche is not so strong after all. He is all too well aware of his failings to live up to his own teachings. He tells us: "When I have looked into my *Zarathustra,* I walk up and down in my room for half an hour, unable to master an unbearable fit of sobbing" (*EH* "Clever" 4; *KSA* 6:287). Why does he sob? One could respond that these are tears of rapture. After all, in the section on *Thus Spoke Zarathustra* in *Ecce Homo,* he speaks of "a rapture whose tremendous tension occasionally discharges itself in a flood of tears" (*EH* "Books" Z 3; *KSA* 6:339). Elsewhere, speaking of his time in Sils Maria, he relates to his friend Gast (as we earlier noted) that his eyes were sometimes inflamed not by "sentimental tears but tears of joy" (letter of August 14, 1881; *SL* 178; *KSB* 6:112). However, consider how Nietzsche describes these particular fits of sobbing. Right before this passage, he says that the great writer (Shakespeare being the comparison here) writes "*only* from his own reality—up to the point where afterward he cannot endure his work any longer." So it is in looking into *himself* that Nietzsche begins sobbing. And he goes on to describe *himself* as "an abyss." Thus, Nietzsche's tears are at once for the nothingness within him and the nothingness without. Here it seems only logical to connect this abyss with the one of which he had written in "Du hast gerufen—Herr ich komme," the abyss that he earlier had said gives him *ein Grauen* [a shudder]. That connection seems even more plausible in that he says his sobbing is "unbearable." What Nietzsche calls "the *free spirit* par excellence" is able to dance "even beside abysses" (*GS* 347; *KSA* 3:583). As the supposedly free spirit with "Dionysian faith" enabling him to say "Yes and Amen" to all that comes, he ought not to be sobbing. Instead, he should have the resolution of the young Fritz to say: "All *life* gives I will joyfully accept: happiness and unhappiness, poverty and wealth, and boldly look even death in the face." *That* would be the expression of the childlike trust after which Nietzsche so desperately seeks. In fact, if Nietzsche were actually to *return* to the mentality of the young Fritz, he might actually be better off. But, lacking that faith, Nietzsche prays to be rescued from *himself,* to become a child.

Perhaps it is only in his madness that Nietzsche finally reaches the Dionysian. It is not merely that he signs a number of letters "Dionysus" or even that he claims to have "become Dionysus" (letter to Cosima Wagner, January 3, 1889; *KSB* 8:573). Rather, it is his signing of other letters as "The Crucified" and saying "I have also hung on the cross" (ibid.) that symbolizes the greatest change. For, if he can *affirm* even the Crucified, then he has truly reached the profoundest level of yes-saying that characterizes the Dionysian. To be able to affirm even Christianity—against which he has railed so vehemently—is finally to become truly Dionysian—and to have left all *ressentiment* behind. But, of course, the price he has to pay to reach the Dionysian is not his soul but his sanity.

Yet that suspension of sanity may be characterized as Nietzsche's own Dionysian "mystical experience." Assuming that sanity ["little reason"] is what has prevented Nietzsche from becoming truly Dionysian, then it must be suspended—or even abandoned. If the cult of Dionysus is all about the suspension of reason and giving oneself over to "Dionysiac drunkenness and mystical self-abandon," then Nietzsche would reach the highest level of the Dionysian only by leaving reason behind. As he puts it: "Singing and dancing, man expresses his sense of belonging to a higher community; he has forgotten how to walk and talk and is on the brink of flying and dancing, up and away into the air above. His gestures speak of his enchantment. . . . he feels himself to be a god, he himself now moves in such ecstasy and sublimity as once he saw the gods move in his dreams" (*BT* 1; *KSA* 1:30). Precisely in such a state of enchantment is how Overbeck finds Nietzsche in those early days of January 1889. Nietzsche both danced and improvised at the piano, accompanying himself with outbursts of wild ideas. And he wrote his last letters in the name of one god or another. Not surprisingly, "Overbeck interpreted these things as a terrifying picture of a kind of holy frenzy, the kind that is found in antique tragedies."[44] But, of course, what would be *more* Dionysian than being caught up in an ecstatic frenzy, a truly "holy" Dionysian frenzy? What could be less surprising than that "when one asks about his state, he responds that he feels well, but that he can only express his state in music"?[45]

Earlier on, Nietzsche had considered the role insanity could play in revealing the deepest possible truths about humanity. "In outbursts of passion, and in the fantasizing of dreams and insanity, a man rediscovers his own and mankind's prehistory. . . . He who, as a forgetter on a grand scale, is wholly unfamiliar with all this *does not understand man*" (*D* 312; *KSA* 3:226). As Nietzsche goes on to say, those who do not understand madness do not understand humanity. So, in madness, Nietzsche may have found his new rhythm after all. Of course, just as the rhythm of the ancient Dionysian cults was inexplicable, so the rhythm of the "insane" Nietzsche is beyond the realm of rational understanding (and so appears to be "simply" madness). Yet, given Nietzsche's exaltation of rapture and abandon, such a transgressive transformation would seem to be the very culmination of Dionysian piety. To be so transformed that one is literally outside of oneself is perhaps the only route left to the decadent Nietzsche.

But how does Nietzsche reach this place of being "beyond"? On the one hand, Pierre Klossowski argues that a kind of "chaos" is present in Nietzsche from the beginning.[46] Thus, his insanity is the end of a lifelong trajectory, the *telos* of the one who wishes to be truly Dionysian. On the other hand, Crawford suggests (as have others) that Nietzsche's madness was perhaps a "simulation" designed as "the perfect culmination of a Dionysian philosophy."[47] Of course, it would be difficult to adjudicate either way. There is good reason to think that Nietzsche truly went mad, but feigning madness as a way to become Dionysian is at least within the realm of possibility. Perhaps Nietzsche believed that it was the only way to overcome his own personal decadence.

In any case, Nietzsche writes a letter to Gast on January 4, 1889, consisting of just one sentence: "Sing me a new song: the world is transfigured and all the heavens rejoice" (*SL* 345; *KSB* 8:575)—and signs it "The Crucified." It would seem Nietzsche has finally found his new rhythm.

NOTES

PREFACE

1. Letter to Carl Fuchs, July 29, 1888 (*SL* 305; *KSB* 8:375).

2. Tracy B. Strong, *Friedrich Nietzsche and the Politics of Transfiguration*, expanded ed. (Urbana: University of Illinois Press, 2000), xxviii.

3. I am well aware that the standard English translation of the title of Albert Schweitzer's famous text is *The Quest "of" the Historical Jesus*. But "quest for" is better English and has become the standard locution. In any case, since the German title is *Geschichte der Leben-Jesu Forschung*, the translators have themselves taken significant liberties in translating that title. See Albert Schweitzer, *The Quest of the Historical Jesus*, ed. John Bowden, trans. W. Montgomery, J. R. Coates, Susan Cupitt, and John Bowden (Minneapolis: Fortress, 2001; 1st pub. 1906).

4. See Walter Kaufmann, *Nietzsche: Philosopher, Psychologist, Antichrist* (Princeton, N.J.: Princeton University Press, 1950). This is the first of what eventually stretched into four editions (the last in 1974).

5. The desire to avoid contradiction and the categorizing of *ad hominem* arguments as "fallacious" are merely two such examples of aspects that Nietzsche seems to have no interest in preserving.

6. Robert C. Solomon and Kathleen M. Higgins, *What Nietzsche Really Said* (New York: Schocken, 2000), while admittedly not a text designed for an academic audience, is exemplary in its clarity, understanding of Nietzsche, and fairness to Nietzsche's views. The basic premise of the book is that Nietzsche has been widely misunderstood, so the goal of the text is to systematically correct those misunderstandings. In that respect, the point of the text is significantly different from one that has what seems to be a similar title—George Allen Morgan, *What Nietzsche Means* (Cambridge, Mass.: Harvard University Press, 1941).

7. Even though Levinas is talking specifically about the project of ontology, his observation that "philosophy consists in suppressing or transmuting the alterity of all that is Other" can easily be read as a hermeneutical indictment. See Emmanuel Levinas, "Transcendence and Height," in *Basic Philosophical Writings*, ed. Adriaan T. Peperzak, Simon Critchley, and Robert Bernasconi (Bloomington: Indiana University Press, 1996), 11.

8. Hans-Georg Gadamer, "Reflections on My Philosophical Journey," in *The Philosophy of Hans-Georg Gadamer*, ed. Lewis Edwin Hahn (Chicago: Open Court, 1997), 46.

9. Hans-Georg Gadamer, "Text and Interpretation," in *Dialogue and Deconstruction: The Gadamer-Derrida Encounter*, ed. Diane P. Michelfelder and Richard E. Palmer (Albany: State University of New York Press, 1989), 51.

10. See Edmund Husserl, *Ideas Pertaining to a Pure Phenomenology and a Phenomenological Philosophy. First Book: General Introduction to a Pure Phenomenology*, trans. Fred Kersten (The Hague: Martinus Nijhoff, 1982), §74.

11. Maudemarie Clark, *Nietzsche on Truth and Philosophy* (Cambridge: Cambridge University Press, 1990), esp. 38–41.

12. I discuss such issues at length—in regard to musical works—in my book *The Improvisation of Musical Dialogue: A Phenomenology of Music* (Cambridge: Cambridge University Press, 2003).

13. Interestingly enough, later in his Epilogue, Strong writes regarding Nietzsche's texts: "We learn from them by finding ourselves in them, which is precisely the source of authority that Nietzsche had found. . . . [Nietzsche] must allow others to find themselves in him" (*Friedrich Nietzsche and the Politics of Transfiguration*, 317). Julian Young speaks of "a regrettable trend in recent discussion of Nietzsche (at least in English), a trend to mere interpretation." He makes it clear that his study, in contrast, is meant as "a *critical* study of Nietzsche's thought." While I completely agree that Nietzsche is all too often studied for mere comprehension, I want to go beyond critique *too*. In so doing, I am merely following Nietzsche's own practice. See Julian Young, *Nietzsche's Philosophy of Art* (Cambridge: Cambridge University Press, 1992), 2.

14. Jacques Derrida, *Of Grammatology*, corr. ed., trans. Gayatri Chakravorty Spivak (Baltimore: Johns Hopkins University Press, 1997), 158.

15. Geoffrey Bennington, *Derridabase*, in Geoffrey Bennington and Jacques Derrida, *Jacques Derrida* (Chicago: University of Chicago Press, 1993), 7.

16. To be sure, he does come close to doing so in *EH* "Books" *CW* 1; *KSA* 6:357, where he speaks of music that is "world-transfiguring" because of its "Yes-saying character" versus the "music of decadence." Here the implication is clear: if music can be used to transform the world, surely it can be used to transform oneself. Thus, what follows can be read as working out that implication.

17. Truth be told, I read Robert Solomon's excellent discussion of Nietzsche's use of the *ad hominem* argument only after writing this section. Since defending *ad hominem* arguments is hardly a popular philosophical position, I'm delighted that he also defends their use—at least in some cases and within certain limits. As he so rightly puts it, "a well-wrought *ad hominem* insight may explain what many pages or hours of analysis and textual exegesis will not." Robert Solomon, "Nietzsche *ad hominem*: Perspectivism, Personality and *Ressentiment* Revisited," in *The Cambridge Companion to Nietzsche*, ed. Bernd Magnus and Kathleen M. Higgins (Cambridge: Cambridge University Press, 1996), 189. Of course, where Solomon and I differ is that *my* goal in reviving the *ad hominem* is to use it as a tool in reading *Nietzsche*.

18. "I hate everything that only instructs me without increasing or directly stimulating my activity," writes Nietzsche (quoting Goethe) at the beginning of "On the Uses and Disadvantages of History for Life" (*UM* II P; *KSA* 1:245). The quotation comes from a letter written by Goethe to Friedrich Schiller, December 19, 1798.

19. "Peter Gast" is the pseudonym Nietzsche invented for his friend Heinrich Köselitz.

20. For an account of this incident (admittedly one-sided, since it is by Derrida himself) and the infamous letter itself, see Jacques Derrida, "*Honoris Causa*: 'This is *also* extremely funny,'" in Jacques Derrida, *Points: Interviews, 1974–1994*, ed. Elisabeth Weber (Stanford, Calif.: Stanford University Press, 1995), 399–421.

21. One might be tempted to respond that taking motives into account is simply unacceptable since our access to others' motives is limited at best (and even knowledge of our own motives is often uncertain). Yet we routinely *do* consider motives in

court cases and in judging both the actions of friends and enemies. That we have limited access to motives means only that we must exercise caution in making judgments on the basis of them, not that we ought not take them into account at all.

22. See Pierre Hadot, *Philosophy as a Way of Life: Spiritual Exercises from Socrates to Foucault,* ed. Arnold I. Davidson, trans. Michael Chase (Oxford: Blackwell, 1995), and *What Is Ancient Philosophy?* trans. Michael Chase (Cambridge, Mass.: Harvard University Press, 2002). Also see Martha Nussbaum, *The Therapy of Desire: Theory and Practice in Hellenistic Ethics* (Princeton, N.J.: Princeton University Press, 1994). Part of Hadot's mission is to counteract what he sees as the disconnection of philosophy from life that has taken place over the centuries. While likewise deploring that separation, I think there has *always* been a connection between one's theory and one's life. That one fails to *see* the connection does not mean that it is not there.

INTRODUCTION

1. Letter to Gustav Krug and Wilhelm Pinder, April 27, 1862 (*KSB* 1:202).

2. *AC* 34; *KSA* 6:207.

3. *GS* 84; *KSA* 3:441.

4. Rüdiger Safranski, *Nietzsche: A Philosophical Biography,* trans. Shelley Frisch (New York: W. W. Norton, 2002), 19.

5. Georges Liébert, *Nietzsche and Music,* trans. David Pellauer and Graham Parkes (Chicago: University of Chicago Press, 2004), 8. This quotation is from *TI* I:33; *KSA* 6:64. A similar statement can be found in a letter of January 15, 1888, to Peter Gast, in which Nietzsche writes: "Life without music is simply an error, a strain, an exile" (*KSB* 8:232).

6. Babette Babich provides a relatively hefty bibliography of studies on Nietzsche and music. However, she notes that it is not uncommon for commentators on Nietzsche to remark that Nietzsche's relation to music has been largely left unstudied. Even in the very journal issue in which her bibliography appears, she points out yet another example of the usual complaint in one of the other articles: "Several commentators have noted, in passing, Nietzsche's predilection for musical metaphor and for particular composers, few, if any, have noted exactly how the art of music functions organically as part of his ongoing philosophical methodology." See her "Nietzsche and Music: A Selective Bibliography," *New Nietzsche Studies* 1 (1996): 64–78. The article to which she makes reference is Gary Lemco, "Nietzsche and Schumann," *New Nietzsche Studies* 1 (1996): 42–56 (the quotation Babich provides from Lemco is on p. 42 of the article).

7. My reading is all the more viable in that the term "cadence" can be applied both to music and to nature. See *The Oxford English Dictionary,* 2nd ed. (Oxford: Oxford University Press, 1999), s.v. "cadence." To the possible objection that I am using the English term "decadence" while Nietzsche always uses the French term *décadence* (instead of the German *Dekadenz*), I would point out that both (and even all three) are derived from the Latin term *decadentia.* Moreover, the English term "cadence" is virtually equivalent to the French *cadence.* Interestingly enough, Babich has used the notion of "cadence" to discuss the "falling out" between

Heidegger and Nietzsche. In one sense, then, her use of "cadence" and my use of "decadence" are similar, though certainly not the same. See her article "A Musical Retrieve of Heidegger, Nietzsche, and Technology: Cadence, Concinnity, and Playing Brass," *Man and World* 26 (1993): 239–60. I know of no one who reads "decadence" in Nietzsche in quite the musical sense that I do.

8. George H. Leiner, "To Overcome One's Self: Nietzsche, Bizet and Wagner," *Journal of Nietzsche Studies* 9/10 (1995): 135.

9. Alistair Kee aptly describes the situation as follows: "Scholars who are not personally interested in religion have decided that it is entirely possible to expound Nietzsche or dialogue with Nietzsche without reference to his views on religion." See Alistair Kee, *Nietzsche against the Crucified* (London: SCM, 1999), 7.

10. John Lippitt and Jim Urpeth, eds., *Nietzsche and the Divine* (Manchester: Clinamen, 2000), xvi.

11. Tyler T. Roberts, *Contesting Spirit: Nietzsche, Affirmation, Religion* (Princeton, N.J.: Princeton University Press, 1998), 5.

12. Kee, *Nietzsche against the Crucified;* Weaver Santaniello, ed., *Nietzsche and the Gods* (Albany: State University of New York Press, 2001); Giles Fraser, *Redeeming Nietzsche: On the Piety of Unbelief* (London: Routledge, 2002); and Julian Young, *Nietzsche's Philosophy of Religion* (Cambridge: Cambridge University Press, 2006). Fraser also sees Nietzsche as influenced by German Pietism. However, on his account, Nietzsche is obsessed with salvation. Conversely, I read Nietzsche as explicitly rejecting all redemptive projects, though retaining the Pietist emphasis on how one lives.

13. Karl Jaspers, *Nietzsche and Christianity* (Chicago: Henry Regnery, 1961), 1–2. Steven C. Aschheim recounts how Nietzsche's thought has been appropriated for Christian purposes, starting even before Nietzsche's death. See Ashheim's *The Nietzsche Legacy in Germany: 1890–1990* (Berkeley: University of California Press, 1992), especially ch. 7. Nietzsche significantly influenced Dietrich Bonhoeffer. For example, Bonhoeffer writes: "The Christian message stands beyond good and evil" and then goes on to add "thus the discovery of what is beyond good and evil was not made by Friedrich Nietzsche . . . it belongs to the original material of the Christian message, concealed, of course, as it is." See *No Rusty Swords: Letters, Lectures and Notes from 1928–1936,* trans. Edwin H. Robertson and John Bowden (New York: Harper & Row, 1965), 41. Karl Barth likewise took Nietzsche's criticism of Christianity seriously enough to write: "With his discovery of the Crucified and His host he discovered the Gospel itself in a form which was missed even by the majority of its champions, let alone its opponents, in the 19th century." Karl Barth, *Church Dogmatics,* vol. III/2, *The Doctrine of Creation,* ed. G. W. Bromiley and T. F. Torrance, trans. Harold Knight, G. W. Bromiley, J. K. S. Reid, and R. H. Fuller (Edinburgh: T&T Clark, 1960), 242.

14. See *KSB* 6:109.

15. Young, *Nietzsche's Philosophy of Religion,* 201. As will become clear, I share with Young the belief that Nietzsche is a deeply religious thinker. Yet, whereas the content of that religion according to Young is a conservative communitarianism, on my account it is a peculiar (and heavily distorted) form of German Pietism.

16. Fraser, *Redeeming Nietzsche*, 2.

17. Thomas Brobjer, "Nietzsche's Atheism," in Lippitt and Urpeth, *Nietzsche and the Divine*, 2.

18. While Nietzsche uses only the French term *décadence*, I will simply substitute "decadence" for *décadence* (except when quoting him).

19. Decadence even makes its way into *Nietzsche contra Wagner*, a reworked compilation of nasty things Nietzsche had earlier written regarding Wagner. In the section "We Antipodes" (a revision of *GS* 370), Nietzsche speaks of selflessness as "the principle of decadence" (*KSA* 6:426–27).

20. *The Oxford English Dictionary*, s.v. "decadence."

21. *Entartung* appears in *Z* I "Gift-Giving Virtue" 1; *KSA* 4:98. We will return to the relation of *Entartung, resssentiment*, and *Nihilismus* to decadence.

22. Letter to Malwida von Meysenbug, October 18, 1888; *KSB* 8:452.

23. Although Roberts is hardly the first to point out that Nietzsche is an ascetic of sorts (and he rightly reminds us that Kaufmann long ago made that claim), he distinguishes between an "ascetic ideal" and "asceticism" (which, as he also points out, both Nehemas and Clark fail to do). See *Contesting Spirit* 78–79, as well as Alexander Nehemas, *Nietzsche: Life as Literature* (Cambridge, Mass.: Harvard University Press, 1985), and Clark, *Nietzsche on Truth and Philosophy*.

24. *Phaedo* 60e–61b, in *The Collected Dialogues of Plato*, ed. Edith Hamilton and Huntington Cairns (Princeton, N.J.: Princeton University Press, 1961). Unless otherwise noted, all further citations of Platonic texts will be from this edition.

25. *EH* "Books" BGE 1; *KSA* 6:350. Although the "yes-saying" aspect of Nietzsche's *askêsis* is clearly the more important aspect, "no-saying" is a crucial step toward "yes-saying." As we will see, the critique that Nietzsche launches against the decadent culture of his day is also very clearly a critique against *himself*.

26. Michel Haar, "Nietzsche and Metaphysical Language," in David B. Allison, ed., *The New Nietzsche: Contemporary Styles of Interpretation* (Cambridge, Mass.: MIT Press, 1985), 30.

1. THE PRAYERS AND TEARS OF YOUNG FRITZ

1. From *Aus meinen Leben* (written at the tender age of thirteen), which was the first of Nietzsche's autobiographical reflections (*KGW* I/1, 4 [77]). Quoted in R. J. Hollingdale, *Nietzsche: The Man and His Philosophy*, rev. ed. (Cambridge: Cambridge University Press, 1999), 17.

2. From *Ecco Homo*, the last of Nietzsche's autobiographical reflections, completed only days before his collapse on the street. See *EH* "Clever" 4; *KSA* 6:287.

3. Resonance here with John D. Caputo's *The Prayers and Tears of Jacques Derrida: Religion without Religion* (Bloomington: Indiana University Press, 1997) goes beyond merely the title. In *Aus meinen Leben*, Nietzsche writes that, when he awoke on July 27, 1849, he heard his mother (with tears in her eyes) say: "Ach Gott! Mein gutter Ludwig ist tot." Upon hearing the news, he himself "wept bitterly" [*weinte bitterlich*] (*KGW* I/1, 4 [77]). As to Nietzsche's last moment of sanity, he is said to have left his lodgings only to discover a horse being beaten in the

Piazza Carlo Alberto. In an act of compassion, Nietzsche threw his arms around the horse's neck to protect it—and then collapsed. It has often been noted that there are remarkable parallels to Raskolnikov's dream of a horse being beaten in *Crime and Punishment* and also what Dostoyevsky says of a character in *A Raw Youth:* "If he saw from the window a peasant shamelessly beating his horse on the head, he would send out at once, and buy the horse at double its value. And he received the gift of tears. If any one talked to him he melted into tears." See Fyodor Dostoevsky, *A Raw Youth,* trans. Constance Garnett (London: Heinemann, 1956), 394.

4. Jacques Derrida makes these claims in *Memoirs of the Blind: The Self-portrait and Other Ruins,* trans. Pascale-Anne Brault and Michael Naas (Chicago: University of Chicago Press, 1993), 122.

5. Carl Pletsch, *Young Nietzsche: Becoming a Genius* (New York: Free Press, 1991), 34.

6. Jörg Salaquarda, "Nietzsche and the Judeo-Christian Tradition," in Magnus and Higgins, *The Cambridge Companion to Nietzsche,* 92. I have found Salaquarda's account helpful in reconstructing the faith of the young Nietzsche. Thomas Brobjer's accounts have likewise been useful. See his "Nietzsche's Atheism" and "Nietzsche's Changing Relation with Christianity," in Santaniello, *Nietzsche and the Gods,* 137–57. Also see Reiner Bohley, "Nietzsches christliche Erziehung," *Nietzsche-Studien* 16 (1987), 164–96, and "Nietzsches Taufe: 'Was, mienest du, will aus diesem Kindlein werden?'" *Nietzsche-Studien* 9 (1980): 383–405.

7. Martin Pernet, "Friedrich Nietzsche and Pietism," *German Life and Letters* 48 (1995), 478.

8. This emphasis on living the Christian life (rather than on salvation) seems almost "this-worldly." Moreover, such an emphasis is in keeping with both the spirit and content of Spener's *Pia Desideria,* the classic work of German Pietism. See Philip Jacob Spener, *Pia Desideria,* trans. Theodore G. Tappert (Philadelphia: Fortress, 1964).

9. Quoted in Hollingdale, *Nietzsche,* 17.

10. Hollingdale prefaces his citation of this prayer by saying "the intensity of [Nietzsche's] religious feeling is startling." But what else would one expect out of Nietzsche than intensity, whether for matters religious or otherwise? It is with the same degree of intensity that Nietzsche rejects this specifically Christian Pietism and embraces his "worldly Pietism." So religious intensity—in whatever form it takes—remains a hallmark of Nietzsche's thought.

11. Much of Nietzsche's poetry functions as a sort of prayer (less obviously in this poem but very clearly so in the next two).

12. Quoted in Philip Grundlehner, *The Poetry of Friedrich Nietzsche* (Oxford: Oxford University Press, 1986), 15–17. Grundlehner provides both German and English versions of Nietzsche's poetry.

13. The connection here to Ludwig Feuerbach's *The Essence of Christianity* seems obvious, though Nietzsche had not read Feuerbach at this point. The following year (1861) he asks for it as a birthday present.

14. Augustine, *Confessions,* trans. Henry Chadwick (New York: Oxford University Press, 1991), X.vii (11). Chadwick translates this quotation as "What

then do I love when I love my God?" Jacques Derrida picks up this question of Augustine and applies it to himself, as someone who also does not believe (unlike Augustine) in the God of Abraham, Isaac, and Jacob, and so calls himself "the last of the Jews." See Jacques Derrida, "Circumfession," in Derrida and Bennington, *Jacques Derrida*, 122.

15. Derrida and Bennington, *Jacques Derrida*, 155.

16. Grundlehner, *The Poetry of Friedrich Nietzsche*, 32–34.

17. Letter to Gustav Krug and Wilhelm Pinder, April 27, 1862 (*KSB* 1:202).

18. Grundlehner, *The Poetry of Friedrich Nietzsche*, 25–26.

19. Paul Deussen, *Erinnerungen an Friedrich Nietzsche* (Leipzig: F. A. Brockhaus, 1901), 4.

20. Neither Brobjer nor Salaquarda, for instance, follow Schmidt's interpretation.

21. Brobjer makes the insightful observation that Nietzsche sees historical analysis as having inevitable negative consequences. Consider what Nietzsche says regarding Christianity: "What one can learn in the case of Christianity" is that everything subjected to historical analysis "ceases to live when it is dissected completely." See Brobjar, "Nietzsche's Changing Relation with Christianity," 146–47, and *UM* 7; *KSA* 1:297.

22. While dropping the study of theology may indicate an important change in Nietzsche's relation to religion, it is worth noting that coordinating the curriculum of the two subjects turned out to simply impossible logistically.

23. Letter to Elisabeth Nietzsche, June 11, 1865 (*KSB* 2:61).

24. In this same letter, Nietzsche speaks of having heard Bach's *St. Matthew Passion* three times that week. He writes that this music represents the "no-saying of the will."

25. Lou Salomé, *Nietzsche*, trans. Siegfried Mandel (Urbana: University of Illinois Press, 2001), 88. The relation between Nietzsche and Salomé is far too complex to be considered here, nor can an adequate assessment be offered of the general reliability of Salomé's account of Nietzsche's thought. But on this particular point, I think Salomé gets Nietzsche exactly right, as will become evident.

26. Martin Heidegger, "The Word of Nietzsche: 'God Is Dead,'" in *The Question Concerning Technology and Other Essays*, trans. William Lovitt (New York: Harper & Row, 1977), 74. We will consider the problematic nature of Heidegger's claim in some detail in the following chapter.

27. Indeed, Nietzsche's reference to himself as "godless" in *GS* 344 is probably best taken as ironic. Both there and in *GM* III:24; *KSA* 5:399, he concedes that he is among those who still have faith in truth, which means that they are *not* truly godless. Instead, Nietzsche goes on to claim that the "true" godless are the Assassins, for whom "nothing is true, everything is permitted" (*GM* III:24; *KSA* 5:399). Of course, it is Nietzsche who is often thought to believe that "everything is permitted" precisely because God does not exist. The logic here is usually attributed to Fyodor Dostoyevsky, who is credited as having said something along the lines of "if there is no God, then everything is permitted." Interestingly enough, no such statement—nor variant thereof—occurs in any of Dostoyevsky's writings. The

idea, however, can be inferred from what Ivan Karamazov says in *The Brothers Karamazov.*

2. THE EUTHANASIA OF CHRISTIANITY

1. *D* 92; *KSA* 3:85–86.

2. My apologies to T. S. Eliot, whose poem "The Hollow Men" (1925) ends, of course, with the well-known stanza *"This is the way the world ends | This is the way the world ends | This is the way the world ends | Not with a bang but a whimper."* See T. S. Eliot, "The Hollow Men," in T. S. Eliot, *The Complete Poems and Plays, 1909–1950* (New York: Harcourt, Brace, & World, 1971), 59.

3. Immanuel Kant, *Religion within the Boundaries of Mere Reason,* trans. Allen Wood, in *Religion and Rational Theology,* trans. and ed. Allen W. Wood and George di Giovanni (Cambridge: Cambridge University Press, 1998), 57–215. David Friedrich Strauss, *The Life of Jesus Critically Examined,* ed. Peter C. Hodgson, trans. George Eliot (Philadelphia: Fortress, 1972), and *The Old Faith and the New,* trans. Mathilde Blind (Amherst, N.Y.: Prometheus Books, 1997). Ludwig von Feuerbach, *The Essence of Christianity,* trans. George Eliot (New York: Harper & Row, 1957).

4. One of Nietzsche's friends checked Stirner's works out of the Basel University library in 1874. It has often been speculated that he did so at Nietzsche's request. It does seem that Nietzsche was at least familiar with Stirner. Carl Albrecht Bernoulli relates Nietzsche's conversation with Ida Overbeck (Franz's wife) in which Nietzsche mentions his interest in Stirner. But then he adds: "Forget it. People will speak of plagiarism, but you will not do that; I know it." See Carl Albrecht Bernoulli, *Franz Overbeck und Friedrich Nietzsche: Eine Freundschaft* (Jena: Eugen Diederichs, 1908), vol. 1, 239. Given the remarkable parallels in their thought, accusations of plagiarism were natural. Yet Nietzsche might equally have been worried about any association of his views with those of Stirner, who was considered a radical figure. For two recent discussions of their connection, see John Glassford, "Did Friedrich Nietzsche (1844–1900) Plagiarise from Max Stirner (1806–56)?" *Journal of Nietzsche Studies* 18 (1999): 73–79, and Thomas Brobjer, "A Possible Solution to the Stirner-Nietzsche Question," *Journal of Nietzsche Studies* 25 (2003): 109–14. Brobjer concludes: "it seems to me highly unlikely that Nietzsche in any sense was profoundly influenced by Stirner" (112).

5. *"Genoi' hoios essi mathôn,"* in Pindar's second *Pythian Ode* 1.73. See Nehemas, *Life as Literature,* 250n3 and ch. 6.

6. See the discussion in Irving M. Zeitlin, *Nietzsche: A Re-examination* (Cambridge: Polity, 1994), 113–22. Max Stirner, *The Ego and His Own,* ed. David Leopold, trans. Steven Tracy Byington (Cambridge: Cambridge University Press, 1995), 139.

7. "Now I know how, have the know-how, to *reverse perspectives,*" says Nietzsche, which he sees as the reason why he alone can attempt a revaluation of values (*EH* "Wise" 1; *KSA* 6:266).

8. Nietzsche claims that "the 'true world' is just *added to it* [the apparent world] *by a lie*" (*TI* III:2; *KSA* 6:75).

9. Santaniello makes the claim (not entirely convincingly) that the ugliest man is none other than Socrates. See her "Socrates as the Ugliest Murderer of God," in Santaniello, *Nietzsche and the Gods*, 73–83.

10. Gilles Deleuze is one of the few who note that Nietzsche presents us with different accounts of the death of God. As he puts it, this death is "sometimes presented as accidental" and "sometimes the effect of a criminal act." See Gilles Deleuze, *Nietzsche and Philosophy*, trans. Hugh Tomlinson (New York: Columbia University Press, 1983), 149.

11. The same account of "death by pity" is to be found in *Z* II "Pitying"; *KSA* 4:115. There "the devil" says to Zarathustra: "God is dead; God died of his pity for man."

12. To be sure, there is yet *another* account of God's death. However, not only is this one specifically of Christ, it also seems to be—in effect—Nietzsche thinking through the logic of the crucifixion. He speaks of the "mystery of an inconceivable, final, extreme cruelty and self-crucifixion of God *for the salvation of man*" (*GM* I:8; *KSA* 5:269). Deleuze cites this section as evidence that "the Jewish God puts himself to death to make himself independent of himself and of the Jewish people" (*Nietzsche and Philosophy*, 153). But it is hard to see this section as providing evidence for such a claim.

13. Jean-Luc Marion, *The Idol and Distance: Five Studies*, trans. Thomas A. Carlson (New York: Fordham University Press, 2001), 1.

14. Heidegger, "The Word of Nietzsche," 61.

15. Ibid., 75.

16. Martin Heidegger, *An Introduction to Metaphysics*, trans. Gregory Fried and Richard Polt (New Haven, Conn.: Yale University Press, 2000), 190–91.

17. Heidegger, "The Word of Nietzsche," 75.

18. Heidegger, like many of his generation, thought of *The Will to Power* as the pinnacle of Nietzsche's thought. Thus, the principle of "will to power" is naturally taken to be central to Nietzsche's philosophy. Walter Kaufmann goes so far as to say that "Nietzsche's conception of power may represent one of the few great philosophic ideas of all time." See Walter Kaufmann, *Nietzsche: Philosopher, Psychologist, Antichrist*, 4th ed. (Princeton, N.J.: Princeton University Press, 1974), xvi. Yet there has been a significant backlash against this view. For example, see Bernd Magnus, "Nietzsche's Philosophy in 1888: *The Will to Power* and the *Übermensch*," *Journal of the History of Philosophy* 24 (1986): 79–98. Magnus divides the world of Nietzsche scholars into "lumpers" (those who take the unpublished texts to be just as authoritative as the published texts) and "splitters" (though who make a sharp division between the published and unpublished texts). As stated previously, my own view is that, while the *Nachlass* should not be given equal weight with published texts, it is an important resource from which one may draw and often serves to clarify what Nietzsche says in his published works. Regarding the "will to power," two Nietzsche commentators have recently written: "Unfortunately, once one has taken the dubious text of that name, *The Will to Power*, out of play, there is surprisingly little in Nietzsche's writings to support these views. The phrase, to be sure, recurs with considerable frequency. Nietzsche was clearly struck by it. . . .

The fact is, most of what Nietzsche says about the will to power is to be found in his unpublished notes, and it is therefore to be regarded with considerable suspicion" (Solomon and Higgins, *What Nietzsche* Really *Said*, 215–16).

19. Bernd Magnus and Kathleen M. Higgins, "Introduction to the Cambridge Companion to Nietzsche," in *The Cambridge Companion to Nietzsche*, 6.

20. Immanuel Kant, *Critique of Pure Reason*, trans. Paul Guyer and Allen Wood (Cambridge: Cambridge University Press, 1998), A x.

21. Richard Rorty, *Philosophy and Social Hope* (New York: Penguin, 1999), xix.

22. Jacques Derrida, "Violence and Metaphysics: An Essay on the Thought of Emmanuel Levinas," in Jacques Derrida, *Writing and Difference*, trans. Alan Bass (Chicago: University of Chicago Press, 1978), 152. Levinas, "God and Philosophy," in *Basic Philosophical Writings*, 148.

3. THE PIETY OF ZARATHUSTRA

1. Letter to Gustav Krug and Wilhelm Pinder, April 27, 1862 (*KSB* 1:202).

2. Quoted in Pernet, "Friedrich Nietzsche and Pietism," 485. Overbeck's unpublished manuscript is in the Basel University library.

3. Regarding Nietzsche's tendency to leave those with a Pietistic faith undisturbed, it is telling that, when Zarathustra comes down from his cave in the mountains at the beginning of *Thus Spoke Zarathustra*, he meets a saint of whom he notes: "Can it be possible? This old saint in the forest has not yet heard anything of this, that *God is dead*." Yet Zarathustra says nothing to contradict or disturb the saint's faith (*Z* I "Prologue" 2; *KSA* 4:14).

4. Elisabeth Förster-Nietzsche, ed., *The Nietzsche-Wagner Correspondence*, trans. Caroline V. Kerr (New York: Boni and Liveright, 1921), 294.

5. An English translation of what is in effect a poster of charges against Christianity is found in Gary Shapiro, *Nietzschean Narratives* (Bloomington: Indiana University Press, 1989), 146. The German text appears in *KSA* 6:254.

6. Fanatic here in the sense of "intense uncritical devotion." See *Merriam-Webster's Collegiate Dictionary*, 11th ed. (Springfield, Mass.: Merriam-Webster, 2003), s.v. "fanatic."

7. Regarding the first book of *Thus Spoke Zarathustra*, Nietzsche writes to Overbeck and says: "This book, about which I wrote to you, the work of ten days, now seems to me like my last will and testament. It contains an image of myself in the sharpest focus, as I am, *once* I have thrown off my whole burden" (letter of February 1883, *SL* 207; *KSB* 6:326). Elsewhere, speaking of the essay *Richard Wagner in Bayreuth*, Nietzsche says: "one need not hesitate to put down my name or the word 'Zarathustra' where the text has the word 'Wagner'" (*EH* "Books" BT 4; *KSA* 6:314). If it makes no difference whether "Nietzsche" or "Zarathustra" replaces "Wagner," then logically it would seem to follow that Nietzsche and Zarathustra are synonymous. So, given both of these passages, there is good reason for taking Zarathustra to represent Nietzsche—at least to a great extent.

8. *Thus Spoke Zarathustra* originally had three parts, with "The Song of Yes and Amen" at the end of the third part. However, Nietzsche later added a fourth part (though only for private circulation among his friends).

9. Higgins also notes that "new festivals, new songs, new recitations are among the means we can use to bridge the chasm of nihilism that separates traditional Christian faith from a newly grounded health, which locates meaning within this life." As much as I agree with Higgins, my point in this chapter is somewhat different from hers. For my point is also that Nietzsche is still indebted to Christian faith (and so *hasn't* simply left it behind and merely adopted its rituals). See Kathleen Marie Higgins, *Comic Relief: Nietzsche's* Gay Science (Oxford: Oxford University Press, 2000), 38, 35.

10. For exposition of the array of interpretations, see Nehemas, *Life as Literature*, 141–56.

11. Robert Gooding-Williams makes a distinction between what he terms "redemption1" (which is "*the redemption of the human past*") and "redemption3" (which is "*the redemption of the will through the act of willing backwards*"). To redeem the past and redeem the will certainly go together, though he is certainly right that they are not exactly synonymous. "Redemption2" is viewing of the past from the spirit of revenge. See Robert Gooding-Williams, *Zarathustra's Dionysian Modernism* (Stanford, Calif.: Stanford University Press, 2001), 205–12.

12. *KGW* I/1, 4 [77]; Hollingdale, *Nietzsche*, 17.

13. As mentioned, this section was originally the ending to *Thus Spoke Zarathustra*. Thus, its function was precisely that of an "amen" at the end of a prayer. Only later did Nietzsche append the fourth section.

14. We noted earlier that the formula for faith seems to be something like "I believe; help my unbelief" (Mk. 9:24).

15. One could even read the title of Nietzsche's second essay of his *Untimely Meditations*—"On the Use and Disadvantage of History for Life"—precisely in this sense.

4. NIETZSCHE'S DECADENCE

1. *EH* "Wise," 1; *KSA* 6:265.

2. *EH* "Wise," 2; *KSA* 6:266.

3. An alternative explanation for this manic-like sense of self-confidence would be that, as a likely advance-stage syphilitic, Nietzsche was undergoing the stage of euphoria and general sense of well-being that often comes before a collapse (which he experienced on January 3, 1889).

4. Referring to *Don Quixote*, he speaks of "the decadence of Spanish culture." See Paul Bourget, "Théorie de la décadence," in *Essais de psychologie contemporaine*, vol. 1 (Paris: Plon, 1926), 3–33. This volume first appeared in 1883, and Nietzsche makes mention of Bourget in letters to Resa von Schirnhofer of March 11, 1885 (*KSB* 7:18) and June 1885 (*KSB* 7:59).

5. Kaufmann, *Nietzsche*, 4th ed., 73n1.

6. Michael Silk, "Nietzsche, Decadence, and the Greeks," *New Literary History* 35 (2005): 595. Nietzsche makes reference to *Verfall* and *Niedergang* as early as 1886, in his newly written prefaces for previously published texts.

7. Given that statement—along with the fact that the list of figures explicitly labeled "decadent" by Nietzsche includes Socrates and Jesus—perhaps it is too

strong to say (as does Daniel W. Conway) that "decadence *enframes* late modernity, imbuing the epoch with an identity and character *all its own*" [my italics]. While modernity is certainly characterized by a heightened, even overwhelming decadence, it is clearly not alone in being decadent. See Daniel W. Conway, "The Politics of Decadence," *Southern Journal of Philosophy* 38 (1999): 24.

8. Here, as with the previous quotation, I cite Nietzsche rather than Silk.

9. "Nietzsche, Decadence, and the Greeks," 595. Silk might be able to draw support from a letter that he does not cite. Writing to Carl Fuchs (mid-April 1886), Nietzsche uses the term *décadence* "not to condemn but only to describe" (*KSB* 7:177). But Nietzsche's use of the term in the texts of 1888 goes far beyond mere description. While there is a sense of inevitability of decadence in the modern age, one may still be criticized for how one *deals* with it.

10. Note what Nietzsche says regarding progress: "Progress is merely a modern idea, that is, a false idea" (*AC* 4; *KSA* 6:171). We turn shortly to why this is a hopeless strategy.

11. Lawrence J. Hatab makes a similar claim, viz., that decadence for Nietzsche is remarkably close to so many things that he rails against: otherworldliness, the ascetic ideal, life-denial, pessimism, optimism, and *Entartung*. See Hatab's "Time-Sharing in the Bestiary: On Daniel W. Conway's 'The Politics of Decadence,'" *Southern Journal of Philosophy* (1999): 38.

12. Of course, Conway makes one very important distinction: "While it is true that [Nietzsche] employed related terms—such as *Entartung, Niedergang,* and *Verfall*—throughout his career to describe the general cultural malaise that gripped European culture, none of these other terms was applied so forcefully and self-consciously to Nietzsche himself. For this reason, in fact, the term 'decadence' acquires a quasi-technical status within the critical apparatus of his post-Zarathustran writings. 'Decadence' thus serves as the central category of Nietzsche's confrontation with modernity in the writings from 1888." With this assertion, I am in complete agreement. See "The Politics of Decadence," 24.

13. Daniel W. Conway, *Nietzsche's Dangerous Game: Philosophy in the Twilight of the Idols* (Cambridge: Cambridge University Press, 1997), 23. Chapter 2 of Conway's text is perhaps the most helpful exploration of decadence in Nietzsche available. Also see Daniel R. Ahern, *Nietzsche as Cultural Physician* (University Park: Pennsylvania State University Press, 1995).

14. Nietzsche writes: "Tell me, brothers: what do we consider bad and worst of all? Is it not *degeneration* [*Entartung*]?" See *Z* I "Gift-Giving Virtue" 1; *KSA* 4:98. While "life-denial" is equivalent with decadence, otherworldliness, truth, pessimism, and optimism are *symptoms* of decadence.

15. For more on decadence in nineteenth-century Europe, see Charles Bernheimer, *Decadent Subject: The Idea of Decadence in Art, Literature, Philosophy, and Culture of the Fin de Siècle in Europe,* ed. T. Jefferson Kline and Noami Schor (Baltimore: Johns Hopkins University Press, 2002). For more on decadence as a concept, see José Luis Bermúdez, "The Concept of Decadence," in *Art and Morality,* ed. José Luis Bermúdez and Sebastian Gardner (London: Routledge, 2003), 111–30.

16. To quote Bourget: "In order for the total organism to function with energy, it is necessary that the composing organisms function with energy, but with a sub-

ordinate energy." See *Essais de psychologie contemporaine*, vol. 1, p. 20. For more on Bourget, see W. D. Williams, *Nietzsche and the French: A Study of the Influence of Nietzsche's French Reading on His Thought and Writing* (Oxford: Basil Blackwell, 1952), 152–56.

17. Max Scheler, *Ressentiment*, ed. Lewis A. Coser, trans. William W. Holdheim (New York: Schocken, 1961), 46.

18. Nietzsche has an additional list of symptoms in *KSA* 13:14 [94].

19. Although it is a common belief that the Hippocratic Oath contains the statement "First, do no harm" [Primum non nocere], such is not the case. Many scholars think that Hippocrates did indeed coin the phrase, though others believe it was Galen (since the phrase is in Latin). In any case, it seems likely that Nietzsche is playing off the common (mis)understanding of the oath.

20. Thomas Hobbes, *Leviathan, Or the Matter, Form and Power of a Commonwealth, Ecclesiastical and Civil* (London: George Routledge and Sons, 1894), I:13.

21. Nietzsche makes this point in yet another sketch for a text never completed, tentatively titled "Philosophy in Hard Times," in *PT* 121.

22. I am indebted to Claudia Crawford on this point. See her "Nietzsche's Dionysian Arts: Dance, Song, and Silence," in Salim Kemal, Ivan Gaskell, and Daniel W. Conway, eds., *Nietzsche, Philosophy and the Arts* (Cambridge: Cambridge University Press, 1998), 310–41.

23. Actually, Nietzsche seems to give us *two* "formulas" for decadence. In this passage, it is fighting against the instincts. In *TI* IX:35; *KSA* 6:133, it is choosing "what is harmful to *oneself,* to be *enticed* by 'distinterested' motives." Of course, in this later passage, Nietzsche actually says that this is "virtually the formula for *décadence* [beinahe die Formel ab für *décadence*]", so perhaps there is merely one formula and another that comes very close. In any case, choosing "what is harmful to oneself" is certainly an instance of going against one's instincts, since we instinctively seek what is beneficial to ourselves (at least according to Nietzsche).

24. See Clark's *Nietzsche on Truth and Philosophy*, ch. 4 and p. 234, where she says, "The ascetic needs the valuation and interpretation of life offered by the ascetic ideal in order to get a sense of power from self-denial. It would not work to say to himself 'I value self-denial only because I get a feeling of power from it.'"

25. *GM* III:23; *KSA* 5:395 and *EH* "Books" GM; *KSA* 6:353. See *Nietzsche on Truth and Philosophy*, 253. Clark considers the possibility of either the *Übermensch* or the eternal recurrence as this "counterideal," ultimately rejecting the former as too close to the ascetic ideal.

26. Nietzsche wrote the preface in the fall of 1886, though the second edition of *The Gay Science* was not published until 1887.

27. Hadot, *Philosophy as a Way of Life*, 91.

28. Ibid., 83.

29. Ibid., 84.

30. There are, of course, at least two senses of "acting by instinct." One would be that of following one's *first* inclination. The other would be that of making a careful, conscious choice that would follow one's instinct(s). The former would not necessarily coincide with the latter.

31. Karl Heussi, *Der Ursprung des Mönchtums* (Tübingen: J. C. B. Mohr, 1936), 13, quoted in Hadot's *Philosophy as a Way of Life,* 128.

32. Roberts makes precisely this point in his *Contesting Spirit,* 80. Indeed, I am particularly indebted to his discussion of Nietzsche's asceticism in general.

33. Michel Foucault, *The History of Sexuality,* vol. I, *The Use of Pleasure,* trans. Robert Hurley (New York: Pantheon, 1985), 74. Interestingly enough, when Nietzsche speaks of what he calls the "religious neurosis," he says that it is "connected with three dangerous dietary prescriptions: solitude, fasting, and sexual abstinence" (*BGE* 47; *KSA* 5:67). Of course, it is difficult to think of "solitude" as a "dietary prescription" (not to mention "sexual abstinence").

34. Michel Foucault, "Friendship as a Way of Life," in Michel Foucault, *Foucault Live: Collected Interviews, 1961–1984,* ed. Sylvère Lotringer, trans. Lysa Hochroth and John Johnston (New York: Semiotext[e], 1989), 309. Obviously, this is still too simple a definition of asceticism. An Epicurean, for instance, may give up certain pleasures precisely in order to gain others.

35. A primary problem of distinguishing between "asceticism" and *askêsis* is that asceticism has its etymological roots in *askêsis.*

36. Kallistos Ware, "The Way of the Ascetics: Negative or Affirmative?" in Vincent L. Wimbush and Richard Valantasis, eds., *Asceticism* (New York: Oxford University Press, 1995), 9.

37. Ibid., 8.

38. And, sadly, one can rather easily point to priests, pastors, and evangelists who preach otherworldly values but just "happen" to cash in rather well on this-worldly values.

39. One can argue that even the renunciation of pleasure need not be interpreted in either moral or religious terms. Nehemas says "the moralization of asceticism occurs when the preexisting prudential structure of behavior which I have been discussing is radicalized and interpreted not as a way of securing certain human pleasures by means of avoiding others, but as the desire to avoid all human pleasures in general." Yet the key here is *not* whether asceticism is "radicalized" but *why* someone renounces pleasure. One might have moral or religious grounds, to be sure, or one might simply view the renunciation of pleasure as a better (i.e., nonmorally better) way to live. See *Life as Literature,* 118.

40. I take this series of adjectives from *Merriam-Webster's College Dictionary,* s.v. "guerrilla." *The Anti-Christ(ian),* for example, was not published until 1895, and then in a carefully edited edition. Even today, amid a flood of Nietzsche scholarship, the work has still received comparatively little attention.

41. The most important work on these prefaces is found in Friedrich Nietzsche, *Ecce Auctor: Die Vorreden von 1886,* ed. Claus-Artur Scheier (Hamburg: Felix Meiner, 1990), in which Scheier provides extensive introductions to each of the prefaces. Also see Keith Ansell-Pearson, "Toward the *Übermensch:* Reflections on the Year of Nietzsche's Daybreak," *Nietzsche-Studien* 23 (1994): 124–45; and Daniel Conway, "Nietzsche's Art of This-Worldly Comfort: Self-reference and Strategic Self-parody," *History of Philosophy Quarterly* 9 (1992): 343–57.

42. Unless otherwise noted, all subsequent quotations in this section come from *EH* "Wise" 7.

43. To observe Nietzsche deconstruct Strauss's prose line by line, see *Unfashionable Observations*, trans. Richard T. Gray (Stanford, Calif.: Stanford University Press, 1995), 71–81; *KSA* 1:229–42. There Nietzsche provides numerous examples of Strauss's stunningly bad prose. Hollingdale, the translator of *Untimely Meditations* (another translation of the same Nietzsche text), claims that such examples would be lost on an English audience and so decides that "the sensible course would therefore seem to be to omit this passage" from his translation (which he does). But, as Gray's translation makes clear, Nietzsche's examples rendered into English are almost as clear—and almost as funny—as in the original German.

44. Of course, this logic of "protesting too much" because of being close to someone (or guilty of precisely what one is protesting) is hardly a quirk unique to Nietzsche.

45. Strong is certainly right when he points out that this admission of proximity to Socrates can be interpreted in many ways, such as that Nietzsche is really in agreement with Socrates, that Nietzsche is "afraid of not being original," or that "the two men have the same doctrine, but for different reasons." Yet these subtleties are, I think, less important than the very fact that Nietzsche finds himself dangerously close to each of these figures. See Strong, *Friedrich Nietzsche and the Politics of Transfiguration*, 113.

46. Salomé, *Nietzsche*, 88 (my italics).

47. Curt Paul Janz, *Die Briefe Friedrich Nietzsches* (Zurich: Editio Academica, 1972), 133–34.

48. The extent to which there really *are* any similarities between the two works is—at the very least—open to question. But I take it that Nietzsche's *perception* of such similarities is what is most significant here.

49. Not surprisingly, Michael Tanner chalks Nietzsche's critique of Wagner up to envy (of Wagner's work being "more dangerous"). There is, no doubt, that *too*. See Michael Tanner, *Wagner* (London: HarperCollins, 1996), 209. However, one can envy someone and still abhor certain features of that person's thought or character.

50. Jörg Salaquarda, "Dionysus versus the Crucified One: Nietzsche's Understanding of the Apostle Paul," in James C. O'Flaherty et al., eds., *Studies in Nietzsche and the Judaeo-Christian Tradition* (Chapel Hill: University of North Carolina Press, 1985), 102–103.

51. Ernst Bertram, *Nietzsche: Versuch einer Mythologie*, 7th ed. (Berlin: Bondi, 1929), 54.

52. Bernoulli, *Franz Overbeck und Friedrich Nietzsche*, vol. 2, 4.

53. Ibid., vol. 1, 316.

54. Edmund Husserl, *Logical Investigations*, trans. J. N. Findlay (London: Routledge & Kegan Paul, 1970), vol. 1, 43.

5. SOCRATES' FATE

1. *TI* II:2; *KSA* 6:67–68. Nietzsche's read of Socrates went strongly against the majority opinion of scholars in Nietzsche's day. Greg Whitlock describes the situation as follows: "The philosophers and philologists of Nietzsche's Germany regarded Socrates with a reverence not unlike the attitude of pious Christians

toward Christ. Indeed, many among the classicists themselves constituted an extension of the millennial cult of Socrates." So Nietzsche, not so surprisingly, boldly takes on the cult figure of his fellow philologists. See Whitlock's commentary to Nietzsche's lectures (*PPP* 258).

2. Here I am using the term "game" simply to denote a more or less enclosed activity that has certain rules and certain basic assumptions. One could—at least with certain modifications—use either Foucault's notion of a "discourse" or MacIntyre's notion of a "practice." See Foucault's essay "The Discourse on Language" in Michel Foucault, *The Archaeology of Knowledge*, trans. A. M. Sheridan Smith (New York: Pantheon, 1972), 215–37; and Alasdair MacIntyre, *After Virtue*, 2nd ed. (Notre Dame, Ind.: University of Notre Dame Press, 1981), 190.

3. Kant, of course, encounters this same problem when he attempts to put reason on trial with itself as judge in the *Critique of Pure Reason*.

4. That is, if I make the claim "my life is meaningless," how meaningful can that claim be (since I am the one making it)?

5. We'll return to this question of whether such a claim is a "faith claim" or "self-evident claim" later.

6. Jacqueline Scott rightly recognizes that assigning value to life is a move of decadence. Yet she is not quite right when she says that "Nietzsche's 'solution' to this problem was to say that some values are less problematic than others." It may well be that some values are less problematic than others, but Nietzsche's "solution" is simply to stop putting any values on life. Not only does he think valuing life is impossible (for the reasons I noted above), but he thinks that valuing life is pernicious. Further, Scott does not make a (crucial) distinction between valuation in general and the valuation of life in particular. See her article "Nietzsche and Decadence: The Revaluation of Morality," *Continental Philosophy Review* 31 (1998): 59–78 (particularly 63).

7. Jacques Derrida, "Plato's Pharmacy," in Jacques Derrida, *Dissemination*, trans. Barbara Johnson (Chicago: University of Chicago Press, 1981), 97.

8. Nietzsche also speaks of Plato engaging in a *Wettkampf* (i.e., *agôn*) with the poets: "That, which, e.g., with Plato, is of special artistic significance in his dialogues, is mostly the result of a contest with the art of the rhetors, the sophists, and the dramatists of his time, invented for the purpose that he at last could say: 'Look, I can do that also, what my great rivals can do; indeed I can do it better than they'" (*HC* 90–91; *KSA* 1:790). Of course, Nietzsche wants to return the truly ancient Greek form of *agôn*. To quote Keith Ansell-Pearson: "Nietzsche's aristocratism seeks to revive an older conception of politics, one which he locates in the Greek *agon*." See his *An Introduction to Nietzsche as Political Thinker: The Perfect Nihilist* (Cambridge: Cambridge University Press, 1994), 33–34.

9. Actually, Nietzsche says almost the exact same thing about Socrates as early as his lectures which he gave in 1872, 1873, and 1876: "Socrates is plebian; he is uneducated and also never went back and picked up his education lost in childhood" (*PPP* 144; *KGW* II/4, TK). Whether Socrates can be termed "plebian" is open to question. His father, Sophroniscus, was a sculptor, as was Socrates early in life. While Socrates received the basic education in gymnastics and music, it seems he was self-taught in other things. That is likely the basis for the charge that

Socrates was "uneducated," as well as perhaps the statement that Socrates makes to the effect that his master (Prodicus) did not train him properly (*Meno* 96d).

10. The story of the physiognomist comes from Cicero, *Tusculan Disputations,* IV, 37, 80.

11. As Daniel Pick puts it, "Nietzsche accepted a great deal of current criminological and eugenic theory, but pushed the implications further than many of the 'prudent' scientists into a kind of extreme provocation." See his *Faces of Degeneration: A European Disorder, c. 1848–c. 1918* (Cambridge: Cambridge University Press, 1989), 226.

12. Jacob Burckhardt, *The Greeks and Greek Civilization,* ed. Oswyn Murray, trans. Sheila Stern (New York: St. Martin's Press, 1998), 128–29.

13. Nietzsche also says that "nothing is as ugly as a human being in the process of *degeneration*" (*TI* IX:20; *KSA* 6:124). So degeneration is linked with one's appearance.

14. *Phaedrus* 246b. There may well be a progression in Plato's thought from a three-soul conception to a tripartite view of the soul. But that difference between his earlier and later philosophy is not significant for our discussion here, since the establishment of the hegemony of reason is the object in either case. See, for instance, T. M. Robinson, *Plato's Psychology,* 2nd ed. (Toronto: University of Toronto Press, 1995), 122–23.

15. *Phaedrus* 247c–e.

16. *Gorgias* 503e–504a.

17. Graham Parkes has made that argument as compellingly as any in his *Composing the Soul: Reaches of Nietzsche's Psychology* (Chicago: University of Chicago Press, 1994).

18. Conway provides an excellent account of *Instinkte* and *Triebe* in *Nietzsche's Dangerous Game,* 30–34. Yet I'm not convinced by his claim that "in *Twilight,* Nietzsche consistently reserves the term *Instinkt* to refer to any specific organization of the drives and impulses, as determined by the dominant mores of the particular people or epoch in question" (pp. 30–31). It's not clear to me that in such claims as "to fight the instincts—that is the formula for *décadence*" (*TI* II:11; *KSA* 6:73) or that "*anti-natural* morality" effectively "turns precisely *against* the instincts of life" (*TI* V:4; *KSA* 6: 85) we have a use of the term *Instinkte* that is distinguishable from that of *Triebe*.

19. *TI* IX:49; *KSA* 6:151–52 presents the interpreter with a slight complication. On the one hand, Nietzsche says that "Goethe conceived of a human being who was strong, highly cultivated," etc. On the other hand, in the same section, Nietzsche claims that Goethe "disciplined himself into wholeness, he *created* himself." Whereas the former sounds as if Goethe merely envisioned such a free spirit, the latter sounds like Goethe actually *became* such a spirit. Given Nietzsche's great admiration for Goethe, the latter interpretation seems more likely, and it is the one that I adopt here.

20. Randall Havas notes that "Nietzsche is often [wrongly] thought to have believed that the tragic Greeks lived with an awareness of something like the contingency or groundlessness of their culture, and that the tragedies served to give voice to that awareness." Instead, Nietzsche sees the tragic Greeks as not seeking

reasons (and having no drive to seek them). See Randall Havas, *Nietzsche's Genealogy: Nihilism and the Will to Knowledge* (Ithaca, N.Y.: Cornell University Press, 1995), 50.

21. *Poetics* 1453a, in *The Complete Works of Aristotle,* ed. Jonathan Barnes (Princeton, N.J.: Princeton University Press, 1984), vol. 2.

22. "Plato, for example, is made by me into a caricature" (*KSA* 12:10 [112]).

23. It is hardly surprising that the relation of Nietzsche and Socrates has been the subject of considerable debate. Very early on, Richard Oehler argued that Nietzsche repudiated Socrates. Since that interpretation proved highly influential in subsequent decades, Kaufmann felt a need to counter it by arguing that Nietzsche was largely favorable toward Socrates. Although Kaufmann does say that Nietzsche's "attitude was 'ambiguous'" (*Nietzsche: Philosopher, Psychologist, Antichrist,* 391), he goes on to give a reading in which Nietzsche turns out to be positively disposed toward Socrates overall. It is interesting that the chapter on Socrates in the first edition (1950) of *Nietzsche: Philosophy, Psychologist, Antichrist* is titled "Nietzsche's Admiration for Socrates," while the fourth edition (1974) has it as "Nietzsche's Attitude toward Socrates." In the first edition, Kaufmann frames his project as a study of "Nietzsche's admiration for Socrates," whereas the latter edition frames it as "an examination of all passages in which Nietzsche discusses Socrates as well as some in which Socrates is not named outright" 391). Werner Dannhauser rightly points out that, in order to argue for his thesis that Nietzsche admires Socrates, Kaufmann makes Nietzsche out to be (1) "more kindly disposed to reason, rational inquiry, and pure theory than he really is," (2) "less radical than he is," and (3) "less shocking and provocative than he really is." Still, the very passage in which Nietzsche accuses Socrates of being against life opens with the words: "I admire the courage and wisdom of Socrates in everything he did, said— and did not say" (*GS* 340; *KSA* 3:569). So one is forced to conclude that Nietzsche recognizes some aspects as worthy of praise and others as worthy of denigration. See Richard Oehler, *Friedrich Nietzsche und die Vorsokratiker* (Leipzig: Dürr, 1904); Kaufmann, *Nietzsche,* 4th ed., 391–411; and Werner Dannhauser, *Nietzsche's View of Socrates* (Ithaca, N.Y.: Cornell University Press, 1974), 38. Hermann Josef Schmidt's *Nietzsche und Sokrates: Philosophische Untersuchungen zu Nietzsches Sokratesbild* (Meisenheim am Glan: Anton Hain, 1969) remains the definitive work on Nietzsche and Socrates.

24. *Phaedo* 118a. Since Asclepius was the god of medicine, sacrificing a rooster to him would indicate that Socrates viewed death as the true cure for decadence. Such an interpretation of this passage gained currency only in the Renaissance.

25. Although Brian Domino is certainly right that "Socrates did not practice dialectic out of revenge, but out of necessity," this last act of Socrates seems to be a kind of revenge. At least Nietzsche sees it as such. See Brian G. Domino, "Vincenzo's Portrayal of Nietzsche's Socrates," *Philosophy and Rhetoric* 26 (1993): 44.

26. Alexander Nehemas, *The Art of Living: Socratic Reflections from Plato to Foucault* (Berkeley: University of California Press, 1998), 14.

27. It was Thucydides who, for instance, said that "war, by taking away the comfortable provision of daily life, is a teacher who educates through violence; and

he makes men's characters fit their conditions." One can hardly imagine a more stark outlook on reality, one that Nietzsche would understandably appreciate. Quoted from Thucydides, *The Peloponnesian War*, bk. III, ch. 82, in Alfred Zimmern, *The Greek Commonwealth*, 4th ed. (Oxford: Clarendon Press, 1924), 420.

6. WAGNER'S REDEMPTION

1. *CW* 3; *KSA* 6:16.

2. Schopenhauer first encountered the *Upanishads* in 1814 (in a Latin translation titled *Oupnek'hat*).

3. Arthur Schopenhauer, *The World as Will and Representation*, trans. E. F. J. Payne (New York: Dover, 1958), vol. II, 349.

4. Ibid., 573.

5. Ibid., 581 and 584.

6. Ibid., vol. I, 125.

7. Ibid., vol. II, 215.

8. Ibid., 170.

9. Ibid., 634.

10. Ibid., vol. I, 374. The German sentence simply reads as follows: "Alle Liebe (ἀγάπη, *caritas*) ist Mitleid."

11. Ibid., vol. II, 645. Of course, the resemblance between Schopenhauer's ethics and Christianity is only to be found in certain—and very limited—respects.

12. Ibid., vol. I, 378–79.

13. Ibid., 380.

14. Ibid., 383.

15. Ibid., 397.

16. Ibid., 398.

17. Ibid., vol. II, 584.

18. Ibid., vol. I, 178.

19. Ibid., vol. II, 373.

20. Ibid., vol. I, 197.

21. Ibid., 205.

22. Ibid., 252–53.

23. Ibid., 254.

24. Ibid., vol. II, 451.

25. "At bottom it is admittedly not 'Schopenhauer as Educator' that speaks here, but his opposite, Nietzsche as Educator" (*EH* "Books" UM 3; *KSA* 6:320). Here we have just one of the many instances of the late Nietzsche emphasizing his independence from Schopenhauer.

26. From "Rückblick auf meine zwei Leipziger Jahre."

27. No better account of the Wagner-Nietzsche relationship exists than Fredrick R. Love, *Young Nietzsche and the Wagnerian Experience* (Chapel Hill: University of North Carolina Press, 1963).

28. *Selected Letters of Richard Wagner*, trans. and ed. Stewart Spencer and Barry Millington (New York: W. W. Norton, 1987), 809. In this same letter, Wagner

also says, "You really are causing me nothing but worry, but it is because I care so very much for you!" The worry was the result of the negative response that *The Birth of Tragedy* had received.

29. Of course, as Martha Nussbaum notes, "Nietzsche was wrong about Euripides." Moreover, she goes on to make the point that, whereas Nietzsche so often departs from the typical scholarly consensus, in this case he has simply adopted the (mistaken) view of his day. See her "The Transfigurations of Intoxication: Nietzsche, Schopenhauer, and Dionysus" in Kemal et al., *Nietzsche, Philosophy and the Arts,* 36.

30. Kaufmann, *Nietzsche,* 4th ed., 131. Young, *Nietzsche's Philosophy of Art,* 27.

31. Young, *Nietzsche's Philosophy of Art,* 150.

32. Once again, the version from the passage in *NCW* varies in a significant way. For, while Nietzsche simply uses the phrase "German music" (in *GS* 370), he changes this to "Wagner's music" in *NCW.*

33. As Agnes Heller puts it: "Nietzsche had to break with Wagner because he had to follow his own star, his own luck, his own fate, his own affect, his own instinct, his own 'will to power'—and so he did." See her *An Ethics of Personality* (Oxford: Blackwell, 1996), 39. Even as early as *Human, All Too Human,* Nietzsche realizes that he needs to find *himself:* "What reached a decision in me at that time was not a break with Wagner: I noted a total aberration of my instincts of which particular blunders, whether Wagner or the professorship at Basel, were mere symptoms. I was overcome by *impatience* with myself; I saw that it was high time for me to recall and reflect on myself" (*EH* "Books" HH 3; *KSA* 6:324).

34. A reference to Senta, heroine of *Der fliegende Holländer.*

35. Houston Stewart Chamberlain, "Notes sur *Parsifal,*" *Revue wagnérienne* 2 (1887–88): 225.

36. Carl Dahlhaus, *Richard Wagner's Music Dramas,* trans. Mary Whittall (Cambridge: Cambridge University Press, 1979), 143.

37. Michael Tanner notes: "As soon as we try to see *Parsifal* as a 'religious work,' it presents nothing else: for everything seems either irrelevant, blasphemous or banal. But seen as the most penetrating study we have of the psychopathology of religious beliefs in artistic terms, it is an incomparably involving experience." Not only do I find Tanner's argument that *Parsifal* is exemplary as a study of "psychopathology of religion" unconvincing (*Parsifal*'s unique conversion experience would be simply one reason why the opera's account of religious belief is suspect), but also I find it highly implausible that Wagner intended it as such. See Michael Tanner, "The Total Work of Art," in *The Wagner Companion,* ed. Peter Burbidge and Richard Sutton (New York: Cambridge University Press, 1979), 209.

38. Dahlhaus, *Richard Wagner's Music Dramas,* 143.

39. Maurice Kufferath, *The Parsifal of Richard Wagner* (New York: Tait, Sons & Co., 1892), 212. Here Kufferath is quoting Paul Lindau, a German critic.

40. Richard Wagner, *Richard Wagner's Prose Works,* vol. I, *Religion and Art,* trans. William Ashton Ellis (New York: Broude Brothers, 1966), 213.

41. Cosima Wagner, *Cosima Wagner's Diaries,* ed. Martin Gregor-Dellin and Dietrich Mack, trans. Geoffrey Skelton (New York: Harcourt Brace Jovanovich, 1978), vol. I, 984 (entry from September 26, 1877).

42. From a letter to Otto Eiser written on February 20, 1877. Quoted in Dieter

Borchmeyer, *Richard Wagner: Theory and Theatre*, trans. Stewart Spencer (Oxford: Clarendon, 1991), 401–402n59.

43. Slavoj Žižek, *The Fragile Absolute—Or, Why Is the Christian Legacy Worth Fighting For?* (London: Verso, 2000), 118–19.

44. Wagner's joy in receiving communion in mentioned in *KSA* 11:26 [377], 11:35 [49], and 12:2 [101].

45. Förster-Nietzsche, *The Nietzsche-Wagner Correspondence*, 294–95.

46. Wagner's opera is clearly based upon Wolfram von Eschenbach's *Parzival*, dating back to the beginning of the thirteenth century. However, Wagner's version is clearly his own, with its Buddhist motifs and strange twists.

47. Of course, there are some eastern traditions in which the gods need themselves to be saved, so perhaps this is not so strange after all.

48. This interpretation is, in essence, that offered by Lucy Beckett in her *Parsifal* (Cambridge: Cambridge University Press, 1981), 146. Liébert interprets this strange ending as follows: "In Wagner's opinion, Christ's message, prisoner of a religion that had betrayed it and become sclerotic in its dogmas and rites, was once again addressed to the whole human species." See Liébert, *Nietzsche and Music*, 121.

49. In titling this section "The Seduction of *Parsifal*," I intend multiple genitives. Without giving an exhaustive list, there is the seduction of Parsifal the character, the seduction that *Parsifal* the opera has on the listener, and the seduction of Wagner himself by the story of Parsifal. There is also the attempted seduction of Parsifal by Kundry, which is countered by a seduction of Kundry (to Christianity) by Parsifal.

50. Philip Pothen makes this point in *Nietzsche and the Fate of Art* (Aldershot: Ashgate, 2002), 173.

51. Elsewhere, Nietzsche writes: "The overture of *Parsifal*, the greatest blessing to be granted to me for a long time. The power and strength of feelings, indescribable, I know of nothing that grasped Christianity so profoundly and so sharply brought it to such a level of empathy. Completely subtle and moving . . . the greatest masterpiece of the sublime that I know, the power and strength in grasping a fruitful certainty, an indescribable expression of greatness of compassion [*Mitleiden*] about it" (*KSA* 12:5 [41]).

52. One could add the following passage: "All things considered, I could not have endured my youth without Wagner's music. . . . From the moment when there was a piano score of *Tristan*—my compliments, Herr von Bülow—I was a Wagnerian. . . . I think I know better than anyone else of what tremendous things Wagner is capable. . . . I call Wagner the great benefactor of my life" (*EH* "Clever" 6; *KSA* 6:289–90). Here it is interesting that Nietzsche actually *overestimates* Wagner's influence: for, when that score of *Tristan* first appeared, Nietzsche's interest was tepid at best (in comparison to Krug's).

7. PAUL'S REVENGE

1. *AC* 42; *KSA* 6:215–16.

2. Jacob Taubes, *The Political Theology of Paul*, trans. Dana Hollander (Stanford, Calif.: Stanford University Press, 2004), 79.

3. Michel Foucault, "Nietzsche, Genealogy, History," in Michel Foucault,

Essential Works of Foucault 1954–1984, ed. Paul Rabinow, vol. I, *Aesthetics, Method, and Epistemology,* ed. James D. Faubion (New York: New Press, 1998), 370–71.

4. Paul Rée, *The Origin of Moral Sensations,* in Paul Rée, *Basic Writings,* trans. Robin Small (Urbana: University of Illinois Press, 2003), 81–167.

5. Already in *Human, All Too Human* Nietzsche had recognized complications of the development of morality, such as parallel developments of notions of good and evil among nobles and slaves (*HH* I:45; *KSA* 2:67).

6. Foucault, "Nietzsche, Genealogy, History," 371.

7. Alain Badiou, *Saint Paul: The Foundation of Universalism,* trans. Ray Brassier (Stanford, Calif.: Stanford University Press, 2003), 21.

8. Quoted in Erik H. Erikson, *Young Man Luther: A Study in Psychoanalysis and History* (New York: W. W. Norton, 1958), 71.

9. Heinz Bluhm also makes this connection in "Nietzsche's View of Luther and the Reformation in *Morgenrote* and *Die fröhliche Wissenschaft,*" *PMLA* 68 (1953): 114. Further, in his article "Nietzsche's Final View of Luther and the Reformation," *PMLA* 71 (1956): 77, Bluhm notes that, for Nietzsche, "there are but two preeminent figures in the entire history of Christianity: Paul and Luther."

10. Interestingly enough, were Nietzsche's account here of Paul correct, then we would have yet another instance of what we have been examining with Socrates, Wagner, and Paul: the state of being particularly harsh with that which (or to whom) one feels so close, since both want to break from the law.

11. Žižek, *The Puppet and the Dwarf: The Perverse Core of Christianity* (Cambridge, Mass.: MIT Press, 2003), 15.

12. Of course, given that the Nag Hammadi library had not been discovered in Nietzsche's time, he was not aware of early competing Gospels. Imagine his interpretation of those (especially the Gospel of Judas)!

13. A reference to I Cor. 1:20: "Has not God made foolish the wisdom of the world?"

14. See Stanislas Breton, *The Word and the Cross,* trans. Jacquelyn Porter (New York: Fordham University Press, 2002). Breton notes that, with the adoption of this new *logos* "we have left the home of Israel just as we have left the home of Greece," the result being that "the Western thinker is divided from *within*" (132).

15. Aaron Ridley makes this point in his *Nietzsche's Conscience: Six Character Studies from the* "Genealogy" (Ithaca, N.Y.: Cornell University Press, 1998), 15.

16. Later, we will consider Nietzsche's own prescription for how one might "spiritualize, beautify, deify a desire."

17. See, for example, Luke 16:15.

18. Israel Eldad, "Nietzsche and the Old Testament," in O'Flaherty et al., *Studies in Nietzsche and the Judaeo-Christian Tradition,* 49. For more on Nietzsche's relation to Judaism, see Gary Banham, "Jews, Judaism and the 'Free Spirit'" and Jacob Golomb, "Nietzsche's Positive Religion and the Old Testament," both in Lippitt and Urpeth, *Nietzsche and the Divine,* 57–76 and 30–56; and Tim Murphy, "Nietzsche's Narrative of the 'Retroactive Confiscations' of Judaism," in Santaniello, *Nietzsche and the Gods,* 3–20. Also see Weaver Santaniello, *Nietzsche, God, and the Jews: His Critique of Judeo-Christianity in Relation to the Nazi Myth* (Albany: State University of New York Press, 1994).

19. Of course, it is not as if one can pinpoint the slave revolt to the Jews *either*. As with any genealogy, the development of the overturning of values takes place in different civilizations and under different conditions. Here, though, I am looking only at the relation between Judaism and Christianity, in order to situate Paul's place in the genealogy.

20. Indeed, the Jewish sect of Jesus' day known as the Sadducees claimed that there is no afterlife.

21. How or how much suffering is redeemed, though, remains a subject of significant dispute among Christians.

22. See the excellent discussion of this problem in Ridley, *Nietzsche's Conscience*, 46–50.

23. For example, consider his claims in I Cor. 9 and II Cor. 11.

24. We are told (Acts 18:3) that Paul actually was a tent-maker, though carpet-weaver comes close.

25. All of the quotations in this paragraph, except as noted, come from *GM* III:15; *KSA* 5:372–75.

26. Joan Stambaugh dwells on this point at length in *The Other Nietzsche* (Albany: State University Press of New York, 1994), chap. 4.

27. Here I am following Conway. See his discussion in *Nietzsche's Dangerous Game*, 109–16.

28. Of course, Socrates becomes a passive nihilist/decadent once he chooses suicide (assuming, of course, that is what he chooses).

29. John Andrew Bernstein, *Nietzsche's Moral Philosophy* (Rutherford, N.J.: Fairleigh Dickinson University Press, 1987), 171.

30. Badiou, *Saint Paul*, 1 and 4.

31. Ibid., 71.

32. Ibid.

33. Norman Wirzba, "The Needs of Thought and the Affirmation of Life: Friedrich Nietzsche and Jesus Christ," *International Philosophical Quarterly* 37 (1997): 398.

34. Here I think Paul Valadier simply misunderstands Jesus' death. He writes: "Dionysus is close to the non-Pauline Jesus. Jesus said yes, he affirmed, but he did not want death. This is the decisive difference between Dionysus and Jesus. Dionysus, the more lucid and vigorous, *wants* to be a martyr: not for himself, but as an inner condition for the affirmation." But why would *wanting* death be an affirmation of *life*? The logic here is simply baffling. In contrast, Jesus' death is all about *overcoming* death, which would seem to be a much stronger—not to mention more coherent—affirmation of *life*. See Paul Valadier, "Dionysus versus the Crucified," in Allison, *The New Nietzsche*, 250.

35. N. T. Wright, *Christian Origins and the Question of* God, vol. III, *The Resurrection of the Son of God* (Minneapolis: Fortress, 2003), 729–30.

36. Badiou, *Saint Paul*, 61.

37. Ibid.

38. For more on Nietzsche's "grand politics," see Ansell-Pearson, *An Introduction to Nietzsche as Political Thinker*, chap. 7.

39. Nietzsche describes human beings as "a rope, tied between beast and

Übermensch." See *Z* I "Prologue" 4; *KSA* 4:16. Although the fourth part of *Thus Spoke Zarathustra* can be read as a repudiation of the *Übermensch,* I will not attempt such a reading here. For a highly insightful reading along such lines, see Daniel W. Conway, "Overcoming the *Übermensch:* Nietzsche's Revaluation of Values," *Journal of the British Society for Phenomenology* 20 (1989): 211–24. For an excellent account of Nietzsche's evolving notion of the *Übermensch,* see Conway's "The Genius as Squanderer: Some Remarks on the *Übermensch* and Higher Humanity," *International Studies in Philosophy* 30 (1998): 81–95.

8. DECONSTRUCTING THE REDEEMER

1. *AC* 28; *KSA* 6:199.

2. *AC* 44; *KSA* 6:218–19.

3. *AC* 39; *KSA* 6:211.

4. Gary Shapiro, "Nietzsche contra Renan," *History and Theory* 21 (1982): 215. For a detailed account of the history of this genre, see Schweitzer, *The Quest of the Historical Jesus.*

5. Strauss, *The Life of Jesus Critically Examined,* 88. His attempt at creating an alternative Christian system is outlined in Strauss's book *The Old Faith and the New.*

6. Michael Tanner, "Introduction," in *Twilight of the Idols/The Anti-Christ* (London: Penguin, 1990), 21.

7. Eugen Biser, "Nietzsche's Relation to Jesus: A Literary and Psychological Comparison," in *Nietzsche and Christianity* [a special edition of *Concilium* 145 (1981)], ed. Claude Geffré and Jean-Pierre Jossua (New York: Seabury, 1981), 63.

8. Shapiro, "Nietzsche contra Renan," 217–18.

9. Tim Murphy, "Nietzsche's Jesus," *Epoché* 20 (1995–96): 38, 40, and 44. See also Murphy, *Nietzsche, Metaphor, Religion* (Albany: State University of New York Press, 2001), especially chap. 7.

10. Readings of Jesus as "idiot" abound. See Karl Schlecta and Herbert W. Reichert, eds., *The International Nietzsche Bibliography* (Chapel Hill: University of North Carolina Press, 1968) for multiple examples. For an example of a reading of Jesus as "Buddha," see Michel Hulin, "Nietzsche and the Suffering of the Indian Ascetic," in Graham Parkes, ed., *Nietzsche and Asian Thought* (Chicago: University of Chicago Press, 1991), 64–75; and Murphy's "Nietzsche's Jesus," 40–42. Robert G. Morrison devotes a short passage to Christianity and Buddhism in his book *Nietzsche and Buddhism: A Study in Nihilism and Ironic Affinities* (Oxford: Oxford University Press, 1997), 27–29.

11. C. A. Miller, "Nietzsche's 'Discovery' of Dostoevsky," *Nietzsche-Studien* 2 (1973): 203.

12. Nietzsche describes this discovery in the same letter to Overbeck in which he discusses Renan (*SL* 260; *KSA* 8:27–28).

13. Nietzsche writes on May 31, 1888, to Gast that he had discovered "das Gesetzbuch des Manu" just the previous week (*KSB* 8:325). Of course, Nietzsche had long been familiar with Buddhism (and the resignation of which he accuses Buddhism—and then ascribes to Christianity—is no doubt due to the influence of Schopenhauer). Yet it is telling, as Nietzsche mentions to Gast, that he had learned

a great deal about how priests control their followers through reading the Law of Manu.

14. Robin A. Roth, "Verily, Nietzsche's Judgment of Jesus," *Philosophy Today* 34 (1990): 366.

15. Elsewhere, Nietzsche says that "Gospel of love" grows "out of the trunk of that tree of revenge and hate, Jewish hate" (*GM* I:8; *KSA* 5:268).

16. Kurt Tucholsky, "Fräulein Nietzsche," in *Gesammelte Werke*, vol. 10 (Hamburg: Rowohlt, 1960), 14. Quoted in Safranski, *Nietzsche*, 11.

17. Thomas Aquinas, *Summa Theologica* III *Supplementum* Q. 94, Art. 1. Quoted in *GM* I:15: *KSA* 5:284.

18. Tertullian, *De spectaculus*, 29. Quoted in *GM* I:15; *KSA* 5:284.

19. Merold Westphal has done a superb job of showing just how well Nietzsche's criticism of Christianity can be taken to heart, as a "theological resource." See his *Suspicion and Faith: The Religious Uses of Modern Atheism* (Grand Rapids, Mich.: Eerdmans, 1993), 219–81, and "Nietzsche as a Theological Resource," in Lippitt and Urpeth, *Nietzsche and the Divine*, 14–29.

20. Ernest Renan, *The Life of Jesus,* trans. Charles Edwin Wilbour (New York: Carleton, 1864).

21. *The Dhammapada: Path of Perfection* (Harmondsworth: Penguin, 1973), chap. 1.

22. Miller, "Nietzsche's 'Discovery' of Dostoevsky," 203; P. Travis Kroeker and Bruce K. Ward, *Remembering the End: Dostoevsky as Prophet to Modernity* (Boulder, Colo.: Westview, 2001), 144.

23. At approximately the time of the composition of *The Anti-Christ(ian),* Nietzsche also writes to Georg Brandes (November 20, 1888) and says: "I am grateful to [Dostoevsky] in a remarkable way, however much he goes against my deepest instincts" (*SL* 327; *KSB* 8:483).

24. Dostoevsky's notebooks for *The Idiot* are helpful for figuring out what Prince Myshkin is supposed to represent. See Fyodor Dostoevsky, *The Notebooks for* The Idiot, ed. Edward Wasiolek, trans. Katharine Strelsky (Chicago: University of Chicago Press, 1967).

25. Fyodor Dostoyevsky, *Selected Letters of Fyodor Dostoyevsky,* ed. Joseph Frank and David I. Goldstein, trans. Andrew R. MacAndrew (New Brunswick, N.J.: Rutgers University Press, 1987), 269–70 and 262.

26. William Hamilton, *A Quest for the Post-Historical Jesus* (New York: Continuum, 1994), 76.

27. Fyodor Dostoevsky, *The Idiot,* trans. Richard Pevear and Larissa Volokhonsky (New York: Alfred A. Knopf, 2001), 74.

28. Ibid., 75.

29. Hamilton, *A Quest for the Post-Historical Jesus,* 78.

30. H. G. Liddell and R. Scott, *Greek-English Lexicon with a Revised Supplement* (Oxford: Clarendon, 1996), s.v. "*idiotês.*"

31. Dostoevsky, *The Idiot,* 508.

32. Kee, *Nietzsche against the Crucified,* 158.

33. Dostoevsky, *The Idiot,* 225–26.

34. Ibid., 61.

35. Murphy, "Nietzsche's Jesus," 37.

36. Dostoevsky, *The Notebooks for* The Idiot, 193.

37. It is extremely difficult to square this portrait of the evangel with what Nietzsche says about him in *Daybreak*. There Nietzsche writes the following: "He who sets such store on being believed in that he offers Heaven in exchange for this belief, and offers it to everyone, even to a thief on the cross—must have suffered from fearful self-doubt and come to know every kind of crucifixion: otherwise he would not purchase his believers at so high a price" (*D* 67; *KSA* 3:64). The kind of figure Nietzsche paints in *The Anti-Christ(ian)* simply doesn't sound like one who's particularly bent on gaining followers (so much so that he's willing to offer heaven as the reward). If the *practice of life* is what makes one "blessed," then what need would there be for heaven as a reward? Instead, it would seem that the practice *is* reward. If Nietzsche had provided a gloss on the passage in *Daybreak*, perhaps a reconciliation of these two portraits might be possible. As things stand, though, they simply seem at odds with each other. Since the portrait in *Daybreak* is an earlier one, the most likely reason for these two different portraits is that Nietzsche came to see the evangel in a different light.

38. The edition that Nietzsche read was Léon Tolstoï, *Ma religion* (Paris: Fischbacher, 1885). Nietzsche even includes citations from the text in his notebooks (*KSA* 13:11 [277]).

39. Matthew 5 is filled with these reversals.

40. Dostoevsky, *The Notebooks for* The Idiot, 193.

41. Stephen N. Williams, "Dionysus against the Crucified: Nietzsche *contra* Christianity: Part II," *Tyndale Bulletin* 49, no. 1 (1998): 149.

9. NIETZSCHE'S MUSICAL *ASKÊSIS*

1. *GS* 84; *KSA* 3:442.

2. Tracy B. Strong, "Nietzsche and the Song of the Self," *New Nietzsche Studies* 1 (1996): 1. Given the force of this claim, it is interesting that Strong's account of Nietzsche's *askêsis* has nothing to do with music. However, the goals of Nietzsche's *askêsis* upon which Strong focuses are ones that definitely typify the free spirit. I turn to Strong's account later in this chapter.

3. Valadier, "Dionysus versus the Crucified," 248.

4. Claudia Crawford, "Nietzsche's Dionysian Arts: Dance, Song, and Silence," in Kemal et al., *Nietzsche, Philosophy and the Arts*, 311.

5. *Phaedo* 60e–61b.

6. Lydia Goehr, *The Quest for Voice: On Music, Politics, and the Limits of Philosophy* (Berkeley: University of California Press, 1998), 1.

7. My account of the ancient Greek conception of *mousikê* is similar to that found in Babette E. Babich, "*Mousikê Technê*: The Philosophical Practice of Music in Plato, Nietzsche, and Heidegger, in *Between Philosophy and Poetry: Writing, Rhythm, History*, ed. Massimo Verdicchio and Robert Burch (New York: Continuum, 2002), 171–205.

8. "Our Western art presupposes the field of tension which is formed between the word and art, between language and music. The *musiké* of antiquity, however,

does not recognize this distinction." Thrasybulos Georgiades, *Music and Language: The Rise of Western Music as Exemplified in the Settings of the Mass,* trans. Marie Louise Göllner (Cambridge: Cambridge University Press, 1982), 134.

9. Simon Hornblower and Antony Spawforth, eds., *The Oxford Classical Dictionary,* 3rd ed. (Oxford: Oxford University Press, 1996), s.v. "music."

10. Ibid., s.v. "Muses"; Liddell and Scott, *Greek-English Lexicon,* s.v. "*mousikos.*" The broad scope of what counted as *mousikê* also explains why the word as used in the *Phaedo* can be rightly rendered in English as "the arts"—and that Socrates could think that philosophizing was what he was being called to do.

11. Goehr, *The Quest for Voice,* 18.

12. Of course, one might argue that, at the time of *The Birth of Tragedy* (1871–72), Nietzsche *did* hold that music provided a kind of "diversion," though of a very exquisite sort. Yet, even though that was likely Nietzsche's view at that time, he undoubtedly *also* thought that music communicates things that speech and writing cannot "capture." Such is not merely Nietzsche's view in his early writings (i.e., when influenced by Schopenhauer) but in his late writings as well. Thus, it is telling that in his own criticism of *The Birth of Tragedy* (from 1886) Nietzsche says that it "ought to have *sung*" (*BT* P 3; *KSA* 1:15).

13. Leiner, "To Overcome One's Self," 132. Although Leiner does not speak of a musical *askêsis* (nor speak of decadence as being "out of rhythm"), his claim that music is central to Nietzsche's self-transformation has important points of resonance with my argument here. In any case, I find Leiner's understanding of the role of music in Nietzsche to be particularly insightful.

14. Frederick R. Love, "Nietzsche, Music and Madness," *Music & Letters* 60 (1979): 196.

15. Wagner, *Richard Wagner's Prose Works,* vol. II, *Opera and Drama,* 209.

16. It almost seems as if Kathleen Marie Higgins misses the depth of what Nietzsche says here. For she claims that "music has the power to render life something other than a mistake, by virtue of the pleasure it offers." While music offers pleasure for Nietzsche, it offers so much more. Even "happiness" is already significantly more than mere pleasure. Of course, she later goes on to note that music for Nietzsche is transformative, in the sense that it has the "power to transform one's perspective" and that it has the "power to heal and stimulate personal growth." It is this transformative power, coupled with the ability to "say" that which cannot be "said" by speech and logic, that makes music so crucial to life. See Higgins's "Music or the Mistaken Life," *International Studies in Philosophy* 35 (2003): 118 and 123.

17. For more on the relation of joy and music, see Michel Haar, "The Joyous Struggle of the Sublime and the Musical Essence of Joy," *Research in Phenomenology* 25 (1995): 68–89. As Richard Schacht puts it: "Music can serve as a model for us in this fashion, for Nietzsche—as a token of a kind of reality to which we can aspire, embodying a kind of value that we can at least to some extent attain." See his "Nietzsche, Music, Truth, Value, and Life," *International Studies in Philosophy* 35 (2003): 143.

18. Writing to Hans von Bülow (October 29, 1872), he says of his improvising: "at times I sink into the perilous realm of the lunatic" (*KSB* 4:77).

19. Leiner, "To Overcome One's Self: Nietzsche, Bizet and Wagner," 133, 135.

20. My discussion of the soul as *oikos* is indebted to both Conway's *Nietzsche's Dangerous Game,* 28–30, and Parkes's *Composing the Soul,* 42–46.

21. Plato, *The Republic of Plato,* trans. Allan Bloom (New York: Basic, 1968), 443d.

22. For a rather different account of Nietzsche's *askêsis* from the one I provide here, see Jim Urpeth, "Nobel *Ascesis* between Nietzsche and Foucault," *New Nietzsche Studies* 2 (1998): 65–91.

23. Walter Lippman, *Musical Thought in Ancient Greece* (New York: Columbia University Press, 1964), 72.

24. Higgins argues that Nietzsche holds the view "that we can communicate at all only because ours is a world in which music is possible." On her read of Nietzsche, music is prior to spoken or written communication. While I find her argument convincing, my argument is somewhat different, viz., that, according to Nietzsche, thinking finds its truest form when it is musical in nature. See her "Nietzsche on Music," *Journal of the History of Ideas* 47 (1986): 663.

25. Babich, "*Mousikê Technê,*" 180.

26. Higgins, *Comic Relief,* 33.

27. Although I discuss a similar point at some length in chapter 10, here it should be mentioned that Zarathustra's "cure" is not soteriological in the sense of needing some sort of "salvation." Rather, Zarathustra's cure is to experience his life as *not needing a cure.* Zarathustra's teachings are precisely that one should be able to will the world *as it is/was.* Being "cured," then, is being able to accept life—just as it is—*with joy.*

28. Compare with *HH* II:165; *KSA* 2:620.

29. Among the first group might be Ludwig *van* Beethoven, whose grandfather was Belgian and came from Mechelen. Of the latter, such Germans are extinct in the sense that German composers of Nietzsche's time have succumbed to decadence.

30. Note that Nietzsche later adds: "When in *this* essay I declare war upon Wagner . . . the last thing I want to do is to start a celebration for any *other* musicians. *Other* musicians don't count compared to Wagner" (*CW* 2nd Postscript; *KSA* 6:46). So Nietzsche is not attempting to put a cult of Bizet in place of one of Wagner. Nietzsche further complicates his comments regarding Bizet when he writes to Carl Fuchs (December 27, 1888) and says: "What I say about Bizet, you should not take seriously; the way I am, Bizet does not matter to me. But as an ironic antithesis to Wagner, it has a strong effect" (*SL* 340; *KSB* 8:554). There are also some marginal notes made on a copy of *Carmen* that Nietzsche sent to Gast that suggest some condescension. See Friedrich Nietzsche, *Randglossen zu Bizets Carmen,* ed. Hugo Daffner (Regensburg: Gustav Bosse, 1912). Despite these complications, Nietzsche *does* draw an important contrast between the two: whereas Bizet "liberates the spirit" (*CW* 1; *KSA* 6:14), Nietzsche asks (rhetorically) "*Does Wagner liberate the spirit?*" (*CW* Postscript; *KSA* 6:42). The answer is clearly "no."

31. "Songs of Prince Free-as-a-Bird" is an appendix to *The Gay Science* that Nietzsche adds in 1887.

32. There is a further complication here. One *could* interpret Zarathustra's sudden affirmation of "eternity" as leaving "Life" (which is here and now) for "eternity" (which is to come). On such a read, Zarathustra has left the immanence of Life

for the transcendence of some otherworld or afterworld. But here I am following a relatively standard interpretation of this passage, in which life is equated with eternity. As Laurence Lampert puts it: "In marrying the woman Eternity, the only woman from whom he has ever desired children, Zarathustra does not marry some woman whom he meets for the first time at the end of his course. For, in marrying Eternity, he marries Life, but in the act of marrying bestows upon her a new name. 'Eternity' is the name that Zarathustra wills Life to take." See Laurence Lampert, *Nietzsche's Teaching: An Interpretation of* Thus Spoke Zarathustra (New Haven, Conn.: Yale University Press, 1986), 240.

33. David B. Allison, "Some Remarks on Nietzsche's Draft of 1871, 'On Music and Words,'" *New Nietzsche Studies* 1 (1996): 18.

34. Strong (in his article "Where Are We When We Are Beyond Good and Evil?" *Cardozo Law Review* 24 [2003]: 549) finds these characteristics in section 4 of the preface (1886) to *Human, All Too Human* (*KSA* 2:17–18). All quotations in the paragraphs that follow are from that section of the preface, except where noted. While these characteristics perfectly typify the free spirit (which means that this passage is useful in telling us *what Nietzsche hopes to accomplish*), the list reads more like a description of the *end product* rather than the *means* (i.e., the *askêsis*) to that end. In that sense this list is less about Nietzsche's *askêsis* (*pace* Strong) than about what that *askêsis* should accomplish.

35. Nietzsche likewise provides a kind of "negative" test as to whether one is a free spirit. As he puts it, "to test whether someone is one of us or not—I mean whether he is a free spirit or not—one should test his feelings toward Christianity. If he stands towards it in any way other than *critically* then we turn our back on him" (*HH* II:182; *KSA* 2:630).

36. Oddly, Hollingdale translates *Krankheit* as "wickedness," which is simply a mistranslation.

37. Elsewhere, Nietzsche writes "*From life's military school.*—What doesn't kill me makes me stronger" (*TI* I:8; *KSA* 6:60). But this passage in *Ecce Homo* significantly expands on that aphorism.

10. WE, TOO, ARE STILL PIOUS

1. *GS* 344; *KSA* 3:574–77.

2. Gianni Vattimo, *After Christianity*, trans. Luca D'Isanto (New York: Columbia University Press, 2002), 2.

3. Michel Haar, *Nietzsche and Metaphysics*, trans. Michael Gendre (Albany: State University of New York Press, 1996), 131.

4. Adrian del Caro, "Nietzschean Self-transformation and the Transformation of the Dionysian," in Kemal et al., *Nietzsche, Philosophy and the Arts*, 70.

5. See Parkes, *Composing the Soul*, 340.

6. *The Oxford Classical Dictionary*, s.v. "Dionysus."

7. Note that Nietzsche was not acquainted with Schopenhauer when he wrote "Dem unbekannten Gott."

8. In *The Birth of Tragedy* itself, there is already an *implicit* connection. But, in the "Attempt at a Self-criticism," Nietzsche writes: "Indeed the whole book

acknowledges only an artist's meaning (and hidden meaning) behind all that happens—a 'god,' if you will, but certainly only an utterly unscrupulous and amoral artist-god" (*BT* P 5; *KSA* 1:17).

9. Michael Allen Gillespie, *Nihilism before Nietzsche* (Chicago: University of Chicago Press, 1995), 221. I have found Gillespie's last chapter ("Dionysus and the Triumph of Nihilism") to be particularly helpful in understanding Nietzsche's shifting conception of the Dionysian.

10. Nietzsche makes a similar statement in *Ecce Homo,* speaking of *The Birth of Tragedy:* "The two decisive innovations of the book are, first, its understanding of the Dionysian phenomenon among the Greeks: for the first time, a psychological analysis of the phenomenon is offered" (the second of Nietzsche's innovations being that of recognizing Socratism) (*EH* "Books" BT 1; *KSA* 6:310). Of course, this claim regarding his appropriation of Dionysus is slightly different from the one quoted above, for here Nietzsche claims to have given the first "psychological analysis of the phenomenon." Such a move is more than simply one of discovering Dionysus.

11. Max L. Baeumer, "Nietzsche and the Tradition of the Dionysian," in O'Flaherty et al., eds., *Studies in Nietzsche and the Classical Tradition,* 2nd ed. (Chapel Hill: University of North Carolina Press, 1979), 166. Baeumer's article provides an excellent overview of the ways in which Dionysus has been appropriated.

12. Del Caro, "Nietzschean Self-transformation and the Transformation of the Dionysian," 75.

13. All of these letters are written on January 1, 3, or 4, 1888 (with one letter undated). An additional letter, to Cosima Wagner (addressed to "Princess Adriadne"), has the statement "I have also hung on the cross," though this letter is unsigned. Nietzsche's collapse occurred the morning of the 3rd. See *SL* 345–46; *KSB* 8:571–77. That Nietzsche also writes a letter to Jacob Burckhardt equating himself with God (though admitting he'd rather just be a Basel professor instead) on the 6th provides commentators with a further reason to dismiss these letters as the products of sheer madness.

14. In this respect, Jerry S. Clegg is perfectly correct when he writes: "Nietzsche never poses as anything other than a religious writer" and that "all his battles are theological ones." However, Clegg's reasoning for Nietzsche's religiosity is much more general than what I am presenting here. He claims: "[Nietzsche] was human, and human beings belong to the species of *homines religiosi*." I have no disagreement with Clegg's claim that, as human being, Nietzsche is inherently a religious being. However, my argument is much stronger, viz., that Nietzsche specifically sees himself as religious and as setting forth a faith. See Clegg's "Life in the Shadow of Christ: Nietzsche on *Pistis* versus *Gnosis*," in Santaniello, *Nietzsche and the Gods,* 161.

15. Del Caro, "Nietzschean Self-transformation and the Transformation of the Dionysian," 89.

16. So Pernet is correct when he writes: "In spite of the sustained attack on Christianity in [Nietzsche's] works, especially his later writings, he himself did not remain untouched by religious belief, especially when that belief took the form of a revivalist pietism." I would only change that last phrase to read "especially

when that belief took the form of a Dionysian pietism." See his "Nietzsche and Pietism," 486.

17. Here I have in mind the "doublet" of which Derrida speaks in Jacques Derrida, *The Gift of Death*, trans. David Wills (Chicago: University of Chicago Press, 1995), 49.

18. Jacques Derrida, *Circumfession*, in Bennington and Derrida, *Jacques Derrida*, 155 and 122.

19. We noted in chapter 8 that the distinction Nietzsche makes here is—at the very least—questionable. One can read the death of the Crucified as an affirmation, rather than a negation, of life.

20. Fraser, *Redeeming Nietzsche*, 74.

21. Ansell-Pearson, *An Introduction to Nietzsche as Political Thinker*, 102.

22. Salomé, *Nietzsche*, 88.

23. Conway, "Overcoming the *Übermensch*," 211–24.

24. One need only consider how poorly Nietzsche's works have sold at this point in his career to realize that he has been highly *ineffective* in influencing his contemporaries. Of course, Nietzsche could also be seen as decadent in that he is not able to will his lack of success (which would be necessary to "affirming all").

25. Such a move would be similar to the demise of the true world. Just as the sixth stage of the true world is one in which any traces of the idea of the true world have vanished, so Nietzsche's "redemption" would be reaching the place where the thought of redemption would simply never occur (see *TI* IV; *KSA* 6:80–81).

26. Fraser, *Redeeming Nietzsche*, 61.

27. Grundlehner, *The Poetry of Friedrich Nietzsche*, 26.

28. Martin Heidegger, "The Self-assertion of the German University" (trans. Karsten Harries), *Review of Metaphysics* 38 (1985): 474.

29. Haar, *Nietzsche and Metaphysics*, 149. Although I am citing Haar's own quotation, that quotation comes from Husserl, *Ideas Pertaining to a Pure Phenomenology and a Phenomenological Philosophy. First Book*, §51.

30. See Gregory of Nyssa, "An Address on Religious Instruction," trans. C. Richardson, in *Christology of the Later Fathers*, ed. Edward Hardy (Philadelphia: Westminster, 1954), 268–325.

31. The section is titled "For the New Year" and was written in late 1881 or early 1882.

32. Luce Irigaray, *Marine Lover of Friedrich Nietzsche*, trans. Gillian C. Gill (New York: Columbia University Press, 1991), 34.

33. In the introduction to his translation of *Thus Spoke Zarathustra*, Hollingdale notes that Nietzsche is strongly influenced by Lutheran Pietism. On that point, I concur. However, I strongly disagree with his assertion that in Nietzsche these doctrines are "transformed and distorted almost beyond recognition." In contrast, I have attempted to show here that the similarities are often uncanny. Hollingdale probably reads Nietzsche's doctrines as "distorted" versions of German Pietistic doctrines largely because he fails to understand German Pietism. For instance, Hollingdale almost gets it right when he associates *amor fati* with the "Lutheran acceptance of the events of life as divinely willed." However, I say "almost" because *amor fati* only has to do with *acceptance* of life's events, not

with the idea of their being *divinely willed*. But, when Hollingdale goes on to connect eternal recurrence with the Christian conception of eternal life, the will to power with "divine grace," the idea of living dangerously with taking up one's cross, and the overman as connected to God and Jesus Christ, he simply misunderstands Christian Pietism. See Friedrich Nietzsche, *Thus Spoke Zarathustra: A Book for Everyone and No One,* trans. R. J. Hollingdale (London: Penguin, 1969), 28–29.

34. One could cite Nietzsche's analyses in *BGE* 19; *KSA* 5:32–34 or *TI* VI; *KSA* 6:88–97, for example.

35. Thus, I think Mathias Risse is completely right when he claims that "the man of guilt and *ressentiment*" is to be replaced by a "joyous and trusting fatalism." See his "Nietzsche's 'Joyous and Trusting Fatalism,'" *International Studies in Philosophy* 35 (2003): 147.

36. Michael Tanner, *Nietzsche* (Oxford: Oxford University Press, 1994), 46.

37. After completing *Twilight of the Idols,* Nietzsche decided to scrap plans for writing a text called *The Will to Power* and instead began work on *Revaluation of All Values* (of which The *Anti-Christ(ian)* was to be the first of four essays). For the preface to *Revaluation of All Values,* see *The Portable Nietzsche,* 568–69.

38. Daniel W. Conway, "Nietzsche's Swan Song: *Eine Kleine Nichtmusik,*" *International Studies in Philosophy* 33 (2001): 65–85.

39. Young, *Nietzsche's Philosophy of Art,* 151.

40. Causality of the will is labeled by Nietzsche as one of "the four great errors" (*TI* VI:3; *KSA* 6:92). Elsewhere, he says: "'the doer' is simply fabricated into the doing" (*GM* I:13; *KSA* 5:279).

41. *Z* IV "Magician" 1; *KSA* 4:316–17.

42. I quote here from Nietzsche's revised version of the poem that appears in *DD* 59–65 (*KSA* 6:398–401).

43. There is, of course, a further complication. Nietzsche envisions Cosima Wagner as Ariadne and *himself* as Dionysus. For instance, he writes a brief sketch for a drama in which he, Cosima, and Richard are the characters. See *DD* 92. Also, on the day of his collapse he addresses what are in effect a series of love letters to Cosima.

44. Claudia Crawford, *To Nietzsche: Dionysus, I Love You! Ariadne* (Albany: State University of New York Press, 1995), 1.

45. Geneviève Bianquis, ed., *Nietzsche devant ses contemporains* (Monaco: Editions du Rocher, 1959), 158. Quoted in Liébert, *Nietzsche and Music,* 204.

46. Pierre Klossowski, *Nietzsche and the Vicious Circle,* trans. Daniel W. Smith (Chicago: University of Chicago Press, 1977), 220.

47. Crawford, *To Nietzsche: Dionysus, I Love You! Ariadne,* 46.

WORKS CITED

Ahern, Daniel R. *Nietzsche as Cultural Physician*. University Park: Pennsylvania State University Press, 1995.

Allison, David B., ed. *The New Nietzsche: Contemporary Styles of Interpretation*. Cambridge, Mass.: MIT Press, 1985.

———. "Some Remarks on Nietzsche's Draft of 1871, 'On Music and Words.'" *New Nietzsche Studies* 1 (1996): 17–41.

Ansell-Pearson, Keith. *An Introduction to Nietzsche as Political Thinker: The Perfect Nihilist*. Cambridge: Cambridge University Press, 1994.

———. "Toward the *Übermensch*: Reflections on the Year of Nietzsche's Daybreak." *Nietzsche-Studien* 23 (1994): 124–45.

Aristotle. *The Complete Works of Aristotle*. Edited by Jonathan Barnes. Princeton, N.J.: Princeton University Press, 1984.

Aschheim, Steven C. *The Nietzsche Legacy in Germany: 1890–1990*. Berkeley: University of California Press, 1992.

Augustine. *Confessions*. Translated by Henry Chadwick. New York: Oxford University Press, 1991.

Babich, Babette E. "*Mousikê Technê:* The Philosophical Practice of Music in Plato, Nietzsche, and Heidegger." In Massimo Verdicchio and Robert Burch, eds., *Between Philosophy and Poetry: Writing, Rhythm, History,* 171–205. New York: Continuum, 2002.

———. "A Musical Retrieve of Heidegger, Nietzsche, and Technology: Cadence, Concinnity, and Playing Brass." *Man and World* 26 (1993): 239–60.

———. "Nietzsche and Music: A Selective Bibliography." *New Nietzsche Studies* 1 (1996): 64–78.

Badiou, Alain. *Saint Paul: The Foundation of Universalism*. Translated by Ray Brassier. Stanford, Calif.: Stanford University Press, 2003.

Baeumer, Max L. "Nietzsche and the Tradition of the Dionysian." In James C. O'Flaherty, Timothy F. Sellner, and Robert M. Helm, eds., *Studies in Nietzsche and the Classical Tradition,* 2nd ed. (Chapel Hill: University of North Carolina Press, 1979), 165–89.

Banham, Gary. "Jews, Judaism and the 'Free Spirit.'" In Lippitt and Urpeth, *Nietzsche and the Divine,* 57–76.

Barth, Karl. *Church Dogmatics*. Vol. III/2, *The Doctrine of Creation*. Edited by G. W. Bromiley and T. F. Torrance. Translated by Harold Knight, G. W. Bromiley, J. K. S. Reid, and R. H. Fuller. Edinburgh: T&T Clark, 1960.

Beckett, Lucy. *Parsifal*. Cambridge: Cambridge University Press, 1981.

Bennington, Geoffrey. *Derridabase*. In Geoffrey Bennington and Jacques Derrida, *Jacques Derrida*. Chicago: University of Chicago Press, 1993.

Benson, Bruce Ellis. *The Improvisation of Musical Dialogue: A Phenomenology of Music*. Cambridge: Cambridge University Press, 2003.

Bermúdez, José Luis. "The Concept of Decadence." In José Luis Bermúdez and Sebastian Gardner, eds., *Art and Morality*, 111–30. London: Routledge, 2003.

Bernheimer, Charles. *Decadent Subject: The Idea of Decadence in Art, Literature, Philosophy and Culture of the Fin de Siècle in Europe*. Edited by T. Jefferson Kline and Noami Schor. Baltimore: Johns Hopkins University Press, 2002.

Bernoulli, Carl Albrecht. *Franz Overbeck und Friedrich Nietzsche: Eine Freundshaft*. Jena: Eugen Diederichs, 1908.

Bernstein, John Andrew. *Nietzsche's Moral Philosophy*. Rutherford, N.J.: Fairleigh Dickinson University Press, 1987.

Bertram, Ernst. *Nietzsche: Versuch einer Mythologie*. 7th ed. Berlin: Bondi, 1929.

Bianquis, Geneviève, ed. *Nietzsche devant ses contemporains*. Monaco: Editions du Rocher, 1959.

Biser, Eugen. "Nietzsche's Relation to Jesus: A Literary and Psychological Comparison." In Claude Geffré and Jean-Pierre Jossua, eds., *Nietzsche and Christianity* [a special edition of *Concilium* 145 (1981)], 58–64. New York: Seabury, 1981.

Bluhm, Heinz. "Nietzsche's Final View of Luther and the Reformation." *PMLA* 71 (1956): 75–83.

———. "Nietzsche's View of Luther and the Reformation in *Morgenröthe* and *Die fröhliche Wissenschaft*." *PMLA* 68 (1953): 111–127.

Bohley, Reiner. "Nietzsches christliche Erziehung." *Nietzsche-Studien* 16 (1987): 164–96.

———. "Nietzsches Taufe: 'Was, mienest du, will aus diesem Kindlein werden?'" *Nietzsche-Studien* 9 (1980): 383–405.

Bonhoeffer, Dietrich. *No Rusty Swords: Letters, Lectures and Notes from 1928–1936*. Translated by Edwin H. Robertson and John Bowden. New York: Harper & Row, 1965.

Borchmeyer, Dieter. *Richard Wagner: Theory and Theatre*. Translated by Stewart Spencer. Oxford: Clarendon, 1991.

Bourget, Paul. *Essais de psychologie contemporaine*. Vol. 1. Paris: Plon, 1926.

Breton, Stanislas. *The Word and the Cross*. Translated by Jacquelyn Porter. New York: Fordham University Press, 2002.

Brobjer, Thomas. "Nietzsche's Atheism." In Lippitt and Urpeth, *Nietzsche and the Divine*, 1–13.

———. "Nietzsche's Changing Relation with Christianity." In Santaniello, *Nietzsche and the Gods*, 137–57.

———. "A Possible Solution to the Stirner-Nietzsche Question." *Journal of Nietzsche Studies* 25 (2003): 109–14.

Burckhardt, Jacob. *The Greeks and Greek Civilization*. Edited by Oswyn Murray. Translated by Sheila Stern. New York: St. Martin's Press, 1998.

Caputo, John D. *The Prayers and Tears of Jacques Derrida*. Bloomington: Indiana University Press, 1997.

Clark, Maudemarie. *Nietzsche on Truth and Philosophy.* Cambridge: Cambridge University Press, 1990.

Clegg, Jerry S. "Life in the Shadow of Christ: Nietzsche on *Pistis* versus *Gnosis*." In Santaniello, *Nietzsche and the Gods,* 159–71.

Conway, Daniel W. "The Genius as Squanderer: Some Remarks on the *Übermensch* and Higher Humanity." *International Studies in Philosophy* 30 (1998): 81–95.

———. "Nietzsche's Art of This-Worldly Comfort: Self-reference and Strategic Self-parody." *History of Philosophy Quarterly* 9 (1992): 343–57.

———. *Nietzsche's Dangerous Game: Philosophy in the Twilight of the Idols.* Cambridge: Cambridge University Press, 1997, 23.

———. "Nietzsche's Swan Song: Eine kleine Nichtmusik." *International Studies in Philosophy* 33 (2001): 65–85.

———. "Overcoming the *Übermensch:* Nietzsche's Revaluation of Values." *Journal of the British Society for Phenomenology* 20 (1989): 211–24.

———. "The Politics of Decadence." *Southern Journal of Philosophy* 38 (1999): 19–33.

Crawford, Claudia. "Nietzsche's Dionysian Arts: Dance, Song, and Silence." In Kemal et al., *Nietzsche, Philosophy and the Arts,* 310–41.

———. *To Nietzsche: Dionysus, I Love You! Ariadne.* Albany: State University of New York Press, 1995.

Dahlhaus, Carl. *Richard Wagner's Music Dramas.* Translated by Mary Whittall. Cambridge: Cambridge University Press, 1979.

Dannhauser, Werner. *Nietzsche's View of Socrates.* Ithaca, N.Y.: Cornell University Press, 1974.

Del Caro, Adrian. "Nietzschean Self-transformation and the Transformation of the Dionysian." In Kemal et al., *Nietzsche, Philosophy and the Arts,* 70–91.

Deleuze, Gilles. *Nietzsche and Philosophy.* Translated by Hugh Tomlinson. New York: Columbia University Press, 1983.

Derrida, Jacques. *Circumfession.* In Geoffrey Bennington and Jacques Derrida, *Jacques Derrida.* Chicago: University of Chicago Press, 1993.

———. *The Gift of Death.* Translated by David Wills. Chicago: University of Chicago Press, 1995.

———. "*Honoris Causa:* 'This is *also* extremely funny.'" In Jacques Derrida, *Points: Interviews, 1974–1994,* ed. Elisabeth Weber, 399–421. Stanford, Calif.: Stanford University Press, 1995.

———. *Memoirs of the Blind: The Self-portrait and Other Ruins.* Translated by Pascale-Anne Brault and Michael Naas. Chicago: University of Chicago Press, 1993.

———. *Of Grammatology,* corrected ed. Translated by Gayatri Chakravorty Spivak. Baltimore: Johns Hopkins University Press, 1997.

———. "Plato's Pharmacy." In *Dissemination.* Translated by Barbara Johnson. Chicago: University of Chicago Press, 1981.

———. "Violence and Metaphysics: An Essay on the Thought of Emmanuel Levinas." In *Writing and Difference*, 79–153. Translated by Alan Bass. Chicago: University of Chicago Press, 1978.

Deussen, Paul. *Erinnerungen an Friedrich Nietzsche.* Leipzig: F. A. Brockhaus, 1901.

Domino, Brian G. "Vincenzo's Portrayal of Nietzsche's Socrates." *Philosophy and Rhetoric* 26 (1993): 39–47.

Dostoevsky, Fyodor. *The Idiot.* Translated by Richard Pevear and Larissa Volokhonsky. New York: Alfred A. Knopf, 2001.

———. *The Notebooks for* The Idiot. Edited by Edward Wasiolek. Translated by Katharine Strelsky. Chicago: University of Chicago Press, 1967.

———. *A Raw Youth.* Translated by Constance Garnett. London: W. Heinemann, 1956.

———. *Selected Letters of Fyodor Dostoyevsky.* Edited by Joseph Frank and David I. Goldstein. Translated by Andrew R. MacAndrew. New Brunswick, N.J.: Rutgers University Press, 1987.

Eldad, Israel. "Nietzsche and the Old Testament." In O'Flaherty et al., *Studies in Nietzsche and the Judaeo-Christian Tradition,* 47–68.

Eliot, T. S. "The Hollow Men." In T. S. Eliot, *The Complete Poems and Plays, 1909–1950,* 56–59. New York: Harcourt, Brace, & World, 1971.

Erikson, Erik H. *Young Man Luther: A Study in Psychoanalysis and History.* New York: W. W. Norton, 1958.

Feuerbach, Ludwig von. *The Essence of Christianity.* Translated by George Eliot. New York: Harper & Row, 1957.

Förster-Nietzsche, Elisabeth, ed. *The Nietzsche-Wagner Correspondence.* Translated by Caroline V. Kerr. New York: Boni and Liveright, 1921.

Foucault, Michel. *The Archaeology of Knowledge.* Translated by A. M. Sheridan Smith. New York: Pantheon, 1972.

———. "Friendship as a Way of Life." In *Foucault Live: Collected Interviews, 1961–1984,* 308–12. Edited by Sylvère Lotringer. Translated by Lysa Hochroth and John Johnston. New York: Semiotext[e], 1989.

———. *The History of* Sexuality. Vol. I, *The Use of Pleasure.* Translated by Robert Hurley. New York: Pantheon, 1985.

———. "Nietzsche, Genealogy, History." In Michel Foucault, *Essential Works of Foucault 1954–1984.* Edited by Paul Rabinow. Vol. II, *Aesthetics, Method, and Epistemology,* 369–91. Edited by James D. Faubion. New York: New Press, 1998.

Fraser, Giles. *Redeeming Nietzsche: On the Piety of Unbelief.* London: Routledge, 2002.

Gadamer, Hans-Georg. "Reflections on My Philosophical Journey." In *The Philosophy of Hans-Georg Gadamer,* ed. Lewis Edwin Hahn, 1–63. Chicago: Open Court, 1997.

———. "Text and Interpretation." In *Dialogue and Deconstruction: The Gadamer-Derrida Encounter,* ed. Diane P. Michelfelder and Richard E. Palmer, 21–51. Albany: State University of New York Press, 1989.

Georgiades, Thrasybulos. *Music and Language: The Rise of Western Music as Exemplified in the Settings of the Mass.* Translated by Marie Louise Göllner. Cambridge: Cambridge University Press, 1982.

Gillespie, Michael Allen. *Nihilism before Nietzsche.* Chicago: University of Chicago Press, 1995.

Glassford, John. "Did Friedrich Nietzsche (1844–1900) Plagiarise from Max Stirner (1806–56)?" *Journal of Nietzsche Studies* 18 (1999): 73–79.

Goehr, Lydia. *The Quest for Voice: On Music, Politics, and the Limits of Philosophy.* Berkeley: University of California Press, 1998.

Golomb, Jacob. "Nietzsche's Positive Religion and the Old Testament." In Lippitt and Urpeth, *Nietzsche and the Divine,* 30–56.

Gooding-Williams, Robert. *Zarathustra's Dionysian Modernism.* Stanford, Calif.: Stanford University Press, 2001.

Gregory of Nyssa. "An Address on Religious Instruction." Translated by Cyril C. Richardson. In Edward Hardy, ed., *Christology of the Later Fathers,* 268–325. Philadelphia: Westminster, 1954.

Grundlehner, Philip. *The Poetry of Friedrich Nietzsche.* Oxford: Oxford University Press, 1986.

Haar, Michel. "The Joyous Struggle of the Sublime and the Musical Essence of Joy." *Research in Phenomenology* 25 (1995): 68–89.

———. "Nietzsche and Metaphysical Language." In Allison, *The New Nietzsche,* 5–36.

———. *Nietzsche and Metaphysics.* Translated by Michael Gendre. Albany: State University of New York Press, 1996.

Hadot, Pierre. *Philosophy as a Way of Life: Spiritual Exercises from Socrates to Foucault.* Edited by Arnold I. Davidson. Translated by Michael Chase. Oxford: Blackwell, 1995.

———. *What Is Ancient Philosophy?* Translated by Michael Chase. Cambridge, Mass.: Harvard University Press, 2002.

Hamilton, William. *A Quest for the Post-Historical Jesus.* New York: Continuum, 1994.

Hatab, Lawrence J. "Time-Sharing in the Bestiary: On Daniel W. Conway's 'The Politics of Decadence.'" *Southern Journal of Philosophy* (1999): 35–41.

Havas, Randall. *Nietzsche's Genealogy: Nihilism and the Will to Knowledge.* Ithaca, N.Y.: Cornell University Press, 1995.

Heidegger, Martin. *An Introduction to Metaphysics.* Translated by Gregory Fried and Richard Polt. New Haven, Conn.: Yale University Press, 2000.

———. "The Self-assertion of the German University." Translated by Karsten Harries. *Review of Metaphysics* 38 (1985): 470–80.

———. "The Word of Nietzsche: 'God Is Dead.'" In *The Question Concerning Technology and Other Essays,* 53–112. Translated by William Lovitt. New York: Harper & Row, 1977.

Heller, Agnes. *An Ethics of Personality.* Oxford: Blackwell, 1996.

Heussi, Karl. *Der Ursprung des Mönchtums*. Tübingen: J. C. B. Mohr, 1936.

Higgins, Kathleen Marie. *Comic Relief: Nietzsche's* Gay Science. Oxford: Oxford University Press, 2000.

———. "Music or the Mistaken Life." *International Studies in Philosophy* 35 (2003): 117–30.

———. "Nietzsche on Music." *Journal of the History of Ideas* 47 (1986): 663–72.

Hobbes, Thomas. *Leviathan, Or the Matter, Form and Power of a Commonwealth, Ecclesiastical and Civil*. London: George Routledge and Sons, 1894.

Hollingdale, R. J. Introduction. In Friedrich Nietzsche, *Thus Spoke Zarathustra: A Book for Everyone and No One*. London: Penguin, 1961.

———. *Nietzsche: The Man and His Philosophy*. Rev. ed. Cambridge: Cambridge University Press, 1999.

Hulin, Michel. "Nietzsche and the Suffering of the Indian Ascetic." In Graham Parkes, ed., *Nietzsche and Asian Thought*, 64–75. Chicago: University of Chicago Press, 1991.

Husserl, Edmund. *Ideas Pertaining to a Pure Phenomenology and a Phenomenological Philosophy. First Book: General Introduction to a Pure Phenomenology*. Translated by Fred Kersten. The Hague: Martinus Nijhoff, 1982.

———. *Logical Investigations*. Translated by J. N. Findlay. London: Routledge & Kegan Paul, 1970.

Irigaray, Luce. *Marine Lover of Friedrich Nietzsche*. Translated by Gillian C. Gill. New York: Columbia University Press, 1991.

Janz, Curt Paul. *Die Briefe Friedrich Nietzsches*. Zurich: Editio Academica, 1972.

Jaspers, Karl. *Nietzsche and Christianity*. Chicago: Henry Regnery, 1961.

Kant, Immanuel. *Critique of Pure Reason*. Translated by Paul Guyer and Allen Wood. Cambridge: Cambridge University Press, 1998.

———. *Religion within the Boundaries of Mere Reason*. Translated by Allen Wood. In *Religion and Rational Theology,* trans. and ed. Allen W. Wood and George di Giovanni, 57–215. Cambridge: Cambridge University Press, 1998.

Kaufmann, Walter. *Nietzsche: Philosophy, Psychologist, Antichrist*. Princeton, N.J.: Princeton University Press, 1950. 4th ed., 1974.

Kee, Alistair. *Nietzsche against the Crucified*. London: SCM, 1999.

Kemal, Salim, Ivan Gaskell, and Daniel W. Conway, eds. *Nietzsche, Philosophy and the Arts*. Cambridge: Cambridge University Press, 1998.

Klossowski, Pierre. *Nietzsche and the Vicious Circle*. Translated by Daniel W. Smith. Chicago: University of Chicago Press, 1977.

Kroeker, P. Travis, and Bruce K. Ward. *Remembering the End: Dostoevsky as Prophet to Modernity*. Boulder, Colo.: Westview, 2001.

Kufferath, Maurice. *The Parsifal of Richard Wagner*. New York: Tait, Sons & Co., 1892.

Lampert, Laurence. *Nietzsche's Teaching: An Interpretation of* Thus Spoke Zarathustra. New Haven, Conn.: Yale University Press, 1986.

Leiner, George H. "To Overcome One's Self: Nietzsche, Bizet and Wagner." *Journal of Nietzsche Studies* 9/10 (1995): 132–47.

Lemco, Gary. "Nietzsche and Schumann." *New Nietzsche Studies* 1 (1996): 42–56.

Levinas, Emmanuel. "God and Philosophy." In Adriaan T. Peperzak, Simon Critchley, and Robert Bernasconi, eds., *Basic Philosophical Writings,* 129–48. Bloomington: Indiana University Press, 1996.

———. "Transcendence and Height." In *Basic Philosophical Writings,* 11–31.

Liébert, Georges. *Nietzsche and Music.* Translated by David Pellauer and Graham Parkes. Chicago: University of Chicago Press, 2004.

Lippitt, John, and Jim Urpeth, eds. *Nietzsche and the Divine.* Manchester: Clinamen, 2000.

Lippman, Walter. *Musical Thought in Ancient Greece.* New York: Columbia University Press, 1964.

Love, Frederick R. "Nietzsche, Music and Madness." *Music & Letters* 60 (1979): 186–203.

———. *Young Nietzsche and the Wagnerian Experience.* Chapel Hill: University of North Carolina Press, 1963.

MacIntyre, Alasdair. *After Virtue.* 2nd ed. Notre Dame, Ind.: University of Notre Dame Press, 1981.

Magnus, Bernd. "Nietzsche's Philosophy in 1888: *The Will to Power* and the *Übermensch*." *Journal of the History of Philosophy* 29 (1986): 79–98.

Magnus, Bernd, and Kathleen M. Higgins, eds. *The Cambridge Companion to Nietzsche.* Cambridge: Cambridge University Press, 1996.

———. "Introduction to the Cambridge Companion to Nietzsche." In Magnus and Higgins, *The Cambridge Companion to Nietzsche,* 1–17.

Marion, Jean-Luc. *The Idol and Distance: Five Studies.* Translated by Thomas A. Carlson. New York: Fordham University Press, 2001.

Miller, C. A. "Nietzsche's 'Discovery' of Dostoevsky." *Nietzsche-Studien* 2 (1973): 202–57.

Morgan, George Allen. *What Nietzsche Means.* Cambridge, Mass.: Harvard University Press, 1941.

Morrison, Robert G. *Nietzsche and Buddhism: A Study in Nihilism and Ironic Affinities.* Oxford: Oxford University Press, 1997.

Murphy, Tim. *Nietzsche, Metaphor, Religion.* Albany: State University of New York Press, 2001.

———. "Nietzsche's Jesus." *Epochê* 20 (1995–96): 32–48.

———. "Nietzsche's Narrative of the 'Retroactive Confiscations' of Judaism." In Santaniello, *Nietzsche and the Gods,* 3–20.

Nehemas, Alexander. *The Art of Living: Socratic Reflections from Plato to Foucault.* Berkeley: University of California Press, 1998.

———. *Nietzsche: Life as Literature.* Cambridge, Mass.: Harvard University Press, 1985.

Nietzsche, Friedrich. *The Anti-Christ(ian)*. In *The Portable Nietzsche*, 568–656.

———. *Basic Writings of Nietzsche*. Edited and translated by Walter Kaufmann. New York: Random House, 1968.

———. *Beyond Good and Evil: Prelude to a Philosophy of the Future*. Edited by Rolf-Peter Horstmann and Judith Norman. Translated by Judith Norman. Cambridge: Cambridge University Press, 2002.

———. *The Birth of Tragedy and Other Writings*. Edited by Raymond Geuss and Ronald Speirs. Translated by Ronald Speirs. Cambridge: Cambridge University Press, 1999.

———. *The Case of Wagner*. In *Basic Writings of Nietzsche*, 611–48.

———. *Daybreak: Thoughts on the Prejudices of Morality*. Translated by R. J. Hollingdale. Cambridge: Cambridge University Press, 1982.

———. *Dithyrambs of Dionysus*. Translated by R. J. Hollingdale. London: Avil, 1984.

———. *Ecce Auctor: Die Vorreden von 1886*. Edited and introduced by Claus-Artur Scheier. Hamburg: Felix Meiner, 1990.

———. *Ecce Homo*. In *Basic Writings of Nietzsche*, 673–791.

———. *The Gay Science*. Edited by Bernard Williams. Translated by Josefine Nauckhoff. Poems translated by Adrian Del Caro. Cambridge: Cambridge University Press, 2001.

———. *Homer's Contest*. In *Prefaces to Unwritten Works*, 81–92. Translated by Michael W. Grenke. South Bend, Ind.: St. Augustine's Press, 2005.

———. *Human, All Too Human: A Book for Free Spirits*. Translated by R. J. Hollingdale. Cambridge: Cambridge University Press, 1986.

———. *Nietzsche contra Wagner*. In *The Portable Nietzsche*, 662–83.

———. *On the Genealogy of Morality*. Translated by Maudemarie Clark and Alan J. Swensen. Indianapolis: Hackett, 1998.

———. "On Moods." Translated by Graham Parkes. *Journal of Nietzsche Studies* 2 (1991): 5–11.

———. "On Music and Words." In Carl Dahlhaus, *Between Romanticism and Modernism: Four Studies in the Music of the Later Nineteenth Century*, 106–19. Translated by Mary Whittall (translation of "On Music and Words" by Walter Kaufmann). Berkeley: University of California Press, 1980.

———. *Philosophy and Truth: Selections from Nietzsche's Notebooks of the Early 1870's*. Edited and translated by Daniel Breazeale. Atlantic Highlands, N.J.: Humanities Press, 1979.

———. *The Portable Nietzsche*. Edited and translated by Walter Kaufmann. New York: Viking, 1954.

———. *The Pre-Platonic Philosophers*. Translated by Greg Whitlock. Urbana: University of Illinois Press, 2001.

———. *Randglossen zu Bizets Carmen*. Edited by Hugo Daffner. Regensburg: Gustav Bosse, 1912.

―――. *Sämtliche Briefe, Kritische Studienausgabe in 8 Bänden*. Edited by Giorgio Colli and Mazzino Montinari. Berlin: de Gruyter/Deutscher Taschenbuch Verlag, 1986.

―――. *Sämtliche Werke, Kritische Studienausgabe in 15 Bänden*. Edited by Giorgio Colli and Mazzino Montinari. Berlin: de Gruyter/Deutscher Taschenbuch Verlag, 1980.

―――. *Selected Letters of Friedrich Nietzsche*. Edited and translated by Christopher Middleton. Chicago: University of Chicago Press, 1969.

―――. *Thus Spoke Zarathustra: A Book for Everyone and No One*. Translated by R. J. Hollingdale. London: Penguin, 1969.

―――. *Twilight of the Idols*. Translated by Richard Polt. Indianapolis: Hackett, 1997.

―――. *Unfashionable Observations*. Translated by Richard T. Gray. Stanford, Calif.: Stanford University Press, 1995.

―――. *Untimely Meditations*. Translated by R. J. Hollingdale. Cambridge: Cambridge University Press, 1983.

―――. *Werke. Kritische Gesamtausgabe*. Edited by Giorgio Colli and Mazzino Montinari. Berlin: de Gruyter, 1967–.

―――. *The Will to Power*. Translated by Walter Kaufmann and R. J. Hollingdale. New York: Random House, 1967.

Nussbaum, Martha. "The Transfigurations of Intoxication: Nietzsche, Schopenhauer, and Dionysus." In Kemal, *Nietzsche, Philosophy and the Arts*, 36–69.

―――. *The Therapy of Desire: Theory and Practice in Hellenistic Ethics*. Princeton, N.J.: Princeton University Press, 1994.

Oehler, Richard. *Friedrich Nietzsche und die Vorsokratiker*. Leipzig: Dürr, 1904.

O'Flaherty, James C., Timothy F. Sellner, and Robert M. Helm, eds. *Studies in Nietzsche and the Judaeo-Christian Tradition*. 2nd ed. Chapel Hill: University of North Carolina Press, 1985.

Parkes, Graham. *Composing the Soul: Reaches of Nietzsche's Psychology*. Chicago: University of Chicago Press, 1994.

Pernet, Martin. "Friedrich Nietzsche and Pietism." *German Life and Letters* 48 (1995): 474–86.

Pick, Daniel. *Faces of Degeneration: A European Disorder, c. 1848–c. 1918*. Cambridge: Cambridge University Press, 1989.

Plato. *The Collected Dialogues of Plato*. Edited by Edith Hamilton and Huntington Cairns. Princeton, N.J.: Princeton University Press, 1961.

―――. *The Republic of Plato*. Translated by Allan Bloom. New York: Basic, 1968.

Pletsch, Carl. *Young Nietzsche: Becoming a Genius*. New York: Free Press, 1991.

Pothen, Philip. *Nietzsche and the Fate of Art*. Aldershot: Ashgate, 2002.

Rée, Paul. *The Origin of Moral Sensations*. In Paul Rée, *Basic Writings*, 81–167. Translated by Robin Small. Urbana: University of Illinois Press, 2003.

Renan, Ernest. *The Life of Jesus.* Translated by Charles Edwin Wilbour. New York: Carleton, 1864.

Ridley, Aaron. *Nietzsche's Conscience: Six Character Studies from the "Genealogy."* Ithaca, N.Y.: Cornell University Press, 1998.

Risse, Mathias. "Nietzsche's 'Joyous and Trusting Fatalism.'" *International Studies in Philosophy* 35, no. 3 (2003): 147–62.

Roberts, Tyler T. *Contesting Spirit: Nietzsche, Affirmation, Religion.* Princeton, N.J.: Princeton University Press, 1998.

Robinson, T. M. *Plato's Psychology.* 2nd ed. Toronto: University of Toronto Press, 1995.

Rorty, Richard. *Philosophy and Social Hope.* New York: Penguin, 1999.

Roth, Robin A. "Verily, Nietzsche's Judgment of Jesus." *Philosophy Today* 34 (1990): 364–76.

Safranski, Rüdiger. *Nietzsche: A Philosophical Biography.* Translated by Shelley Frisch. New York: W. W. Norton, 2002.

Salaquarda, Jörg. "Dionysus versus the Crucified One: Nietzsche's Understanding of the Apostle Paul." In O'Flaherty et al., *Studies in Nietzsche and the Judaeo-Christian Tradition,* 100–129.

———. "Nietzsche and the Judeo-Christian Tradition." In Magnus and Higgins, *The Cambridge Companion to Nietzsche,* 90–118.

Salomé, Lou. *Nietzsche.* Translated by Siegfried Mandel. Urbana: University of Illinois Press, 2001.

Santaniello, Weaver, ed. *Nietzsche and the Gods.* Albany: State University of New York Press, 2001.

———. *Nietzsche, God, and the Jews: His Critique of Judeo-Christianity in Relation to the Nazi Myth.* Albany: State University of New York, 1994.

———. "Socrates as the Ugliest Murderer of God." In Santaniello, *Nietzsche and the Gods,* 73–83.

Schacht, Richard. "Nietzsche, Music, Truth, Value, and Life." *International Studies in Philosophy* 35, no. 3 (2003): 131–46.

Scheler, Max. *Ressentiment.* Edited by Lewis A. Coser. Translated by William W. Holdheim. New York: Schocken, 1961.

Schlecta, Karl, and Herbert W. Reichert, eds. *The International Nietzsche Bibliography.* Chapel Hill: University of North Carolina Press, 1968.

Schmidt, Hermann Josef. *Nietzsche und Sokrates: Philosophische Untersuchungen zu Nietzsches Sokratesbild.* Meisenheim am Glan: Anton Hain, 1969.

Schopenhauer, Arthur. *The World as Will and Representation.* Translated by E. F. J. Payne. New York: Dover, 1958.

Schweitzer, Albert. *The Quest of the Historical Jesus.* Edited by John Bowden. Translated by W. Montgomery, J. R. Coates, Susan Cupitt, and John Bowden. Minneapolis: Fortress, 2001.

Scott, Jacqueline. "Nietzsche and Decadence: The Revaluation of Morality." *Continental Philosophy Review* 31 (1998): 59–78.

Shapiro, Gary. "Nietzsche contra Renan." *History and Theory* 21 (1982): 193–222.

———. *Nietzschean Narratives.* Bloomington: Indiana University Press, 1989.

Silk, Michael. "Nietzsche, Decadence, and the Greeks." *New Literary History* 35 (2005): 587–606.

Smith, Houston Chamberlain. "Notes sur *Parsifal.*" *Revue wagnérienne* 2 (1887–88): 220–26.

Solomon, Robert. "Nietzsche *ad hominem:* Perspectivism, Personality and *Ressentiment* Revisited." In Magnus and Higgins, *The Cambridge Companion to Nietzsche,* 180–222.

Solomon, Robert, and Kathleen M. Higgins. *What Nietzsche Really Said.* New York: Schocken, 2000.

Spener, Philip Jacob. *Pia Desideria.* Translated by Theodore G. Tappert. Philadelphia: Fortress, 1964.

Stambaugh, Joan. *The Other Nietzsche.* Albany: State University Press of New York, 1994.

Stirner, Max. *The Ego and His Own.* Edited by David Leopold. Translated by Steven Tracy Byington. Cambridge: Cambridge University Press, 1995.

Strauss, David Friedrich. *The Life of Jesus Critically Examined.* Edited by Peter C. Hodgson. Translated by George Eliot. Philadelphia: Fortress, 1972.

———. *The Old Faith and the New.* Translated by Mathilde Blind. Amherst, N.Y.: Prometheus Books, 1997.

Strong, Tracy B. *Friedrich Nietzsche and the Politics of Transfiguration.* Expanded edition. Urbana: University of Illinois Press, 2000.

———. "Nietzsche and the Song of the Self." *New Nietzsche Studies* 1 (1996): 1–14.

———. "Where Are We When We are Beyond Good and Evil?" *Cardozo Law Review* 24 (2003): 535–62.

Tanner, Michael. "Introduction." In Friedrich Nietzsche, *Twilight of the Idols/The Anti-Christ,* 7–24. London: Penguin, 1990.

———. *Nietzsche.* Oxford: Oxford University Press, 1994.

———. "The Total Work of Art." In Peter Burbidge and Richard Sutton, eds., *The Wagner Companion,* 140–224. New York: Cambridge University Press, 1979.

———. *Wagner.* London: HarperCollins, 1996.

Taubes, Jacob. *The Political Theology of Paul.* Translated by Dana Hollander. Stanford, Calif.: Stanford University Press, 2004.

Tolstoï, Léon. *Ma religion.* Paris: Fischbacher, 1885.

Tucholsky, Kurt. "Fräulein Nietzsche." In *Gesammelte Werke,* vol. 10, 9–15. Hamburg: Rowohlt, 1960.

Urpeth, Jim. "Nobel *Ascesis* between Nietzsche and Foucault." *New Nietzsche Studies* 2 (1998): 65–91.

Valadier, Paul. "Dionysus versus the Crucified." In David B. Allison, ed., *The New Nietzsche,* 247–61. Cambridge, Mass.: MIT Press, 1985.

Vattimo, Gianni. *After Christianity.* Translated by Luca D'Isanto. New York: Columbia University Press, 2002.

Wagner, Cosima. *Cosima Wagner's Diaries*. Edited by Martin Gregor-Dellin and Dietrich Mack. Translated by Geoffrey Skelton. New York: Harcourt Brace Jovanovich, 1978.

Wagner, Richard. *Richard Wagner's Prose Works*. Translated by William Ashton Ellis. New York: Broude Brothers, 1966.

———. *Selected Letters of Richard Wagner*. Translated and edited by Stewart Spencer and Barry Millington. New York: W. W. Norton, 1987.

Ware, Kallistos. "The Way of the Ascetics: Negative or Affirmative?" In *Asceticism,* ed. Vincent L. Wimbush and Richard Valantasis, 3–15. New York: Oxford University Press, 1995.

Westphal, Merold. "Nietzsche as a Theological Resource." In Lippitt and Urpeth, *Nietzsche and the Divine*, 14–29.

———. *Suspicion and Faith: The Religious Uses of Modern Atheism*. Grand Rapids, Mich.: Eerdmans, 1993.

Williams, Stephen N. "Dionysus against the Crucified: Nietzsche *contra* Christianity: Part II." *Tyndale Bulletin* 49, no. 1 (1998): 131–53.

Williams, W. D. *Nietzsche and the French: A Study of the Influence of Nietzsche's French Reading on His Thought and Writing*. Oxford: Basil Blackwell, 1952.

Wirzba, Norman. "The Needs of Thought and the Affirmation of Life: Friedrich Nietzsche and Jesus Christ." *International Philosophical Quarterly* 37 (1997): 385–401.

Wright, N. T. *Christian Origins and the Question of God*. Vol. III, *The Resurrection of the Son of God*. Minneapolis: Fortress, 2003.

Young, Julian. *Nietzsche's Philosophy of Art*. Cambridge: Cambridge University Press, 1992.

———. *Nietzsche's Philosophy of Religion*. Cambridge: Cambridge University Press, 2006.

Zeitlin, Irving M. *Nietzsche: A Re-examination*. Cambridge: Polity, 1994.

Zimmern, Alfred. *The Greek Commonwealth*. 4th ed. Oxford: Clarendon, 1924.

Žižek, Slavoj. *The Fragile Absolute—Or, Why Is the Christian Legacy Worth Fighting For?* London: Verso, 2000.

———. *The Puppet and the Dwarf: The Perverse Core of Christianity*. Cambridge, Mass.: MIT Press, 2003.

INDEX

BRUCE ELLIS BENSON is Professor and Chair of the Philosophy Department at Wheaton College. He is author of *Graven Ideologies: Nietzsche, Derrida, and Marion on Modern Idolatry* and *The Improvisation of Musical Dialogue: A Phenomenology of Music*. He is coeditor (with Kevin Vanhoozer and James K. A. Smith) of *Hermeneutics at the Crossroads* (Indiana University Press, 2006).